MW00856168

OPEN SOCRATES

OPEN SOCRATES

*The Case for a
Philosophical Life*

A GNES C ALLARD

W. W. NORTON & COMPANY

Independent Publishers Since 1923

For information about permission to reproduce selections from this book,
write to Permissions, W. W. Norton & Company, Inc., 500 Fifth Avenue,
New York, NY 10110

For information about special discounts for bulk purchases, please contact
W. W. Norton Special Sales at specialsales@wwnorton.com or
800-233-4830

Manufacturing by Lake Book Manufacturing
Book design by Lovedog Studio
Production manager: Julia Druskin

ISBN 978-1-63149-846-6

W. W. Norton & Company, Inc., 500 Fifth Avenue, New York, NY 10110
www.wwnorton.com

W. W. Norton & Company Ltd., 15 Carlisle Street, London W1D 3BS

1 2 3 4 5 6 7 8 9 0

Contents

OPEN SOCRATES

The Man Whose Name
Is an Example

THERE'S A QUESTION YOU ARE AVOIDING. EVEN NOW, AS you read this sentence, you're avoiding it. You tell yourself you don't have time at the moment; you're focused on making it through the next fifteen minutes. There is a lot to get done in a day. There are the hours you spend at your job, the chores to take care of at home. There are movies to be seen, books to be read, music to be listened to, friendships to catch up on, vacations to be taken. Your life is full. It has no space for the question, "Why am I doing any of this?"

If that question does arise, you are ready to reply that you *have* to do most of the things you're already doing. A job is a source of things one *has* to do, in that you depend on the money it provides, and many people—clients, patients, students, co-workers, readers, bosses, customers, mentees—depend on your work. If a job involves research, there might be a problem that *has* to get solved. In school, students are told what they *have* to do—attend class, complete assignments, study for exams. You also have obligations to your family members and friends, to live up to your (mostly tacit) agreements with them. And then there are other extraneous obligations—political activism, community involvement, religious commitments—that a person might feel called upon to fulfill. All of these are "necessities," and they bypass the "why" question.

That doesn't cover everything you do in a day; no one would claim they "have to" pursue the simple pleasures of entertainment or companionship. But in those cases, the question is not so much "Why?" but "Why not?" Between the things you need to do and the things you like to do, your days are packed with activity. If you keep tacking one fifteen-minute period onto another, eventually it adds up to a life.

True, you might sometimes have to pause to ask: Should I take a vacation? Move? Have a(nother) child? Or you might find yourself faced with a moral dilemma or a romantic crisis. But in those cases you frame "What should I do?" as a question about which option fits best with what you had antecedently determined that you have to do and like to do. You are careful to keep your practical questions from exploding beyond narrow deliberative limits within which you confine them in advance. It is fine to be open-minded and curious about all sorts of questions that don't directly impinge on how you live your life—How do woodpeckers avoid getting concussions?—but you are vigilant in policing the boundaries of practical inquiry. You make sure your thinking about how your life should go doesn't wander too far from how it is already going.

You appear to be afraid of something.

I. TOLSTOY

At around age fifty, the great Russian novelist Leo Tolstoy (1828–1910) experienced his life unraveling. He reports:

> My life came to a halt. I could breathe, eat, drink, sleep and I couldn't *not* breathe, eat, drink, sleep; but I had no life because I had no desires in the fulfillment of which I might find any meaning. If I desired something, then I knew in advance that whether I fulfilled my desire or not, nothing would come of it. If an enchantress had come and offered to fulfill my desires for me, I wouldn't have known what to say.[1]

A person moves through life by envisioning positive outcomes either for herself, or those around her, and working to bring them about. If there is nothing that could happen that would satisfy you, motivational collapse ensues. The fact that Tolstoy could face such a collapse is an alarming indictment of the very concept of success, since very few human lives have been characterized by more substantial success than Tolstoy's. Tolstoy's life "came to a halt" after he had written and been recognized for *War and Peace* and *Anna Karenina*, and, more generally, when his life was going just about as well as it could possibly go for a person.

> And this happened to me at a time when on every side I had what is considered to be perfect happiness: it was when I wasn't yet fifty. I had a kind, loving, and loved wife; good children; and a large estate which without labor on my part grew and increased. I was respected by family and friends, was praised more than ever before by the world at large, and without especial self-deception could consider myself to have fame. Moreover, I not only wasn't sickly physically or spiritually but on the contrary had both spiritual and physical strength such as I seldom encountered in my contemporaries: physically I could mow the hay and keep up with the peasants; mentally I could work for eight or ten hours at a stretch without feeling any consequences from the effort.[2]

Tolstoy's crisis was caused by his inability to answer certain questions. He has everything he ever wanted in life—literary fame, a loving family, wealth, physical and mental stamina—but finds himself plagued by the thought that he cannot understand *why* he cares about any of those things:

> Before occupying myself with the Samara estate, the education of my son, the writing of a book, I had to know why I would be doing that. *As long as I didn't know why, I couldn't do anything.* As I thought about estate

management, which engaged me a lot at the time, there would suddenly come into my head the question: "Very well, you'll have sixteen thousand acres in the province of Samara, and three hundred horses, and then what?" I was completely thrown and didn't know what more to think. Or starting to think about how I was educating my children, I would say to myself, "Why?" Or considering how the welfare of the people might be achieved, I suddenly would say to myself, "But what's it to do with me?" Or thinking about the fame my works would bring me, I would say to myself, "Very well, you'll be more famous than Gogol, Pushkin, Shakespeare, Molière, than all the writers in the world—so what?"

And I couldn't answer anything, anything at all.[3]

The above quotations are from a work called *Confession*, in which Tolstoy describes the period of his life when he struggled with these questions, found them unanswerable, and reached a devastating conclusion: "The thought of suicide came to me as naturally as once there had come thoughts of the perfection of life."[4]

Throughout *Confession*, Tolstoy is tormented by the problem of how to move on: How do I go back to a life centered on writing novels, managing my estate, attending to my family? How do I go back to *anything* I could have previously recognized as life? He cannot answer, and the result is that he becomes "convinced of the need for suicide."[5] By his own lights, what Tolstoy discovered is that the examined life was not worth living.

Although he found an escape from these questions—and from suicide—in religious faith, Tolstoy is clear that faith is a way of setting them aside, not an answer to them. He expresses envy for the simple existence of peasants who, at least in Tolstoy's imagining, enjoy blissfully unexamined lives from birth to death.

Confession reads as a cautionary tale: Stay away from fundamental questions! Keep yourself busy enough to ensure your gaze never has time to turn inward, because, once it does, you put yourself on the road to self-destruction. Even if you escape the temptations of suicide, you'll never recover your once untroubled calm. You can't answer these questions, and you can't unask them, so the best strategy is to keep the lid on Pandora's box secured as tightly as you can.

Taking life fifteen minutes at a time is a Tolstoyan strategy. The name for the opposite strategy is "Socratic."

II. SOCRATES

The event that nearly ended Tolstoy's life is the same as the one that got Socrates' started. Like Tolstoy, the philosopher Socrates found himself confronted with profound questions he did not know how to answer; and yet Socrates came to the conclusion that this confrontation was the best, not the worst, thing that ever happened to him. Whereas Tolstoy struggled, with only partial success, to find a way to return to his old life, Socrates never once looked back. He pursued happiness not by avoiding or moving on from these questions, but by diving headlong into them, to the point of forsaking the thought of ever doing anything else with his life. Tolstoy found that the "why" question made existence unbearable: "I had no life."[6] Socrates described the prospect of spending an eternity inquiring into it as "an extraordinary happiness."[7]

Who is this Socrates? Everyone has heard his name, and most people are aware of the basics: he lived thousands of years ago in Athens, Greece, and is somehow the father of Western philosophy, though exactly how is a mystery, since people struggle to say what he actually believed.

Socrates left no writing behind, but we know many biographical details about him from other sources. We know, for example, that he was an Athenian citizen born around 469 BCE, that his father was a stonecutter, his mother a midwife; that he was married, and had children; that he rarely left Athens; that he fought in the Peloponnesian War; and that in 399 BCE he was charged by the city of Athens with impiety and corrupting the youth, put on trial, found guilty, and executed. He was famous for interrogative conversations—with leading Athenians, with visiting dignitaries, and with promising youth—in which he regularly exposed his interlocutor's pretensions to wisdom. He was also famously ugly—bug-eyed, snub-nosed, and goatish, in a city where personal beauty was as highly prized as wealth or fame.

Our earliest major source for Socrates is Aristophanes' *Clouds*, a comic play that mocks Socrates and his practice of refutation. Our other main sources are the works of Xenophon and Plato, who each wrote texts that were similar to plays, though some of them are narrated in the third person. These texts are called "Socratic dialogues," and they present Socrates talking to a great variety of people on a great variety of topics—love, death, politics, punishment, household management, the interpretation of poetry, the proper use of oratorical skills, and much more. Both Plato and Xenophon were close associates of Socrates, so when they portrayed him they were able to draw on their memory of what they had witnessed, participated in, or heard reports of; but in neither case should their dialogues be understood as transcripts of actual conversations. Nor were Plato and Xenophon the only authors of Socratic dialogues. The Socratic dialogue became a genre in the period after Socrates' death, with many writers trying their hand at depicting Socrates in conversation. Although most of the entries in this genre were lost, the fact that Socrates inspired so much writing by other people says something about the kind of cultural significance he had. As does the fact that in the centuries that followed Socrates' death, when philosophical schools were proliferating, not only the Academics—the school descended from Plato's Academy—but also the Stoics, the Cynics, and the Skeptics treated him as a paradigm for their (sharply differing!) conceptions of what a philosopher should be.

Plato's dialogues are the exclusive source for the Socrates you will encounter in this book, just as they are the starting point for most of the philosophizing done in Socrates' wake. (Few would disagree with the claim that Plato's is the more interesting Socrates. And that includes Xenophon scholars.) To this day, Plato's Socratic dialogues remain the standard text used in college courses to introduce students to the very idea of philosophy.

Socrates was a particular, historical individual; but he was and is more than that. Plato reports that during Socrates' lifetime his contemporaries were already imitating him, to the point of copying his habit of walking barefoot.[8] Then as now, Socrates presented himself as a person one can become, as a *kind* of person, someone imitable enough to have his persona replicated in so many dialogues and plays.

Socrates was not only famously ugly, but also poor, and he often remarked on his lack of intellectual gifts. He confesses to having a bad memory, and denies any facility with speechmaking, those being the two essential markers of intelligence in fifth-century Athens. In a society that prized manliness and male-coded attributes, Socrates described his life project in feminine terms, saying that he is a kind of midwife to ideas, and cites a woman—Diotima—as his teacher. Beauty, wealth, eloquence, and a decidedly manly self-presentation may have been prerequisites for conventional success as an Athenian citizen, but Socrates represents a new model for human excellence.

Unlike Tolstoy, or Plato, or Xenophon, or Aristophanes, Socrates did not write great books. And yet he is responsible for one truly great creation: the character of Socrates. Socrates made himself into someone that other people could be. He fashioned his very person into a kind of avatar or mascot for anyone who ventures to ask the sorts of questions that disrupt the course of a life.

IF YOU ARE ON trial for your life, and you have the chance to tell the jury one story about yourself, then you will take great care to select the right one.

Socrates, finding himself in just such a situation, chose to talk about the time that his friend Chaerephon took a trip to the oracle at Delphi. The oracle, which was held to communicate the will of

Apollo, was the supreme religious authority for people throughout the Greek world. Chaerephon asked the oracle whether there was anyone wiser that Socrates; its answer was "no." Upon hearing this, Socrates is shocked:

> When I heard of this reply I asked myself: "Whatever does the god mean? What is his riddle? I am very conscious that I am not wise at all; what then does he mean by saying that I am the wisest? For surely he does not lie; it is not legitimate for him to do so."[9]

This is not the normal reaction to being told, by an official representative of God, that you are special. Most of us harbor secret hopes of finding out that we are in some way distinctively, uniquely better than everyone around us. If you are a normal person, you would bathe in the glow of the oracle's answer, treating it as the confirmation you had been waiting for your whole life: I'm a secret genius! Socrates, by contrast, insists that he knows perfectly well that his wisdom is in no way extraordinary, and eventually finds a way of understanding the oracle's pronouncement as confirmation of *that* view:

> What is probable, gentlemen, is that in fact the god is wise and that his oracular response meant that human wisdom is worth little or nothing, and that when he says this man, Socrates, he is using my name as an example, as if he said: "This man among you, mortals, is wisest who, like Socrates, understands that his wisdom is worthless."[10]

Socrates is saying: the god only appears to be singling me out. According to Socrates' interpretation of the oracle, the message is that no human being is possessed of any kind of extraordinary wisdom. The god wasn't specifically talking about Socrates; rather, Socrates merely served as *an example*. When the god used the name

"Socrates," he was referring not to the concrete individual who was the son of Sophroniscus and the husband of Xanthippe, but to *a kind of person*, namely anyone who understands the fact that no human being is wise. If you understand this, that is enough to make you "a Socrates."

Socrates thought that anyone could become a Socrates; moreover, he had a habit of demanding that they do so. For instance, when talking to the orator Gorgias, he says:

> I'd be pleased to continue questioning you if you're the same kind of person I am, otherwise I would drop it.[11]

And he challenges Gorgias:

> So if you say you're this kind of person, too, let's continue the discussion; but if you think we should drop it, let's be done with it and break it off.[12]

Notice that Socrates is, implicitly, making a very strong claim here. He equates being willing to continue the discussion with saying, "I'm the same kind of person as you, Socrates." Only a Socrates can talk to Socrates.

Socrates is successful at inducing Socratism in others, as is clear from Gorgias' response:

> Oh yes, Socrates, I say that I myself, too, am the sort of person you describe.[13]

What sort of person is Gorgias agreeing to be here? Socrates is careful to spell it out:

> And what kind of person am I? One of those who would be pleased to be refuted if I say anything untrue, and who would be pleased to refute anyone who says anything

untrue; one who, however, wouldn't be any less pleased to be refuted than to refute.[14]

Because Socrates understands that he is not wise, he is pleased to be shown to be wrong—and that is the kind of person he also needs Gorgias to be. One might have expected Gorgias to resist this, and press Socrates to accept the commonsense view that being refuted is worse than refuting someone else. The norm, in Gorgias' time as in our own, is for people to become angry and offended when shown to be wrong, and proudly delighted to show others that they are wrong. Socrates announces that he doesn't play by those rules: "I count being refuted a greater good, insofar as it is a greater good for oneself to be delivered from the worst thing there is than to deliver someone else from it."[15] Athenians were inclined to dismiss comments of this kind as ridiculous, or naïve, or simply to express incredulity:

> Tell me, Socrates, are we to take you as being in earnest now, or joking? For if you *are* in earnest, and these things you're saying are really true, won't this human life of ours be turned upside down, and won't everything we do evidently be the opposite of what we should do?[16]

Those are the words of a man who has been quietly observing Socrates interact first with Gorgias, and then with another man, Polus, until the moment arises when the observer, whose name is Callicles, cannot contain himself any longer. And yet, even as such interlocutors questioned whether they could take Socrates seriously, he also brought them around, and they started to see the problem with arguing to win. Talking to Socrates is like encountering argument in the wild, in its natural habitat. By comparison, your usual argumentative practices come off as unnaturally distorted by social considerations: the same kind of animal, but trapped in a cage in the zoo. Socrates' interlocutors couldn't help finding themselves inspired to want to become the kind of people who think ignorance is the worst thing there is. That is why the space around Socrates becomes peopled by Socrateses. It is a space dedicated both to acknowledging one's ignorance in the face of, and to overcoming one's fear of, the "why?" question.

When Socrates is on trial—as least in Plato's representation of that event, the *Apology*—he goes beyond simply defending himself against the official charges to argue that not even his accusers really believe that he is guilty of impiety or corrupting the youth. Then why were they trying to put him to death? Socrates' answer is: fear of being asked "Why?" He tells the jury members who voted against him that they did so in vain. They voted to kill him, he says to them, "in the belief that you would avoid giving an account of your life," but imitators would rush forward to take his place, so that in the end "there will be more people to test you." He claims that "if you kill the sort of man I say I am, you will not harm me more than yourselves."[17] As Socrates understands it, the jury's quarrel is not with an individual—the elderly son of a stonecutter—but with the very idea of a person who lives as if there is no good greater than knowledge and no human project more important than inquiry. The jury's real target is not Socrates but his creation—the sort of man Socrates says he is. As Socrates suggests, *that* creature is a hydra who sends forth multiple heads to replace each one you sever.

Socrates predicted that after his death, the world would be filled with Socrateses. Was he right?

III. Where Is Socratic Ethics?

English economist John Maynard Keynes (1883–1946) famously claimed that anti-intellectuals are more intellectual than they realize:

> Practical men, who believe themselves to be quite exempt from any intellectual influences, are usually the slaves of some defunct economist. Madmen in authority, who hear voices in the air, are distilling their frenzy from some academic scribbler of a few years back.[18]

If we concede to Keynes that many practical men unwittingly draw on the ideas of economists, we may find ourselves wondering: Where do the economists get their ideas? The answer, for defunct and non-defunct alike, is ethical philosophy.

Economists draw on the tradition of ethical theorizing that springs from the writings of English philosophers Jeremy Bentham (1748–1832), John Stuart Mill (1806–1873), and Henry Sidgwick (1838–1900), which tells you to perform the action that is likely to result in as many benefits to as many beneficiaries as possible. The benefits are typically understood in terms of the presence of pleasure and the absence of pain, and the beneficiaries are typically assumed to be human beings, but both of those terms can be broadened— from pleasure to any good state of affairs, from human beings to any sentient being. This theory is called "Utilitarianism."

I am not sure which "mad authorities" Keynes had in mind, but people in positions of political, legal, or religious authority tend to rely on scribblers who, whether they know it or not, are themselves relying in some way on the scribblings of Immanuel Kant (1724–1804). Kant was a German philosopher who articulated a form of ethics that is focused on the ways that dignity—the infinite worth of every rational being—constrains how we are allowed to treat one another. This system features a "categorical imperative," or absolute prohibition, against using a human being as a mere tool for the benefit of others.

If the practical men and the economists and the authorities and the scribblers are all getting their ideas from philosophers, the natural follow-up question is: Where do the philosophers get their ideas? The answer is, other philosophers. Bentham and Mill and Sidgwick are drawing on a tradition that goes back to ancient Epicureanism, and Kant is similarly indebted to ancient Stoicism. But now we must take the final step: Where did the Epicureans and the Stoics get their ideas? Like Keynes' madmen, they too, heard voices: the Epicureans heard the voice of the body, as it screams out to us, in the language of pleasure and pain, and demands that we promote and protect and serve it. The Stoics heard the voice of the group, when it draws each individual's attention to the fact that she is part of a larger community, and demands that she regulate her behavior accordingly.

The Stoics and the Epicureans did not simply channel those voices, but reformed them, making them more reasonable and consistent, so that they could become the basis of a systematic approach to the conduct of life. Subsequent philosophers made further contributions toward the universalization and stabilization of each system. The later revivals of these two traditions have been very successful: utilitarianism and Kantianism continue to underwrite our lives to this day. Yet neither was so successful as to avoid conflict with the other. The action that best promotes the greatest good for the greatest number is not guaranteed to be the same, in all cases, as the action that shows respect for the dignity of another person. (This conflict is what the set of philosophical thought experiments called "trolley problems" is designed to reveal.)

The predicament of the anti-intellectual is worse than Keynes recognized: he is the secret slave of not one but two masters, and these masters are at war with one another. But the darkest secret of all is that these warring masters are merely feeding him back, in disguised form, the *savage commands*, either of his own body (Save me!) or of his own group (Cooperate with us!).

In the twentieth century, a movement arose—called "Neo-Aristotelianism" or "Virtue Ethics"—aiming to do for Aristotle what Kant did for Stoicism in the eighteenth century and what Bentham, Mill, and Sidgwick did for Epicureanism in the nineteenth. The Aristotelian insists that the two commands can be harmonized with one another through *habituation*, which is the Aristotelian term for the moral training that occurs during one's upbringing. Someone who has been well habituated pursues happiness and pleasure for herself by means of behaving respectfully toward others, which is to say, she aims at virtue. Neo-Aristotelianism has been less influential than Kantianism or Utilitarianism, perhaps because its more recent revival has given it less time to be widely adopted, or perhaps because its philosophical foundation is more complex than the other two theories, or perhaps because Aristotle's explicit restriction of the audience of ethical theory to those who have been "well habituated" is not as plausible to a modern audience as it was to his contemporaries.

What about Socrates? Why isn't there a Neo-Socratic ethics? Why hasn't Socratic ethical thought been revived as the basis of an ethical framework that might compete with those drawn from other ancient sources? The answer is that Socrates' ethics is typically understood in purely negative terms. The characterization offered by the Roman statesman and philosopher Cicero (106–43 BCE) is representative:

> The method of discussion pursued by Socrates in almost all the dialogues so diversely and so fully recorded by his hearers is to affirm nothing himself but to refute others, to assert that he knows nothing except the fact of his own ignorance, and that he surpassed all other people in that they think they know things that they do not know but he himself thinks he knows nothing, and that he believed this to have been the reason why Apollo declared him to be the wisest of all men, because all wisdom consists solely in not thinking that you know what you do not know.[19]

In this view, the reason we can't live our lives Socratically is that Socrates, unlike Kant, or Mill, or Aristotle, didn't have answers. Socrates could criticize the overconfident answers of others, but had nothing to offer in their stead. "Being like Socrates" just means being open-minded, and willing to admit when you are wrong, and unafraid to ask challenging questions. This is not an ethical theory. It is more like a critical-thinking "sauce" that can be poured over any ethical theory, or simply over common sense. Whereas "Kantian" or "Aristotelian" refers to a set of ideas about how to live, "Socratic" refers to a style.

So goes one story about Socrates. This book tells a different one. It argues that people have overestimated the degree to which a Socratic approach can be layered on top of what we were doing anyways. When Socratism is adopted as a style, it has a tendency to land the one who so stylizes themselves in a performative contradiction. For example, consider the plight of my own university, the University of Chicago, declaring its commitment to "the principle of complete freedom of speech on all subjects" by insisting that "this principle can neither now nor at any future time be called in question."[20] Apparently, our freedom to question extends to all subjects *but one*. People will announce, "Question everything!" without noticing that they have just uttered not a question, but a command. If the Socratic method is a tool, it is a strange kind of tool, one that has the audacity to dictate both how it should be used, and for what purposes.

How should the method be used? With another person, who has taken on a role distinct from yours. One of you offers answers to some fundamental question, while the other explains why he or she cannot accept those answers. Thinking, as Socrates understands it, is not something that happens in your head, but rather out loud, in conversation. Socrates argues that it is only by recognizing thinking as a social interaction that we can resolve a set of paradoxes as to how thinking can be open-minded, inquisitive, and truth-oriented. The Socratic motto is not, "Question everything," but "Persuade or be persuaded."

When it comes to the purpose of the Socratic method, Socrates had colossal ambitions. He believed that all of the trouble we have leading our lives, all of our dissatisfactions, all of our failures to progress, all of our moral imperfections, all of the injustices we commit, large and small, stem from one source: ignorance. Socrates' claim that "I know that I know nothing" isn't an empty gesture of skepticism, but rather a plan for life. It tells you that the key to success, whether you are navigating difficulties in your marriage, your terror at the prospect of death, or the politicized minefield of social media, is to have the right kinds of conversations. Given that we cannot lead lives based on knowledge—because we lack it—we should lead the second-best kind of life, namely, the one oriented toward knowledge.

Socrates discovered that between the acknowledgment of one's own ignorance and the ideally knowledgeable life lies a substantive ethics of inquiry. The way to be good when you don't know how to be good is by learning. You should do everything in such a way as to be learning what the right thing to do is, and this means getting other people to show you when you are wrong. Instead of implementing a principle—such as "Achieve the greatest good for the greatest number!" or "Obey the categorical imperative!"—you should inquire. Socrates insists that there is no greater benefit he could receive from another person than being shown why he is wrong, and that the only sure way to treat another human being with respect is to either answer their questions or question their answers.

Socrates turns a spotlight on all the places where we have dressed up our ignorance as something else—a lack of willpower, or selfishness, or laziness, or badness—in order to evade the imperative to inquire. According to Socrates, whenever we say, "I knew what the right thing to do was, I just couldn't get myself to do it," we are flattering ourselves, ascribing to ourselves knowledge we evidently lack, and whenever we say, "He knew what the right thing to do was, he just decided not to do it," we are creating excuses for the exercise of vengeance. Socrates denies that it is possible to act against one's better judgment, and he denies that anyone ever deserves to be harmed. There is only one problem, which is ignorance, and there is only one solution, which is to learn.

When inquiry informs your love life, your approach to death, and your politics, the result is not simply a continuation of business as usual. For example, we will see that when it comes to politics, Socrates holds that free speech is achieved neither by debate nor by persuasion; that political battles, including war, are simply philosophy gone awry; and that true egalitarianism is fully compatible with the pursuit of status. Socratic ethics does not confine itself to adding an air of skepticism to the small subdivision of life explicitly occupied with intellectual pursuits; it inserts itself everywhere, into every interaction, infusing every corner of life with the demand to become more intellectual.

Ultimately, our difficulties seeing that Socrates' ethics forms a distinct alternative to Kant's or Mill's or Aristotle's are rooted in the imitability of the character of Socrates. Socrates' greatest strength has also turned out to be a weakness. We, especially those of us who identify as intellectuals, experience ourselves as fully saturated by critical-thinking sauce. We feel sure that we already are being Socratic. We are not entirely wrong. Before Socrates, bold claims to possessing deep wisdom were a sign of elite status; after Socrates, epistemic humility and skeptical disavowals become the surer mark of culture and sophistication. Being gracious to those who criticize you, welcoming disagreement, refusing to straw man your opponent—all of these now-commonplace norms bear the mark of Socrates.

But our Socratism has been much diluted from the original formula. So, although it has become a matter of routine to praise open inquiry into any topic, and especially into what are labeled as "fundamental questions," the ones doing the praising are rarely doing much inquiring. If someone teaches a class by asking questions, even if they are only using those questions to fish for the specific answers they had in mind, that is called, wrongly, "the Socratic method." The value of skeptical caution, open-mindedness, and intellectual humility are familiar talking points among people who, by and large, agree with Tolstoy that only the unexamined life is livable. All of these normalizers of Socrates miss what Callicles saw: that Socratic skepticism, the Socratic method, Socratic inquiry, and Socratic humility are not ways of conducting business as usual. We are all halfheartedly imitating—or as Keynes might say, "slaves to"—a man who, if he were around today, would be disappointed in us. The reason why we aren't inclined to acknowledge the existence of Socratic ethics is that the existence of Socratic ethics is an indictment of us.

In this book, I aim to reintroduce Socratic ethics as a novel and distinctive ethical system, complete with its own core theses and distinctive ethical recommendations. Unlike the other three traditions, Socratic ethics does not take its bearings from the savage commands of one's body, or one's group. Unlike the other three traditions, Socratic ethics does not present itself as a finished system, but rather awaits its own elaboration by those who now do, and those who in the future will, understand themselves as Socratics. A follower of Socrates is ethically required to inquire into Socratism, whereas no such intellectual requirements constrain someone who wants to be a good Kantian, a good Utilitarian, or a good Aristotelian. Those traditions purport to rest on a bedrock of ethical knowledge that is immediately available to be acted on: no further philosophizing is required. Socrates boasts of no such bedrock. Nonetheless, Socratic ethics offers concrete practical guidance: it tells you that you should live a philosophical life, and helps you see how to do so.

IV. An Incautionary Tale

The book that you are currently reading is an incautionary tale. It is the counterpoint not only to *Confession*, but also to the countless other stories, novels, essays, and speeches that echo Tolstoy's message of fear and despair. Many of those warnings are written by professional philosophers, who, far from being immune to Tolstoyan terror, are in many ways especially susceptible to it. Academic philosophers are, in my experience, eager to allow that one can live a perfectly happy and fulfilled life without ever engaging in philosophy. They are also careful to shield the rest of their lives from their philosophical activities: they would readily admit to taking off their philosopher hat when walking into their homes, when socializing with friends—even friends who are philosophers!—and, more generally, whenever things get serious. Even the practitioners of philosophy are wary of philosophy.

Those who praise philosophy tend to take care to praise it in limited doses. Callicles, a Socratic interlocutor mentioned above, speaks approvingly of young people asking "why?" questions, and compares philosophizing to lisping: charming and delightful right up until someone reaches the age for serious, manly pursuits. It is common today to hear advisors to young people unwittingly echoing Callicles, praising a philosophy major on the grounds that it gives you "analytic tools" and "critical thinking skills" valued by employers. The message is: Do philosophy, but don't overdo it.

We live inside a bubble of caution and wariness that can only be sustained by maintaining the conviction that, when it comes to the question of how to live our lives, we are already being intellectual and critical and thoughtful enough. The assumption is that no one—not even a professional academic philosopher—needs to be living their whole life in a philosophical manner.

This book is an argument to the contrary: it makes the case for a philosophical life. That case has three parts. We begin, in part one, by pulling at the threads that Tolstoy urged us to leave alone. The kinds of questions Tolstoy warned us against asking form a special class: I call them "untimely questions." Untimely questions are marked by the fact we need answers to them before we are prepared to ask them. Our default answers—the ones available to us absent philosophizing—come from unreliable sources: our bodies, and other people. These sources issue savage commands, contradicting one another and themselves, leading us to act in confused and haphazard ways. One approach to this problem is to try to "tame" the savage commands. Thus Utilitarianism aims to rehabilitate the bodily command; Kantianism the command of the group; and Aristotelianism tries to harmonize the two commands with one another. But those are not the only possible methods for dealing with untimely questions—there is also the Socratic one.

Part two explains the Socratic approach to untimely questions: don't rely on the default answers, not even on tamed versions of them. Instead, inquire into them, with an open mind, pursuing truth, and avoiding falsity. Following this formula is, however, less straightforward than it appears. Each of its three parts—inquiry, open-mindedness, and truth-seeking—conceals a paradox. The paradox as to how inquiry is possible is called "Meno's paradox": How can one search for what one does not yet know? How will one recognize it when one finds it? Open-mindedness is paradoxical because it requires a person to be willing to admit that she is wrong—which, if you consider it carefully, is a form of self-awareness that is not easy to make sense of. It is not hard to admit that you *were* wrong, but very hard to admit that you *are* wrong. This is called "Moore's paradox." The third paradox is about pursuing the truth and avoiding falsity, two activities that, far from being identical, turn out to be in tension with one another. In order to believe truths you must believe *something*, and that means you run the risk of believing something false. You could avoid false belief by believing nothing at all, but that would frustrate the aim of believing truths.

Socrates' solution is to give one person the task of asserting truths, and the other person the job of avoiding falsehoods. If they work together, the second refuting the first, they can achieve both goals. We also get solutions to the other two paradoxes: someone who refutes you serves as a mirror in which you can see your own errors reflected, and they allow you to search for answers to questions—even untimely ones. Socrates discovered that by working together with another person, we make possible forms of thinking, self-knowledge, and questioning that are foreclosed to the person who works alone. Speech can free thought from the blindness and bias and provinciality endemic to being just one mind.

If you face up to the difficulty of understanding what it means to truly think critically, the result is a much more demanding "Socratic method" than the one to which we are accustomed. In part three, we examine that method's demands in the three areas of human life where Socrates thought our ignorance loomed largest: politics, love, and death. Two and a half millennia later, these remain humanity's problem areas. Even as the explosion of scientific and technological knowledge has created massive improvements in many areas of our lives, we remain at sea when it comes to managing politics, handling love affairs, and confronting our own deaths. Socratic ethics is the ethics of living a truly philosophical life, and it tells you that the way you should conduct yourself in each of these three domains is: inquisitively. It promises to make people freer and more equal; more romantic; and more courageous.

The details of inquisitive living may well appear odd or downright unacceptable to us: from the *Phaedo*, we learn that Socrates believes in life (before birth and) after death; from the *Symposium* and *Phaedrus*, that he embraces (a distinctively Socratic version of) polyamory and rejects (so-called "Socratic") irony; from the *Gorgias* that he denies that it is so much as *possible* to fight injustice. Socrates says that vice is ignorance, that falling in love is an attempt to ascend to another plane of existence, and if he were around today, he would accuse all of us of treating corpses in a superstitious manner. He insists that everyone desires the good, and that treating others unjustly is worse, for the person who does so, than being unjustly treated herself. In his hands, both "freedom of speech" and "egalitarianism" become not political ideas, but intellectual ones. He thinks that philosophy is a preparation for death.

Couldn't Socrates have gotten it wrong on one or more of these questions? Of course. He admits this regularly; we will encounter an especially startling example, taking place in the final hour of his life, in the final chapter. Followers of Socrates will feel welcome to disagree with him, so long as we can explain why. We Socratics are not beholden to Socrates, the protagonist in Plato's dialogues; nor are we beholden to Socrates, the historical individual. The one to whom we are beholden is the character—that is, the ideal—created by the historical Socrates. We want to be the kind of person that the historical Socrates, no doubt imperfectly, tried to make himself into; it was that same kind of person that Plato, again, no doubt imperfectly, tried to copy. It is un-Socratic to treat a Platonic text dogmatically, but it is also un-Socratic to dismiss the ideas in that text simply because they strike us as "upside-down."

Again, this book is an incautionary tale. I will show you what a philosophical life looks like, but I can't say whether the sight of it will fill you with Socratic hope and energy or plunge you into Tolstoyan despair. If you are willing to take the risk, read on.

A Note on the Use of Plato's Dialogues
Chapters 1 to 5 bounce around among Plato's Socratic dialogues (*Alcibiades, Apology, Charmides, Clitophon, Crito, Euthydemus, Euthyphro, Gorgias, Hippias Minor, Laches, Lysis, Meno, Protagoras*), but from chapter 6 onward, each chapter is chiefly devoted to one dialogue, as follows:

    chapter 6, Moore's Paradox: *Alcibiades*
    chapter 7, Meno's Paradox: *Meno*
    chapters 8 and 9, Politics: *Gorgias*
    chapter 10, Love: *Symposium*
    chapter 11, Death: *Phaedo*

Part One

＊

UNTIMELY QUESTIONS

Chapter 1

The Tolstoy Problem

My question, which at the age of fifty brought me to the point of suicide, was the very simple question that lies in the soul of every human being, from a silly child to the wisest sage—the question without which life is impossible, as I experienced in actual fact. The question is this: What will come from what I do and from what I will do tomorrow—what will come from my whole life?[1]

IN MIDDLE AGE, TOLSTOY CAME TO THE TERRIBLE CONclusion that the question "without which life is impossible" is also intractable, in that no matter how much he thought about it, he would never be able to answer it. If Tolstoy is right that this question "lies in the soul of every human being," then his predicament is far from unique. Nor does he seem especially well placed to fall into bottomless despair. Quite the contrary: one might have thought that if anyone would have been in a position to find the meaningfulness of their life to be self-evident, it would have been someone like Leo Tolstoy. So why aren't all of us haunted by Tolstoy's problem?

It is tempting to answer that Tolstoy was depressed. When you hear that anyone is contemplating suicide, it is hard not to jump to a medical diagnosis; so much the more so when the person in question is spectacularly successful. The natural explanation for why someone thinks their life is going badly when it gives every outward sign of going well is that there is something off with the part of the body whose malfunctioning characteristically escapes the mind's notice: the brain. But when it comes to Tolstoy, we are in an awkward position to draw these conclusions. The basis on which we presume to diagnose him, namely, the book in which he describes his crisis, constitutes an eloquent argument for feeling just the way he does. He held that there are facts about the human condition which, if you attended to them, would make you "mentally ill," too.

This is why the psychologist and philosopher William James (1842–1910), discussing *Confession* in his book *The Varieties of Religious Experience*, insists that Tolstoy's "melancholy," as James described it, "was not merely an accidental vitiation of the humors," but rather "the escape from falsehoods into what for him were ways of truth." James continues: "And though not many of us can imitate Tolstoy, not having enough, perhaps, of the aboriginal human marrow in our bones, most of us may at least feel as if it might be better for us if we could."[2]

If most people find themselves unbothered by Tolstoy's question, is it because they have a real answer to it, or because they have the power to ignore it?

I. QUESTIONS THAT COME TOO LATE

If you stood under the immediate threat of violence—unless you take action, you or a loved one will be harmed—the last thing it would make sense to do would be to ask about the meaning of life. In movies, people frequently are provided with good reasons to cut off conversations because "we have to go, now!" Many of us have become gifted at endowing everyday tasks with such urgency: I "must" go to the store, I "have to" get to work, I "need to" call my parents, I am "very busy"—after all of which I probably "deserve" a break during which the last thing I want to do is embark upon an exhausting existential inquiry. We learn to take life fifteen minutes at a time. And if you add up enough of those fifteen-minute periods, the sum total is a whole life. This is what T. S. Eliot refers to when he writes, "I have measured out my life with coffee spoons." We find a way to avoid ever asking, "What will come from my whole life?"

One can avoid Tolstoy's crisis by placing one foot after another, and attending either to whatever strikes one as the greatest danger—either physical or moral—to be avoided, or, alternatively, the greatest source of pleasure or entertainment to be pursued. Whether we see life, pessimistically, as an ongoing crisis punctuated by periods of relief, or, more optimistically, as an ongoing source of pleasure punctuated by periods of crisis, we will find it replete with reasons for postponing philosophical inquiry. If we postpone for long enough, death will rescue us from ever having to come to terms with the meaninglessness of life.

I believe that Tolstoy identified a special class of question that I am going to call "untimely questions." An untimely question is a question that comes at the wrong time—namely, after it has been answered. Untimely questions are remarkable not only because they are hard to answer, but, first and foremost, because they are hard to ask; and they are hard to ask not only because it is hard to pose them to others, but, first and foremost, because it is hard to pose them to oneself. We are familiar with the circumstances under which a person will be unable to get others to engage with her question—when they won't let her talk, or when she doesn't want to admit that she doesn't know the answer, or when there is simply no one around. But can't one always pose a question to oneself? No. Some questions are so elusive that if you write them down on a piece of paper, and then go on to read what you have written out loud to yourself, over and over again, to the point where even after you stop talking, the words of the question are echoing through your head, you still won't be *asking* the question. You'll be going through the motions of inquiry without actually inquiring into anything.

The reason why you can't ask yourself untimely questions is that you think you already have the answer to them, and the reason you think you have the answer is that you are *using* the answer. Such questions don't show up to you as *questions*; by the time you get them in view, you find that they have hardened into the shape of answers. Untimely questions come too late. "What will come of my entire life?" was, for Tolstoy, such a question, but in other places he is more specific. Recall:

> Before occupying myself with the Samara estate, the education of my son, the writing of a book, I had to know why I would be doing that. *As long as I didn't know why, I couldn't do anything.* As I thought about estate management, which kept me very occupied at the time, there would suddenly come into my head the question: "Very well, you'll have sixteen thousand acres in the province of Samara and three hundred horses, and then what?" I was completely thrown, and didn't know what more to think. Or, starting to think about how I was educating my children, I would say to myself, "Why?" Or considering how the welfare of the people might be achieved, I suddenly would say to myself, "But what's it to do with me?" Or thinking about the fame my works would bring me, I would say to myself, "Very well, you'll be more famous than Gogol, Pushkin, Shakespeare, Molière, than all the writers in the world—so what?" And I couldn't answer anything, anything at all.[3]

Why seek material prosperity? Why educate my children? Why care about the welfare of the people? Why does literary fame matter? These are untimely questions, and they form a contrast with the sorts of questions that float free of what we are currently doing, questions where open-mindedness is possible, questions whose answers we needn't rely on already knowing. Those sorts of questions come at the right time.

At this point you might reply that a person does not "need" an answer to this, or any other, question in order to live: Food, water, air, and shelter are the sorts of things a person needs in order to survive—not answers to questions! It is true that food and water are the sorts of things that, if withdrawn from a person, remove the possibility of survival. No answer can substitute for any of those things: man cannot live on ideas alone. But there are questions whose answers constitute a person's basis for living. This is because, first, living, for a human being, essentially involves acting; second, every action is for the sake of some goal; and, third, a goal is an idea about what matters. Ideas are, in fact, prerequisites for the kind of living that we human beings do. Indeed, even breathing is, as Tolstoy noted in his suicidal despair, strictly speaking, optional. We go on breathing because we chose to do so.

Human existence requires a biological infrastructure; human agency requires, in addition, a conceptual infrastructure. Though everything from changes at the cellular level to involuntary reflexes illustrate the fact that our bodies can be moved in ways we don't control, most of what we refer to under the heading "human life" concerns all the ways we *do* exercise some control our bodies: we choose where to go and how to behave when we get there, we decide what words to assert, we do our best to hurl ourselves into one future rather than another. To engage in these acts of self-control and self-management, we have to believe that something is worth pursuing. Recall Tolstoy: "As long as I didn't know why, I couldn't do anything." Every belief that we might act on is the answer to some "why" question. But that means whichever answer we're currently acting on the basis of closes the corresponding question. The difficulty is that we can't make use of the answer and ask ourselves the question at the same time.

Suppose I firmly believe that cloning is immoral. I won't be able to ask myself, "Is cloning immoral?" because, when I check in with my beliefs, I see that one of them already answers the question. In order to inquire into that question, I would have to take "cloning is immoral" off of the list of my beliefs. At that point I could look into whether I can derive it from other beliefs that I have, or whether any new information I might acquire could settle the question for me. But if what I am currently doing is advocating against cloning, then I cannot take "cloning is immoral" off of the list of my beliefs, because I'm relying on its presence. If someone asked me, "Why are you doing what you are doing?" I need to be able to answer, "Because cloning is immoral."

If it strikes you as somehow brutal and uncaring that Tolstoy is willing to countenance such thoughts as "Why should I care about my children" and "So the peasants are suffering, what's it to me?" your judgmental response—How dare he?!—points to the unaskability of the corresponding question. You are not supposed to regard those questions as open, precisely because you are supposed to already be using the answers, in the caring that you are currently doing. But in that case, how was Tolstoy, who did care about his children, and about the welfare of the peasants, able to ask himself those questions? The answer is that he wasn't. He could say the words of the questions to himself, but he couldn't ask them.

II. WHAT TOLSTOY COULDN'T DO

Though Tolstoy repeatedly *refers* to the process of inquiry into fundamental questions, his text betrays no sign of his having performed such inquiry: actual philosophical reasoning and argumentation are strikingly absent from it.

Consider Tolstoy's initial response to his own questions:

> At first I thought that these were just pointless, irrelevant questions. I thought all this was known and that if and when I wanted to take up finding the answers, it wouldn't be much work for me—it was only that now I didn't have the time to do that, but when I turned my mind to it I would find the answers.[4]

Tolstoy's description of how we use trivializing rationalizations to keep such questions at bay likely rings true for many people. But one might expect that the result of rejecting this approach would be a recognition of those questions as worthy of sustained intellectual effort. By Tolstoy's report, however, despair set in immediately:

> I understood that this was no casual exhaustion but something very important, and that if these same questions kept on being repeated, then one must answer them. And I tried to answer. The questions seemed such stupid, simple, childish questions. But as soon as I tackled them and tried to find the answers, I at once became certain first that these were not childish and stupid questions but the most important and profound questions in life, and second that I could not, just could not answer them, however much I thought about it.[5]

Note the simultaneity of question and answer: "*As soon as* I tackled them and tried to find the answers, I *at once became certain* . . . that I could not, just could not answer them." Tolstoy jumps very quickly from acknowledging that these questions must be answered to certainty that they cannot be. The claim that it is immediately obvious that philosophical questions cannot be answered is no less evasive than Tolstoy's initial claim that it is immediately obvious that philosophical questions are easy to answer. In one way Tolstoy's attitude toward these questions undergoes a profound transformation: from casual dismissal to reverential awe. Eventually, this awe takes a religious form. But Tolstoy's attitude never at any point becomes inquisitive; in one way or another, inquiry always gets ruled out in advance.

Though he reiterates this negative conclusion many times over the course of his autobiographical account, he never actually explains how he arrived at it. Consider another of his descriptions of that conclusion: "I couldn't attribute any intelligent meaning to a single act or to the whole of my life. I was surprised that I couldn't understand that at the very beginning. All this had been known to everyone for so long."[6] Though he has moved from his initial description of the questions as "pointless" and "irrelevant," his description of the meaninglessness of life as "known to everyone" is likewise evasive: Does everyone really know that neither one's life, nor any act contained therein, has any meaning? How do they know this?

Tolstoy never explains why the questions he asked himself were impossible to answer, or what makes these questions so "important and profound." He does not even leave the reader with much clarity as to what the questions are—or how many of them there are. Sometimes, as in the passages above, the "questions" are in the plural: these are his questions about the value of wealth, literary fame, or parenting. At other times he seems to see but a single question, though he formulates it in multiple ways that are not obviously identical to one another:

> The question without which life is impossible . . . is this: What will come from what I do and from what I will do tomorrow—what will come from my whole life? . . . Expressed differently, the question would be this: Why should I live, why should I wish for anything, why should I do anything? One can put the question differently again: Is there any meaning in my life that wouldn't be destroyed by the death that inevitably awaits me?[7]

This list of questions itself raises many questions, for example: Is the final question really equivalent to all of the others? What could it mean for something to "come from" a whole life—especially given that literary fame doesn't count as an answer? Should one expect that a question such as "Why should I educate my children?" will be answered by the same "meaning" that would also underwrite "Why should I pursue a literary career?"

It is evident that Tolstoy was in anguish over questions about the meaning of his own life, but it is less evident that he actually succeeded in asking those questions. He regularly leaps from a highly imprecise statement of some form of the question to despair over the impossibility of arriving at any kind of answer. Tolstoy offers no development or discussion of the questions that, by his own admission, obsessed him to the point of driving him toward suicide. He does not articulate what the steps in offering an answer might look like, or draw any distinctions relevant to the answering of the question. Tolstoy's text is characterized by a jerky movement, as though he is being repeatedly brought up short by the prospect of an impossible investigation. This leads him to feel that he has come up against the meaninglessness of life:

> How can a man see this and go on living—that is what's astonishing. You can only live as long as you're drunk with life; but when you sober up, you can't help but see that all this is just a fraud, and a stupid fraud.[8]

Over and over again he describes himself decisively concluding against the meaning of life and in favor of suicide. He describes this conclusion in the firmest possible terms: "Life is a meaningless evil, that is unquestionable."[9] Why then, doesn't he commit suicide? He says that something—which he describes variously as "habit," "weakness," or "intoxication"—inhibits him from carrying out the deed:

> If in drunken moments I did not have so much desires as the habits of old desires, then in sober moments I knew that it was delusion, that there was nothing to desire. I could not even desire to know the truth because I guessed wherein it lay. The truth was that life is nonsense.[10]

Tolstoy describes an odd confluence of attitudes about suicide. On the one hand, he fears committing it: he removes the ropes from the room where he undresses every night to prevent himself from hanging himself on the beam between the cupboards; he avoids hunting lest he encounter an irresistible temptation to turn his rifle on himself. At the same time, he classifies these fears as "delusion" and "intoxication" by contrast with the "truth" that life is meaningless and suicide is required. He calls his approach "the way of weakness." By weakness, Tolstoy means "understanding the evil and meaninglessness of life, to continue to drag it out, knowing in advance that nothing will come of it."[11] He describes people like him as "the weakest, most illogical" and "most stupid of men."[12]

He admires those "strong and logical people" who, in his position, commit suicide, and is ashamed to classify himself as belonging to the category of people who "know that death is better than life but, not having the strength to act intelligently—to end the fraud quickly and kill themselves—they seem to be waiting for something." He asks himself, "If I know what is best and it is in my power, why not take the best?"[13]

There is an obvious objection to the claim that suicide is a coherent response to despair about meaning. If human life is meaningless, if there is *nothing* that we can do that would matter in any way, then that line of reasoning applies equally to suicide. To put it another way: if you think that suicide is valuable enough to perform, you think that *something* is valuable and now it seems you are no longer a nihilist. Tolstoy does not refute this objection, or even consider it, because he does not arrive at the idea of suicide by a process of systematic thought. Faced with despair over a set of questions he can neither avoid nor confront, he finds himself blown back and forth between the unthinkability of suicide and the necessity of it, oddly confident about his ability to determine which of those states counts as "sobriety," which as "intoxication."

I have been drawing your attention to two striking features of the account Tolstoy provides in *Confession*. The first is that although Tolstoy repeatedly refers to fundamental questions about the meaning of life, he never succeeds in asking himself those questions. The second is that he firmly, passionately, and with certitude espouses a conclusion—life is meaningless, suicide is mandated—to which he has not reasoned and from which his behavior repeatedly *wavers*.

III. ENTER SOCRATES

In the *Protagoras*, Socrates tells a funny story of being awakened very early in the morning by a young Hippocrates:

> This morning just before daybreak, while it was still dark, Hippocrates, son of Apollodorus and Phason's brother, banged on my door with his stick, and when it was opened for him he barged right in and yelled in that voice of his, "Socrates, are you awake or asleep?"
>
> Recognizing his voice, I said, "Is that Hippocrates? No bad news, I hope."
>
> "Nothing but good news," he said.
>
> "I'd like to hear it," I said. "What brings you here at such an hour?"
>
> "Protagoras has arrived," he said, standing next to me.
>
> "Day before yesterday," I said. "Did you just find out?"
>
> "Yes! Just last evening." As he said this he felt around for the bed and sat at my feet and continued: "That's right, late yesterday evening, after I got back from Oenoë. My slave Satyrus had run away from me. I meant to tell you that I was going after him, but something else came up and made me forget. After I got back and we had eaten dinner and were about to get some rest, *then* my brother tells me Protagoras has arrived. I was getting ready to come right over to see you even then, until I realized it was just too late at night. But as soon as I had slept some and wasn't dead-tired any more, I got up and came over here right away."[14]

Hippocrates resembles a chicken with his head chopped off. He is rushing around, chasing after Satyrus, meaning to tell Socrates about this but forgetting, barging in on Socrates before sunrise, far too early to politely call on Protagoras, and awakening Socrates by asking whether he is awake!

Hippocrates' outward behavior displays incoherence and thoughtlessness, and when Socrates scratches the surface, we see more of the same. He goes on to question Hippocrates: Why is Hippocrates so excited to meet Protagoras? Because Protagoras is a sophist, replies Hippocrates. But what is a sophist? asks Socrates. Hippocrates turns out to be unable to answer, offering only empty phases such as "someone who has an understanding of wise things"—which ones? What is a sophist good at?—"making people clever speakers"—on which subjects?[15] Eventually Hippocrates admits that he just does not know what he's rushing into: "By God," he said, "I really don't know what to say."[16]

Socrates chastises Hippocrates:

> You hear about him in the evening—right?—and the next morning, here you are, not to talk about whether it's a good idea to entrust yourself to him or not, but ready to spend your own money and your friends' as well, as if you had thought it all through already and, no matter what, you had to be with Protagoras, a man whom you admit you don't know and have never conversed with, and whom you call a sophist although you obviously have no idea what this sophist is to whom you are about to entrust yourself.[17]

Note Socrates' criticism that Hippocrates is behaving "as if you had thought it all out." Hippocrates had not even asked himself the questions to which he confidently assumed an audience with Protagoras was the answer. When we settle on answers to the central questions of our lives without ever having opened up those questions for inquiry, that is a recipe for wavering. A mind tasked only with thinking its way through the next fifteen minutes is likely to find itself acting inconsistently, routinely undoing what it confidently did earlier.

Hippocrates and Socrates do eventually head over to where Protagoras is staying, and Socrates and Protagoras end up in a conversation about the relationship between being a good person (having "virtue") and having knowledge. At the end of this conversation Socrates points out that the conversation itself has wavered:

> It seems to me that our discussion has turned on us, and if it had a voice of its own, it would say, mockingly, "Socrates and Protagoras, how ridiculous you are, both of you. Socrates, you said earlier that virtue cannot be taught, but now you are arguing the very opposite and have attempted to show that everything is knowledge—justice, temperance, courage—in which case virtue would be eminently teachable. . . . Now, Protagoras maintained at first that it could be taught, but now he thinks the opposite, urging that hardly any of the virtues turn out to be knowledge. On that view, virtue could hardly be taught at all."
>
> Now, Protagoras, seeing that we have gotten this topsy-turvy and terribly confused, I am most eager to clear it all up, and I would like us, having come this far, to continue until we come through to what virtue is in itself . . . if you are willing, as I said at the beginning, I would be pleased to investigate them with you.[18]

Socrates diagnoses their mistake as trying to answer the question of whether virtue can be taught or whether virtue is knowledge without asking, "What is virtue?" They presupposed they had an answer to that question, but in fact they had never even asked it. The result is that they wavered. Protagoras is impressed with Socrates, but turns down the invitation to inquire:

> Socrates, I commend your enthusiasm and the way you find your way through an argument. I really don't think I am a bad man, certainly the last man to harbor ill will. Indeed, I have told many people that I admire you more

than anyone I have met, certainly more than anyone in your generation. And I say that I would not be surprised if you gain among men high repute for wisdom. We will examine these things later, whenever you wish; now it is time to turn our attention elsewhere.[19]

Protagoras thinks that he must turn his attention elsewhere, away from inquiry. He needs to get on with the next fifteen minutes of his life. Socrates encounters a similar scenario in another dialogue, with Euthyphro, who complains that "whatever proposition we put forward goes around and refuses to stay put where we establish it."[20] The conversation ends when Socrates insists, "We must investigate again from the beginning . . . "[21] and Euthyphro replies "some other time, Socrates, for I am in a hurry now, and it is time for me to go."[22]

In the *Alcibiades*, a dialogue we will examine in more detail in chapter 6, Socrates takes it upon himself to draw a young, ambitious person's attention to the fact that he has never asked himself the most basic ethical questions. That failure manifests as wavering:

> SOCRATES: So if you gave conflicting answers about
> something, without meaning to, then it would be
> obvious that you didn't know it.
> ALCIBIADES: Probably.
> SOCRATES: Well then, you tell me that you're wavering
> about what is just and unjust, admirable and contempt-
> ible, good and bad, and advantageous and disadvanta-
> geous. Isn't it obvious that the reason you waver about
> them is that you don't know about them?[23]

Yet another dialogue, the *Lesser Hippias*, ends with an exchange in which Socrates admits his own wavering:

> HIPPIAS: I can't agree with you in that, Socrates.

SOCRATES: Nor I with myself, Hippias. But given the argument, we can't help having it look that way to us, now, at any rate. However, as I said before, on these matters I waver back and forth and never believe the same thing.[24]

Socrates diagnoses his own wavering in the same way as he diagnoses Alcibiades': "I go back and forth about all this—plainly because I don't know."[25] What causes Socrates to waver is his failure to have inquired sufficiently; to this extent, he is in the same boat as everyone else. The difference between Socrates and those around him is that he wants to do something about this problem. Socrates thinks that his circumstances call for inquiry, whereas his interlocutors are inclined to cut off the inquiry and move on with their lives. As Socrates sees it, by preemptively closing the questions, they consign themselves to a lifetime of wavering.

IV. EVERYBODY WAVERS

One cannot but sympathize with Tolstoy's self-representation as someone who is inquiring assiduously, laboriously, energetically:

And I searched for explanations of my questions in all the branches of knowledge that human beings have acquired. And I searched long and agonizingly and not just out of idle curiosity; I didn't search limply but I searched agonizingly, persistently, day and night; I searched as a dying man searches for salvation, and I found nothing.[26]

Nonetheless, Tolstoy's "I found nothing" should shock any reader. How could it be that Tolstoy found absolutely *nothing* to address the question of the meaning of life in *all the branches of knowledge that human beings have acquired*? Has the whole human intellectual endeavor been a total failure? One might have thought that there would be *something* useful for thinking about the meaning of life in the vast ocean of human intellectual output—in fact, I would contend that there is much that is useful to be found even in that tiny portion of the sea constituted by Tolstoy's own literary output.

The Socratic interpretation is that Tolstoy did not try and fail; rather, he failed to try. He confused his own failure to ask a question with a conclusive "unquestionable" discovery that there was no possible answer. Although Tolstoy regularly refers to "my reasoning," the absence of philosophical thinking in his text suggests that his conclusions were not products of reasoning, but substitutes for it. Sometimes, when we are very determined not to ask a question, we make a claim of having very decisively answered it.

Tolstoy was not able to ask himself whether his existence mattered, because he could not pause the activity of living for long enough to inquire into an answer. Tolstoy imagined that he had formed a settled judgment against the meaning of life, but he had not. Rather, he failed to articulate any kind of sustained argument against the meaning of life, and his incessant wavering made it impossible to find any sense of closure or contentment in the conclusion he pretended to have decisively arrived at:

> If I had simply understood that life has no meaning, I might have known that calmly, could have known that this was my fate. But I couldn't be content with that. If I had been like a man in a forest from which he knows there is no way out, I could have lived; but I was like a man lost in a forest who has been overcome by terror through being lost, and he rushes to and fro trying to find the road; he knows that every step makes him more lost, and he can't stop rushing about.[27]

We might be reminded here of young Hippocrates rushing around in the early morning hours.

Wavering is not a phenomenon consigned to the ancient world, though it has gone by many names. The philosopher Bertrand Russell called one species of it "emotive conjugation":

> I am firm, you are obstinate, he is a pig-headed fool. I am righteously indignant, you are annoyed, he is making a fuss over nothing. I have reconsidered the matter, you have changed your mind, he has gone back on his word.[28]

Russell is noticing the form of wavering that arises from the ways in which ethical language is hostage to its user's approval: we call self-confidence "arrogance" when we dislike it; we call youthfulness "immaturity" when we dislike it; we call revenge "accountability" when we like it; we call consequences "punitive" when we dislike them (otherwise we just call them consequences). Consider the difference between "tribalism," which always references something we don't like, and "loyalty," which is what we call the same phenomenon when we approve of it. Likewise, consider how we applaud someone's behavior as "cooperative" when we like the fact that she is doing what works for others, and reject her behavior as "conformist" when she's once again doing what works for others, but this time we happen to dislike it. Those who risk their lives for a cause they believe in count as "courageous" to those who also believe in the cause, whereas disbelievers are likely to say these people are "fools" or "indoctrinated."

Folk wisdom is another place to see wavering. Pick a maxim or adage and you can usually articulate a counter-maxim that people will use to cover the case where they wish to praise the opposite: "Look before you leap," *but* "He who dares, wins"; "Slow and steady wins the race," *but* "Time waits for no man"; "Birds of a feather flock together," *but* "Opposites attract"; "Silence is golden," *but* "The squeaky wheel gets the grease." And so on.

You waver when you decide that one thought is suitable for one context and a different one for another, even though you cannot specify any relevant difference between the two contexts. Did I say

"Silence is golden" on the basis of a principle that allows me to determine when it is or is not the time to be a squeaky wheel? Or did I say "Silence is golden" simply because, in the here and now, I don't want you to talk? Whereas other people criticize Socrates for being repetitive, he criticizes them for wavering—or, as he puts it, refusing to say the same things about the same subjects. In the *Gorgias* Socrates is discussing the central question of politics—who should rule—and he says:

> Do you see, my good Callicles, that you and I are not accusing each other of the same thing? You claim that I'm always saying the same things, and you criticize me for it, whereas I, just the opposite of you, claim that you never say the same things about the same subjects.[29]

There is no domain where our wavering is more obvious than it is in politics, and there is no one who finds it more obvious than our political opponents. If you are in favor of free speech, except when it comes to people you disagree with, those people will see you as wavering. If you think a president whose term is coming to an end should still get to choose a Supreme Court justice—but only when that president belongs to your party—the opposite party will say you are wavering. If you cite empirical research only when it supports the position you antecedently championed, and call that "following the science," those who hold the other position will say you are wavering.

Wavering often takes the form of weakness of will, where we commit ourselves to one course of action, and end up acting against our better judgment, instead. Remember Tolstoy's reference to "the way of weakness" in which I do something worse even though "I know what is best and it is in my power." We say we *know* that we should exercise more and spend less time on our phones and be nicer to our parents and keep our kids away from video games and eat more vegetables and read more novels and be more conscious about our consumption choices and so on and so forth, but quite often we don't act in accordance with this supposed knowledge—instead, we act exactly as people would act who didn't know those things.

V. FICTION AS REFUGE

Most of the time, when we waver, we don't notice that we are wavering. We become adept at avoiding having to acknowledge our wavering. We *rationalize*. When Tolstoy is wearing his novelist hat, he sees this phenomenon quite clearly. For example, in *War and Peace*, Pierre wrangles with himself over whether or not he should go to a party at Anatole Kuragin's house:

> "I should like to go to Kuragin's," thought he.
>
> But he immediately recalled his promise to Prince Andrew not to go there. Then, as happens to people of weak character, he desired so passionately once more to enjoy that dissipation he was so accustomed to that he decided to go. The thought immediately occurred to him that his promise to Prince Andrew was of no account, because before he gave it he had already promised Prince Anatole to come to his gathering; "besides," thought he, "all such 'words of honor' are conventional things with no definite meaning, especially if one considers that by tomorrow one may be dead, or something so extraordinary may happen to one that honor and dishonor will be all the same!" Pierre often indulged in reflections of this sort, nullifying all his decisions and intentions. He went to Kuragin's.[30]

Pierre gives Andrew his word of honor that he won't go to Kuragin's party, then enters a carriage, and almost immediately directs the driver to Kuragin's. The paragraph above describes the thoughts he has along the way. Notice that Pierre not only decides to go to Kuragin's, but also convinces himself that he has carefully reasoned his way to the conclusion that it would be best to go—when in fact, as Tolstoy tells us, that question was closed from the outset: "He desired so passionately . . . that he decided to go." Passionate desire, not inquiry. Passionate desire pressures us to think no more than fifteen minutes ahead.

But imagine *being* Pierre, and acknowledging what is happening: maybe the truth is that drinking and partying really are my central concerns; I'm like an animal, battered around by pleasure and convention; there's nothing my life is about. No one could bear to see himself as one of those "people of weak character." The only way to get through the next fifteen minutes is to convince yourself that you're doing something much nobler than getting through the next fifteen minutes. And so you produce, as Pierre does, as Tolstoy does, the illusion of a synoptic perspective on your life as a whole.

If we never inquire into untimely questions, the thinking we use to guide our lives will be unstable. We will never be able to rely on it for very long—perhaps no more than fifteen minutes or so—before it is subject to being overturned. But we don't experience these overturnings, because we are accustomed to smoothing over the bumps created by wavering. Again, we rationalize. This is why it comes as a shock to his interlocutors when Socrates, using his probing questioning, forces the wavering into the light. Socrates brought the Tolstoy problem to the attention of people who would otherwise never have noticed it.

There are so many questions about human life that we never stop to ask ourselves, because we are too busy moving on with our lives, deploying our answers. They are questions about how to treat other people fairly, what kind of greatness to pursue in life, what it means to love and be loved, how we should face death, how society should be organized, who our real friends are, how to raise our children, what the demands of justice are, and quite generally, what to do with our lives. These are questions about the things that matter most to us, about projects we have a standing investment in, questions we have always already answered. We cannot "step back" to a detached position from which having no answer at all is permissible: question and answer are magnetically attracted to one another, and the space for thought is eliminated. So we get by without asking untimely questions—or we appear to ourselves to get by, while actually wavering. We waver in our actions, we waver in our thoughts, and we waver most of all when pressed to explain ourselves.

When Tolstoy has Pierre excuse his promise-breaking on the grounds that "all such 'words of honor' are conventional things with no definite meaning, especially if one considers that by tomorrow one may be dead," it is clear that the reader is meant to see right through this. We should not fall for Pierre's grandiose nihilism. And yet Tolstoy falls for his own. The reader of *Confession* can see clearly that Tolstoy closed the questions before ever opening them; that he is pretending at profundity even with his despair ("the truth was that life was meaningless"); that the deepest abyss is one he never allows himself to confront. But Tolstoy cannot see this. It is a commonplace that the self is a blind spot, and that we detect others' rationalizations more easily than our own, but behind this commonplace lies the troubling fact that each person routinely fails to confront the most important questions about their lives.

Fiction was a place where Tolstoy could dramatize, from a safe distance, his own brush with the meaninglessness of life. The Tolstoy problem haunts so much of Tolstoy's fiction: many of his characters confront the question, "What will become of my whole life?" His novella *The Death of Ivan Ilyich* is straightforwardly centered on the Tolstoy problem. It tells the tale of the collapse of Ivan's infrastructure of ideas in the face of the terrifying prospect of death. We will return to that novella, and some of Tolstoy's other fictionalizations of the Tolstoy problem, in the final chapter of this book; I draw attention to them here only to note the larger pattern, that Tolstoy was evidently fascinated with the Tolstoy problem, and that he had an easier time giving free rein to this fascination in fictional form.

We see through others' conceits more readily than our own, and there is even a profession—that of novelist—that capitalizes on this asymmetry. The Italian novelist Elena Ferrante hypothesizes that the writing of fiction prevents someone from employing the strategies of avoidance that we ordinarily use to get through our lives:

> To tolerate existence, we lie, and we lie above all to ourselves. Sometimes we tell ourselves lovely tales, sometimes petty lies. Falsehoods protect us, mitigate suffering, allow us to avoid the terrifying moment of serious reflection, they dilute the horrors of our time, they even save us from ourselves. Instead, when one writes one must never lie. In literary fiction you have to be sincere to the point where it's unbearable, where you suffer the emptiness of the pages.[31]

Ferrante finds in fiction a refuge from the lies: an opportunity to sincerely and directly address what must otherwise be skirted around. Many readers of fiction find in it a similarly liberating experience. All fiction offers up the possibility of escape from everyday life, but great fiction allows us to explore what we otherwise look away from. Books and movies offer opportunities to ponder the great questions about the meaning of marriage, of friendship, of career, of politics, of suffering—and, yes, also of life and death.

Fiction can make untimely questions askable—but only in relation to fictional characters. That is a serious limitation. We approach the lives of others with a kind of boldness that seems impossible for our own. When we come back to reality, and to the course of our own lives, we are, like Tolstoy, stuck "telling ourselves tales." When Ferrante describes "the terrifying moment of serious reflection," it is clear that she has confronted the Tolstoy problem.

Tolstoy laments: "How often I envied the peasants for their illiteracy and lack of education." William James accurately channels Tolstoy's combination of condescension and admiration toward the peasantry: "Yet how believe as the common people believe, steeped as they are in grossest superstition? It is impossible,—but yet their life! their life! It is normal. It is happy! It is an answer to the question!"[32] The ideal, for Tolstoy, would be never having to confront the Tolstoy problem in the first place. Tolstoy held that reasoned thought is useless when it comes to the most fundamental problems. If Tolstoy were correct, the best course for those unlucky enough to cross paths with the Tolstoy problem might be to postpone and postpone, fifteen minutes at a time, until one runs out the clock.

Ferrante thinks that seriously reflecting on life is terrifying, and Tolstoy thinks that its logical conclusion is suicide. Both allow us, as readers, some access to the untimely questions that drive their fictional characters to waver so disastrously. Neither countenances the possibility of sincerely articulating and carefully examining the conceptual framework of one's own real, ongoing, life. In much the way that a painting presents us with a landscape but prevents us from entering it, novelists give us a view onto the promised land, but not more.

Socrates believed that "the unexamined life is not worth living for a human being,"[33] and that belief motivated him to make time for untimely questions. Whereas the nonphilosopher is "is always in a hurry when he is talking; he has to speak with one eye on the clock," the philosopher resists taking life fifteen minutes at a time: "He talks in peace and quiet, and his time is his own." Socrates says that "it does not matter to such people whether they talk for a day or a year, if only they may hit upon that which is."[34] Socrates thought that the Tolstoy problem could be solved.

VI. UNWAVERING ACTION

But why should we care whether we solve the Tolstoy problem? There is a tense moment toward the end of one dialogue where Socrates' interlocutor—a young visitor from Thessaly by the name of Meno—casts doubt on the value of inquiry. Why should we care whether or not we can inquire into untimely questions? Socrates has to admit that even without inquiring, we are not wanting for answers to these questions. What makes a question untimely is precisely that it comes to us already answered. Socrates explains that by pursuing knowledge—which is to say, by seeking a solution to the Tolstoy problem—we *stabilize* those answers:

> MENO: That . . . makes me wonder, Socrates . . . why knowledge is prized far more highly than right opinion, and why they are different.
>
> SOCRATES: Do you know why you wonder, or shall I tell you?
>
> MENO: By all means tell me.
>
> SOCRATES: It is because you have paid no attention to the statues of Daedalus, but perhaps there are none in Thessaly.
>
> MENO: What do you have in mind when you say this?
>
> SOCRATES: That they too run away and escape if one does not tie them down but remain in place if tied down.
>
> MENO: So what?
>
> SOCRATES: To acquire an untied work of Daedalus is not worth much, like acquiring a runaway slave, for it does not remain, but it is worth much if tied down, for his works are very beautiful. What am I thinking of when I say this? True opinions. For true opinions, as long as they remain, are a fine thing and all they do is good, but they are not willing to remain long, and they escape from a man's mind, so that they are not worth much until one ties them down by (giving) an account of the reason why.[35]

Socrates is here distinguishing an opinion that one simply has from an opinion that is formed by way of an inquisitive process. When the opinion is the conclusion of a process of inquiry, whose steps can in turn be retraced ("an account of the reason why"), our wavering stops. "After they are tied down, in the first place they become knowledge, and then they remain in place. That is why knowledge is prized higher than correct opinion, and knowledge differs from correct opinion in being tied down."[36] The thinking that we do in pursuit of an answer holds that answer fixed. Knowledge is simply the name for an answer that is the product of a completed inquiry into a question. Wavering, by contrast, is a sign that one has cut off an investigation before it came to a close—or that one never even opened it.

When it comes to untimely questions, the challenge is not simply to find answers. We can have those without inquiring. We can even have *true* answers ("right opinion") without inquiring. What inquiry gets us are answers that are both true and stable. When we have not really reasoned our way to a conclusion, it is easily reversed—especially under conditions of urgency. The preference for knowledge over mere "right opinion" is the preference for answers that have been stabilized by inquiry.

But why is stability—the avoidance of wavering—so important? I have said that human action differs from mere behavior through its conceptual infrastructure: action is based on ideas about what is good, ideas that supply the motivating goal of the action. The fact that you think those ideas are true is the only reason you are doing anything at all. The question is: How long will these ideas last? For how much time will you continue to think that they are true? If you are only trying to make it to the end of your action without being confronted by the fact that you have lost faith in the ideas underwriting it, then they might only need to last fifteen minutes or so. But in that case your action does not really have a conceptual infrastructure; it only appears to you that it does for the duration of the time during which you are acting. In retrospect—viewing the completed action from the standpoint of a time when you no longer hold the relevant idea—you would be forced to acknowledge there was no point to what you did.

Of course, you would only be forced into such an acknowledgment if, having wavered, you also chose to look back. If you confine your gaze—never looking back, never looking too far ahead, always only making it through the next fifteen minutes—you can avoid being confronted with evidence of your wavering. But suppose you succeed at this: you put one foot in front of another, over and over again, all the way to the end, which is to say, right up until the moment that your journey is cut off by death. What will you have achieved? The answer is that you will have maintained the appearance, to yourself and others, that your behavior has a conceptual infrastructure. It will seem to be true that all your various doings hang together, bound by some through-line that makes them intelligible as parts of a whole life. You will have put on a good show of being someone whose life is supported by ideas, someone who knows what they are doing.

But the only explanation for why a person would put on this show is that she wants it to be reality. Some part of her desperately wants to live a life that makes sense. The philosophical project springs from this desire. The inquiry into untimely questions is the search for a life that doesn't need to be shielded from reflection, a life you live *by* understanding it. Viewed in this light, "philosopher" is not the name of a profession. It is just a way—an especially open, direct and straightforward one—of being a person.

Chapter 2

Load-Bearing Answers

S OCRATES DIED BY DRINKING HEMLOCK. BEFORE THE
city of Athens compelled him to drink it—an event dramatized
in Plato's *Phaedo*—he awaited execution in a prison cell, and his
friend Crito came to visit him. Crito offered to bribe the guards so
as to help Socrates escape prison and death, and Socrates persuaded
him that escaping would be wrong—their conversation is dramatized in another dialogue, the *Crito*. Before that happened, Socrates
was convicted of impiety by an Athenian jury, and before he was
convicted, he made a speech of self-defense, which is dramatized
in the *Apology*. Before he visited the courtroom to defend himself,
Socrates made an earlier visit to the same courtroom, to hear what
his three accusers (Meletus, Anytus, and Lycon) charged him with;
and before he arrived at the courtroom that first time—when he
was standing just outside it—he ran into a religious prophet named
Euthyphro, and they had a conversation about piety. This conversation, dramatized by Plato in the *Euthyphro*, is thus the first in a
chain of dialogues that end in the death of Socrates.

Euthyphro has come to the courtroom to prosecute his own father
for murder. If we would be surprised to hear a son announce such a
plan, a contemporary of Euthyphro would have been shocked. Athenian law categorized murder as a crime against the family of the victim, not the state; in that respect, such a lawsuit resembles our civil
cases more than our criminal ones, and it would normally only be
brought on behalf of, not against, a family member. In fact, Euthyphro's is the only case of a son prosecuting his father that we know

of from ancient Athenian legal history.[1] We can almost see Socrates' eyebrows rising:

> SOCRATES: Whom do you prosecute?
>
> EUTHYPHRO: One whom I am thought crazy to prosecute.
>
> SOCRATES: Are you pursuing someone who will easily escape you?
>
> EUTHYPHRO: Far from it, for he is quite old.
>
> SOCRATES: Who is it?
>
> EUTHYPHRO: My father.
>
> SOCRATES: My dear sir! Your own father?
>
> EUTHYPHRO: Certainly.
>
> SOCRATES: What is the charge? What is the case about?
>
> EUTHYPHRO: Murder, Socrates.
>
> SOCRATES: Good heavens! Certainly, Euthyphro, most men would not know how they could do this and be right. It is not the part of anyone to do this, but of one who is far advanced in wisdom.
>
> EUTHYPHRO: Yes, by Zeus, Socrates, that is so.
>
> SOCRATES: Is then the man your father killed one of your relatives? Or is that obvious, for you would not prosecute your father for the murder of a stranger.[2]

The story only gets more bizarre from here. The man killed was not only *not* a relative of Euthyphro's—he was himself a killer. What happened was this: A family servant killed a household slave, Euthyphro's father sent for a priest in order to determine the appropriate punishment, and meanwhile bound the killer hand and foot and threw him into a pit. The killer died of exposure before Euthyphro's father heard back from the priest, and Euthyphro thinks his father is guilty of murder for not taking proper care of the killer while he lay in the pit.

Socrates, having heard this story, jumps at the chance to interrogate a person who could confidently navigate this ethical quandary:

> SOCRATES: Whereas, by Zeus, Euthyphro, you think that your knowledge of the divine, and of piety and impiety, is so accurate that, when those things happened as you say, you have no fear of having acted impiously in bringing your father to trial?
>
> EUTHYPHRO: I should be of no use, Socrates, and Euthyphro would not be superior to the majority of people, if I did not have accurate knowledge of all such things.
>
> SOCRATES: It is indeed most important, my admirable Euthyphro, that I should become your pupil, and as regards this indictment, challenge Meletus about these very things.[3]

Meletus is the ringleader of the trio whose accusations of impiety Socrates is about to hear. The philosophical conversation that ensues, between Socrates and Euthyphro as they stand on the threshold of the courtroom, concerns the nature of piety. When Euthyphro prosecutes his father, he runs the risk of being accused of impiety; and it is likewise on charges of impiety that Socrates will, in that same courtroom, be tried and sentenced to death. Whatever piety is, it matters a great deal to Socrates, to Euthyphro, and to the Athenians before whom they will plead their cases.

Each of Plato's Socratic dialogues features a conversation with high stakes. When talking to a child, Socrates' question is: "Am I right in assuming, Lysis, that your father and mother love you very much?"[4] When Lysis answers yes, Socrates offers an argument to the contrary. He asks power-hungry Alcibiades whether he really thinks he has what it takes to be a ruler. When Socrates asks orators to explain what oratory is, the implied challenge is: Are you able to make a speech about what speeches are, or will that leave you tongue-tied? When talking to a professional virtue teacher, Protagoras, Socrates questions whether virtue can be taught. In conversation with Hippias, a self-proclaimed expert in everything, Socrates argues that the expert is the one who will be capable of the most evil. Socrates asks Ion, a rhapsode who makes his living by reciting Homer, whether Homer really knew what he was talking about. When he runs into Lysimachus and Melesias, who are debating the proper military education for their sons, and the generals Laches and Nicias, who are advising them, he asks whether any of them know what courage is. In a conversation with a young man from a noble family and the guardian charged with making sure he is educated into his proper place in the aristocracy Socrates asks about the meaning of *sōphrosynē*. *Sōphrosynē* is notoriously difficult to translate—it has been rendered as "moderation," "temperance," "discipline," and "self-control"—but it can be described as "an aristocrat's virtue par excellence, involving a sense of dignity and self-command."[5] Thus Socrates is asking the parties to aristocratic education whether they understand its goal. The topic of the *Phaedo*, the dialogue featuring Socrates' death, is whether there is life after death—Socrates has, up until this moment, tended to believe that there is, but decides that this is the opportune moment to subject that belief to sharp critique. He asks his friends, all of them devastated by the unbearable prospect of his death, to remain calm, refrain from crying, and inquire alongside him.

Euthyphro's last words in the dialogue, after Socrates encourages him to continue the conversation in spite of many failed attempts to explain piety, express the frustration and beleaguerment typical of Socrates' interlocutors: "Some other time, Socrates, for I am in a hurry now, and it is time for me to go."[6] And yet what is surprising about these conversations is not the fact that the interlocutor is eager to rush off at the end, but that they stay as long as they do. Likewise, though Socrates is eventually put to death for his philosophizing, it is amazing how long he is permitted to spend doing exactly that: he reached the ripe old age of seventy. The story of Socrates is mostly the story of people putting up with the treatment described above. Each of his conversations is a high-wire act in which Socrates manages to sustain an inquiry into the very question his interlocutor is least likely to tolerate. These are untimely questions. Let's examine them more carefully.

I. WHAT IS AN UNTIMELY QUESTION?

Some of Socrates' interlocutors are initially taken aback by how easy his questions seem. Here is how Meno responds to being asked to define "virtue":

> *It is not hard to tell you*, Socrates. First, if you want the virtue of a man, *it is easy to say* that a man's virtue consists of being able to manage public affairs . . . if you want the virtue of a woman, it is *not difficult to describe*: she must . . . be submissive to her husband; the virtue of a child, whether male or female, is different again, and so is that of an elderly man, if you want that, or if you want that of a free man or a slave. And there are very many other virtues, so that *one is not at a loss to say* what virtue is.[7]

Meno remarks on how easy this question is four times over the course of a short speech. Euthyphro similarly thinks he will have an easy time explaining what he means by "piety." But Socrates has only to apply the lightest pressure to their answers for this appearance of ease to dissolve. Meno, for example, has not considered the fact that there must be something that all of the characters he describes—man, woman, child, slave—have in common, insofar as they deserve to be called "virtuous." When pressed to explain what this common element might be, Meno makes a second attempt at defining virtue: "to be able to rule over people, if you are seeking one description to fit them all." But Socrates immediately points out

that this description does not fit those whose virtue Meno believes
lies in their *being* ruled. Meno's definition fits the position he sees
himself as occupying in this story, that of being in charge. And this
is connected to the fact that Meno is giving the answer that guides
his own life: his answer is not just an answer, but a kind of plan he
takes himself to be currently following.

Euthyphro initially defines piety as follows: "I say that the pious is
to do what I am doing now, to prosecute the wrongdoer, be it about
murder or temple-robbery or anything else, whether the wrongdoer
is your father or mother or anyone else."[8] At first, Socrates' interlocutors often conflate the activity of *defining* the concept in question
with that of showing how it applies to and affirms their own behavior.* In the *Gorgias*, Socrates asks his interlocutor—an orator—to
define oratory, and he says it is "the most admirable of the crafts."[9]

There is a pattern to how many people respond to Socrates' questions: they first feel that the questions are so straightforward as to
hardly deserve consideration, and then give "answers" that amount
to performative self-affirmations. This pattern is not a sign of any
arrogance peculiar to Socrates' milieu. It is, instead, a direct conse-
quence of how Socrates has chosen his questions. Someone who asks
a child, "Do your parents really love you?" cannot expect the child
to approach this question in a detached, reflective manner. The child
needs to believe that his parents love him, and, more generally, people need to approve of the choices that they are, at that very moment,
making. Socrates' questions pinpoint beliefs the person needs to
have—and his questioning applies targeted pressure on that critical,
load-bearing, spot.

What does it mean to say that we "need" some belief? Imagine

---

* Socrates is relentlessly consistent in prioritizing definition over praise: at
a drinking party where participants have been taking turns offering flowery
speeches of praise to the god of love, Erōs, Socrates, ever the wet blanket,
insists on beginning his own speech by defining love—and goes on to insist
that Erōs is not even a god.

we are walking together chatting, and you ask me, "Which way is the supermarket?" I say, "I'm going that way right now, do you want to come with me?" Or even more simply, I might answer, "Just follow me!" Notice that my response to you does not require me to revisit the question "How does one get to the supermarket?" I don't open an inquiry into a question that I take myself to have already answered. If, by contrast, you had asked me directions to somewhere I was not going—e.g., the post office—I might have had to pause for a moment, consider my mental map of my neighborhood, locate myself in it, and then offer you instructions: "You will have to turn left at the next intersection." A belief that one needs to have is a belief that one is acting on.

I give directions differently when I'm already heading to the same destination. I don't pause to consider how an action should be performed when I am already performing that action. Notice that my failure to employ the reflective, detached, post office procedure when asked about the supermarket is not a sign of misplaced self-confidence; the difference in how I answer is simply a function of the fact that the relevant belief is already *operational*. When I talk to you about the location of the supermarket, I am handing you a special kind of thought—one that is, as it were, currently moving my legs forward.

But suppose you gave me good reason for thinking that I might be headed in the wrong direction: "That supermarket is closed today; you should go to a different one." If your claim is credible, its effect on me will be visible: I will stop. Now, I both can and must ask myself which way I should go. The moment this becomes an open question for me is the moment I put my walking on hold for long enough to inquire into it. Once stopped, I can approach this problem in the same detached, speculative manner I had earlier adopted for the post office, because I am not acting on any answer to it.

One mark of an untimely question is the availability of one's answer. It is not only that one (feels certain that one) has an answer, but that, because that answer is currently at work in propelling one forward, the expression of the answer takes the form of *using it* ("Follow me!") rather than *explaining it* ("This is how . . . "). It is akin to the difference between responding to "Do you have a pencil?" with "Yes," and responding by handing over a pencil. When the question is untimely, we "hand over" an answer that is guaranteed to be found on the tip of our tongue, because we were already speaking it—to ourselves. Or at least we assumed we were. Socrates catches people in the awkward moment of transfer where everyone suddenly realizes that the hand that both parties had supposed to be holding the pencil is, in fact, empty.

In this story, "Which way is the supermarket?" was an untimely question, but a relatively lightweight one. A small amount of pressure—for instance, your telling me it is closed today—would be enough to get me to stop using that answer. At that point I would be free to stop walking and ask myself which way I should go. To be clear, I have at all points been free to *go* somewhere else. My freedom of movement has never been in question: no one is forcing me to go to the supermarket, and none of the paths before me are blocked. But in order to exercise the freedom to go wherever I want to go, I give up some freedom to think about whatever I want to think about. I regain the freedom to ask myself the question, "Which way is the supermarket?" or more broadly, "Where should I go?" only once I *stop* using an answer to that question. This doesn't mean I have to literally stop moving my legs, because I might keep walking from the force of habit, or because I found some new reason for walking, such as the desire to save myself from the embarrassment of pausing in front of a shop window and having the people inside notice my confusion. I could keep walking, but I could not keep *walking to the supermarket*. In the case of the supermarket, we can see that the project is not very fundamental to my life, by noting how easy it is to come to be arrested by a thought such as "Maybe I need to go to a different supermarket?"

Not all projects are so easily put on hold. For example: I am a mother all the time. Even when I'm away from my children, I cannot pose to myself a question such as "What does it take to be a good mother?" without thinking about whether my own mothering meets the standard I am describing. I can't step off the mothering treadmill long enough to consider the question in a dispassionate and detached way. The same is true of other substantial roles, such as being a student. Unless a student is somehow truly alienated from their education—just going through the motions to please others—they will be unable to approach the question as to what makes for a good student in an impartial and dispassionate manner. Their answer will have the marks of being currently in use, because they can't take time off from this pursuit. Time off from studying, such as vacations or study breaks, cannot be equated with time off from taking the concept "student" as crucial to one's self-understanding. One could stop being a student by dropping out of school, and perhaps one could stop being a parent by cutting off contact with one's children, but those are high costs to pay for opening up a question. And notice that the person who paid those costs and became "open" to these questions by divesting themselves from the corresponding commitments would be precisely the one who had little reason to care about the answers.

What makes a question untimely for a given person is the fact that she is enacting its answer, but there are important differences between the size and scope of our practical projects. Untimely questions about being a mother and student refer to activities that represent a more substantial investment of our agency than untimely questions about being a shopper, which makes the former more interesting but also more elusive. The most interesting and most elusive questions will be the ones whose answers we must give at every moment of our lives, for their whole duration. In terms of the degree to which we, as agents, rely on them, these answers bear the heaviest load.

Socrates tends to drive his inquiries toward such questions. One example is: Am I a just (i.e., good) person? This question becomes the subject of Socrates' conversation with Alcibiades in the dialogue of the same name:

SOCRATES: When you were a boy I often observed you, at school and other places, and sometimes when you were playing knucklebones or some other game, you'd say to one or another of your playmates, very loudly and confidently—not at all like someone who was at a loss about justice and injustice—that he was a lousy cheater and wasn't playing fairly. Isn't that true?

ALCIBIADES: But what was I to do, Socrates, when somebody cheated me like that?

SOCRATES: Do you mean, what should you have done if you didn't actually know then whether or not you were being cheated?

ALCIBIADES: But I *did* know, by Zeus! I saw clearly that they were cheating me.

SOCRATES: So it seems that even as a child you thought you understood justice and injustice.

ALCIBIADES: Yes, and I *did* understand.

SOCRATES: At what point did you find it out? Surely it wasn't when you thought you knew.

ALCIBIADES: Of course not.

SOCRATES: Then when did you think you didn't know? Think about it—you won't find any such time.[10]

Mothers can think back to before they were mothers, and students can look ahead to when they won't be students, but there are some projects that take up our whole lives. We can ask someone, "Why did you decide to have children?" or "Why did you decide to go to graduate school?" but we cannot ask, "Why did you decide to be a good person?" No one will be able to account for that decision; as far back as we stretch our minds, we will find that the decision was already in place. Nor will we be able to think back to a time when we were too confused or puzzled about what justice was to have the kinds of responses Alcibiades had to being cheated at games: an attitude of wonder or detached inquisitiveness seems misplaced here.

One doesn't need to be very old to confront questions of justice, and as soon as one does, one finds that one is already in the business of indignantly insisting on one's rights.

One can wonder, in a detached and curious spirit, whether there is life on other planets or how fast the fastest bird flies; one cannot wonder disinterestedly whether some harm that has been done to us is unjust. By the time a question of justice arises, one finds oneself needing to hit the ground running with an answer. There is no space for either a practical, deliberative activity such as "deciding," in which one evaluates a proposed option for goodness; nor is there space for an inquisitive activity such as scientific analysis, in which one evaluates the truth of a claim—and this is what leads to our fighting about claims of justice ("Lousy cheater!").

II. Untimely, Not Subjective

Our standing investment in the answers to untimely questions explains their contentiousness much better than the usual explanation, which is to dismiss these questions as "subjective." To see why, consider what sorts of disagreements give rise to fights:

> SOCRATES: I don't suppose you've ever seen or heard people disagreeing so strongly about what is healthy and unhealthy that they fight and kill each other over it, have you?
>
> ALCIBIADES: Of course not.
>
> SOCRATES: But I know you've seen this sort of dispute over questions of justice and injustice; or even if you haven't seen it, at least you've heard about it from many other people—especially Homer, since you've heard the *Iliad* and the *Odyssey*, haven't you?
>
> ALCIBIADES: I certainly have, of course, Socrates.
>
> SOCRATES: Aren't these poems all about disagreements over justice and injustice?

ALCIBIADES: Yes.

SOCRATES: It was over this sort of disagreement that the Achaeans and the Trojans fought battles and lost their lives, as did Odysseus and the suitors of Penelope.[11]

Socrates says that we fight when we disagree about justice, but not when we disagree about health. We cannot explain this difference by claiming that questions of health are unimportant, because sometimes those questions are, quite literally, a matter of life and death.

But don't we sometimes fight over health? It is true that we become angry when health concerns are ignored or overstated, especially by public authorities, or when the irresponsible choices of some endanger the health or safety of others. In each of these cases, however, considerations of health are bound up with those of justice: deception, misinformation, and reckless endangerment are moral and political concerns, not medical ones.

If you think a high-protein diet is healthier and I think a high-carbohydrate diet is healthier, or if you favor treatment X for a particular disease and I favor treatment Y—even if these are matters of life and death—we won't necessarily fight. We might fight, if one of us feels the other's position is due to culpable negligence in gathering or interpreting data—but that is to turn the question once again into one of justice. Assuming no accusations of wrongdoing are at play, even a disagreement over a matter of life and death can be quite peaceable: each of us waits to hear the other's reasons, ready to change her mind in the presence of sufficient evidence.*

We make space for reasonable disagreement and suspension of judgment in matters of life and death, and this is appropriate. For

---

* The fact that it is possible for these discussions to become heated just shows that there is another way in which questions of health can become mixed up with questions of justice. When participants feel that the underlying question being adjudicated is not one about health, but about their own authority or intellectual competence, then disagreement gets translated into disrespect.

vulnerable creatures, death and illness are part of life. We try to avoid them when we can, but understand that we cannot escape them altogether. We acknowledge no such limits in relation to injustice. In the *Euthyphro*, Socrates traces this key difference to the question of measurement:

> SOCRATES: What are the subjects of difference that cause hatred and anger? Let us look at it this way. If you and I were to differ about numbers as to which is the greater, would this difference make us enemies and angry with each other, or would we proceed to count and soon resolve our difference about this?
>
> EUTHYPHRO: We would certainly do so.
>
> SOCRATES: Again, if we differed about the larger and the smaller, we would turn to measurement and soon cease to differ.
>
> EUTHYPHRO: That is so.
>
> SOCRATES: And about the heavier and the lighter, we would resort to weighing and be reconciled.
>
> EUTHYPHRO: Of course.
>
> SOCRATES: What subject of difference would make us angry and hostile to each other if we were unable to come to a decision? Perhaps you do not have an answer ready, but examine as I tell you whether these subjects are the just and the unjust, the noble and the shameful, the good and the bad. Are these not the subjects of difference about which, when we are unable to come to a satisfactory decision, you and I and other people become hostile to each other whenever we do?[12]

It is tempting to think, "The reason we don't fight over size, or shape, or weight, or number is that those questions are mundane and unimportant." But that is not any more true than the corresponding claim about health. Questions of weight or size can be the difference between a bridge that stays up and one that collapses; and when we study the healing properties of a drug, or the prophylactic power of a vaccine, we are doing so by way of such "mundane" measurements. Social scientists use measurement to explore questions about what forms of social organization are most beneficial for human beings. Measuring is how we check what works and what doesn't; measurement matters.

The question, then, is why we fight over what we *can't* measure. Is it because we need our disputes to be decidable, and when we can't decide them by measurement, we try to decide them by fighting? This cannot be quite right, because there might be a contingently undecidable question: when we disagree on a question where measurement would be impractical, or where the relevant measuring device doesn't exist yet, we do not immediately turn to fighting.

It is at this point in the discussion that people invoke the objective/subjective distinction. They say: The reason we do not fight over what can be measured is that there is an answer out there. Whether we know it or not, there is an objective truth of the matter. We fight only when the question is "subjective," in the sense that each person sets her own answer, without outside constraint. The claim is: We fight when there is no independent fact of the matter about how things are, apart from how the warring parties think that they are.

But this explanation is not consistent with the observation that there are plenty of questions that are subjective that we do not fight over, questions such as "Is chocolate ice cream tastier than vanilla?" and "Are airplane trips fun?" We might argue sportively over which movie is best or what kind of music is most charming or which joke is funniest, but until the point where these questions get entwined with questions of justice—or otherwise secure untimely status, as they might for those whose identities are bound up with certain favorite novels or films—we do not tend to become angry, hostile, or defensive.

When I am angry at you for (as I see it) having treated me unjustly,

I think there *is* a fact of the matter, and I think that it says that you are wrong and I am right. I see that as objective truth, and I see it with a blazing certainty; the fact that you think otherwise doesn't make the matter "subjective"—it makes you wrong! Likewise, if I learn that you disapprove of my parenting, or dismiss me as a worthless student, I *might* brush this off with an indifferent gesture: "That is your subjective opinion; I have my own." But if I don't—which is to say, if I care enough about what you think to be angered, insulted, and hurt by your estimation of me—then I do not see our difference of opinion as being "merely subjective."

The idea that the dispute is "merely subjective" is more likely to reflect the point of view of an onlooker who wishes the parties to stop their squabbling. The parties themselves fight because they see the question as in some way objective—decidable in the light of the truth, in spite of the impossibility of measurement.

Insofar as we treat gustatory preferences, or disagreements about art, or even religious disagreements, as subjective matters, we won't fight over them. Insofar as we do fight over them, we take there to be constraints governing what our interlocutor ought to believe, regardless of whether she recognizes the existence of those constraints. We fight or argue over the matter in order to bring our interlocutor's behavior or speech in line with those constraints. So we shouldn't conflate the question of whether we think there's a fact of the matter about something with the question of whether we can use a measurement procedure to decide the question.

To recap: We fight over questions that cannot be decided by measurement—but not over all such questions, because we do not fight over matters of taste, nor over questions where the instrument of measurement has simply not been invented yet. What questions, then, do we fight over? We fight over those questions whose answers are practically operative, rendering the suspension of judgment impossible. Untimely questions best explain why we fight when we do.

It is not an accident that the Trojan War was fought over a question of justice as opposed to one about weights and sizes. If you and

I disagree over the size of some object, we can each set aside what we think for long enough to go measure it. Even if I have an opinion, I'm able to "step back" from my opinion while we take the time to measure it. The art of measurement exists because sizes, shapes, and weights are things that people are able to tolerate not knowing: a "blank" is permitted to occupy the place where the answer should be. Not so with questions of ethics. People are prepared to fight and even kill over those disagreements. Their inability to inquire into them stems from the fact that they are currently making use of the answers.

Measurement exists only where detachment is possible. This holds true not only for natural scientific properties such as weight and size and health, but also for social scientific phenomena. When economists, psychologists, or sociologists wish to investigate some aspect of human behavior, they can formulate the question as one of measurement only because they have not presupposed that they already know the answer. Questions of measurement require the one asking to "go out and check." This is why untimely questions are never answerable through measurement, but the converse does not hold: a question that is not amenable to measurement isn't necessarily untimely. We might be unable to use measurement to decide the question for other reasons, such as the absence of the relevant measuring apparatus, or because it is a subjective matter of taste.

It is a mistake to use the word "objective" to mean measurable, since "objective" picks out the larger category of questions where there is a fact of the matter about who is right and who is wrong. As mentioned, we all think questions of justice have this property—at least when we are worked up about them. What is distinctive about questions of measurement is not that they are "objective" but that *it is easy to separate the asking of the question from the answering of it.*

Questions amenable to measurement are readily detachable from the project of living of one's life. Instead of saying that questions of justice are "subjective," we should say that when it comes to a question of justice, my pursuit of the answer is inflected by my personal investment in how it gets answered: while asking it, I am necessarily already engaged in answering it.

Recall Alcibiades insisting that he knows the answer to the question of justice, and that he has always known it:

> SOCRATES: So it seems that even as a child you thought
>   you understood justice and injustice.
> ALCIBIADES: Yes, and I *did* understand.[13]

Calling a question of justice "subjective" is a confused way of getting at the mysterious fact that the answers to such questions seem to have always been with us.

III. Load-Bearing Beliefs

We navigate our lives by way of answers as to what things matter or have meaning. These answers map the world for us: without a sense of what to aim at, we are floating, purposeless. Most of the answers that anchor our agency in the world concern our relationships with the people we are close to. It is with reference to those people that our abstract commitments to being an empathetic, kind, loving, helpful person become concrete directives with action-guiding force; and so when, for example, some of those people die, or betray us, we experience a profound disruption and disorientation. We cannot live without answers, and so when some of our most important answers are, or stand to be, removed from us, we experience that event in the form of strong, negative emotions.

These negative emotions are the most straightforward indication that not every case is like the supermarket case. Our inability to simply stop engaging in certain activities—loving someone who has died, caring about a job we've been fired from—serves as a way of demarcating those questions that are fundamental, those answers that bear a heavy load. Emotions such as rage and despair are how we respond when something happens to us that we were counting on not happening.

You might not notice it, but as you make your way through each day, there are many, many things you are counting on. For example, you are counting on the fact that you will not die today. Our load-bearing answers to untimely questions tend to give rise to predictions that specify what needs to be true in the future in order for my answer to guide my action in the present. If I orient my life around the prospect of becoming a mother, or going to college, or being publicly recognized for my efforts, or being reunited with a loved one, I am going to need to have a belief about whether or not these things will happen. I might not have a lot of *evidence* as to whether these projects will succeed, but an agnostically detached attitude—"I simply don't know what will happen"—will be hard for me to sustain. No one can live without making predictions about those parts of the future that are of special concern to them.

People who are getting married are likely to find the question as to whether they will stay married to be untimely, and parents are in the same position with respect to questions about the health and happiness of their children. On these matters, people don't simply suspend judgment; and they will find it much more difficult to approach them probabilistically—"there is a 60 percent chance things will work out"—than outsiders do. Whereas you might be able to engage in a detached, impartial inquiry into whether my spouse will ever cheat on me or whether my best friend will ever reveal secrets of mine she has promised to keep, those questions tend to arrive in my mind already answered. Each of us is counting on the future unfolding in some ways rather than others, even though we cannot fully control whether it does.

The name for these load-bearing predictions is "hope." And it is worth observing that hope is fragile. It is difficult to sustain, since it comes with the prospect of grief and loss if we are disappointed, so at times we recoil against it by "detaching" ourselves from the goal—or pretending to: "I know it won't happen and I don't care." People are sometimes plunged into exaggerated certainty that they will fail or be frustrated in their aims—during these times, they might be far more pessimistic than they have reason to be. At other times, they might jump to the opposite extreme. When you are counting on the future to unfold in a particular way, because your ability to orient yourself within it depends on its unfolding in that way, you become inclined to flip back and forth—to waver—between positive and the negative certainty, alternating moments of hopefulness with those of despair. When something matters to our ability to navigate our lives, we *need* to have a belief about what will happen, because we make use of that belief, in the activity of living. For the same reason, those who trust are, in many contexts, given to waver into distrust: trust is that species of hope that pertains to whether others will hold up their end of the bargain.

Almost any belief can become load-bearing. Consider Bertrand Russell's praise for how the logician Gottlob Frege responded to the demonstration that his axiom system was inconsistent:

> As I think about acts of integrity and grace, I realize that there is nothing in my knowledge to compare with Frege's dedication to truth. His entire life's work was on the verge of completion, much of his work had been ignored to the benefit of men infinitely less capable, his second volume was about to be published, and upon finding that his fundamental assumption was in error, he responded with intellectual pleasure clearly submerging any feelings of personal disappointment.[14]

One doesn't usually receive so much credit for being willing to accept that one claim follows logically from another. For example, it happens to be true that when I learned that Frege's axioms allow for the construction of a set (call it, "S") of all sets that are not members of themselves, and that this amounts to a contradiction (Is S a member of itself? If yes, then it does not belong to S, if not, then it does), I responded to this discovery with intellectual pleasure. Although Russell describes Frege's intellectual pleasure as "almost superhuman"; he wouldn't praise me in those terms. This is because the claim in question doesn't have the same load-bearing role in my life as it did in Frege's.

For a different kind of example, contrast the juror in a criminal trial with the defendant's mother: the juror might begin the trial without any opinions as to whether the defendant committed the crime, but the mother, sitting in the audience, hears the evidence from a very different position. While the juror might gradually become more convinced of guilt as the evidence mounts, the mother's epistemic path is more likely to take the shape of "flipping" from hopeful certainty of his innocence to despair and rage over his guilt. The fact that some question really matters to you affects how "freely" and "open-mindedly" you can think about it, because certain answers might make life unlivable for you. The point is not that the mother cannot rationally track the evidence. The point is that for the mother, unlike the juror, there is a psychological cost to such a rational response—it requires her to rebuild her life on a new foundation. For this reason, impartiality constitutes a much greater achievement for the mother than for the juror.

Calling attention to the demands of agency puts hostile encounters in a new light: the reason we fight over certain questions is not that they are "subjective," but because our answers to them are in use. Similar observations apply to concepts such as "partiality" or "bias." There is a limit to how much weight advice such as "be more objective" and "be more impartial" can carry, because the root of the problem is that we have to investigate our lives while living them. The cognitive distortions produced by powerful emotions such as sadness and anger are occupational hazards for the occupation that is: living a life.

IV. Sadness versus Anger

What is the difference between sadness and anger? That is an example of the kind of question that I see as paradigmatically philosophical. We feel viscerally that there is a big difference, and that it has been staring us in the face all our lives; we would readily describe ourselves as *knowing* that and how they are different. We might even find ourselves echoing Meno: "It is not hard to tell you" what this difference is, in fact "it is easy to say," and the difference between sadness and anger is "not difficult to describe," so that "one is not at a loss to say what it is." But after we got through that speech, what would we actually say?

Consider the difference between what I feel when I learn that someone I love is killed in a freak accident and what I feel when I learn that that person is murdered. In both cases, my loved one experiences profound harms; in both cases my life becomes unmoored from some of its goals. But in the second case, I feel something in addition to what I feel in the first. Whereas in the first I only feel sadness (at the loss), in the second I also feel anger (at the violation). Likewise, the mother in the trial might feel both anger—at the justice system, or at her son, or at both—and sadness.

Or compare the disappointment of failing at the career of my dreams because I am simply not as talented as my competitors with the anger I feel when my job search fails due to discrimination. There seems to be a big difference between the experience of loss and the experience of being wronged, or slighted, or treated unjustly. This difference is important to understanding untimely questions—or rather, it is important to understanding how to classify the answers we give to those questions.

A good place to start, in explaining the difference, is by noting that you can be angry at people but you cannot be sad at them. You can be sad *about* what you have lost, and one of the things you can lose is another person, for instance when they die or move far away from you, and you can be sad *for* another, if they have lost something or someone. But there is a reason we do not describe ourselves, in any of these scenarios, as being "sad at" anyone. Unlike sadness, anger is motivating: the angry person thinks that there is something to be done in relation to what she is angry about, some goal to be achieved in light of the violation—and that goal involves the person she is angry "at." The "at" captures the sense in which her motivation has a target. She might describe her goal in relation to that person as, "making them pay"; "getting them to regret what they did"; "ensuring they see justice"; "receiving restitution from them"; "holding them accountable"; and so on. But however we phrase it, there is something that the angry person wants to do, and she wants to do it *to* the person she's angry "at."

In fact, anger is not only motivating but *very* motivating: it is well known as a particularly powerful and all-consuming driver of action, thought, and feeling. When I am angry enough, I do not care that I am hungry. Anger presents itself as a problem that can be solved and it aims at this solution. Anger may not be a desire, but it operates akin to desire: anger aims at its target in much the way that desire aims at satisfaction. Sadness, by contrast, can only be made to wane under the force of time or distraction: it ebbs away, but we do not "resolve" or "fix" it.

We experience anger as a *rectifiable* disruption of an answer to an untimely question, and this rectification essentially involves other people. I cannot be angry without being angry at, and the target of my anger must be a person, or a group of people.* In fact, the recti-

---

* Allowing that at times a person can be angry at "the system" or "the world," I nonetheless hold that these are fringe cases, intelligible as anger only with reference to the more central cases, in which anger has a sharper, more personal, target. Anger at oneself is, likewise, a non-paradigmatic kind of anger. As in the case of self-deception, self-praise, self-promising (see chapter 6, p. 194), we can make sense of the reflexive variant of the concept to the degree that we can make sense of treating oneself as other. Usually, we can do this only to a limited extent. For example, when we "punish ourselves" we are pantomiming punishing another, as is evident from the fact that anyone will-

fication involves other people in two ways: first, there is the person I am angry at, but often there is also the group of people I am angry *alongside*. Anger is in many ways a collective phenomenon: if I am angry, I want other people to be angry on my behalf (and may well get angry at them for failing to do so). Even if I stand alone in my anger, as a beacon of integrity, the passion that burns within me is a social one: to fix the social order by modifying the minds of others. It may be true that misery loves company, but unlike anger, sadness is not a socially directed emotion; it doesn't drive one to adjust the social order.

Anger points to the presence, in us, of shared or collective answers to untimely questions. If there is something that I value privately—a beautiful cup—and it shatters, I will be sad. This cup was a (small) part of my answer to "How should I live?"—look at the cup, use the cup, show the cup off to other people—and now, due to events outside my control, I can no longer enact that answer. Sadness is immobilizing and disaffecting, there is nothing that it makes one do, and indeed it inclines one to spend some time doing just that: nothing. I can't make the cup unshatter, and so there is nothing to be done.

You might have thought that the same would be true of anger: if I am angry that you wronged me, that wronging is in the past and cannot be changed. The reason why there is nonetheless something to be done about anger is that anger is fundamentally directed *at* the wrongdoer, on the grounds that the wrongdoing indicates *a failure to give a shared answer*. So, for example, if you violate my rights, that indicates that you do not see respect for my rights as an answer to an untimely question about how you ought to treat me. But I believed that "respect one another's rights" was an answer we were giving together—a collective answer. And so, my anger moves me to try to restore that answer as a collective answer, by somehow *forcing* you to give it, or ensuring that you will give it in the future,

---

ing to punish themselves with the violence they would be prepared to mete out onto another—a black eye, for instance—would be seen as mentally ill.

or bringing it about that you are no longer part of the collective who gives that answer—because you are now dead, or an outcast. Setting aside what happens to you, a sufficient amount of clamor and outrage on my behalf may satisfy me, because it indicates that I am part of a group who gives the answer, restoring the status of the answer as "collective." When I am angry, I am in an unstable state where I feel that something that is supposed to be collective is being held only by me, and I must rectify that situation.

Consider this example from Sophocles' *Antigone*. A watchman has come to tell Creon that someone has violated his royal edict decreeing that the body of Polyneices remain unburied. Creon is enraged, suspects the watchman of having been bribed into performing the burial himself, and orders the watchman to find out who did it—or face torture.

> *Now listen here. So long as I am reverent to Zeus*
> *I am under oath, and you can be absolutely sure*
> *That if you don't find the hand behind this burial*
> *And bring him so I can see him with my own eyes,*
> *Death alone will not be good enough for you—*
> *Not till I've stretched you with ropes and you confess*
> *To this outrageous crime. That will teach you*
> *Where to look to make a profit. And you will learn:*
> *Never accept money from just anyone who comes along.*
> *Those who take from a source that is wicked, you'll see,*
> *Are ruined far more often than saved.*[15]

There is too much passion in this speech for us to interpret these proclamations about what is "good enough" for the wrongdoer, what Creon wants to "teach" him, what he will "learn" and "see," as simple sarcasm. Creon is truly unsettled by the thought that the watchman may have been bribed to break the law. This possibility shakes Creon's hold on what constitutes, for him, a fundamental norm: that his word, as king, ought to be obeyed. He does not know how to be a king—how to act, in the role that gives his life meaning—if his edicts are not met with obedience. The answer "Creon is in charge" must be given by others; it is a shared or collective answer.

And so, Creon seeks to extract the truth—the "lesson" Creon wishes to teach—from the mouth of the wrongdoer. What does Creon get from this act of ventriloquism? The answer is: a more forceful version of what he gets by vociferously condemning "the outrageous crime." When angry, we raise our voices, as though that were a way to forcibly inscribe the rules into the minds of others. In this state, our own answers to the salient untimely question do not suffice for us. We need the other party—or perhaps society as a whole—to echo us, so that we can once again come to see the answer as a collective one. Holding the wrongdoer accountable promises to rehabilitate the answer by restoring its shared status.

Some answers to untimely questions are given only individually, whereas others are collective, given by one because they are given by a group. The first kind of answer exposes a person to sadness, or fear, or despair; the second kind, to anger. That is the difference between sadness and anger, a difference whose roots we will explore in the next chapter. The terrible violence that anger renders us capable of reveals how much is at stake: when people feel that the answers on which their lives depend are slipping away from them, they become willing to do almost anything in order to secure them. This is because nothing—including the consequences of violence—matters unless these answers are secured. The answers are *how* things matter.

If nothing mattered to you, many impediments would be removed from your life. You wouldn't get into fights, the stakes would never seem high, you wouldn't find any questions "touchy" or "sensitive," and you would have no trouble taking an unbiased, impartial, detached perspective on things. You would never rage against your fellow man or feel despair or grief. If you don't care about anything, including the fact that you don't care about anything, you are invulnerable. But also: invulnerability is wasted on you. Your detachment from what matters has made it impossible for you to live.

The load-bearing answers we give to untimely questions are both the sources of all our problems and the sources of all our reasons to care that we have problems. If we could *ask* the corresponding questions, we might be able to produce better answers, which would give rise to fewer problems. But it is not clear how someone is supposed to ask a question to which she thinks she has an answer, when she is currently using that answer to guide her life. She is not going to saw off the branch she is standing on.

The question we should be asking ourselves is: How did she get on that branch in the first place?

Chapter 3

Savage Commands

A LL AROUND YOU, THE AIR IS THICK WITH COMMANDS. You can't escape them. They follow you wherever you go. You don't see them: they're invisible. You can't hear them: they're inaudible. You feel them. The feeling is pain, accompanied by the prospect of pleasure.

Even when the command takes the form of some relatively sophisticated attitude such as ambition, or jealousy, or existential ennui, it has physical manifestations. When the command is urgent, you feel it in a particular part of your body, or by way of your heart pounding, or the breath catching in your throat, or an inability to move, or an inability to stop moving. Before it gets urgent you may not have any strong feeling associated with its presence; nonetheless, you know what to anticipate.

Even a relatively unsophisticated command, such as what we get from feeling hungry (Eat!) or tired (Sleep!), is associated with mental images and fantasies and ideas about actions we could perform in relation to the pain. The pain promises to go away if you do one thing, to increase if you do anything else. The pains don't always keep their promise: sometimes obedience leads to more pain—you eat and then get a stomachache. And sometimes disobedience works out just fine—you ignore your terror of public speaking, get up on the stage, and somehow the world doesn't end.

These commands are *savage*, employing the tools of the torturer—pain, fear of more pain, the purely contrastive pleasure of temporary release from pain—to get you to do what you may see no other reason to do. The commands are also unreliable, since they have a history of not always panning out. Like a capricious tyrant, they are prone to reversals, filling you with regret for having acted as they ordered. Why do we obey such savage and inconsistent masters?

The answer is not: because they overwhelm us. It is rare that you are so hungry that you couldn't restrain yourself from eating what was in front of you, if you knew, for instance, that it was someone else's food. When we disobey a command, it is usually at the prompting of another command—for instance, the command to observe social niceties might trump the command of hunger. We don't obey these commands because any one of them moves us with overpowering force. We obey whichever is strongest, because we have no other options. These commands are our answers to untimely questions. To see how we ended up with them, you only have to turn back the clock.

As soon as you were born, you had to hit the ground running. You were forced to start leading your life even though you had no idea how to do so. What did you do? You screamed, you wiggled, and you took in information about how the world reacted to your screams and wiggles: Does this make the pains go away? Does that? By the time we have the conceptual wherewithal to wonder about how we should live our lives, we've long been taking heaps of answers for granted.

FROM A YOUNG AGE, I was mostly left to my own devices after school. My dad was not the interfering type, and my mom, who was, was busy interfering in other people's lives, which is to say, saving them from dying of cancer. But I recall one day my mom came home from work early and was surprised not to find me there. I had, unbeknownst to her, developed the habit of reading a book on the way home from school; I was working my way alphabetically through the junior high school library. What should have been a twenty-minute walk often took me hours.

That day, when I got home, she peppered me with questions about where I'd been, what homework I had, when I was planning to do it, whether I had any tests coming up, my time-management plans. In retrospect I can see she must have been worried about me—all of this took place before portable phones—but at the time I thought she was trying to suddenly take charge of my life.

I wasn't exactly annoyed or angry at her. Instead, I had an odd feeling of detachment: Today is the day you want to start parenting me? But I already have a way of doing things. I felt sure that the next day would be much like the previous ones: I'd get a new book from the library, wander home over hours, pausing whenever I reached a particularly exciting passage, rely on my peripheral vision to cross the street while I read, ignore my homework until the last possible minute. None of that was how my mother wanted me to live, but I felt sure I'd keep living that way. And I was right.

As a parent, I'm now on the other side of this conflict, but the basic story is the same. Every time I approach my kids in a corrective mode, to nudge them toward what I see as a superior way of living, I feel as though I've walked onto the stage of a play where the characters were given their direction at some previous time, by some other person. Sometimes it amazes me: How could it be that I missed my chance to give them *my* instructions, given that I've been around since the minute they were born?

The truth is that parental instruction is almost always corrective rather than primordial.* You wouldn't give a two-year-old a lecture about homework; you would give the lecture to a ten-year-old, precisely when she refuses to do it. The sign that a child is ready to hear your instruction is that she is acting in conflict with it.

The question "How should I live?," posed to oneself, faces a resistance similar to the resistance parents face when trying to correct

---

* There are a few counterexamples to this principle, where we are inclined to give our kids "the talk." The talk might be about sex, or drugs, but the thing to notice about parenting is that on most topics there is no talk. We wait to correct, instead.

their children. By the time that question shows up on the scene, there is already a way in which you are living. That means it's too late to ask, How should I live? You can say those words out loud, you can inflect your voice at the end so that it sounds like a question, but you're fooling yourself if you think you're opening some kind of inquiry. Our attempts at self-parenting—at taking ourselves firmly in hand, giving ourselves a good shake, and confronting ourselves with the basic or fundamental questions about the meaning of life— all of that is liable to feel otiose, as though we are decorating the surface of life, leaving its deep structure untouched.

When you need answers to a question before you know how to ask it, that is when you become susceptible to a form of speech that can only be described as a command. Think about it this way. If I ask you what I should do and, in answer to my question, you reply, "Do jumping jacks," you're giving me advice, or making a suggestion, or maybe making a guess as to what you think I'd like to hear. That's one scenario. We get an entirely different scenario if you say the same thing—"Do jumping jacks"—but you say it of your own accord, not as a reply, without me having asked you anything at all. If you just walk up to me and say, "Do jumping jacks," you are commanding me. A command answers the question "What should I do?" when no one asked it. In general you can't reconstruct the original question based on the answer alone— "Reykjavik" could be the answer to a lot of different questions— but commands are a case where you can do so, because of the form that the answer takes.

We are the sorts of beings who need answers before developing the ability to ask questions, and who therefore rely on answers to unasked questions. Which is to say: commands.

In the previous chapter, we described the answers to untimely questions as "load-bearing," insofar as they guide our actions over long stretches of time, rendering us vulnerable to intense emotion if disrupted. In this chapter, we will see that to the extent that the corresponding questions were never asked, we can also call these answers "commands." It is only if we become dissatisfied with all of the ways in which we are being commanded that we will be moved to seek out a different kind of answer, by inquiring. This is why Socratic ethics opens with a critique of commands.

I. The Bodily Command and the Kinship Command

Socrates describes bodily appetite as a source of answers to unasked questions: "Wouldn't you say that the soul of someone who has an appetite for a thing . . . nods assent to it as if in answer to a question?"[1] Aristotle gives a similar gloss on the distinction between mere sense perception and desire: "To perceive then is like bare asserting or thinking; but when the object is pleasant or painful, the soul makes a sort of affirmation or negation, and pursues or avoids the object."[2] Perception tells me what is the case—it informs me as to what items populate the world—whereas desire dictates which of those items should serve as my target. It is one thing to perceive a glass of water on the table before me, alongside a book and a pen. When I'm thirsty, I pick out the water from the other items *as* the answer to an unasked question; thus, my thirst can be understood as an affirmative reply or as a nod of assent.

Someone motivated to pursue something is armed with an answer to the question, "What should I do?" For example, someone who feels thirst thinks that she should drink: "The soul of the thirsty person, insofar as he's thirsty, doesn't wish anything else but to drink, and it wants this and is impelled towards it."[3] When it comes to getting fed or hydrated or staying warm or facing some imminent threat, our bodies are ready to issue loud and definitive answers to the question "What should I do?" The questions never had to be asked; the answers somehow just came to us of their own accord. It is not quite right to say I am commanding myself, since the voice that arises in me is not one that I speak, whether silently or aloud. I am the cause of the voice, but not because I decided to say something. Those who are puzzled by the fact that human beings are capable of such half-baked ideation should consider the phenomenon of dreams.

Our bodies are not the only source of savage commands. Each of us stands in a variety of overlapping relationships with other people, relationships that are predicated on bonds of reliance, support, and identification with them. The Greek word for this kind of bond is *philia*, which is usually translated "love" or "friendship," but *philia* is broader than either of those words. People in Socrates' world saw themselves as standing in a relation of *philia* to their fellow citizens as well as their parents, children, siblings, and friends; and they would speak of *philia* in contexts—for instance, those of business—where we would use a weaker word than "friend," such as "associate." *Philia* covers all the various ways in which I use the concept "mine" to talk about other people: my family, my friends, my city, my military regiment. Nowadays, we might include: my religious denomination, my social class, my educational or professional cohort.

Perhaps due to improved technology for travel and communication, less geographically bound categories have, in the modern world, become available as groups with which to identify oneself. Sexual orientation, gender, disability, and race are now grounds for ties of belonging, and some people feel solidarity with those who share their personality type, aesthetic sensibility, or hobby.

There isn't a perfect English word that covers this broad and heterogenous set of connections we have with others, so I will take some liberties with the word "kinship"—usually restricted to family relationships grounded in marriage—and stretch it to cover all of this territory. The bonds I have described can be thought of as a wide variety of ways in which I can see another as "akin" to myself. When someone is my kin, their opinions matter to me just by virtue of the fact that they belong to some group, where the group in question can be defined geographically, or on the basis of an identity category, or in terms of blood relations, or in some other way.

The essential feature of kinship bonds is that they offer *commu-*

nal answers to questions such as: Which people and places and activities matter most to us? Which days do we celebrate? Under what circumstances are we willing to fight and die? Do we believe in God? What kinds of jobs, social gatherings, hobbies, music, home décor, dress, and so on are appropriate for people like us? Who is in charge of our group? More generally: How should we behave in relation to each other? The kind of question that is answered, and the kind of answer that is given, varies depending on the kinship group, but a common denominator is that the members of one's kinship group are enjoined to help one another—or at the very least, not to do one another harm. We feel called upon to help friends or loved ones in their time of need, and the same holds, though more weakly, for anyone we characterize as a "fellow human being." For most of us, humanity is the largest kinship group we see ourselves as belonging to, though there are people who see themselves as parts of an even larger "family" that includes all sentient life, or even all life.

The body offers an answer to what I should do in the form of the approving nod of appetitive pleasure or the "no" of pain. Kinship does the same, but it does so by allowing an individual to delegate the project of answering to the group. A kinship relation dictates that "this is how *we* live, here is how *we* do things, these are the things *we* care about, this who *we* are committed to protecting and providing for." Belonging to the group gives you an answer. Much of a person's basic ethical "stance" is underwritten by one or another kinship relation. Group membership, in effect, stands in for the kind of justification one might have arrived at, had one been in a position to ask who or what one should care about.

Whereas the bodily command operates by way of the carrot of pleasure, comfort, and safety, and the stick of pain and the fear of death, the kinship command operates by way of the carrot of status, honor, affection, and camaraderie, and the stick of the fear of exclusion and the various social emotions (shame, pity, sympathy, envy, and so on). The two commands serve up different forms of existential threat: the former pertains to my biological existence, whereas the latter concerns my social existence, which is to say, how my place in my community is demarcated by others' opinions of me.

The Greek word *doxa* means both "opinion" and "reputation," but it is not a homonym, as these are not two independent meanings. "My" reputation is not something I can ever have in my own possession: it is located outside me—outside my body—in the minds of other people in my community. My reputation is identical to—the same object as—other people's opinions. It is because my peers own a piece of me that if they reject or mock or disavow me, I come to be in a state of social nonexistence. The emotion associated with the prospect of such rejection is *shame*. The archetypical shame-inducing event is finding oneself naked among fully clothed associates. Clothing signals a person's social place—stripped of it, she is an animal among humans, bereft of a social role, lacking a social existence.

English words for the phenomenon of psychosocial dependence rely on the prefix "self-" to such a degree that one could interpret this as a linguistic protest against what's being described. Someone's "self-esteem" or "self-regard" or "self-image" or "self-respect" or "self-confidence" is largely a function of how others treat her. Imagine yourself in a version of *Gulliver's Travels* where the first place you come to is inhabited by people who revere and adore you as the most charming and insightful person around, and later you arrive at the land of magnetically charismatic geniuses, relative to whom you come off as an insipid dolt. It is unlikely that your "self-image" would be very stable over the course of this adventure. Given the degree to which a sense of self-worth is determined extrinsically, it would be more accurate to call it a "sense of other-worth."

In his book *Death and the Afterlife*, philosopher Samuel Scheffler asks the reader to imagine an "infertility scenario" in which we learn that the last generation of human beings has just been born.[4] He suggests that even without the prospect of any violent end—everyone currently alive gets to live out a full human life—the knowledge of the imminent death of the species would be massively destructive of general human morale. He calls attention to the feeling of existential horror that many of us feel at the prospect of the end of humanity, and puzzles over the fact that a person's terror at group annihilation is often more profound than the terror she has in relation to her own death. Why would it become difficult to feel one's life had meaning in the infertility scenario? I would argue: We rely on the continuity of kinship relations—the fact that "our people," in some sense of "our," will live on—in order to be at peace with our own individual deaths. The disparity Scheffler notes, between our ability to accept that we will die but our inability to accept the same about the species, is thus evidence for the grip that the kinship answer has on us. This helps explain the willingness people sometimes have, in the context of war or other crises, to sacrifice their lives for their kin: they see the relevant question about their existence as a question about a group.

And now that we see what lies at the essence of the kinship command—it is given to one because it is given to all—we can draw the boundary between the two types of commands a bit more precisely. While the core cases of bodily command will involve literal bodily functions—food, sex, warmth—the body can drive us to pursue many ends beyond those, propelling us toward a great variety of forms of entertainment and self-protection. Socrates says that the body "fills us with wants, desires, fears, all sorts of illusions and much nonsense . . . and it is the body and the care of it, to which we are enslaved, which compel us to acquire wealth."[5] Our bodies do not content themselves with commands to eat this or drink that. They also command us to acquire the resources that will allow us to fulfill such commands in the future. Thus, the pursuit of wealth is driven by the body, as is our anxious investment in our health, itself backed by our fear of death.

Our bodies are able to organize us in their service, to the point where even bodily restraint is typically driven by the body. Socrates comments that a person who holds off from indulging in pleasure due to a fear of painful consequences is really driven by "a kind of licentiousness." He uses a monetary metaphor to describe what such people are doing: they "exchange pleasures for pleasures, pains for pains and fears for fears, the greater for the less like coins."[6] Someone who endures pain only for the sake of enduring less pain in the future is being ordered around just as blindly by his body as the person who yields to immediate pleasure. Most of the language of self-care—relax, take time for yourself, don't stress, don't overwork—is a version of the bodily command. If someone says that it is "good for you" to unwind or recharge they are channeling the bodily command, encouraging you to think of yourself as a custodian of your own pleasures and pains. "The bodily command" is thus a label for all of those imperatives that address me as me, as an individual animal, not as a member of a social group.

Intimate relationships—between best friends, or lovers, or close siblings—straddle the divide between body and kin. To the extent that my intimate associate is someone to whom I am obligated, with whom I stand in bonds of reliance, to whom I owe loyalty, who holds me to account for living under a set of shared norms, they count as my kin, which is to say, there are some answers that each of us only gives because we give them together. But to the extent that they are someone whose presence relaxes me, whose sense of humor delights me, whose sparkling wit engages me, the sight of whose face brings a smile to mine, someone I greet with warm affection after any time apart, someone whose absence pains me, and so on, then my attachment to them is a bodily one, which is to say, whether or not I *have to* be around them, I want to. Most intimate associations are a site of both bodily and kinship commands.

The bodily command and the kinship command underwrite much of what we do, think, and feel. And yet, Socrates criticizes both. He draws an analogy between how our bodies mislead us in perception, and how they mislead us when it comes to choice. Just as "things of the same size appear . . . larger when seen near at hand and smaller when seen from a distance. . . . And similarly for thicknesses and pluralities. . . . And equal sounds seem louder when near at hand, softer when farther away," so too, the body subjects us to practical illusions:

"The power of appearance often makes us wander all over the place in confusion, often changing our minds about the same things and regretting our actions and choices with respect to things large and small."[7] Socrates says that "the body confuses the soul. . . . It fills us with wants, desires, fears, all sorts of illusions and much nonsense."[8] My body might tell me that I have to do one thing at one time, but, at a later time, fill me with regrets and pains for having obeyed it.

The commands generated by other people—one's kin group—have the same fluctuating character. Socrates often laments the inconsistency of such injunctions, and the consequent impossibility of consistently appeasing "the many" (he also calls them "the majority" or "the people" or "most people").

Those people who easily put men to death and would bring them to life again if they could, without thinking; I mean the majority of men.[9]

Would that the majority could inflict the greatest evils, for they would then be capable of the greatest good, and that would be fine, but now they cannot do either. They cannot make a man either wise or foolish, but they inflict things haphazardly.[10]

Socrates criticizes Callicles on the grounds that "You keep shifting back and forth. If you say anything in the Assembly and the Athenian demos [i.e., citizenry] denies it, you shift your ground and say what it wants to hear."[11] Later, Socrates repeats the accusation, explaining why Callicles is unable to be convinced by Socrates' arguments: "It's your love for the people, Callicles, existing in your soul, that stands against me."[12]

Both the bodily command and the kinship command make us waver. They might give us a loud, clear answer as to what we ought to do, but the answers don't last. By frequently reversing themselves, they prompt us to take life fifteen minutes at a time.

But isn't this familiar territory? Doesn't everyone already under-stand the dangers of bodily self-indulgence and group conformity? Socrates shows that the answer is no: people wildly underestimate just how much these commands poison our minds, to the point where we've normalized the incoherent babbling that comes out of our mouths when we have to explain what it's like to be driven by them. I'm talking about two phenomena in particular: weakness of will and revenge.

II. WEAKNESS OF WILL

In the *Protagoras*, Socrates imagines a conversation with people who claim to err knowingly, at the command of their bodies: they say they are "overcome by pleasant things like food or drink" and "do those things all the while knowing they are ruinous."[13] They claim to be "unwilling to do what is best, even though they know what it is and are able to do it," and to "act that way . . . because they are overcome by pleasure or pain."[14] Socrates first clarifies that by "best" they mean best as far as the bodily command is concerned, which is to say: con-ducing to more pleasure and less pain. These actions strike them as objectionable not on the grounds of any kinship concern—they are not worried that they are acting immorally, or that others will look down on them or criticize them for behaving that way—but from the simple calculus of pleasure and pain associated with the body. They indulge, and end up with more pain than pleasure overall.

We can all relate: we stay up too late, we overeat, we avoid answer-ing emails, we make impulse purchases, and we are not always sur-prised when these things do not end up working out for us. Like Socrates' interlocutors, we might ascribe such choices to being "overcome by pleasure or pain." The person who makes such a claim is called either "akratic" (an English word formed off of the ancient Greek word for the condition, *akrasia*), or "weak-willed." The weak-willed or akratic person insists that they wavered with their eyes open.

Socrates' claim is that this story doesn't hold together:

> What you're saying is ridiculous—someone does what is
> bad, knowing that it is bad, when it is not necessary to do
> it, having been overcome by the good.[15]

Akratics represent themselves as freely choosing "more bad things for the sake of fewer good things." But no one would make such a choice. If offered $100 and $10, no one who wanted money would choose the $10 because they were "overwhelmed by the desire for money." Socrates imagines the weak-willed person objecting:

> But Socrates, the immediate pleasure is very much differ-
> ent from the pleasant and the painful at a later time.[16]

Socrates explains:

> I would reply, "They are not different in any other way
> than by pleasure and pain, for there is no other way that
> they could differ. Weighing is a good analogy; you put
> the pleasures together and the pains together, both the
> near and the remote, on the balance scale, and then say
> which of the two is more. For if you weigh pleasant things
> against pleasant, the greater and the more must always be
> taken; if painful things against painful, the fewer and the
> smaller. And if you weigh pleasant things against painful,
> and the painful is exceeded by the pleasant—whether the
> near by the remote or the remote by the near—you have
> to perform that action in which the pleasant prevails; on
> the other hand, if the pleasant is exceeded by the painful,
> you have to refrain from doing that."[17]

If getting the $10 now is of more value to you than getting $100 in a year—for instance, because you owe $10 and your creditor will kill you if you don't pay immediately—then you're not choosing the lesser good by choosing $10, and there's no mistake. Socrates imagines asking: "Within yourself, does the good outweigh the bad or not?"[18] The answer must be "It does not; for if it did, the person who we say is overcome by pleasure would not have made any mistake." So, if you choose $10 now because it's more valuable to you, you haven't made a mistake. But if $100 later is worth more to you, why would you choose $10? You wouldn't. According to Socrates, the case the akratic wants to describe, where they recognized that one option was better and still freely chose the other, simply can't happen.

And yet we seem to be attached to the phenomenon of "acting against our better judgment" or "knowing full well I shouldn't eat another cookie but still eating it." Recall Tolstoy's reference to the "way of weakness" in which he purports to make the worse choice even though "I know what is best and it is in my power." Doesn't this sort of thing happen all the time? Socrates' answer is, no, it doesn't ever happen, because it can't. You could be *forced* to eat a cookie when you knew that was the inferior choice, because someone shoved the cookie down your throat, but you couldn't *choose* to eat it when you knew that was the worse option, because we never do that. You can no more choose what you know to be worse than you can believe what you know to be false. So what's really going on?

Simple: your body commands you to eat that cookie, presenting that as the best possible option because its judgment about pleasure is distorted by the proximity of the cookie. By the time you are ready to regret the choice, the cookie is far away again (in the past), and your body is now prepared to tell you that you made a mistake. To this description you object: even as I was eating the cookie, I knew it was a mistake! Socrates will correct you: even as you were eating the cookie, you were able to represent to yourself the future state in which you would regret it, and that upcoming command hovered like a specter—Socrates' word is *phantasma*—above what you were doing. Don't confuse your ability to notice that you'd make a different command under different circumstances with actually giving yourself that counterfactual command. Just because you understand that you will regret this choice in the future, it doesn't follow that you do regret it now.

Consider how you're able to think back, while enduring the stomachache the cookie gave you, and recall the appeal it once held. That you can do so doesn't mean you approve of your decision to eat it. You might well regret having eaten it. But while regretting having eaten the cookie, you also remember what it was like to see the cookie in such a positive light that you opted to eat it. A similar point holds if we wind the clock back, and consider the moment when you decided to eat the cookie: in spite of deciding to eat it, you might have been able to imaginatively project forward into a future where you would regret this decision. Socrates can allow that now you regret and remember enjoying, and that back then you enjoyed and anticipated regret. What Socrates denies the akratic, then, is the point of stability they are trying to insist on when they say, "I knew all along this was a mistake." The weak-willed person has deluded themselves into thinking that they waver less than they do; they think that, while relying only on their bodies, they can somehow get a stable grip on what's best for their bodies. But that is not true. The body can't take care of itself: it wavers, judging X to be better than Y at one moment, and Y to be better than X in the next. There is nothing that it knows all along. That is the moral of the story of akrasia.

But there is another, equally important moral to the story, which is how we talk ourselves into not seeing the first moral. It is worth quoting at greater length a passage I excerpted from above:

> For I say to you that if this is so, your position will become absurd, when you say that frequently a person, knowing the bad to be bad, nevertheless does that very thing, when he is able not to do it, having been driven and overwhelmed by pleasure; and again when you say that a person knowing the good is not willing to do it, on account of immediate pleasure, having been overcome by it. Just how

absurd this is will become very clear, if we do not use so many names at the same time, "pleasant" and "painful," "good" and "bad"; but since these turned out to be only two things, let us instead call them by two names, first, "good" and "bad," then later, "pleasant" and "painful." On that basis, then, let us say that a person knowing bad things to be bad, does them all the same. If then someone asks us: "Why?" "Having been overcome," we shall reply. "By what?" he will ask us. We are no longer able to say "by pleasure,"—for it has taken on its other name, "the good" instead of "pleasure"—so we will say and reply that "he is overcome." "By what?" he will ask. "By the good," we will say, "for heaven's sake!" If by chance the questioner is rude he might burst out laughing and say: "What you're saying is ridiculous—someone does what is bad, knowing that it is bad, when it is not necessary to do it, having been overcome by the good."[19]

We have developed the habit of using multiple words for the same thing, in order to hide from ourselves the absurdity of our own behavior. Even when the downside of eating the cookie is (future) pain, and the upside is pleasure (in the present), we represent the action as "doing what's *bad* because we are overcome by pleasure" rather than "doing what's *painful* because we are overcome by pleasure," because if we said the latter we would immediately grasp how silly we sounded. Likewise, we insist that "the immediate pleasure is very much different from the pleasant and the painful at a later time," even when we also think we have taken this temporal difference into account in our understanding of eating the cookie as *more painful overall*. As Socrates notes, "They are not different in any other way than by pleasure and pain, for there is no other way that they could differ."[20] When you shine the light of reason on the way we talk about ourselves, you see that we are being ridiculous.

What is remarkable about akrasia is that it is an absurdity hiding in plain sight. For many of us it rears its head multiple times a day. Our mechanism for conducting our lives doesn't work, and we see that it doesn't work, we watch it not working, but we nevertheless tell ourselves, "What I am doing is bad, but I'm doing it because it is also good, I don't mean good in one way and bad in another, I mean bad overall but a good kind of badness, so that it also seemed good overall—in the sense that I wanted to do it, though I knew it was bad, and I wasn't taken in by the seeming, except I also was. This is normal." Socrates says: All you have to do is pay attention to the words coming out of your own mouth to see that what you're saying can't be a description of what's happening. You're saying that you have some kind of a grip on how you should be acting, but what's actually happening is that you're wavering, because you can't keep that grip for more than fifteen minutes at a time. You waver in how you act and then you waver in how you talk about how you didn't waver when you acted. You can't even stabilize your *sentences* for more than a few seconds at a time!

We've allowed our talk to waver in this way, just because the phenomenon is so common and normal and natural that we can't believe it could be a sign that something is going deeply wrong. But it is. Our problems talking about what is happening reflect a problem in the happening itself. There's a crack at the foundation of human motivation, but we've looked at it so many times that we've convinced ourselves that it is part of the design. In fact, there are two such cracks.

III. Revenge

Just as our bodies routinely lead us to choose what is, in bodily terms, worse, our kinship attachments routinely lead us to choose, what is, in kinship terms, worse. We intentionally harm our kin, and we do so under the guise of kinship. The names we give to this phenomenon range from "accountability" and "justice" to "punching up" and "indignation" and "self-defense" and "retribution," but I'm going to call it by the name we use for it when we are suffering the harm: "revenge." Revenge is when love wavers into hate. This fact about love—that it disposes us to hate—is, like weakness of will, so routinely subjected to disguises and rationalizations that it is hard to see clearly. It sounds crazy to say that revenge is an act of love—that it is hateful love—but in fact that description is not crazy. What's crazy is the thing itself.

Let's go step by step, starting with a definition of revenge:

X is getting revenge on Y when, first, X sees the way he is treating Y as good because Y sees it as bad; and, second, X justifies his behavior on retaliatory grounds.

By retaliatory I mean to include, but not restrict myself to, the case where Y did, or was perceived to have done, something wrong first. Sometimes X is incensed at Y in the absence of wrongdoing: X objects not to anything Y has done but to who Y is, resulting in a spiteful desire to take Y down a peg. I think that desire—spite—belongs to the revenge family, as does what we might call "pre-venge," where X harms Y in anticipation of Y's wronging X. So I'm using "revenge" somewhat broadly, to include all the cases where you behave hatefully toward someone—treating harms to them as goods—and understand your behavior as a fitting response to how they have acted, or to how they will act, or to who they are.

Socrates' analysis of all three flavors of revenge shares the basic structure of his analysis of weakness of will: revenge is a form of wavering thinly disguised as non-wavering by a proliferation of terms. As in the case of weakness of will, we use multiple words for the same thing so as to conceal our inconsistency. The fundamental directive of the body is to pursue as much pleasure as possible, so when it leads you to pursue less, that is wavering; the fundamental directive of kinship is to benefit one's associates, and so when it leads you to harm them, that is wavering. Socrates does not offer up an argument against taking revenge, because he does not need to—any more than he needed to argue against acting akratically. As soon as he gets us to stop using many words for the same thing, the self-contradiction—of being commanded to hurt by the command to help—becomes apparent.

Socrates' views on revenge are clearest in the moment when he refuses the opportunity to take it himself. When Socrates is about to be executed, he is encouraged, by his friend Crito, to seek revenge. Crito says that Socrates, in allowing himself to be executed, is playing into the hands of his enemies and being a coward: when someone tries to destroy you, you are supposed to fight back.[21] Crito wants to bribe the guards so that Socrates can run away. Although lawbreaking would ordinarily count as wrongfully harming one's city, Crito insists that it is justified for Socrates to turn on Athens because Athens wronged Socrates first.[22]

Socrates' approach to revenge is simple: you shouldn't ever do bad things. It's never good to do bad things. Bad things don't become good because of who they're done to, or what someone did first, or because they're done in self-defense. No matter what someone did in the past, or will do in the future, they do not "deserve" harm. Being bad is not a way to be good. Harming people isn't good; it's bad. All the ways we talk ourselves into doing bad things are thinly disguised contradictions. Here is the passage from the *Crito* in which Socrates explains that:

> SOCRATES: Do we say that one must never in any way
> do wrong willingly, or must one do wrong in one way
> and not in another? Is to do wrong never good or
> admirable, as we have agreed in the past, or have all
> these former agreements been washed out during the
> last few days? Have we at our age failed to notice for
> some time that in our serious discussions we were no
> different from children? Above all, is the truth such
> as we used to say it was, whether the majority agree
> or not, and whether we must still suffer worse things
> than we do now, or will be treated more gently, that
> nonetheless, wrongdoing or injustice is in every way

harmful and shameful to the wrongdoer? Do we say
so or not?

CRITO: We do.

SOCRATES: So one must never do wrong.

CRITO: Certainly not.

SOCRATES: Nor must one, when wronged, inflict wrong
in return, as the majority believe, since one must never
do wrong.

CRITO: That seems to be the case.

SOCRATES: Come now, should one do harm to anyone or
not, Crito?

CRITO: One must never do so.

SOCRATES: Well then, if one is done harm, is it right, as
the majority say, to do harm in return, or is it not?

CRITO: It is never right.

SOCRATES: Doing harm to people is no different from
wrongdoing.

CRITO: That is true.

SOCRATES: One should never do wrong in return, nor do
any person harm, no matter what he may have done
to you . . . consider very carefully whether we have
this view in common, and whether you agree, and let
this be the basis of our deliberation, that neither to
do wrong nor to return a wrong is ever correct, nor is
doing harm in return for harm done.[23]

This passage shares the language-unifying character of the passage about akrasia in the *Protagoras*. Socrates is noting that we
have a collection of phrases—such as "doing injustice," "doing
harm," "doing wrong," "doing wrong in return," and "behaving
shamefully"—that, in the context of the kinship command, all
mean the same thing. Nonetheless, we hide behind this proliferation of terms in order to talk ourselves into the idea that sometimes,
instead of helping our kin, we should harm them. But if we shine the

light of reason on the words we speak, we will have to accept that all of these phrases mean the same thing, that there is just no good way to be bad, and that the kinship command routinely commands us to waver.

Just as we were careful to distinguish weakness of will from cases where there's actually an advantage to having the pleasure sooner (if $10 now is more valuable to you than $200 later, there's no mistake), we should likewise distinguish revenge from what is going on when an action that would otherwise count as hurting (such as cutting someone's body) is done in order to help, for instance by a surgeon. Socrates is not raising any objection to violence, or killing, so long as they are justified by the good to be achieved, rather than understood as "deserved" in the light of evils done.

In revenge, the bad that is going to be done to a person is vaunted *as* the good to be achieved. When we get revenge on someone, we see ourselves as harming them, and, at the same time, as achieving a good result. Moreover, we identify these two events: the harm to them *is* the good we're bringing about. Socrates' insight is that this thought—doing good by doing bad—is essentially confused. If I harm you vengefully and call that justice, I must see what I'm doing as, on balance, good; but I also have a representation of how you see it, as being something that is, on balance, bad and harmful. Thus, I see one and the same action, at one and the same time, as good —that's my point of view on it, this is justice being done—and as bad, harmful, and evil—that's your point of view *as imagined by me*. The more vengeful I am, the more I seem to myself to agree with your point of view, which is to say, to think that you are *correct* to represent what I am doing to you as evil and harmful and even unjust. And thus I might describe myself as doing something "bad." Speaking as me, I don't really think that what I am doing is bad, but speaking as you, I do. Just as weakness of will entails a prudent image—a kind of "phantasm"—of my future regret, revenge entails an empathetic image, a phantasm of your emotional repudiation of the revenge I am enacting against you.

This reveals an important truth about empathy. If empathy is the psychological power to import the feelings of others, it follows that empathy is a prerequisite for revenge. Empathy is what allows us to channel the suffering we inflict on others to a sufficient degree to take revenge on them. If this is surprising, that is because we usually use the word "empathy" in a laudatory way that conceals the existence of what we might call "dark empathy." When I channel your feelings, I can *react* to those feelings in a way that reverses their valence for you. Thus, I can empathetically import your joy, and be pained by it (envy), or empathetically import your suffering, and be pleased by it (Schadenfreude). By contrast, in the more heartwarming manifestations of empathy, the ones we usually have in mind when calls for more empathy abound, I am pained by (my representation of) your being pained and feel joy at (my representation of) your joy. But there is a common ground: all forms of empathy, be they dark or heartwarming, begin with my feeling what you feel. Empathy is not a virtue, but a power. Almost every adult has this power to some degree, though some of us have more of it than others, and it can be used for good or ill.

The importance of "dark empathy" to revenge can be made clearer by contrasting vengeful punishment with the kind of punishment of which Socrates approves, beneficent punishment.[24] The beneficent punisher dismisses the unrepentant criminal's point of view on the punishment—"Don't hurt me!"—as a mistake akin to the sick person's mistake when they resist medical treatment. The beneficent punisher is able to straightforwardly see themselves as helping the criminal become (psychologically) healthy. When faced with a repentant criminal, who joyfully welcomes punishment because they correctly understand that it is really a benefit, the beneficent punisher's task only becomes that much more cheerful.

The vengeful punisher, by contrast, is flummoxed by the repentant criminal's request for punishment. The vengeful punisher only understands the practice of punishment when it is accompanied by a vision of the punishment as being, on net, bad. The vengeful person's mirage of agreeing with the point of view of the (unrepentant) victim is, once again, structurally analogous to the akratic's mirage of agreeing with her future self. This mirage leads the vengeful person to say things like, "Yes, I'm harming him, and that's bad, but sometimes it is good to harm people." That makes no sense. Doing bad things isn't good. The fact that something is a bad thing to do can never be what makes it good. No one deserves to be harmed.

The Socratic position on revenge can be summed up as a set of truisms: "No one deserves to be harmed"; "It's never right to do what's wrong"; "Being bad can never be what makes something good." Why would we ever waver from these truisms? The answer is: kinship.

Socrates noticed a simple fact about revenge that we tend to ignore, which is that it is only possible to take revenge against kin. First, because anger is a prerequisite for vengeance and harms only incite anger within the context of the right kinship relation. I might get angry at my husband if he forgets my birthday, or my child if he puts off his homework for too long, or my nurse if I feel her bedside manner is lacking, but I don't expect birthday recognition from the nurse or a skillful bedside manner from my child. If you are my fellow citizen, and you do not vote, I might get angry at you, but I am unlikely to mind if you are a foreigner, and you don't vote in the elections of your own country. Notice that even when it comes being violently attacked, I might say I would be angry at *anyone* who did this, but in fact I am only angered insofar as I see that anyone as a *someone*, which is to say, a fellow human being. When a boulder or wild beast hurtles toward me, what I feel is fear, not anger. Harms don't generate indignant concerns about "accountability" unless they strike you as, in some way, disrespectful or offensive, which is to say, as violations of kinship norms.

Second, note that the vengeful person is treating another person in a way that she would ordinarily see as forbidden, were it not for whatever it is she is retaliating for. The constraints on what she would be allowed to do to the person absent the retaliatory justification spell out the relevant kinship relation. She is violating behavioral norms governing how one generally treats one's spouse, or mother, or neighbor, or fellow human being, on the grounds that the person in some way "deserves it." So, for instance, you can get revenge on your spouse by just ignoring them, or leaving dirty dishes in the sink, whereas in order to get revenge on a stranger you need to violate those norms that apply to how we treat any human being—physically harm them, insult them, or intentionally impede one of their projects. When you get revenge, you treat someone in precisely the way that you are forbidden to treat precisely that person. The phenomenon of revenge reveals that the kinship command is capable of ordering us around in a self-destructive way.

The conventional view is that enemies deserve revenge. Socrates comes up against this view in *Republic*, Book I, when his interlocutor describes revenge as *justice* by insisting that a just person harms their enemies.[25] But consider how one becomes an enemy. The status of "enemy" is the product of some event—the person did something wrong, or belongs to a group associated with some wrongdoing— that transformed them from a creature one was prohibited from harming (kin) into someone you can be praised ("justice") for harming. Socrates insists, against Polemarchus, that you should *help* your enemies. Why? Because of who your enemies are: your spouse, when he forgot your birthday, your mother, when she makes unreasonable demands, your fellow citizen, when he expresses irritating political views. Your enemies are people who used to be your friends.

This holds for war, too. Each side sees the "rightness" of their attempt to kill people on the other side—who are, after all, fellow human beings—as predicated on the fact that the other side committed some wrong, or, at any rate, is now trying to kill them. We distinguish between the killing of enemy combatants and the killing of innocent civilians on the basis of the idea that violence can be justified if it takes the form of fighting *back* against someone understood as "the aggressor" or "the enemy."

It is worth noticing that even outside the context of war, our intuitions about permissible violence track the idea of fighting back much more closely than the idea of self-protection. For example, if too many people board a lifeboat fleeing the *Titanic*, and you push the weakest ones into the water to drown in order to save your own life, your act would usually not be vindicated as "self-defense." Our common understanding of self-defense includes *a culprit* and that means that self-defense, as it is usually understood, hides within it the notion of revenge. The guilt of the party under attack matters more to us than the positive, lifesaving value that the act of violence stands to achieve. Guilt transforms kin—whom you were not permitted to harm—into anti-kin.

And "guilt" can be construed broadly: many are eager to join the opposition against whichever of two parties is larger, stronger, wealthier, or more powerful, treating anyone with these traits as likely sources of evil; whereas others are ready to interpret the behavior of those in specific groups—ones to which their own group has long been opposed—as acts of aggression. The full menu of classic revenge, spiteful revenge, and pre-vengeful revenge allows a person to justify almost any attack on anyone else as being in some sense a case of retaliation against an enemy.

Revenge makes the world go round. In so many contexts, both intimate and public, we intentionally inflict harms on those we would otherwise see ourselves as prohibited from harming. We tell ourselves that we are in special circumstances in which something's being bad makes it good. Socrates predicts that few will be able to stand along him and acknowledge how little sense that makes:

> One should never do wrong in return, nor do any person harm, no matter what he may have done to you. And *Crito, see that you do not agree to this, contrary to your belief. For I know that only a few people hold this view and will hold it, and there is no common ground between those who hold this view and those who do not, but they inevitably despise each other's views.* So then consider

very carefully whether we have this view in common, and whether you agree, and let this be the basis of our deliberation, that neither to do wrong nor to return a wrong is ever correct, nor is doing harm in return for harm done. Or do you disagree and do not share this view as a basis for discussion? I have held it for a long time and still hold it now, but if you think otherwise, tell me now.[26]

Just as the no-akrasia principle dictates that the body cannot care for the body, the no-revenge principle makes the corresponding point in relation to the kinship command: it cannot provide stable guidance as to how one should treat those around one. Most people will agree that if someone harms you then you are permitted some amount of hostility toward them; most people are adept at clothing harms to others in the language of justice when they need to. Crito had initially described Socrates' unwillingness to break the law as giving in to his enemies and choosing the easiest path instead of the good and courageous path.[27] Crito was ready to reword the injustice of breaking the law as, actually, under the relevant circumstances, a means of achieving justice—until Socrates interferes.

Socrates is prepared to tell his close friend that there might be an unbridgeable gap between them, that they might be people who despise each other, who have no mutual understanding. Socrates is unwilling to hate anyone, but he is only willing to truly *love* those people who can see that the aims of kinship—benefits to one's associates—will not be achieved if the kinship command is left to its own devices. He loves Crito only conditionally, where the condition in question is that Crito refuse to yield uncritically to the demands of kinship.

It is worth underlining just how unusual Socrates' condition is. Imagine: Your two young daughters get into a fight, because the older snatches a dress from the younger, and the younger one responds by pulling her older sister's hair.[28] What do you, the parent, say? You might scold both girls—the older one for dress-snatching, and the younger one for hair-pulling—but would you scold the young one as much as the older one? After all, she was provoked. Do you think: It was understandable that she treated her sister unjustly, given that her sister had treated her unjustly? That is the logic of revenge, and parents tend to accept it. If your kids have ever said to you, "I wasn't the one who started it," that's a sign that you taught them the logic of revenge. Socrates calls this bad parenting; he doesn't acknowledge such a state as "being provoked." Pulling your sister's hair isn't any better if she did something bad first, because hurting people is never good. On his terms, most of us teach our kids to make a significant mistake.

The Socratic view on revenge is not that it is immoral, but that it is impossible. Socrates, who fought in the Peloponnesian War, objects not to violence as such, but to vengeance as a justification for violence. The pacifist thinks that you *shouldn't* kill people whereas Socrates thinks that you *can't* do good by doing bad. The Socratic position on vengeance should also be distinguished from the attitude of a martyr who accepts mistreatment placidly, with equanimity, by turning the other cheek. The reason why Socrates tried so hard to persuade the Athenians not to kill him is that he thought they would be committing a terrible injustice.* Socrates was no martyr, and when they made their decision clear he objected to it vehemently. The one thing he did not try to do is hurt them back, because he understood that he could not be just by being unjust. Revenge simply makes no sense.

The vengeful person insists that the wrongness of the wrong thing they are doing—the fact that their victim is suffering, or dead—is

---

* If Socrates denies that revenge is possible, why does he object to it? Socrates denies that it is possible to act against one's better judgment, or to do good by doing bad, so in this sense he denies both weakness of will and revenge, but he does not deny the destructive character of the phenomena that are (he thinks, wrongly) described in those ways. That is, he thinks it is perfectly possible, and lamentable, to waver catastrophically at the behest of the bodily or the kinship command.

what makes it right or fitting or necessary or good. It is this way of speaking that Socrates objects to—though, as in the case of weakness of will, his point is not ultimately about language. Rather, he's using the way our language wavers to direct us to how our thoughts and actions waver. What we're trying to do, when we aim to commit revenge, is something that cannot be done.

A vengeful person might, in response to Socrates' argument, make the following move: "I don't want to do good by doing bad, I just want to do bad. My motive is purely to hurt." Socrates' reply is that this person has mischaracterized his motivation, and he offers an argument to that effect in the *Gorgias*, when he explains how you would actually treat someone if you really wanted to hurt them as much as possible. In a remarkable passage, Socrates lays out a recipe for ruining someone's life. Take a person who is poised to become the next Stalin or Hitler, and clear all of the obstacles out of the way of their path toward the most complete injustice. If they steal money, make sure they get to keep it and spend it as unjustly as possible, on themselves and on others. Insulate them from any possible feedback that would allow them to come to understand how evil they really are, make sure they are never punished, and ideally make them immortal, "never to die at all but to live forever in corruption."[29] *That*, says Socrates, is how you would treat someone if you wanted to do maximal harm to them: you would ensure that they live the worst possible life forever, with no way out. That is what pure hate looks like. When you are enacting revenge, you don't treat people that way. Revenge is animated by the desire to teach people lessons and set them straight. (Recall Creon: "That will teach you. . . . And you will learn.") Revenge is not pure hate, it is loving hate.

Many people disavow revenge, but allow it into their lives under a different name. The distance between theory and practice is a result of the rephrasings our kin groups normalize—we learn to talk around the incoherent wavering of kinship-induced revenge, just as we talk around the incoherent wavering of body-induced akrasia. Revenge is a passion that tells you that the bit of cruelty you are thinking of enacting will be righteous and glorious. When you feel this passion, what you are feeling is the kinship command malfunctioning. This corresponds to the akratic experience of the bodily command malfunctioning: "I know I'm going to regret this later." Revenge and akrasia teach us that our default systems for managing our lives are defective: they make us waver.

IV. THE SOCRATIC PROPOSAL

I've called the commands of our body and our kinship group "savage commands," borrowing that phrase from the *Crito*. In that same passage, Socrates both uses the term and identifies another path. He says that the laws, as he understands them, don't make such commands. Rather, they "only propose things."

> We [i.e., the laws of Athens] say that the one who disobeys does wrong . . . [when] he neither obeys us nor, if we do something wrong, does he try to persuade us to do better. Yet we only propose things, we do not issue *savage commands* to do whatever we order; we give two alternatives, either to persuade us or to do what we say.[30]

The modus operandi Socrates attributes to the laws when he personifies them—"persuade or be persuaded"—bears a striking resembles Socrates' own.[31] Socrates has projected the Socratic method onto the laws. For example, look at what he said to Crito a little earlier in their conversation:

> Let us examine the question together, my dear friend, and *if you can make any objection* while I am speaking, make it and I will listen to you, but if you have no *objection* to make, my dear Crito, then stop now from saying the same thing so often, that I must leave here against the will of the Athenians. I think it important *to persuade*

you before I act, and not to act against your wishes. See whether the start of our inquiry is adequately stated, and *try to answer what I ask you* in the way you think best.[32]

The Socratic method is an alternative to savage commands. It takes the form of a proposal: either you are going to be convinced by me, to go along with what I think, or you are going to convince me to go along with what you think. Socrates is not going to tell Crito what to do, nor does he permit Crito to tell him what to do ("Stop saying I must leave"). Instead, they are to jointly organize themselves into two distinct roles. These roles are sometimes translated to mean "persuade or obey" but it's worth emphasizing that in Greek it's the same word in the active and passive voice: "obey" is another way of translating the word we can also translate as "be persuaded."[33] These roles can also be put in terms of refuting and being refuted, since Socratic persuasion works by way of refutation; or of asking and answering questions, since Socrates refutes people by questioning their answers. Both refutation and inquiry are suggested, if not foregrounded, in the passage just above: "if you can make any objection" and "try to answer what I ask." Persuade or be persuaded, refute or be refuted, ask questions or answer them: exactly why these formulations are equivalent will become clearer in part two, in which we will examine the Socratic method in depth. For the moment I want to speak to how they might, collectively, represent a genuine alternative to the savage commands of body and kin.

Consider Socrates' complaint that Crito has been "saying the same thing so often, that I must leave here against the will of the Athenians." Is this fair? Crito has not simply repeated that command; he has given Socrates a slew of reasons to escape. For instance, Crito points to the fact that Socrates' children need him: if Socrates dies "they will probably have the usual fate of orphans."[34] Crito also worries that he himself will look bad: "Many people who do not know you or me very well will think that I could have saved you if I were willing to spend money, but that I did not care to do so. Surely there can be no worse reputation than to be thought to value money more highly than one's friends."[35] In addition, Crito hopes to entice Socrates with the prospect of a warm welcome in Thessaly: "I have friends there who will greatly appreciate you and keep you safe."[36] Why does Socrates discount these arguments?

In attempting to motivate Socrates with the stick of fear for his loved ones and the carrot of safe haven in Thessaly, Crito is throwing Socrates back on the savage commands of kinship ("Protect your family and friends!") and body ("Preserve your safety!"). If "Do jumping jacks, I won't say why!" is a savage command, so is "Do jumping jacks or your kids get hurt!" or "Do jumping jacks and you get a prize!" A penalty or reward might suffice to change your mind, but Socrates is not in the business of changing minds. He's in the business of *either* changing minds *or* having his own mind be changed, which is to say, the business of figuring out which of those two things should happen. This requires looking into why a person was inclined to do whatever they were going to do, and checking to see whether it makes sense: on examination, does their speech waver, or not? Crito's arguments are attempts to tip the scales in favor of the outcome that Socrates is resisting, while leaving shrouded in darkness Socrates' grounds for resisting it. Crito is giving Socrates incentives, without engaging Socrates' reasons for believing that escaping would be unjust.

That is why Socrates dismisses "those questions you raise about money, reputation, the upbringing of children," and insists that "the only valid consideration . . . is whether we should be acting rightly in giving money and gratitude to those who will lead me out of here, and ourselves helping with the escape, or whether in truth we shall do wrong in doing all this."[37] Socrates wants Crito to help him ask the question, "Should I escape from jail?" even though both Socrates and Crito already think that they have answers to that question. An untimely question is a closed question: already answered. Nonetheless, Socrates thinks that he and Crito can open it, together. How? By way of the Socratic method: persuade or be persuaded.

If, when you try to articulate what you are doing to someone else, you find yourself babbling, contradicting yourself, unable to make sense of the words coming out of your own mouth, then even you will become aware that you can't expect to persuade anyone. This happens to teachers all the time: you learn what you really understand, and what you only appeared to yourself to understand, when you put your supposed knowledge to the test by trying to explain it to someone.

It's one thing to be motivationally driven to engage in akrasia or take revenge; it's another to try to explain to someone else why those would be the right course of action. The pressure of objection, refutation, and explanatory clarity exposes the savageness of the command driving you, to the point where you would not be able to demand that anyone else act the way you are acting. This wouldn't stop you from acting on the basis of a savage command—but in doing so, you would be turning your back on having Socrates as a friend. "Persuade or be persuaded" means refusing to live on the basis of the kinds of answers that only sound like good answers before you've explicitly posed the relevant question.

Everything we do, every choice we make, every action we take, is underwritten by some answer to the question "What should I do?" Socrates' alternative to savage commands allows us to transform our default answers into something different: inquisitive answers. These inquisitive answers will, in the end, either correspond to what an interlocutor such as Crito had (before asking the question) thought they should do, or not. The first case would be the one where Crito persuades Socrates to flee, the second where Crito is persuaded that Socrates should not flee. Either way, Crito will have asked the question to which his decision is an answer, and the sign of this will be the ability to explain himself.

For any given command, we have the idea of setting it aside in favor of something more important. Many people would pride themselves on being able to rise above hunger, or exhaustion, or conformity pressures, if the stakes are high enough. Socrates asks us to imagine becoming people who, instead of setting one command aside in favor of another, discover something better to do with our lives than follow commands. What if you lived, not off of commands, but off of an understanding of what you were doing? Liberation from commands begins with questions.

A QUESTION MAY BE lingering with the reader from our discussion of revenge: Does Socrates really think that the worst thing you can do to someone is make them evil? What about making them suffer terrible physical pain, or forcing them to see their loved ones slaughtered? Aren't there two very different states we might refer to with the phrase "a bad life," namely, *unhappiness* and *immorality*? In the next chapter, we will examine why Socrates denied that we can draw this distinction in the way in which we are accustomed to. And not only Socrates: the varying philosophical traditions that emerged in Socrates' wake had sharply differing views on most core ethical questions, but they agreed with one another, and with Socrates, on this point.

Chapter 4

Socratic Intellectualism

A RE SOCRATES AND I BEING FAIR TO THE NATURAL human inclinations toward pleasure and sociability? Do they really serve as such poor guides for life? Even if you accept the argument that weakness of will and revenge show us how body and kin (respectively) incline to savage self-contradiction, you might think that tamed versions of these commands could escape those problems. Couldn't we appease the body without overvaluing proximate pleasures, and, to take the taming a step further, without ignoring the needs of other people? Isn't there a way to prevent kinship from turning on itself, and, better yet, to make the great variety of demands springing from the great variety of kinship groups consistent with one another? Could the demands of kinship perhaps be, quite generally, harmonized with those of the body?

Socrates never asked himself these questions, but later philosophers did. They sought to rehabilitate one or both of the savage commands in the wake of criticisms leveled by Socrates. In this chapter, we will take a look—though it will have to be a cursory, synoptic one—at both the ancient seeds, and the modern fruits, of those efforts.

There are three main strands of ethical theorizing in the West: the first is Kantian ethics, also known as "deontology" or, in one of its currently popular forms, "contractualism"; the second is what Jeremy Bentham, John Stuart Mill, and Henry Sidgwick called "Utilitarianism," and that some of its modern day proponents generalize to a position they call "consequentialism"; the third is Virtue Ethics, which, being inspired by the thought of Aristotle, also goes by the name "Neo-Aristotelian ethics." The fundamental principle of Kantian ethics is that of constraining one's actions by respect for humanity (in one's own person and that of others); that of Utilitarian ethics is to bring about the greatest good for the greatest number; and that of Virtue Ethics is to act virtuously, which is to say, do whatever the decent (just, kind, courageous, prudent, and so on) person would do if he were in the situation you are in.

I will do more to explain these theories, and how they differ from one another, in what follows, with a view to claiming that the ethical theory presented in this book represents a genuine alternative to all three. Indeed, as I suggested in the introduction to this book, one of my purposes is to develop and propose a new strand of ethical thought, one we could label "Neo-Socratic," in that it is, first, based on the thought of Socrates; but, second, extrapolates and generalizes that thought into a method of continued relevance for the living of one's life; and third, differs not only in what it prescribes but in its very foundations from the ethical systems derived from Kant, Mill, and Aristotle.

However, before I get to describing differences, I will begin with a surprising point of agreement. Common sense distinguishes between what justice demands and what is personally advantageous: although it is valuable to do what is just, and it is valuable to do what benefits oneself, everyday intuition says that these two values do not always overlap, and one can be torn between them. The surprise is that not only does Socrates disagree with common sense on this point, but so do all the other ethical theories described above. Let's begin with Socrates.

I. The Just and the Advantageous

At one point, Socrates' interlocutor Alcibiades makes the claim that "the just differs from the advantageous." When Alcibiades distinguishes between what is just and what is advantageous, he is really distinguishing between the kinship answer and the bodily answer.

Alcibiades uses words such as "just," "admirable," "proper," and "right" to describe his implicit, socially absorbed knowledge of how a person *should* act: this is the kinship answer. He contrasts justice with being motivated to pursue one's own private advantage, for example in a case where one's survival is on the line. Socrates clarifies: the idea that "the just" differs from "the advantageous" amounts to the claim that some just things, though admirable, are bad.

> SOCRATES: So all just things are admirable.
>
> ALCIBIADES: Yes.
>
> SOCRATES: Now what about admirable things? Are they all good, or are some good and others not good?
>
> ALCIBIADES: What I think, Socrates, is that some admirable things are bad.
>
> SOCRATES: And some contemptible things are good?
>
> ALCIBIADES: Yes.
>
> SOCRATES: Are you thinking of this sort of case? Many people get wounded and killed trying to rescue their friends and relatives in battle, while those who don't go to rescue them, as they should, escape safe and sound. Is this what you're referring to?[1]

What Alcibiades is envisioning, when he claims that justice and advantage conflict, is the fact that the demands of one's body to escape wounds or death can stand in tension with the bonds of solidarity to behave admirably or justly in rescuing friends and relatives. When Alcibiades insists that what is just or admirable isn't necessarily good, he is talking from his experience of situations where what the kinship answer tells you to do will often be exactly what the bodily answer tells you to avoid.

If weakness of will is how the bodily command wavers—undermining itself—and revenge is how the kinship command wavers, the scenario under discussion between Socrates and Alcibiades is one in which the person wavers because the two commands come into conflict with one another. Alcibiades wants to describe this scenario—in which one is subject both to the command "Run away to save yourself!" and "Stay and fight to save your kin!"—as an experience of being torn between the value of advantage and the value of justice. He transforms a division of voices into a division into two distinctive goods, and Socrates objects. Consider an analog. Suppose you seek investment advice and your two friends, A and B, give you different advice, each insisting that following the other's advice would be a mistake. You wouldn't be inclined to conclude that "there are two kinds of money out there, each valuable in its own way: A is telling me how to maximize A's kind of money, whereas B is advising me on how to maximize B's kind." Rather, you'd understand, first, that A and B are both trying to help you get as much as possible of one same thing—money—second, that they disagree about how to do that, and third, they cannot both be right. Likewise, thinks Socrates, the bodily and kinship command are both trying to tell you what the best thing to do is, they are giving you different answers, and these answers cannot both be right. To the extent that you find one compelling, that speaks against your having reason to trust the other. To the extent that you find them both compelling, that speaks to your being confused.

Let's look at how Socrates conveys his analysis of the conflict between the two commands to Alcibiades:

> SOCRATES: You agreed that the rescue is admirable, in
> that it's courageous. Now consider this very thing—
> courage. Is it good or bad? Look at it like this: which
> would you rather have, good things or bad things?
> ALCIBIADES: Good things.
> SOCRATES: Namely the greatest goods?
> ALCIBIADES: Very much so.
> SOCRATES: And wouldn't you be least willing to be
> deprived of such things?
> ALCIBIADES: Of course.

> SOCRATES: What would you say about courage? How
> much would you have to be offered to be deprived
> of that?
> ALCIBIADES: I wouldn't even want to go on living if I
> were a coward.
> SOCRATES: So you think that cowardice is the worst
> thing in the world.
> ALCIBIADES: I do.
> SOCRATES: On a par with death, it would seem.
> ALCIBIADES: That's what I say.[2]

When he asks Alcibiades, "How much would you have to be offered to be deprived of that?" we can imagine Socrates offering Alcibiades financial compensation for cowardice. Alcibiades' indignant rebuff suggests that no amount of bodily goods could compensate him for a sacrifice in the sphere of goods the body wholly ignores. To one sufficiently inflamed by the spirit of the kinship command, only honor matters. Cowardice is the worst thing in the world—but so is death. Can there be two worst things? Socrates will go on to show him that there cannot. The first step is to observe that Alcibiades can no longer say that what is just but not advantageous is bad:

> SOCRATES: Then when you say that rescuing one's
> friends in battle is admirable but bad, you mean
> exactly the same as if you'd called it good but bad.[3]

Socrates completes the argument by showing Alcibiades that all the terms now line up:

> SOCRATES: So if we find that something is admirable,
> we'll also find that it's good—according to this
> argument, at least.
> ALCIBIADES: We'll have to.

SOCRATES: Well then, are good things advantageous, or not?

ALCIBIADES: Advantageous.

SOCRATES: Do you remember what we agreed about doing just things?

ALCIBIADES: I think we agreed that someone who does what's just must also be doing what's admirable.

SOCRATES: And didn't we also agree that someone who does what's admirable must also be doing what's good?

ALCIBIADES: Yes.

SOCRATES: And that what's good is advantageous?

ALCIBIADES: Yes.

SOCRATES: So, Alcibiades, just things are advantageous.[4]

Alcibiades' predicament should be recognizable to anyone who has ever taken it for granted that "what's in my self-interest and what's moral can diverge" or that "fulfilling my duties to others can come at a substantial cost to my happiness." Most of us are, like Alcibiades, drawn to the conceit that we have the resources to distinguish between what is just and what is to our advantage. It seems obvious that there is a particular *way* that the body picks out something as good—it points us to what's in our personal interest—whereas our kin groups point us to what's good from the point of view of the group: the courageous, the admirable, the right, the fair. These cues lead us to conclude that the world contains two distinctive types of goods that we might pursue. Socrates thinks that is a mistake. We've mapped our own subjective confusion about the good—our inability to decide what's best, our inclination to waver back and forth between two incompatible answers to that question—onto the world, as if it were a divide in the things themselves.

At the heart of Socrates' argument is the claim that all of us would rather have good things than bad things, and that we are "least willing to be deprived" of "the greatest goods."[5] Socrates would say that "self-interest" and "happiness" and "advantage" are one set of names we apply to this greatest good, and "duty," "morality," "justice," and "what is good for others" are another set of names *for the same thing*. The first set of names reflect the influence of the bodily command, the second that of the kinship command, so there is a *subjective* difference between them; nonetheless, there aren't two kinds of goods "out there." There is no objective difference; there is no distinctive kind of good to which the bodily command, or the kindship demand, directs us. When Alcibiades goes back and forth between describing the good as "the just," and describing it as "the advantageous," he is not describing two things out there. He's just wavering. There's only one thing out there: the good.

And yet: surely there is more to be said on behalf of each of these commands than what the philosophically inexperienced Alcibiades manages to blurt out the first time he is pressed to articulate his intuitions. Perhaps it was in anticipation of such skepticism that Plato goes over this territory many, many times. The most obvious examples are provided by Socrates' long exchanges with Callicles and Thrasymachus, each of whom enters their respective conversation with Socrates determined to uphold the thesis that what is moral and what is in a person's interest can diverge. Socrates pursues their arguments down many twists and turns, all of which result in dead ends. The question of the diversity of goods also rears its head inside longer exchanges on different topics, such as when Socrates gets Protagoras to agree that when a courageous man advances toward danger, he goes "toward the more honorable, the better, and more pleasant."[6] According to Socrates, those are not three different things; they are one thing. (At his trial, when Socrates has been accused of corrupting the youth, and he accuses his accusers of being unable to supply a motive for this crime— because how could anything but harm accrue to a person who harms those around him?—the unity of the good once again lurks in the background.)*

II. Taming the Savage Commands

Still, even if we considered the sum of Socrates' conversations on the question, the result would not be anything close to a conclusive case against taking guidance from body or kin. This is because Socrates is always limited by his interlocutors' answers, and his interlocutors share the assumption that the road from savage commands to ethical theory is very short—indeed, immediate. One might assert that, once tamed from its original wild, wavering self-contradictions, a savage command does point us to a distinctive object and offers us a vision of the good. Perhaps it takes philosophical work, the work of organizing and ordering the various forms that the command takes, and separating legitimate instances of it from the illegitimate ones, to bring the true object of the command into view. Socrates did not encounter anyone who had done this work, but he did inspire later thinkers to take it up.

What if, instead of considering the untutored versions of the bodily or the kinship command, we considered the *maximally rational versions* of those commands? This is the task to which the two dominant strands of ethical theorizing in the West have set themselves.

Ancient Epicureanism offered the first attempt at an enlightened version of the bodily answer. It was an entire worldview organized around the possibility of identifying, in a consistent way, the set of

---

* Some more examples: When Socrates gets Polus to agree that being unjust harms you (*Gorgias*, 475c) and being justly punished benefits you (*Gorgias*, 487c–c); when Socrates confronts Laches with a paradox that arises from the latter's desire to contrast acting courageously with the pursuit of what's advantageous (*Laches*, 192d–193e); when Socrates accepts the burden of showing that justice is personally advantageous (*Republic*, book II).

pleasures that are natural to us. The philosopher Epicurus (341–270 BCE) enjoins a person to eliminate unnecessary sources of pain (among them, the fear of death), and to select pleasures carefully:

> And it is just because this [i.e., pleasure] is the first innate good that we do not choose every pleasure; but sometimes we pass up many pleasures when we get a larger amount of what is uncongenial from them. And we believe many pains to be better than pleasures when a greater pleasure follows for a long while if we endure the pains. So every pleasure is a good thing, since it has a nature congenial [to us], but not every one is to be chosen. Just as every pain too is a bad thing, but not every one is such as to be always avoided. It is, however, appropriate to make all these decisions by comparative measurement and an examination of the advantages and disadvantages. For at some times we treat the good thing as bad and, conversely, the bad thing as good.[7]

When Epicurus speaks of "comparative measurement," he is describing what later philosophers will call a "hedonic calculus." Epicureans showed that it is possible to pursue pleasure without heedlessly opting for the pleasure that is closest at hand. Pleasure lovers who consider the consequences of their choices, and who give future pleasures their proper weight, are also lovers of prudence. The careful, calculative selection of pleasure is the Epicurean response to the problem of weakness of will.

I mentioned in chapter 3 that intimate friendship naturally straddles the boundary between body and kin; Epicureans take pains to drag it all the way onto the side of the body: "The wise man feels no more pain when he is tortured than when his friend is tortured, and will die on his behalf; for if he betrays his friend, his entire life will be confounded and utterly upset because of his treachery."[8] So long as the Epicurean is able to translate whatever values he wishes to preserve into the language of pleasure and pain, and these pleasures and pains can be weighed against one another, the resulting hedonism becomes a stable guide for life.

Bentham, Mill, and Sidgwick cite Epicurus as a precursor to their own "Utilitarian" view, which offers a systematic way of ensuring consistency in bodily answers: whereas my body tells me what *I* have to do *now* in order to avoid what feels like *my* death, the Utilitarian systematization of this answer tells me that every such demand matters equally.[9] This means my future pains matter as much as my present ones, and this also means yours matter as much as mine. In order to figure out what ought to be done, one must do the math. The problem may be complex, and there may be many unknowns, but in principle there is an answer—a fixed and unwavering one—as to what I ought to do: whatever will maximize pleasure and minimize pain for humanity considered as a totality (and, potentially, for the totality of all sentient beings).

Ancient stoicism offered the first attempt at an enlightened version of the kinship answer. My kin are the people who are "mine" or on my side. Stoic cosmopolitanism posits a world community that includes everyone in this group, as the Roman philosopher Seneca (4 BCE–65 CE) writes:

> Let us grasp the idea that there are two commonwealths— the one, a vast and truly common state, which embraces alike gods and men, in which we look neither to this corner of earth nor to that, but measure the bounds of our citizenship by the path of the sun; the other the one to which we have been assigned by the accident of birth.[10]

The Stoics believed that our truest attachments are not to our families, or associates, or country, but to a world order governed by fixed universal laws. If you understand your place within this larger order, you will see that within it there can be no conflicting interests, and that you never have any reason for revenge. They advocated against all passions, but especially against anger. The Greek Stoic Epictetus (50–135 CE), for instance, instructs his reader on how to feel pity, instead of anger, for wrongdoers.[11] When human beings or even animals more generally appear to be pursuing pleasure and avoiding pain, according to the Stoics what is really going on is that they are moved to act in a manner that befits the kind of creature they are: in effect, Stoics analyze appetitive motivation in terms of an animal's kinship relation *to itself.* When you appear to be selfishly following the individual dictates of your particular body, what you are really doing is participating in a larger whole by following the rules that govern the kind of thing you are.[12]

Stoic cosmopolitanism is the ancestor of Kantian deontology, which offers an account of kinship grounded in the power of practical rationality. The correct action, on Kant's theory, is the one that is consistent with respect for the activity of rational thought—in myself and in every other rational being—and thereby allows me to see myself as a member in an (ideal) universal community of beings capable of mutual recognition. Kant calls this community "the kingdom of ends." Kantianism includes a test—called "the categorical imperative"—that provides a fixed and unwavering answer as to whether an action is permitted or not. The power of reason is here understood as the power of an individual to legislate for oneself—to give oneself rules that work universally, for every member of one's kind.

III. UTILITARIANISM, KANTIANISM, VIRTUE ETHICS

Classical Utilitarianism foregrounds the maximization of pleasure, offering up a way to stabilize the bodily answer, whereas deontology foregrounds respect for each individual's place in a larger whole, stabilizing the kinship answer. The first type of ethical theory centers ethics around experience ("I feel pleasure and pain"), the second around membership ("I belong to the group of rational beings"). It is important to note that while both counsel rationality, it is of different kinds. One operates by creating a giant aggregate of everyone's experiences, positive or negative, which is then the target of maximization. The other gives a central place to the idea of a moral law. Law is a kinship concept, addressed to a creature who understands itself not as part of an aggregate but as belonging to a kind: a group of individuals who likewise subject themselves to that same law. Utilitarian rationality takes a calculative form; it works by cost-benefit analysis. In contrast, deontological rationality takes a legalistic, regulative form—it works by subjecting what you were antecedently inclined to do to a constraint. The first is a way of caring about advantage, the second about justice.

Mill's and Kant's own intellectual descendants have tended to remove many traces of the original commands by pushing their theories in a more abstract direction: Utilitarians today often call themselves "consequentialists," to mark their willingness to broaden the scope of what gets maximized, from pleasure alone to whatever the best outcomes are. A parallel point can be made about modern-day Kantians. For example, consider the "contractualism" of T. M. Scanlon, who does not mention membership in an ideal community, or the categorical imperative, but nonetheless gestures in those directions by defining an act as wrong if it violates principles that anyone would reasonably accept as a basis for general agreement. Other contractualists, such as John Rawls and Christine Korsgaard, likewise invoke idealized acceptance procedures descended from Kant's categorical imperative.

Even if consequentialists don't mention pleasure and even if contractualists don't mention citizenship, the former nonetheless describe rationality in calculative and maximizing terms, whereas the latter describe it in legalistic and regulative (restraining) terms. In each case, the original savage command makes itself known in the shape into which it organizes rationality.

Both traditions have a response to the Socratic complaint, articulated at the end of chapter 3, about our blind obedience to savage commands. Contractualists and other modern-day Kantians deny that morality makes us hostage to inarticulate commands: the cleaned-up kinship command is *so* clean, they insist, that it constitutes the only possible rule in accordance with which a rational being could, on full reflection, choose to live. Blind obedience to arbitrary commands— "heteronomy" in Kant's lingo—is precisely the fate of beings who *don't* give themselves the moral law; by contrast, obedience to the categorical imperative is self-rule, or "autonomy." The Utilitarian (or, more generally, consequentialist) way of managing our rebellious impulses is to embrace them. Whatever it is you were hoping to get out of whatever you were going to do, they are proposing a way to get *more* of that. There is no possible reason to rebel, since none of the goods in the service of which you might rebel lie outside all the good that can be brought about by your actions. But notice that the measures taken to render the two commands rebellion-proof also serve to obscure the divide between the just and the advantageous. The war between the just and the advantageous becomes a war that cannot be articulated *within* Kantianism or Utilitarianism, because it is the war *between* those theories.

This war is characteristically fought in ethics classrooms, by means of a set of hypothetical scenarios known as "trolley problems." Suppose a trolley is barreling down tracks to which a dozen people have been tied, and you are positioned to be able to switch it over to a different track, where only one person is tied. Your inner Utilitarian might well urge you to make the switch, on the grounds that one death is better than twelve. Now suppose that instead of being positioned at the switch, you are standing at a bridge that overlooks the tracks, such that in order to save the twelve you have to push someone off the bridge. Only one man is large enough to stop the trolley. Should you push him off the bridge? Your inner Utilitarian may at this point take a backseat to your inner Kantian, who tells you that violently hurling someone to their death counts as "using him as a mere means," which is to say, refusing to afford him the recognition they are due as a fellow rational creature.

Our responses to these scenarios don't take a consistently Kantian or a consistently Utilitarian shape, revealing that each theory leaves something unaccounted for. The Kantian cannot see the good of acting on one's inclination, against duty; he thinks you never have any reason to act in such a mistaken way. The Kantian finds himself in the same position as Alcibiades when, having insisted that cowardice is the worst thing there is, he sees no way to assert that death is an evil. Likewise, the Utilitarian cannot see the good of achieving less pleasure—or less well-being, or more relief from suffering, or however one wants to consequentialize it—when one could achieve more. The idea that a person can be torn between the value of justice and the value of personal advantage is not available to the Kantian or the Utilitarian any more than it is to Socrates. This is where, as mentioned above, Socratism is in fact similar to Kantianism and Utilitarianism.

Trolley problems are traditionally understood as a basis for objecting to the completeness of either Kantianism or Utilitarianism as a system. It would be premature to pass judgment here on these objections without careful consultation not only of the large literature on trolley problems, but also the other debates between deontology and consequentialism, and, in addition, the intramural disputes between the myriad factions into which each one has splintered. That said, the very existence of all this scholarship attests to the reality that the fault line over which Alcibiades (and Callicles, and Thrasymachus, and so on) stumbled runs deep. Post-Socratic ethical theory does reveal the possibility of a more systematic and coherent articulation of the objects of the two commands, the goods pertaining to the body and the goods pertaining to kinship. But it also reveals, at the same time, how difficult it is to construct a single system that includes both of these sorts of goods. It seems that if you allow the one, you exclude the other.

In short, the distinction we take for granted every time we blithely notice a conflict between justice and advantage is one that philosophers have not settled how to draw. We think we are speaking from some stable position when we insist that there is a difference between justice and advantage, but Socrates would say we are merely being blown back and forth. We can now supplement what he would say: we are being blown back and forth between an impulse whose best available rational articulation takes a calculative form, and an impulse whose best available rational articulation takes a legalistic form.

But wait: Isn't there another option? Utilitarianism and Kantianism tend to dominate the landscape not only of Anglo-American academic ethics, but also of the disciplines that engage with it—law, political theory, medicine, economics, and so on. Nonetheless, they are not the only games in town. Virtue Ethics, the theory that traces its origins to Plato's student Aristotle, attempts to harmonize the two commands without subordinating either to the other. The Virtue Ethicist believes that to exercise virtue—to behave as a just, and courageous, and wise, and decent person does—is at once the greatest source of pleasure for the individual who so behaves, and at the same time the greatest source of benefit for his society. The work of harmonizing the two commands is not theoretical, but practical: they will come into line given the presence of a supportive culture, the right social norms, the best laws, a good upbringing, and so on. The claim is that if one is raised well in a good society, one becomes habituated to responding as a decent person would in each specific case. Such a person will not hear the command of the body separately from the command of social pressure, because both of these voices will have been harmonized into the single song of virtue. The virtuous person will heed this voice not as one succumbs to the onerous demands of a tyrannical master, but as one rejoices at the opportunity to do something beautiful and noble. The Greek word *kalon*, which I am translating as "beautiful" and "noble," deftly combines into a single concept the personal allure of pleasant experience and the social appeal of recognition and honor.

Whereas Kantians command you to constrain your actions to those that are consistent with respect for humanity (in your own person and in that of others) and Utilitarians enjoin the production of good outcomes for everyone, proponents of Virtue Ethics simply tell you to be a decent, kind, fair, brave person. As long as you were well brought up, you will be equipped to act in accordance with those ideals, as each situation requires, without wavering.

So what does a Virtue Ethicist say about trolley problems? She will be happy to accede to the complexity of our natural response: it is sometimes virtuous to kill one to save twelve, and sometimes it is not. The Virtue Ethicist does not feel compelled to give you a theoretical account of which kinds of cases will fall into each category, because she takes ethical knowledge to be knowledge not of universal principles but of particulars. Aristotle describes a virtuous soul as similar to a healthy eye: the virtuous person can simply see what the right thing to do is in each case.

Notice that this means that such a person will, once again, *not* be torn between justice and advantage. The Virtue Ethicist holds that in a well-ordered society of well-brought-up people there will not be much of a conflict between what is in someone's personal interest and what is in the interest of the group. If *you* frequently find yourself torn in this way, something has gone wrong either with you or with the world you live in. Thus, Aristotle agrees with Socrates: there is really no tension between the value of justice and the value of advantage, these are not two separate goods, and any appearance that they are must be chalked up to error—either an error in the way you see things, or an error in the way your society is organized, or (likely) both.

Kantians, Utilitarians, and Aristotelians all end up taking Socrates' side against Alcibiades. When we refer, alongside Alcibiades, to the clash between justice and advantage, we are confessing our inability to give a coherent, non-wavering answer to the question "How should I act?" The theories of Kant, Mill, Aristotle, and Socrates are designed precisely to yield such an answer.

IV. The Socratic Difference

The crucial question for anyone proposing a novel ethical theory is: How does it differ from the offerings already on the menu?

Socrates believed that savage commands are not the only sources of answers to untimely questions, denying that we are forced to rely on even the cleaned-up versions of those commands posited by the other three traditions. For Socrates, what appears to be a difficulty with *life*—that it puts us in situations in which we must make "tough choices" between personal and social value—is in fact a difficulty in our *thinking* about life. What is tough about tough choices is only that we are consigned to approaching them in slavish subjection to savage commands. "What should I do?" is a single question: if you find yourself giving two incompatible answers, that is your ignorance talking. More specifically, what is doing the talking is not any conception you have of the good—if you had one, it would be *one* conception—but two savage commands, each of which has you at its beck and call, neither of which is willing to explain itself.

For Socrates, ethics consists in inquiring into untimely questions, rather than in finding ways to read answers off of (either, or both) of the savage commands. Socrates' identification of the quest to be a good person with a quest for knowledge underlies the distinctively Socratic denial that anyone ever acts against their better judgment ("weakness of will") or does what they know to be wrong. If, unlike Socrates, you think you already know the answers to untimely questions, then you need to explain why you yourself sometimes fail to act on them. How does the Utilitarian explain not donating more to charity? How does the Kantian explain her little white lies? The answer is that neither believes that *knowing* what you should do suffices for *action*—they posit an additional something, call it "will-power," or "effort," or "commitment" or "respect," that one has to add to moral knowledge to make it effective.

Kantianism and Utilitarianism must allow for the possibility of residual, untamed savagery, and they can, though only at the cost of invoking an entity, such as "the will," which will be tasked with battling it. The savagery might come in the form of the command that has supposedly been tamed, for instance the Utilitarian failing to overcome the irrational selfishness of a body that demands *my pleasure now!*, or it might come in the form of the continued force of a command that has supposedly been superseded, such as the Kantian caving to the impulse to tell a small lie that will make everyone happier. The Virtue Ethicist, by contrast, must count motivational failures as cognitive failures. This is perhaps one reason why Virtue Ethics has had less of an impact outside of the discipline of academic philosophy than the other two approaches: you cannot preach Virtue Ethics without, often dubiously, claiming to have yourself achieved a measure of moral perfection, and you cannot preach it *to* anyone other than those who have already been well brought up, which is to say, the choir.

Socrates would charge all of these views with creating a false ceiling: what they are calling "knowledge" is not yet knowledge. Another, higher kind of knowledge is possible. The mystery substance with which they insist knowledge be supplemented is, according to Socrates, a fiction constructed to cover the ignorance born of prematurely arrested inquiry. If you actually knew what you should do, you would do it. So long as you don't know, holds Socrates, the proper ethical attitude is an inquisitive one.

Let me emphasize that I am not putting forward this series of Socratic critiques *as valid*. I am only putting them forward *as Socratic*. The brief overview I've offered in this chapter cannot hope to have done justice to the three rich philosophical traditions, each with histories spanning thousands of years. My aim has only been to situate Socratic ethics in a broader field of alternative approaches to the problem of answering untimely questions—I have pointed to some shared agreement, namely the response to Alcibiades, and to some disagreements. I do not take myself to have offered a detailed comparison between Socratic ethics and its competitors, let alone any reason to reject them in favor of him. As Socrates insists to Polus in the *Gorgias*, before you praise something, you need to say what it is that you are praising. When it comes to Socratic ethics, we are still at the stage of saying what it is—and that is a big enough task for one book. The comparative evaluation will have to await another.

The ethical theories currently being used to navigate human life have their roots in the ancient world: in the thought of Aristotle, of the Stoics, and of the Epicureans. If we turn the clock back only slightly earlier, to the man who set all of those thinkers off on their divergent philosophical journeys, we gain access to a very different approach to the question, "How should I live?"—namely, an inquisitive one. You might wonder, if this alternative is available, why hasn't it been taken up? Why isn't Socratic ethics already a well-established tradition of its own?

The answer is that Socrates' ethics is intellectualist, and people have a strong and deep aversion to intellectualism. Let me explain.

I have already mentioned two distinctive features of Socrates' ethics: that we do not yet have the answers, and that philosophizing is the way to get them. If you put these together, you get the third and perhaps most surprising feature: viewing the activity of philosophical theorizing as itself having ethical significance. When Utilitarians debate Kantians, or Kantians argue among themselves, or Virtue Ethicists vie for recognition in an ethical landscape that persistently treats them as second-class citizens, all participants tend to treat these debates as something of an intellectual sideshow to whatever is going on in what they are prepared to call "the real world." While the specialists are arguing among themselves, people are being born and dying, they are fighting for political victories and military ones, they are making and enjoying art, they are working to provide for their families, or working to earn money to donate it to charities, or working on scientific breakthroughs that will benefit humanity, or taking care of those who cannot care for themselves, and so on. According to other ethical traditions, those sorts of events bear the hallmarks of real life. Socratics, by contrast, believe that arguing about how one should live *is* real life. Although it is often necessary to spend some or much of one's time otherwise, inquiry is the best thing one can do with one's life, given that one does not know how to lead it. The hard work of struggling to be a good, virtuous, ethical person—Socrates understands that work as, first and foremost, intellectual work.

These three features of Socratism—that we don't now know, that if we knew we would act on our knowledge, and that intellectual conversations are the road to becoming a good person—add up to an "intellectualism" that many people find so implausible as to be ready to dismiss it without serious consideration. "What philosophers and non-philosophers alike have often found disappointing in Socrates is his intellectualism," writes Socrates scholar Heda Segvic.[13]

Even Socrates' fans and defenders tend to share this bleak assessment of intellectualism—the label is almost exclusively treated as an insult—and so they perform interpretative backflips to argue that: he did not, could not, *really* think that weakness of the will is impossible;[14] that he did not quite hold the view that all desire is only for what is, as a matter of fact, good (a view that would entail that good and bad people could only be differentiated by what they know, which is to say, intellectually);[15] that he allowed for emotion and motivation to make knowledge-independent contributions to ethical life;[16] that he did not really believe that we could have ethical knowledge that would be on par with the kind of knowledge we now have about how to make shoes or clocks;[17] that he did not really think that virtue, which is to say, knowledge, could suffice for happiness;[18] and generally, that he's not as much of an intellectualist as he initially appears to be.[19] My own approach to Socrates might be described as "hard-line intellectualist"—I think that Socrates is just what he seems to be, namely someone who believes that we don't know, that if we knew we would act on our knowledge, and that philosophy— the pursuit of such knowledge—is the only sure road to becoming a better person. Why is this collection of views so implausible?

If you posed this question to the many scholars who try to save Socrates from his own intellectualism, they would say "because it is obvious that someone could have knowledge—such as the knowledge that it is wrong to steal, or kill—but be unwilling to act on it." Socrates' response is: What makes you think that was knowledge? The real source of the opposition to Socratic intellectualism is not the commonsense observation that people often act in ways they are ready to repudiate, but the insistence that what we sometimes act against deserves to be called "knowledge."

Socratic intellectualism turns its back on a very basic human need: the need to *already* know. Kantianism, Utilitarianism, and Virtue Ethics tell us that we *already know* how to live, that the formula for how to do so is simply a matter of cleaning up the bodily command, or cleaning up the kinship command, or of looking to the best ways in which the people around us have found to satisfy both at the same time. These ethical theories address the urgent demand for answers *now*. The human need to know how to live subjects us to its desperate logic: *Because I must know, it must be the case that I do know.* The passionate confidence with which people are inclined to proclaim their ethical beliefs—often with little ability to defend those beliefs—stems not from flightiness but from a seriousness about the project of living their one and only life. Could it really be true that we will have to go through our whole lives, from birth to death, without ever knowing whether we are doing it right? The answer is yes. If the encounter with Socratic ethics is destabilizing—being refuted was, for Socrates' interlocutors, like having the ground shift underneath their feet—those who inhabit it accept a much deeper instability: there is no firm ground, and you don't ever get to take foundations for granted.

In (implicitly) describing Kantianism, Utilitarianism, and Virtue Ethics as uninquisitive, I do not mean to level a charge of dogmatism against any individual: the philosophers who embrace these views tend, like all philosophers, to be open to counterargument, careful not to overclaim, and charitable in interpreting their intellectual opponents. Nonetheless, each of the three theories present their foundations as settled in a way that Socrates' does not. That is why it makes sense to speak of a Stoic sage, or an Epicurean sage, or an Aristotlean sage ("the *phronimos*,") but the very idea of a "Socratic sage" is a contradiction, because a person who had arrived at knowledge would no longer have need of an inquisitive ethics, and thus would no longer be a Socratic. I think this feature—*the impossibility of sages*—speaks to an advantage of Socratic intellectualism, but the advantage will be easier to articulate if we consider not sages, but utopias. If a sage is a perfect person, then a utopia is a sage writ large: a perfect society.

V. The Paradox of Utopia

If asked to sketch an ideal society, the Kantian, or Utilitarian, or Virtue Ethicist does not find that her ethics stands in the way of doing so. And indeed some proponents of each of these theories have provided quite detailed sketches: John Rawls' *A Theory of Justice* is a Kantian utopia of sorts, and Aristotle's description of his preferred constitution in the *Politics* is an Aristotelian one; to the extent that Utilitarians have tended to hesitate, it is because they are not sure they know how exactly to bring about the world that they take to be self-evidently the best. In his great treatise on Utilitarianism, *The Methods of Ethics*, Henry Sidgwick explains the difficulty:

> We require to contemplate not so much the end supposed to be attained—which is simply the most pleasant consciousness conceivable, lasting as long and as uninterruptedly as possible—but rather some method of realising it, pursued by human beings; and these, again, must be conceived as existing under conditions not too remote from our own, so that we can at least endeavour to imitate them. And for this we must know how far our present circumstances are modifiable; a very difficult question, as the constructions which have actually been made of such ideal societies show.[20]

Utilitarianism, like Kantianism and Virtue Ethics, is hospitable to the idea of utopia. This is a problem for these theories, because there is a problem with utopia. A good place to see the problem is to consider an encounter, not with a fictional or conceptual or notional utopia, but with one located in the real world, in upstate New York, in the Appalachian highlands ten miles above Lake Erie. A visitor writes:

A few summers ago I spent a happy week at the famous Assembly Grounds on the borders of Chautauqua Lake. The moment one treads that sacred enclosure, one feels one's self in an atmosphere of success. Sobriety and industry, intelligence and goodness, orderliness and ideality, prosperity and cheerfulness, pervade the air. It is a serious and studious picnic on a gigantic scale. Here you have a town of many thousands of inhabitants, beautifully laid out in the forest and drained, and equipped with means for satisfying all the necessary lower and most of the superfluous higher wants of man. You have a first-class college in full blast. You have magnificent music—a chorus of seven hundred voices, with possibly the most perfect open-air auditorium in the world. You have every sort of athletic exercise from sailing, rowing, swimming, bicycling, to the ball-field and the more artificial doings which the gymnasium affords. You have kindergartens and model secondary schools. You have general religious services and special club-houses for the several sects. You have perpetually running soda-water fountains, and daily popular lectures by distinguished men. You have the best of company, and yet no effort. You have no zymotic diseases, no poverty, no drunkenness, no crime, no police. You have culture, you have kindness, you have cheapness, you have equality, you have the best fruits of what mankind has fought and scrambled and striven for under the name of civilization for centuries. You have, in short, a foretaste of what human society might be, were it all in the light, with no suffering and no dark corners.[21]

This report comes from William James, who visited the Chautauqua Institution, as it is now called, back in 1900. At that time, it was a quarter century old; as of the publication of this book, it has been in existence for 150 years.

Chautauqua seems to check all the utopian boxes. It is hard to see what grounds a Utilitarian, or a Kantian, or an Aristotelian would have for objecting to it, since it is a world in which both the bodily command and the kinship command get their due. James himself finds nothing to fault in how it is organized, or in what goods and services it provides, suggesting that if he had been tasked with describing an ideal society, he would have produced a blueprint for something much like Chautauqua. So one is stunned to see him recount what happened when he departed from this paradise:

> I went in curiosity for a day. I stayed for a week, held spell-bound by the charm and ease of everything, by the middle-class paradise, without a sin, without a victim, without a blot, without a tear. And yet what was my own astonishment, on emerging into the dark and wicked world again, to catch myself quite unexpectedly and involuntarily saying: "Ouf! what a relief. Now for something primordial and savage, even though it were as bad as an Armenian massacre, to set the balance straight again. This order is too tame, this culture too second-rate, this goodness too uninspiring. This human drama without a villain or a pang; this community so refined that ice-cream soda-water is the utmost offering it can make to the brute animal in man; this city simmering in the tepid lakeside sun; this atrocious harmlessness of all things—I cannot abide with them.[22]

I don't think there's a single parenthetical more shocking to me in all of philosophical writing than the one containing the phrase "an Armenian massacre," above. James is saying that his week in a perfect idyll was so horrific that it made the experience of *genocide* look alluring! His explanation is that what he was missing was the element of *struggle* in life:

> The ideal was so completely victorious already that no sign of any previous battle remained, the place just resting on its oars. But what our human emotions seem to require is the sight of the struggle going on. The moment the fruits are being merely eaten, things become ignoble. Sweat and effort, human nature strained to its uttermost and on the rack, yet getting through alive, and then turning its back on its success to pursue another more rare and arduous still—this is the sort of thing the presence of which inspires us, and the reality of which it seems to be the function of all the higher forms of literature and fine art to bring home to us and suggest. At Chautauqua there were no racks, even in the place's historical museum; and no sweat, except possibly the gentle moisture on the brow of some lecturer; or on the sides of some player in the ballfield.[23]

There is a deep problem here. If James wants struggle and effort and difficulty, why couldn't you dig a few pits in Chautauqua and disguise them well, so that people would fall in and then have to struggle to get out of? What if one citizen were designated "town villain" and he occasionally wreaked havoc and needed punishment? No, I can hear James replying, it needs to be a *real* struggle, with *real* villains. But a real struggle must be directed at some goal, the real punishment of real villains must have some end in view, and James would be hard pressed to articulate what more fitting end we could be struggling toward than: ending poverty, disease, crime, inequality, and massacres; ample educational and recreational opportunities for all; perhaps even perpetually running soda-water fountains. All of that is to say: the world James sees us as struggling to bring about is Chautauqua. And, then, when he finds himself actually inhabiting his utopia, he finds he'd rather be in a massacre! It makes no sense to insist that we spend our lives struggling and toiling to bring about a world that, if we were in it, we'd recoil from. We might call this "the paradox of utopia," and it characterizes the entire tradition of utopian writing.

Readers of Plato's *Republic*, Thomas More's *Utopia*, or Francis Bacon's *New Atlantis* rarely find themselves longing to live in the "perfect" worlds these authors have constructed. We might go case by case with our excuses: we dislike the fact that Kallipolis is founded on a noble lie, that More's "utopia" features slavery, that Bacon's Bensalem is so scholastic and so obsessed with "The Spirit of Chastity," and so on. But as one considers other utopias, too, there appears something suspicious about the reality that we *always* have some problem or other with them. When I teach Genesis, I find that few students really view leaving the Garden of Eden as a punishment. They're *glad* we got kicked out. It is not an accident that much utopian writing takes the form of satire (Samuel Butler, Jonathan Swift). It comes naturally to us to present a utopia sarcastically: "as *though* this were a utopia!"

The paradox of utopia is that we don't seem to like it very much. And now we can return to Socrates, because our dislike for utopia is a point in favor of Socratic intellectualism. Socrates will not accept that the problem could be with perfection itself; he will not permit us to say that some life, or some society, is "too happy." Instead, he will diagnose the problem as this: every utopia that has ever been constructed has been an imperfect person's idea of a perfect place. When we encounter a world that matches our template for what a happy world would look like, and recoil from the prospect of living there, that is a sign that our template might not be so good. Our "utopias" reflect our ignorance about fundamental questions; they write it large enough for us to see it clearly. The paradox of utopia suggests that our thinking about how we should live may not yet be complete.

VI. PLATO AND SOCRATES

Recall this exchange from the opening of the chapter:

> SOCRATES: What would you say about courage? How much would you have to be offered to be deprived of that?
> ALCIBIADES: I wouldn't even want to go on living if I were a coward.[24]

The prospect of being paid in exchange for cowardice elicits in Alcibiades a very recognizable form of scorn, one that results from viewing the demands of the body through the lens of kinship. We experience the demands of kinship as elevating us above the selfishness of merely catering to our bodies, which is also why Kantians look down their noses at Utilitarians. It seems doubtful whether kinship will ever allow itself to be organized "from below" by the demands of the body; nor do the demands that issue from one's various kin groups always cohere with one another. Plato describes this situation by claiming that there is a part of the soul that reflects the demands of kinship—he calls it "the spirited part." It needs to be ruled—it cannot rule itself—but it will not submit to rule by the part of the soul that reflects the needs of the body, which he calls "the appetitive part." Thus he posits a third part of the soul, "the rational part," which he describes as natural ruler over the other two: "in the civil war in the soul [the spirited part] aligns itself far more with the rational part." The rational part is suited to rule because it possesses answers of a very different sort from those located in the other two parts. Consider this observation from book VI of the *Republic*:

In the case of just and beautiful things, many people are content with what are believed to be so, even if they aren't really so, and they act, acquire, and form their own beliefs on that basis. Nobody is satisfied to acquire things that are merely believed to be good, however, but everyone wants the things that really *are* good and disdains mere belief here.

Every soul pursues the good and does its utmost for its sake. It divines that the good is something but it is perplexed and cannot adequately grasp what it is or acquire the sort of stable beliefs it has about other things, and so it misses the benefit, if any, that even those other things may give.[25]

When it comes to justice, someone might be content to let the social expectations that come packaged with anger guide her; when it comes to aesthetic appreciation, she might be willing to hand that task over to her body's pleasure and pain responses.[26] One need look no further than social media to see examples of outrage that seems driven less by the nature of a given injustice and more by the expectation that others will join in the response. So long as we enjoy a movie, or some food, or some music, taking pleasure in the various looks, smells, sounds, or tastes, we are often prepared to set aside any worries about whether the object of our appetitive responses is "really" or "objectively" beautiful.

But there is something in us that approaches ethics differently, some part that "wants the things that really are good and disdains mere belief here." Plato is describing the desires of the rational part of the soul, whose journey begins when "it divines that the good is something but it is perplexed and cannot adequately grasp what it is," and ends when it arrives at stable and secure knowledge.

It is worth emphasizing that the tripartite soul is Platonic, not Socratic. The scholarly consensus takes Plato to be departing from the thought of Socrates in the later books of the *Republic* (that is, after book I), and I agree with that consensus. Socrates is not inclined to explain our departures from prudence and justice by invoking battles among soul-parts, any more than he is inclined to explain them by invoking mysterious motivational entities, such as "the will." He believes in the unity of the soul just as he believes in the unity of the good. If beauty and justice are different from goodness, that can only be because, in our confusion, sometimes goodness appears to us in the form of beauty, sometimes in the form of justice. What Plato offers us in the *Republic*, with his extended and elaborate discussions of the kind of upbringing required for a person to be just, and his description of Kallipolis, a utopia organized toward the production of such upbringings, is already halfway to Aristotelian Virtue Ethics.

But even if we recognize all of the ways Plato departs from Socrates, and specifically acknowledge that the representation of the soul as containing an appetitive *part* and a spirited *part* is un-Socratic—because Socrates would instead just speak of a single soul, confused about what to do, hearing all sorts of conflicting commands, and whose confusion calls for no impossible feat of psychic surgery, only the very possible acquisition of knowledge—we should nonetheless grant that the *addition* of a rational part to the other two reflects an importantly Socratic insight.

Rationality, as Plato depicts it, is not only a means of smoothing out the demands of body or kin, but represents a full-fledged alternative, a third and independent source of answers to the question of how we should live. Unlike the other two parts, it doesn't ever issue savage commands; rather, it is a faculty for truthful inquiry whose inquisitively produced directives never need to be tamed. They come pre-tamed by the fact that they are answers to a question *that was asked*. The idea that the function of thought is not only to help us get what our body tells us we need, or to behave how our kin want us to behave, but to ask the very questions to which the other two commands provide automatic answers—this is the most important lesson that Plato learned from Socrates.

If you want to know what it would be like to act on the basis of a very different *kind* of answer to questions about how you—and we—should live, an answer that is not the answer of one's body, or one's group, the first step is learning how to ask those questions. If the method of Kantianism is legalistic and regulatory; and the method of Utilitarianism is calculative and maximizing; and the method of Virtue Ethics is to consult one's well-habituated faculty of practical judgment, in what more precise terms can we describe the Socratic method? That is the question part two of this book is devoted to answering.

Part Two

✳

THE
SOCRATIC
METHOD

Introduction to Part Two:

Three Paradoxes

Y OUR ANSWERS TO UNTIMELY QUESTIONS STEM FROM savage commands. Suppose you want to replace them with better answers. What should you do? Simple: keep an open mind and inquire, moving toward what's true and away from what's false.

Can that really be all there is to it? Yes. That is the Socratic method. It is by following that formula that Socrates secured for himself much better answers to untimely questions than the standard-issue versions supplied by his body or kinship groups. But, as you might expect, there is a catch: following the formula, using the method, is not as straightforward as it appears to be. When we try to follow it, we find that each of the three ingredients—open-mindedness, inquiry, and separating truth from falsity—conceals a paradox.

Open-mindedness means being able to admit that you are wrong. This sounds easy enough until you insist that the last three words be interpreted literally. Set aside being able to admit that you were wrong in the past, or that you are the sort of creature who is liable to go wrong, or that what you think at this very moment might be shown to be wrong at some future time, or that there might be some people out there right now who believe that you are wrong. Let's focus on your ability to know (now) that you are in the wrong (now). If that's what open-mindedness amounts to, being open-minded seems to entail believing what you also know to be false!

If you are wondering why a person who can admit that she *was* or *might be* wrong isn't sufficiently open-minded, recall that with untimely questions, there is no suspension of judgment. If someone wants to criticize your answer to an untimely question without offering you a replacement, the only way you can be receptive to such criticism is by being able to see what is wrong with what you think *even as you continue to think it*. Either we cannot be open-minded about untimely questions, or we must somehow be able to think, "p is wrong, even though I believe p." This is called "Moore's paradox," and it is the subject of chapter 6.

What is inquiry? We cannot simply equate inquiry with the asking of questions, because some questions are rhetorical, sometimes we are only asking a question to be polite, and even when neither of those two circumstances obtains, we often seek knowledge not from any inquisitive motive but simply because the information is instrumental to the removal of some practical obstacle. ("Where's the post office?"; "How do I turn on the printer?") We tend to prefer problem-solving to inquiry, which is why, quite often, when faced with a genuine question, our first instinct is to try to turn it into a problem. For instance, Einstein, when confronted with "What is time?" turned it into "How would clocks behave under various circumstances?"

We are eager to operationalize questions—to turn them into problems—by introducing measurement. So, for example, when confronted with questions such as What is it to be angry? or smart? or good at policework?, people are inclined to look to bodily indicators such as heart rate and skin temperature, or scores on IQ tests, or number of cases closed. The advantage of turning a question into a problem of measurement is that it becomes clear what it would mean to have a solution to it. Now consider this: If I were to treat a question as a proper question, rather than a problem in disguise—which is to say, to ask that question purely for the sake of answering it—could I tell when I had in fact arrived at the answer? This is called "Meno's paradox," named after the Socratic interlocutor Meno, who challenged Socrates with one of the most difficult questions in all of the dialogues: "If you should meet with it, how will you know that this [i.e., the answer] is the thing that you did not know?" We will discuss that question in chapter 7.

However, before discussing Socratic open-mindedness or Socratic inquisitiveness we must address the paradox that calls into question whether such a person as Socrates is even possible. It was obvious to everyone who encountered him that Socrates was a gadfly who busied himself with the negative, destructive activity of refutation—but Socrates also characterizes himself as a midwife who helpfully, constructively births the ideas of others. How can he be both? How is the negative project of avoiding falsehood related to the positive project of seeking the truth? I call this "the Gadfly-Midwife paradox." In order to explain how there is one Socrates, rather than two, we are going to have to settle the question of how a person can go about *both* pursuing truth *and* avoiding falsity, when, on the face of it, these tasks are in tension with one another. To get a sense of the nature of the tension, consider that those who want truths must come to have beliefs, whereas the only sure way to avoid falsity is not to believe anything at all. The Gadfly-Midwife paradox is the one we will take up immediately, in chapter 5.

My initial characterization of the Socratic method—inquire open-mindedly, moving toward truth and away from falsity—is likely to have struck you as disappointingly banal. The banality comes from the fact that you already knew that was what you had to do. Before reading this book, you would likely have given similar instruction to anyone who wanted to learn anything. There is an important sense in which explaining the Socratic method is not a matter of offering new information. Instead of adding to our store of knowledge—as the biographer, or the cartographer, or the biologist might—Socrates demonstrates that we already have, in us, ideas we do not quite know how to live up to. Learning philosophy is less like filling a void and more like untying a knot. Philosophy begins not in ignorance, not in wonder, but in error.

I will show you that when you try to make sense of seeing that one is (not was) in the wrong, of posing questions (not problems), and of combining (in one act of thought, not two) the pursuit of truth and the avoidance of falsity—you will find that you are stuck. You

don't know how to proceed. I am going to argue that the key to getting unstuck, in all three cases, is relocating that act of thought—the
act of thought that is inquisitive, open-minded, and oriented both
toward truth and away from falsehood—from its usual home inside
one person's head into the shared space of the conversation that
passes between two people. Socrates found a way for two people,
together, to ask and answer untimely questions that neither could
inquire into on their own. Socrates overturned the conventional
wisdom that thinking is something that each of us can do, on our
own, without much effort. Instead, he found that it was a communal
feat—and he showed us how to pull it off.

Chapter 5

The Gadfly-Midwife Paradox

I N AN ESSAY CALLED "ON THE GRADUAL CONSTRUCTION
of Thoughts During Speech," German playwright Heinrich
von Kleist (1777–1811) gives his reader advice for what to do when
"there is something you want to know and cannot discover by meditation."[1] Kleist says you should seize upon "the first acquaintance
whom you happen to meet," not in order to extract from them the
knowledge you seek but, rather, to hand it over to them: "You yourself should begin by telling it all to him." Kleist expects that in the
past "you spoke with the pretentious purpose of enlightening others." He instructs you to change course: "I want you to speak with
the reasonable purpose of enlightening yourself." Kleist reports that
when he is stuck on a mathematical problem, he explains it to his sister, whose very presence, in spite of her lack of mathematical training, works its magic: "I have only to begin boldly, and . . . to my
surprise, the end of the sentence coincides with the desired knowledge." He says Molière did something similar with his servant girl,
and that the phenomenon is commonplace in public speaking. "I
believe that, at the moment when he opened his mouth, many a
great orator did not know what he was going to say."

Kleist anticipates that his reader will be surprised by his advice:
"I can see you opening your eyes wide at this." We tend to assume
that we couldn't have more to say to another person than we would
to ourselves—that if I have anything to tell you, I could as well have
told it to myself. We are familiar with the fact that we often communicate less than what we believe—when we lie, or conceal our views,

or simply refrain from expressing them—but it is surprising to think that the reverse also happens, that there are contexts where we can be *more* generous with others than with ourselves.

Kleist's insight—that I can give you more than what I seem to myself to have—is Socratic. It is also very alien to us, so alien that we are not ready to receive it until we remove the assumption that stands between it and us. The full depth of the insight is alien even to Kleist, whose failure to identify the relevant assumption and to detangle the troublesome knots to which that assumption gives rise consign him to appreciating only the thinnest edge of the Socratic wedge. When tasked with explaining how it is that we can give more than we have, Kleist observes: "The human face confronting a speaker is an extraordinary source of inspiration to him." This is not exactly wrong, but in his focus on speechifying to a silent, ignorant audience, Kleist misses how much potential hides behind the human face. "Socrates converses with Alcibiades not by saying words to his face, but by addressing his words to Alcibiades, in other words, to his soul," says Socrates to Alcibiades.[2] Speaking to the soul of a person—which entails letting them talk back to you—allows you to share something with them that you don't have.

What blocks us from fully appreciating the Socratic insight here is our tendency to assume that thinking is like breathing: something each person does for themselves. If each of us must do her own thinking, then no one has more to offer to another than what she has privately constructed, albeit perhaps quite recently, in the workshop of her mind. Kleist suggests that the presence of others incites one to speed up the construction process, for example, when we think they might be about to interrupt our mathematical exegesis:

> During this process nothing is more helpful to me than a sudden movement on my sister's part, as if she were about to interrupt me; for my mind, already tense, becomes even more excited by this attempt to deprive it of the speech of which it enjoys the possession and, like a great general in

an awkward position, reaches an even higher tension and increases in capacity.

Kleist recognizes that other people often supply us with the energy or optimism for constructing thoughts; Socrates goes one step further and suggests that we can construct thoughts *with* other people. But in order to take this second step with him, we have to learn to recognize the pervasive distortion created by the assumption that thinking is a private, inner, mental activity. The distortion extends to our experience of Socrates himself, generating a kind of double vision that leaves us seeing two Socrateses.

I. THE TWO SOCRATESES

In the *Apology*, Socrates describes Athens as a sleeping horse, and himself as a gadfly sent by the gods to awaken it from ignorance. He stings and reproaches his fellow citizens, asking them questions that reveal the absence of the knowledge they felt sure they had. His refutations put people in a state of confusion in which they do not know where to go, what to do, which way to turn. The Greek word for this state is *aporia*: etymologically, it is composed of the word from which we get "pore" and a privative prefix meaning "not," so literally it refers to the absence of a route or a way forward or path by which to proceed.

Socrates shocks people into recognizing just how lost they are, by making them aware that they are in fact missing what they purport to know. People subjected to this treatment describe themselves as feeling numb, unable to speak, as seeing their words waver back and forth. Unsurprisingly, they find this disconcerting. The individual who goes around removing others' pretensions to wisdom is going to find himself surrounded by a lot of grumpy and resentful people— that much is obvious to anyone, or at least, to anyone but Socrates, who, having taken up the project of systematically refuting all the politicians in Athens, reports with surprise the moment when "I realized, to my sorrow and alarm, that I was getting unpopular."[3] So that's the first Socrates: the refutational gadfly.

The other Socrates is Socrates the midwife. In the *Theaetetus*, Socrates claims that not only was his mother a midwife, but he, too, is a kind of midwife—only for men rather than women,[4] and for the soul rather than the body. Though he is himself "barren" of insights, others are not. When people converse with him, "they discover within themselves a multitude of beautiful things, which they bring forth into the light. But it is I," he boasts, "with God's help, who deliver them of this offspring."[5] Going along with the "midwife" image is Socrates' claim, in the *Meno* and *Phaedo*, that what his interlocutor is doing is "recollecting" something they already knew, and he is only helping them in that process: bringing hidden wisdom to light.[6] In the *Symposium*, the upshot of philosophical learning is not being purged of false beliefs but something undeniably positive: giving birth to true virtue and thereby earning immortality. In the *Charmides*, he describes his philosophical activity as having the goal "that the state of each existing thing should become clear."[7] In the *Gorgias* he says, "All of us ought to be contentiously eager to know what's true and what's false about the things we're talking about. That it should become clear is a good common to all."[8] At the end of that dialogue he describes the conclusions that he has arrived at multiple times, through multiple routes, with multiple people—Gorgias, Polus, and Callicles—as now "held down and bound by arguments of iron and adamant."[9]

In these passages Socrates seems to suggest that he is engaged in activity that makes positive progress toward figuring out the truth. Socrates the midwife is someone whom it would be natural to experience as productive and helpful. Talking to him gives you more than what you had when you entered the conversation; you are on firmer ground, you are *less* lost. The expected response to encountering such a person would be gratitude.

So, what is Socrates? Is he the gadfly who leaves people stunned, bereft, lost, and confused, or the midwife who helps birth their beautifully clear idea-babies? Is he engaged in a fundamentally negative refutational activity, of clearing away pretensions to knowledge, or in a fundamentally positive inquisitive one, of finding new items that one can add to what one claims to know? I call this "the Gadfly-Midwife paradox."

It could also be called the paradox of Socratic humility. Socrates was famous among his contemporaries for the fact that he reputedly "knew that he knew nothing," or "knew his own ignorance"—this is sometimes called "Socratic humility." He frequently disparages his own cognitive powers—his memory, his ability to speak well—and also makes specific denials with respect to his knowledge of piety, virtue, courage, and so on. This is midwife Socrates: empty, lowly, ready to occupy a subordinate position. Barren, with no ideas of his own, he is reduced to making himself useful by facilitating the thinking of others. He routinely praises the greater knowledge of his interlocutor.

But Socrates was also famous for his habit of besting the most impressive minds of his day in one-on-one showdowns that were often public. The person who is focused on publicly taking others down a peg—and who is good at it—isn't typically the most humble person in the room. Socrates the gadfly, negative Socrates, displays the intellectual resources required to foil the most brilliant people. Socrates routinely comes up against sophists, orators, and members of the Athenian intellectual elite angling to display their virtuosity at his expense. Time after time, Socrates prevails.

How could one person be known both for his humility and for his competitive argumentative prowess? The mystery of Socrates is that the two central facts about him don't seem to fit together. Is Socrates as arrogant as he seems, or as ignorant as he claims to be? Which is he, a provocative gadfly or a cooperative midwife?

Those first encountering Socrates tend to interpret him as either all gadfly or all midwife. Pure gadfly Socrates is personally invested in demonstrating how little others, especially those of high status, actually know. This Socrates is perceived as arrogant and triumphal by virtue of his attraction to and success at such intellectual combat; he is also perceived as mocking or disparaging his interlocutors. When it comes to Socrates' famed "knowledge of his own ignorance," readers who favor gadfly Socrates emphasize the knowledge part—and all the self-importance that goes along with it.

Pure midwife Socrates is the intellectual hero whose sincere attempts to learn are maligned and misunderstood by his uncooperative interlocutors—who are the arrogant ones. Midwife Socrates is just trying to make "the truth of each existing thing become clear." He is honestly inquiring, sincerely hoping that Euthyphro will tell him what piety is, that Laches will tell him what courage is, and so on; he is not trying to refute anyone. Refutation is, if it occurs, an accidental side effect of his noble quest for knowledge. What sets Socrates apart from everyone else is a simple receptive willingness to learn from the people around him. On this interpretation, Socrates' "knowledge of his own ignorance" is nothing but naïve innocent ignorance. This Socrates is ever hopeful that the next intellectual encounter will be the one that enlightens him.

More sophisticated readers combine the two identities in various ways: there is, for example, Socrates the altruistic gadfly who stings people for their own benefit; and there is also Socrates the skeptical gadfly who doubts there is any knowledge to be had at all. If one leans in the direction of gadfly Socrates, as interpreters from Aristotle onward have tended to do, one might wonder whether we could assign the positive project of knowledge acquisition to Plato—in this view, Socrates refutes and destroys while Plato is the theory builder and creator. The scholarly consensus on the chronology of Plato's dialogues sees roughly three groups.[10] In what scholars call his early period, Plato wrote dialogues such as the *Apology*, *Laches*, *Euthyphro*, *Protagoras*, *Gorgias*, *Hippias Minor*, *Crito*, and *Phaedo*. These dialogues showcase the person and views of the historical Socrates, with a special focus on the events surrounding his death.[11] Scholars then identify a middle period (including *Symposium*, *Phaedrus*, *Republic*), in which Plato is beginning to produce and put forward some of his own original ideas, and a late period, where he does so to an even greater degree. In late dialogues such as *Sophist*, *Statesman*, and *Laws* Socrates either does not appear or is not the main speaker. In late dialogues such as *Philebus* and *Theaetetus*, where the midwife image is located, Socrates is the main speaker but is often understood as, at least in part, playing the role of a mouthpiece for Plato. Might we, then, segregate gadfly Socrates from midwife Socrates by identifying only the gadfly character with the historical Socrates, and the midwife with Plato?

No. Even in the early dialogues, Socrates routinely presents the positive pursuit of knowledge as his goal. While it is true that Socrates depicts himself as a refutational gadfly in the *Apology*, when he is actually engaged in (what look to us to be) refutations—with interlocutors such as Laches, Protagoras, Hippias, Gorgias, and so on—he is remarkably consistent in representing his motivations in a positive manner. He says that he is talking to his interlocutors in order to learn. Here's a representative passage:

> "Protagoras," I said, "I don't want you to think that my motive in talking with you is anything else than to take a good hard look at things that continually perplex me. I think that Homer said it all in the line, Going in tandem, one perceives before the other. Human beings are simply more resourceful this way in action, speech, and thought. . . . How could I not solicit your help in a joint investigation of these questions?"[12]

So, even though the actual midwife image appears in a dialogue usually considered to be late, we can't relegate midwife Socrates to later dialogues. Another alternative is to adopt a sequential interpretation, not across the dialogues, but within each of them: what if Socrates first refutes, and then inquires. Could it be that Socrates acts as gadfly, and acts as midwife, in that order?

II. THE TWO-STAGE VIEW

If you accepted that Socrates has both a destructive and a constructive role, you might be inclined to assume that he switches from the first to the second. I call this "the two-stage view." It breaks Socrates' activity into a preliminary, destructive, error-identification component and, once that has been completed, a secondary, productive search component. Negative refutation paves the way for positive inquiry. Socrates' interlocutors enter the field of conversation laden with "baggage": a dismissive attitude toward the project of seeking after such items as knowledge, justice, and virtue, grounded either in the conceit of already possessing those things, or in a cynical denial of their value.* On the two-stage view, Socrates begins by clearing away bad answers to his questions, thereby motivating his interlocutor to be the kind of person inclined to participate in the search. Socrates can then transition from this initial adversarial stance to the positive, constructive stage of his method in which he and his interlocutors jointly inquire after a satisfactory answer.

We can look beyond the dialogues, to book III of Augustine's *Confessions*, to see a clear example of the two-stage approach. Augustine (354–430), then a student at Carthage, is steeped in heretical beliefs and a sinful, sensually indulgent lifestyle. His devout mother Monica approaches a bishop whom she hopes will set her son straight.

---

* Note that the two-stage view was evidently in the air in Plato's day, since Xenophon expresses it when he says that a sufficiently humble and devoted interlocutor met with an entirely positive and didactic response from Socrates: "Socrates, for his part, seeing how it was with him [Euthydemus], avoided worrying him"—which is to say, Euthydemus was already so humble that Socrates did not see the need to "worry" him by refuting him—and instead Socrates "began to expound very plainly and clearly the knowledge that he thought most needful and the practices that he held to be most excellent" (*Memorabilia* 4.2.40). This is exactly the Socrates we don't find in the Platonic dialogues; Plato, I propose, held the two-stage view to be a misunderstanding of Socrates.

Augustine reports that she "asked him [that is, the bishop] to make time to talk to me and refute my errors and correct my evil doctrines and teach me good ones." A literal translation of that last phrase— *dedocere me mala ac docere bona*—would reveal two forms of the word "teach": "to unteach me evil things and teach me good things." On the two-stage view, refutation constitutes the therapeutic "unteaching" stage that must precede any positive teaching. Monica sees the bishop as having the sort of intellectual and religious prowess necessary both to eradicate Augustine's errors, and to implant truths where they used to be. She expects him to, first, establish a clean slate, and, second, to serve as a teacher.

The bishop declines Monica's request. His rationale is that her son's mind is too infected with heresy to be receptive to the truth. As Augustine recounts:

> For he answered that I was still unready to learn, because I was conceited about the novel excitements of that heresy, and because, as she had informed him, I had already disturbed many untrained minds with many trivial questions. "Let him be where he is," he said; "only pray the Lord for him. By his reading he will discover what an error and how vast an impiety it all is."

The bishop claims that he is unable to teach Augustine because something else has to clear the way first. The bishop evidently specializes in stage two. Some of Socrates' contemporaries saw him as the counterpart to this bishop: someone who relegates himself to the unteaching stage of education. We find this perspective on Socrates in a dialogue called the *Clitophon*.[13]

Clitophon is an associate of Socrates who represents himself as having fully internalized the negative and motivating parts of Socrates' process, and complains about Socrates' failure to provide the positive goods. He avows that he has an excellent understanding of exactly why the usual approach to questions of justice and virtue is wrong, and that he fully appreciates the need for better answers. He reports that "I was therefore very interested in what would come next after such arguments."[14] He describes his frustration at what he experiences as Socrates' unwillingness to get to stage two:

> When I had endured this disappointment, not once or twice but a long time, I finally got tired of begging for an answer. I came to the conclusion that while you're better than anyone at turning a man towards the pursuit of virtue, one of two things must be the case . . . either you don't know it, or you don't wish to share it with me. And this is why, I suppose, I go to Thrasymachus and to anyone else I can: I'm at a loss.[15]

Notice that Clitophon's vision of what happens in the second stage is that Socrates finally discloses the truth in one fell swoop. Clitophon understands his own slate of conventional views about morality as having been wiped so thoroughly clean that the only option is for Socrates to write the answers on it. Clitophon treats refutation as the prelude to indoctrination—and is disappointed that the indoctrination never comes.

A glance through Plato's dialogues confirms Clitophon's observation that there is no separate second stage. In the *Laches*, after Socrates has refuted Laches' initial definition of courage as endurance, he doesn't begin stage two—instead he moves on to refute Nicias' definition of courage. The same thing happens in the *Gorgias*. Socrates spends the whole time refuting—first Gorgias, then Polus, then Callicles. When he is done refuting one interlocutor, he doesn't transition to a more positive activity; instead, he moves on to refuting the next person. The *Meno* might be the best candidate for a two-stage interpretation. Yet even after Meno wants to give up, claiming to have been struck numb by Socrates, Socrates offers him a hypothesis such that Meno can continue to give answers and Socrates can continue to refute them. Socrates doesn't seem to ever complete the refutation stage; we don't see him "moving on," in the way that the two-stage interpretation would predict.[16]

In the *Euthydemus* Socrates encounters two men, Euthydemus and Dionysiodorus, who boast of having great wisdom to sell, and who offer to demonstrate it. Socrates preempts their demonstration with a question: he wants to know whether, in addition to being able to fill willing customers with their wisdom, they are able to convert the unwilling to wanting to buy it. Socrates wants to know whether they are capable of *motivating* someone toward the pursuit of the thing that they claim to offer, or whether they have delegated that work to another party.[17] They answer that they are also able to convert, and Socrates exhorts them to demonstrate *only* that power and hold off on demonstrating how they fill others with their wisdom.[18] If Clitophon had been present, he would have thrown up his hands at Socrates' refusal to receive "the goods" from Euthydemus and Dionysiodorus: "Look at Socrates, avoiding stage two again!" Is Socrates somehow obsessed with the demolition of the conceit of wisdom, to the exclusion of the acquisition of it?

Clitophon is not the only one who gets annoyed by Socrates' failure to move on to stage two. When Critias asks him to do so, Socrates says the problem is that he does not know the answers:

> You are talking to me as though I professed to know the answers to my own questions and as though I could agree with you if I really wished. This is not the case—rather, because of my own ignorance, I am continually investigating in your company whatever is put forward.[19]

This speech leads Critias to expect that Socrates will now transition from recalcitrant refuter into docile recipient of Critias' wisdom—but in fact what Socrates does next is what Socrates always does, namely, to go on to refute the answer Critias offers. After enduring a few back-and-forth exchanges of such refutations, Critias explodes at Socrates in Clitophonic irritation:

> I think you are quite consciously doing what you denied
> doing a moment ago—you are trying to refute me and
> ignoring the real question at issue.[20]

Critias here contrasts what he takes Socrates to have been claiming to be doing—"investigating in your company"—with what he
now thinks Socrates was really doing: "trying to refute me." Critias
feels Socrates doesn't want answers, he doesn't want to move on to
stage two, he doesn't care about making positive progress on "the
real question." All he ever wants to do is destructively refute people.
Critias is vexed that Socrates claims to be a helpful midwife, when
he's really nothing but an irritating gadfly.

Socrates' response to Critias' outburst is, as far as the Gadfly-
Midwife paradox is concerned, the most important passage in the
entire Platonic corpus:

> Oh come, how could you possibly think that even if I were
> to refute everything you say, I would be doing it for any
> other reasons than the one I would give for a thorough
> investigation of my own statements—the fear of uncon-
> sciously thinking I know something when I do not. And
> this is what I claim to be doing now, examining the argu-
> ment for my own sake primarily, but perhaps also for the
> sake of my friends. Or don't you believe it to be for the
> common good, or for that of most people, that the state
> of each existing thing should become clear?[21]

The thing to notice about this passage is how seamlessly Socrates
transitions from depicting negative refutation to depicting the fruits
of positive inquiry. Socrates begins by saying he refutes people for
the same reason that he welcomes refutation, namely, to reveal blind
spots and expose false claims to knowledge. Socrates is acknowledging that he actively seeks to prove people wrong. That's the gadfly
talking. But in the last sentence, seemingly just by way of rephrasing

what he has said before, he describes his goal as being "that the state of each existing thing should become clear"—that's where Socrates the midwife rears her head. Notice what he doesn't do in this passage: he doesn't assert that proving people wrong serves as a ground-clearing preliminary stage in an inquisitive process. Recall his earlier claim that "I am continually investigating in your company whatever is put forward." Socrates' view seems to be that his investigations are, at one and the same time, blind spot–exposing and existence-clarifying. Critias and Clitophon may have a two-stage interpretation of the Socratic process, but Socrates himself doesn't.

Clitophon reports, grumpily, that as a result of Socrates' refusal to give him answers, he's been forced to turn himself over to people who will: public intellectuals such as the sophist Thrasymachus and the orator Lysias. He says, "And this is why, I suppose, I go to Thrasymachus and to anyone else I can: I'm at a loss." These people confidently offer up, usually in exchange for money, a set of doctrines about how to be a winner at life—or in some specific and important domain of life, such as public speaking. When Socrates turns away from the positive part of Euthydemus and Dionysiodorus' offerings, he is turning away from such "answers." Socrates seems to think, contra Clitophon, that if the negative, motivating part of the process is done properly, that itself will amount to positive progress toward knowledge—not by filling someone with (possibly erroneous) doctrines but rather through a shared inquiry into the truth.

I think the most natural conclusion to draw about Socrates' own solution to the Gadfly-Midwife paradox is that Socrates *equates* the negative process of refutation and the positive process of discovery. Socrates the gadfly *is* Socrates the midwife. Socrates engages in productive inquiry by doing nothing other than refuting people. Which is to say, when he destructively, negatively, refutes people, that constitutes a positive, productive search for the truth. Socratic conversation is inquisitive refutation. Before I explain how this works, I want to explain why we should have thought, before encountering such a thing, that it couldn't possibly exist.

III. James versus Clifford

Two thousand years after the death of Socrates, William James dropped a bombshell:

> We must know the truth; and we must avoid error—these are our first and great commandments as would-be knowers; but they are not two ways of stating an identical commandment, they are two separable laws.[22]

It should come as a shock to hear someone assert that the pursuit of truth and the avoidance of error don't go hand in hand. You might protest: if someone believes the truth, then it follows that she avoids error. James has to admit that you are right: if S believes p, and p is true, then S has also succeeded in avoiding error with respect to p. Every truth held constitutes an error avoided. So what's the problem?

The problem is this: when you talk about truths held and errors avoided, you are looking at an end result, which obscures the tensions intrinsic to the process of arriving at that result. Let's wind the clock back on our friend S, back to before she believed p, back when there was some doubt in her mind as to *whether* p. The road split before her. She opted for the path of believing p, and was thereby correct—she succeeded at the task of having truth—but only by risking a failure at the task of avoiding falsehood. Every time you stand at the crossroads of doubt, there is a path open to you that guarantees success at the task of avoiding error. That is the path of suspended judgment: don't form a belief as to whether p. Whereas in order to end up with truth you must court falsehood.

The reason why pursuing the truth requires courting falsehood is that in order to have a true belief about some subject matter you must, in the first instance, have some belief or other about that subject matter. If you don't believe anything you have definitively failed at the task of believing what's true—but you have just as definitively succeeded at the task of avoiding error. The two tasks may line up in retrospect; they do not line up in prospect. If you are giving someone instructions, and you instruct them that they must acquire a true belief, that is not at all the same instruction as the instruction to avoid error at all costs. As James writes:

> Believe truth! Shun error!—these, we see, are two materi-
> ally different laws; and by choosing between them we may
> end by coloring differently our whole intellectual life. We
> may regard the chase for truth as paramount, and the
> avoidance of error as secondary; or we may, on the other
> hand, treat the avoidance of error as more imperative, and
> let truth take its chance.[23]

James articulates this dilemma as a response to his contemporary, the philosopher and mathematician William Clifford (1845–1879), whose essay "The Ethics of Belief," comes down firmly on the side of error avoidance.[24] Clifford writes that "Belief is desecrated when given to unproved and unquestioned statements."[25] He enjoins every person to "guard the purity of his belief with a very fanaticism of jealous care, lest at any time it should rest on an unworthy object, and catch a stain which can never be wiped away."[26] Clifford describes those who believe on the basis of insufficient evidence, *even if the belief is true*, as "sinful."[27]

Clifford's advice is that whenever you stand at the crossroads of doubt, you should prioritize the avoidance of falsehood by suspending belief. James disagrees:

> Believe nothing, [Clifford] tells us, keep your mind in
> suspense forever, rather than by closing it on insufficient
> evidence incur the awful risk of believing lies.[28] . . . Clif-
> ford's exhortation has to my ears a thoroughly fantastic
> sound. It is like a general informing his soldiers that it is
> better to keep out of battle forever than to risk a single

wound. Not so are victories either over enemies or over nature gained.[29]

There is a foolproof strategy to avoid believing anything false: Believe nothing! Given that you can only believe one of two contradictory claims, there is no similarly foolproof strategy to believe everything true. Still, you'll raise your odds if you always hold some belief or other, about every matter. So, if you have the goal of avoiding falsehood, you should always suspend judgment (be skeptical), and if you have the goal of securing truths, you should never suspend judgment (be credulous).

Why not think that James and Clifford are both right, and that one needs to *combine* the activities of scouting for truth and testing for falsity? James' point is, you can't. The goal of avoiding falsehood and the goal of securing truths are in tension with one another. There isn't an obvious or easy way of doing both at the same time. Trying to be credulous and skeptical at the same time is like trying to go forward and backward at the same time, or trying to build what you are concurrently tearing down. Clifford agrees with James about this tension, though he thinks the skeptical motive should dominate:

> No man holding a strong belief on one side of a question, or even wishing to hold a belief on one side, can investigate it with such fairness and completeness as if he were really in doubt and unbiased; so that the existence of a belief not founded on fair inquiry unfits a man for the performance of this necessary duty.[30]

Clifford thinks that unless one's agency and attention are directed skeptically from the outset, one will not be in a position to identify error later on. One cannot count on "running into error"; instead, one should focus one's effort and attentions on spotting it, so that whatever truth arrives does so only by having overcome one's resistance to it.

Clifford's solution is that you should always prioritize error avoidance. James does not adopt the opposite extreme position—he acknowledges that you should *sometimes* prioritize error avoidance, for instance in abstract intellectual inquiry. James merely wants to demonstrate that there are more practical cases—such as that of friendship, self-confidence, and religion—where we should prioritize truth acquisition:

> Do you like me or not?—for example. Whether you do or not depends, in countless instances, on whether I meet you half-way, am willing to assume that you must like me, and show you trust and expectation. The previous faith on my part in your liking's existence is in such cases what makes your liking come. But if I stand aloof, and refuse to budge an inch until I have objective evidence, until you shall have done something apt, as the absolutists say, *ad extorquendum assensum meum*, ten to one your liking never comes. . . . There are, then, cases where a fact cannot come at all unless a preliminary faith exists in its coming.[31]

James wants to invoke this "preliminary faith," which he also calls a "will to believe," only in areas of inquiry where the question is momentous, and where there is a need to act:

> Wherever the option between losing truth and gaining it is not momentous, we can throw the chance of gaining truth away, and at any rate save ourselves from any chance of believing falsehood, by not making up our minds at all till objective evidence has come. In scientific questions, this is almost always the case; and even in human affairs in general, the need of acting is seldom so urgent that a false belief to act on is better than no belief at all.[32]

I find this attempt at a territorial compromise with Clifford to be unpersuasive. Scientists invest large amounts of money, effort, and time into testing a given hypothesis; a mathematician might spend months or years of her life struggling to prove a conjecture; a high school student, writing a paper on *King Lear*, reads through the text searching for evidence of the thesis statement she settled on in advance. The claims into which they pour these efforts are not chosen lightly. The considerations James raises about friendship—that one would give up quickly without faith that this was headed somewhere—apply very well to the pursuit of abstract inquiry. Even in theoretical pursuits, we are forced to invest in the truth of an idea in advance of decisive evidence.

If not science, is there any area of human life where the Jamesian demand for a will to believe can be safely set aside? Yes: the domains where it is least likely to be true that "a fact cannot come at all unless a preliminary faith exists in its coming" will be those that are far from where we invest our efforts. Sometimes we say, about a question, "I am just curious." This is a sign that one feels one can allow oneself to be a pure Cliffordian, suspending judgment until enough information happens to roll in to "extract assent." Personally, I feel this way about much gossip; about the existence of extraterrestrial life; about the solution of famous mysteries (the Voynich manuscript, the Tamám Shud case); and so on. As a nonscientist, I also feel this way about a lot of science. I am inclined to approach assertions that fall into this region with an attitude of skeptical detachment—I might be willing to form a firm judgment eventually, but I will have to be driven there. If a question strikes you as one that leaves you fully free to indulge in the luxury of indefinitely holding out for objective evidence, you can call it a "Cliffordian question."

Do Cliffordian questions have any kind of Jamesian counterparts? I think so. When faced with the question, "What are you doing?" it's hard to avoid a Jamesian response. Consider what I'm doing, right now. I'm engaged in a bunch of bodily movements—tapping with my fingers on the keyboard, looking at a screen, breathing— but those movements are not the whole story of what is happening with me right now. I also possess a bunch of intentions. In general, over the course of this chapter I intend to be talking to you about the Gadfly-Midwife paradox—not just talking *at* you but talking *to* you, communicating the reasons to think there is such a paradox, as well as suggestions about how, and how not, to approach it. That's a general intention I have throughout the chapter. At this specific moment, as I write this sentence, I intend to be engaging your interest and holding your attention by using a vividly reflexive example about how I'm intending to do just that.

That is what I *intend* to be doing: to communicate with you, to engage you. And if you asked me "What *are* you doing?" I would give those same answers. I'm communicating, I'm engaging. There is a remarkable coincidence between my answers to the question "What do you intend to be doing?" and my answers to the question "What are you doing?" The philosopher Elizabeth Anscombe noticed this coincidence. She pointed out that although a person usually finds out what other people are doing by observation—which is to say, by going out and looking at the evidence—a person doesn't find out what he himself is doing in that same way.[33] When I say "I'm talking," I do so without *checking* whether my lips are moving, even if I'm looking in a mirror. The way I know I'm talking is that that's what I intend to be doing. I parlay my awareness of what I intend to be doing into an assertion about what I am doing. It is not surprising that I would have direct non-observational cognizance of an intention, since it is a mental state, but it is surprising that I could claim to have direct non-observational knowledge of a worldly happening, which is what an action is.

Do I actually have such knowledge? As philosophers writing in response to Anscombe noticed, the move from what I intend to be doing to what I am doing is fraught with epistemic danger. Suppose I am copying out a passage from William James' *Writings: 1878–1899* into this chapter, or rather, that's what I think I'm doing, and what I would answer to anyone who asked me what I was doing, but when I look up from the book, at the screen, I don't see any of James' words. My fingers were mispositioned on the keyboard and what I've typed is gibberish.[34] I *intended* to be copying out the passage, but that isn't what I was actually doing. Given that "knowledge" is a success term—you don't count as knowing that p if p turns out to be false—we shouldn't follow Anscombe in describing agents as having non-observational *knowledge* of what they are doing. Agents can be wrong about what they are doing, so they don't count as *knowing* what they are doing. Still, a person clearly stands in *some especially non-skeptical relation to those events in the world that are her own actions.*

One way to capture this point is to say: the readiness to move from awareness of what I intend to be doing to a conclusion about what I am actually doing displays a characteristically Jamesian optimism. An expression of intention that takes the form of a description of an action—"I am currently explaining the Gadfly-Midwife paradox to you"—is a great example of "a fact that cannot exist at all unless a preliminary faith exists in its coming." The existence of "Anscombean practical knowledge" is hard to defend in the face of counterexamples such as the case where I intend to be typing a word, but don't know whether I am doing so. But even if we don't have *knowledge* of what we are doing, it seems true to say some of our *beliefs* about what we are doing are distinctive: they seem to have been freed from the usual demand to check whether what we believe is actually the case. We could call these "Jamesian beliefs."

If we contrast the detached, curious indifference with which we face Cliffordian questions with the unavoidable investment we have in Jamesian beliefs—think about how unsettling it can be to learn that you're not doing what you intended—we can see that it makes a big difference whether we prioritize the absence of error or the presence of truth. But most questions are *not* Cliffordian questions, and most beliefs are *not* Jamesian beliefs, and that means that most of the time, neither of the two demands can be comfortably set aside. How do we combine the uncombinable? How do we follow two rules when we can't follow both at the same time? How do we achieve knowledge? We might try a two-stage approach. For example, we could start by wiping the slate clean using Cliffordian doubt so as to provide a basis for our eventual construction of a Jamesian edifice. Alternatively, the first stage might involve helping ourselves to some Jamesian intuitions, and we follow up with Cliffordian winnowing: deleting as many intuitions as we cannot render consistent with one another.

The first approach should bring to mind Descartes, who wrote:

> Some years ago I was struck by the large number of falsehoods that I had accepted as true in my childhood, and by the highly doubtful nature of the whole edifice that I had subsequently based on them. I realized that it was necessary, once in the course of my life, to demolish everything completely and start again right from the foundations if I wanted to establish anything at all in the sciences that was stable and likely to last.[35]

The second one sounds more like Aristotle:

> We must, as in all other cases, set the phenomena before us and, after first discussing the difficulties, go on to prove, if possible, the truth of all the reputable opinions about these affections or, failing this, of the greater number and the most authoritative; for if we both resolve the difficulties and leave the reputable opinions undisturbed, we shall have proved the case sufficiently.[36]

The problem with the Cartesian approach is that it's easy to get carried away with step one. Most readers of Descartes' *Meditations* find his argument for skepticism—the doubts raised by the whispers of the evil demon—much more compelling than his eventual antiskeptical resolution of those doubts. Although Descartes gives two arguments for the existence of God in the *Meditations*, neither is his claim to fame. Which is to say, when you start with Clifford you're apt to get stuck with Clifford.

The problem with the Aristotelian approach is that someone could succeed in reconciling the phenomena to one another but still, due to being insufficiently skeptical about the "reputable opinions," fall pretty far short of the truth—to the extent of, for example, producing arguments in defense of slavery and infanticide. Which is to say, Jamesian faith in intuitions tends to land you in Jamesian dogmatism. (There is, of course, a direct link between these two approaches: Descartes' method of doubt is inspired by a desire to liberate science from the elaborate edifice of Aristotelian scholasticism.)

IV. Inquisitive Refutation

Socrates didn't think we have to work in stages, nor was he forced to prioritize either the pursuit of truth or the avoidance of error. Instead, he conceived of learning as a social activity where one person prioritizes the pursuit of truth and the other person prioritizes the avoidance of error. The Jamesian rule and the Cliffordian rule don't conflict if they are given to two different people. This insight is at the very heart of the Socratic method, of Socratism, and of Socratic ethics.

Socrates claims, in the *Theaetetus*, that the distinctive form of social interaction that he pioneered allowed its participants to make astounding intellectual progress. The people who enter into conversations with him do not do so already laden with wisdom: "At first some of them may give the impression of being ignorant and stupid," and yet they exit those conversations having made "a progress which is amazing both to other people and to themselves." And this is not because Socrates transfers his own wisdom to them: even though they discover those things *with* Socrates, they do so not because Socrates taught them anything: "it is clear that this is not due to anything they have learned from me." Rather, the progress is a result of the interaction between the asserter's putting forward claims and the refuter's refuting them.

A careful look at Socrates' description of his midwifery shows that it seems to consist of . . . being a gadfly:

> And the most important thing about my art is the ability to apply all possible tests to the offspring, to determine whether the young mind is being delivered of a phantom, that is, an error, or a fertile truth.[37]

It is the job of Socrates' interlocutor to give answers to questions, whereas Socrates' job is that of refutation, which is to say, applying tests to those answers. Socrates is amazed that sometimes people get "into such a state with me as to be literally ready to bite when I take away some nonsense or other from them." Such people fail to understand the role that Socrates' refutations are playing in a larger process. Recall Critias accusing Socrates of "just trying to refute":

> And I think you are quite consciously doing what you denied doing a moment ago—you are trying to refute me and ignoring the real question at issue.

And recall Socrates' response:

> "Oh come," I said, "how could you possibly think that even if I were to refute everything you say, I would be doing it for any other reasons than the one I would give for a thorough investigation of my own statements—the fear of unconsciously thinking I know something when I do not. And this is what I claim to be doing now, examining the argument for my own sake primarily, but perhaps also for the sake of my friends. Or don't you believe it to

be for the common good, or for that of most people, that
the state of each existing thing should become clear?"[38]

When Socrates is describing only his part of the knowledge project, he describes the benefit in Cliffordian terms: warding off false
claims to knowledge. That's the bit he contributes: Socrates is the
master of the Socratic role; he's a genius at parrying claims to knowledge. But when his destructive testing is combined with his interlocutor's insistence on knowing—which is to say, when he and Critias
are working together—they stand to gain more than just knowledge
of ignorance. They stand to gain knowledge of "the state of each
existing thing." The Socratic solution to the problem articulated by
James is to treat inquiry as a human interaction: inquisitive refutation is possible because there are two people doing it. That it is
possible for two people to work together in the pursuit of knowledge
comes, to those unaccustomed to it, as a big surprise.

V. A Division of Labor

Socratic inquiry appears, at first, to be an instance of the adversarial
division of labor. An adversarial division of labor is one that calls
for competition between agents performing the tasks into which the
labor has been divided; it stands in contrast to a cooperative division
of labor, in which the various sub-tasks complement each other.

So, for example, a cooperative division exists between various
stages in an assembly line, or in a household where one person does
the cooking and the other does the cleanup. If I do a good job cooking,
that does not make it more difficult for you to succeed as a cleaner. By
contrast, if our jobs stand in an adversarial arrangement—if you are
the prosecutor and I am the defense attorney; or if you are the product tester and I am the product maker; or if you the speaker arguing
for one policy in a debate and I am the speaker arguing for another;
if you are one presidential candidate and I am the other—then your
success poses a threat to mine. Our interests conflict.

In a simple kind of criminal trial, the prosecutor aims for a conviction, and the defense attorney aims for an acquittal. By placing these two parties in a zero-sum game—a contest they cannot both win—we hope that the criminal justice system as a whole can achieve the goal of justice, which requires both defending the innocent and convicting the guilty. The same conflict of interest exists between the product tester, insofar as he is instructed to break the product, and the product maker, insofar as she is instructed to make it unbreakable. Two candidates for the same office are said to be running *against* each other, and debaters are likewise arguing *against* each other. In all of these cases, the zero-sum competition between the adversaries results (in theory) in a systemic benefit to some broader group. This happens due to the mediation of a third party who adjudicates the contest: the jury decides on conviction or acquittal, the manager chooses whether or not to move ahead with the product, the voters select their representative, the audience of the debate determines who convinced them.

Socratic inquiry, in which one person tries to maintain the correctness of a given answer to a question, and the other tries to show them that it has not yet been answered, or has been answered incorrectly, might appear to share these features of adversarial division of labor: being zero-sum, being competitive, and involving the adjudication of a third-party moderator or audience. (Recall that many of the dialogues were conducted in front of some kind of audience.) In fact, however, as Socrates repeatedly emphasizes, it shares none of them.

When Socrates and Protagoras reach a stalemate as to the length of speeches that should be permitted in their conversation, the suggestion that they choose a moderator is met with approval by everyone—except Socrates.[39] Socrates insists that the kind of activity he's engaged in does not require a moderator. If Protagoras wishes to question Socrates instead of answer questions, Socrates is amenable, but those are the only two options: ask questions or answer them. There is no third role. To Crito, Socrates' formula is persuade or be persuaded. There are no moderators, because there is no conflict of interest. Recall what Socrates said to Protagoras:

> "Protagoras," I said, "I don't want you to think that my motive in talking with you is anything else than to take a good hard look at things that continually perplex me. I think that Homer said it all in the line, Going in tandem, one perceives before the other. Human beings are simply more resourceful this way in action, speech, and thought. . . . How could I not solicit your help in a joint investigation of these questions?"[40]

Socrates is regularly in a situation where he has to try to disabuse his interlocutor of the notion that what is going on between them is taking place in an adversarial or competitive context. He tells Gorgias, "I'm afraid to pursue my examination of you, for fear that you should take me to be speaking with eagerness to win against you, rather than to have our subject become clear."[41] But if refutation is, in truth, a cooperative, collaborative process, why does it *appear* so adversarial to those whom Socrates refutes? The answer is that they are convinced that they can do, by themselves, what Socrates is trying to help them do. Socrates comes across as someone who offers to cooperatively divide the task of shopping—and then follows you around the supermarket taking things out of your cart and putting them back on the shelf. If he seems to be interfering with *your part* of the work, that's only because you've inflated the size of your part.

There is a tension between the Jamesian demand to know the truth and the Cliffordian demand to avoid the false *when one person is responsible for satisfying both demands*, but if they are distributed over two people, the tasks turn out to be complementary. Spreading out the work of thinking over two people is a way of allowing both demands to constrain the process of thinking. And yet the tension between the two demands seems to persist, for Socrates' interlocutors, in spite of his presence. They do not jump at the opportunity he offers them, to divide the labor of thought. People find it hard to accept that thinking is a social activity. We persist in seeing it as a private, inner activity. When someone is trying to think with you, you experience that as competitive—as though they were vying, with you, to be "the thinker." You see the activity of thinking as indivisible, because, at bottom, you're sure that you can do it on your own. You find it incredible and unacceptable that thinking is something you need help to do. Each of us envisions ourselves as a kind of house, and inside that house is a special being—we call it "a mind," and it has the power to figure out answers to questions. We conceive of thinking as a "mental activity," which is to say, an activity of this "mind."

Which is not to say that we demand the mind always be on duty. We are happy—often, more than happy—to take time off. Clitophon, for example, invites Socrates to go ahead and do the thinking for the both of them. He is ready to sit back and let Socrates dictate the answers to questions, and he is frustrated by Socrates' apparent uncooperativeness. He cannot see that he is telling Socrates, "Do something you need my help to do, but without my help!" When Gorgias and Protagoras are irritated by being refuted, the conceit of each man is that he can think on his own; likewise, Clitophon's irritation is driven by the conceit that Socrates can think on his own. Recall Critias' complaint:

> I think you are quite consciously doing what you denied doing a moment ago—you are trying to refute me and ignoring the real question at issue.[42]

Critias can be read as demanding: either go ahead and do the thinking, or step back and let me do it! It is difficult for Socrates' interlocutors to understand the novel way in which he is proposing to cooperate with them, and their misunderstanding distorts their conversations into competitions.

The misunderstanding endures, to this day, even among philosophers: we are inclined to retreat from conversation to a shelter we call thinking. When someone has a good rebuttal, we sometimes say, "I'll have to think more about this," as though the real test comes when I import the claim into my inner sanctum, the place where Thinking happens. We breathe a sigh of relief when some dispute comes to an end and we can, as we say, sit back and think. Arguing is stressful—thinking, we tell ourselves, is enjoyable. Socrates would say: that's because you're not actually thinking.

The demand to choose between the pursuit of the truth and the avoidance of error comes as an insult to a person who was taking for granted that they had been doing both. Socrates tells us that our minds are not as powerful as we thought they were. When we shelter from the demands and pressures of the outside world and quietly engage in an activity we call "thinking to ourselves," that is not in fact when thinking happens. Thinking happens during the uncomfortable times when you permit others to intrude into your private mental world, to correct you.

Socrates' real claim to fame is not any kind of secret special knowledge—he was not holding out on Clitophon. Nor does the distinctness of Socrates lie, as many of his followers believed, in an impossibly high standard for knowledge. Socrates was neither possessed of knowledge he refused to share nor did he believe that real knowledge was unattainable. Socrates thought knowledge was there for the taking, and spent his life trying to take it. He was neither a sadist who took pleasure in exposing the weaknesses of others nor a freelance therapist out to rehabilitate the broken citizens of Athens. He was always clear that what drives him, Socrates, to ask people questions is quite simply the desire to know the answers to those questions. Socrates was not an extremist about knowledge and he was not an extremist about altruism. All he was doing was trying to inquire, open-mindedly, into untimely questions—but he understood this as a social process. It is easier to believe in the existence of two Socrateses than to believe that there was ever one person who denied that thinking is a private mental activity.

Our project, then, is to dismantle the illusion of the two Socrateses, which is to say, to inquire into what it means for a social situation to offer up discoveries that are unavailable to the individual. This is easier said than done. It is one thing to say that Socrates inquires by refuting, and a very different thing to actually reconcile refutation with inquiry. The difficulty lies in the fact that in both cases, we are inclined toward misunderstanding, and these misunderstandings are precisely why our double vision persists.

In the next two chapters we will confront the paradoxes that hide just under the surface of the ways in which we usually think, first, about the practice of showing someone to be wrong, and next, about the practice of asking questions in order to find something out. It is only after untangling those two knots that we will be ready, in the final part of the book, to apply the Socratic method to untimely questions in three areas: love, death, and politics.

Chapter 6

Moore's Paradox of Self-Knowledge

D O YOU KNOW WHAT IT'S LIKE TO BE WRONG? I'M NOT asking whether you know what it's like to *have been* wrong. If you find yourself recollecting something you were wrong about in the past, what you are effectively doing is thinking about how right you are now: At least you're not making that mistake anymore! It would be a very different matter to recognize that you are, currently, thinking about something incorrectly.

Error does not tend to survive introspective awareness of itself: when you catch your mind in going astray, at that very moment your mind cleans up its act. As soon as you realize it's a mistake to think something, you become unable to make the mistake of thinking that. You can still think *about* it, as, for example, something you used to think, or something someone else might think. You can look *at* the erroneous thought, but you can no longer look at the world *through* it. Our errors are blind spots, which is why real open-mindedness is so difficult.

We often speak as though a person could simply *choose* to be more open-minded than they are, as though each person had, somewhere deep within themselves, a "consider the possibility that you are wrong" lever. We criticize stubbornness and obstinacy in a person as if these conditions were born of unwillingness to simply push the lever.

And it is true that in many contexts I can, in fact, decide to be self-critical: I may believe that I have vetted this paragraph for typos, or that I have added up a series of numbers correctly, but I can always double-check. When I am about to propose a plan to a group of people I might try to anticipate their objections, so as to come prepared with responses. I can consider the possibility that I am wrong, and thus it appears that the lever exists. The problem is that the set of occasions when people most need to pull it—when they are wrong about something fundamentally important, something that approaches the heart of how they live their lives—are also the occasions when the lever seems stuck. And it is precisely on those occasions that we blame people for obstinacy.

When I construct objections to my own plan or check my arithmetic, I suspend my commitment to seeing my plan as the right one, or to arriving at a particular sum. In these cases, I'm able to step back from my conclusion, in order to examine it. But there are other conclusions where this method won't work, because I can't step back from them. Considering the possibility that I am wrong about those conclusions would seem to require me to call into question the very belief that I cannot let go of—which is to say, to open myself up to seeing that I'm wrong, *while I remain wrong*. But is that even possible?

Socrates showed that the answer was yes. Even when open-mindedness is most difficult, it is still possible. How? Not by simply trying harder. Socrates does not believe in such things as "force of will," and for the same reason he does not think that what obstinate people are missing is any kind of willingness. Socrates grants that there are circumstances when the lever really will not move under your own efforts. What he discovered was how another person could help you push it.

I. Do You Want to Rule the World?

There was once a young man who wanted to rule the world, but never dared give voice to that wish. He couldn't admit to the people around him that he hungered to rule over them; he couldn't even admit it to himself. All of that changed on the day he met Socrates, and Socrates said to him:

Suppose one of the gods asked you, "Alcibiades, would you rather live with what you now have, or would you rather die on the spot if you weren't permitted to acquire anything greater?" I think you'd choose to die. What then *is* your real ambition in life? I'll tell you. You think that as soon as you present yourself before the Athenian people—as indeed you expect to in a very few days—by presenting yourself you'll show them that you deserve to be honored more than Pericles or anyone else who ever was. Having shown that, you'll be the most influential man in the city, and if you're the greatest here, you'll be the greatest in the rest of Greece, and not only in Greece, but also among the foreigners who live on the same continent as we do.

And if that same god were then to tell you that you should have absolute power in Europe, but that you weren't permitted to cross over into Asia or get mixed up with affairs over there, I think you'd rather not live with only that to look forward to; you want your reputation and your influence to saturate all mankind, so to speak. I don't think you regard anybody as ever having been much to speak of, except perhaps Cyrus and Xerxes. I'm not guessing that this is your ambition—I'm sure of it.[1]

Alcibiades wants to rule, and he wants to rule over *everyone*. If he were consigned to rule only over the Athenians, or only over the Greeks, that achievement would be so puny as to merit suicide. Alcibiades does not think life is worth living unless he is the greatest and most influential man in the entire world. Socrates expects to shock Alcibiades with this description of his own lust for power, and he does. A desire to rule the world was no more socially acceptable in Socrates' time than it is in ours, but Socrates is not interested in criticizing Alcibiades. Rather, Socrates wants Alcibiades to confront who he really is and what he really wants, without a care for seeming sane and palatable and normal. Socrates wants Alcibiades to take himself seriously, so that he can examine himself with an open mind.

By the end of the dialogue, things have gotten serious indeed. Alcibiades has come to accept a new truth about himself—not that it is wrong to want to rule the world, but that he in particular is unfit to do so. And Socrates pushes him a step further, convincing Alcibiades that "before one acquires virtue it's better to be ruled by somebody superior than to rule," and that "it's appropriate for a bad man to be a slave."[2] When these principles are taken together with what the two of them have learned, over the course of the dialogue, about Alcibiades—how ignorant he is when it comes to justice—the implication is so shocking that Socrates doesn't quite want to spell it out for Alcibiades:

> SOCRATES: Can you see what condition you're now in?
> Is it appropriate for a free man or not?
> ALCIBIADES: I think I see only too clearly.[3]

Without saying it directly, Socrates has landed on the most offensive and outrageous insult you could make to an aristocratic Greek: "You deserve to be a slave." But Alcibiades, who wants to rule the world, accepts that this insult is true. There is a sharp divergence between the reality of Alcibiades' condition and the self-image with which he identifies—and in the dialogue we see this divergence gradually become available *to Alcibiades himself.* The contrast is all the more salient if we consider it against the sweep of Alcibiades' life.

Alcibiades' ambitions were, if oversized, not entirely irrational: he was stunningly handsome, well educated, and descended on both sides from powerful noble families. He was a persuasive and charismatic speaker, and "an ancient equivalent of a record-breaking sports superstar" owing to his Olympic victories in chariot races.[4] The encounter with Socrates that is related in the *Alcibiades* occurs on the eve of Alcibiades' entry into public life, at the age of about eighteen. This is a moment when all believed him to be destined for political and military greatness—especially Alcibiades himself, who, in the historian Thucydides' (460–400 BCE) account, seeks election as a general by announcing "Athenians, I more than others am entitled to command . . . and I consider myself deserving as well."[5]

Once he has the ear of the Athenians, Alcibiades pushes them to embark on an ambitious military conquest of Sicily. It ends disastrously. During the expedition, Alcibiades was recalled by Athens to stand trial on charges of impiety—he was thought to be involved in a religious scandal—and he chose, instead, to flee, to defect to the side of the enemy (Sparta), and to advise them on how to defeat the Athenians. Later, Alcibiades would fall out of favor with the Spartans and shift his allegiance to the Persians, playing the Athenians and the Spartans against each other.

The Athenians' love-hate affair with Alcibiades did not end with his initial act of betrayal: four years after the Sicilian Expedition they recalled him to command a naval fleet, the successes of which eventually led them to reverse his condemnation for impiety—only to go on to dismiss him again shortly thereafter, due to a military defeat. After this, Alcibiades retired, though there were subsequent calls for his return; his final attempt to offer advice to the Athenians met with rejection, and then the next year he was assassinated, probably by Spartans, at the age of forty-six. We have no contemporaneous accounts of Alcibiades' death, and although the details in Plutarch's account—written six hundred years later—are almost certainly inaccurate, they convey his iconic status:

> The party sent to kill him did not dare to enter his house, but surrounded it and set it on fire. When Alcibiades was aware of this, he gathered together most of the garments and bedding in the house and cast them on the fire. Then, wrapping his cloak about his left arm, and drawing his sword with his right, he dashed out, unscathed by the fire, before the garments were in flames, and scattered the Barbarians, who ran at the mere sight of him. Not a man

stood ground against him, or came to close quarters with him, but all held aloof and shot him with javelins and arrows. Thus he fell.[6]

The nineteenth-century historian and lexicographer William Smith summed up his death and life in these terms:

> Thus perished miserably, in the vigour of his age, one of the most remarkable, but not one of the greatest, characters in Grecian history. With qualities which, properly applied, might have rendered him the greatest benefactor of Athens, he contrived to attain the inhumane distinction of being that citizen who had inflicted upon her the most signal amount of damage.[7]

Alcibiades was not, in fact, well suited to rule the Athenians, the Spartans, or the Persians, let alone all of them taken together. We can see this, and no doubt there were some people during Alcibiades' lifetime who could see it—but how was Socrates able to get Alcibiades *himself* to see it? The dialogue presents a stunning reversal, in which a man who thinks he should rule the world, a man given to statements such as "I, more than others, am entitled to command," instead erupts, repeatedly, in moments of pained self-awareness:

> Well, Socrates, I swear by the gods that I don't even know what I mean. I think I must have been in an appalling state for a long time, without being aware of it.[8]

Plato's *Alcibiades* tells the story of Alcibiades becoming aware that he is making a mistake, even as he continues to make it—moreover, the reader knows he will continue to make it, all the way up to his death.

II. MOORE'S PARADOX

Honey never spoils. This is true, though many people are unaware of it. Consider the sentence, "Jones believes that honey spoils, though in fact he's wrong about that: it doesn't spoil." This sentence might be true, and I might know that it's true, and you might know that it's true, and everyone in Jones' family might know that it's true, but there is one person who will struggle mightily with such a sentence, and that person is Jones. Imagine Jones trying to agree with us: "Yes, all of you people are right: I believe that honey spoils, though in fact it doesn't spoil." We would feel unsure how to interpret his words. We might doubt his sincerity. Sincere assertions license belief ascription: if Jones tells you that honey never spoils, and he is being sincere, then you can attribute to him the belief that honey never spoils. So, what can he mean by going on to express the belief that it does? And yet notice that the state of affairs he is struggling to tell you about— where the world is one way, but his mind represents it as being a different way—is one that can certainly occur. Moreover Jones, unless he has delusions of epistemic grandeur, knows that it can occur.

Sentences that fit the pattern, "p is the case, but I believe it isn't"—or its subtly different variant "p is the case, but I don't believe it is"—are sometimes called "Moore sentences" after the philosopher G. E. Moore (1873–1958), who first singled them out for philosophical attention. It is important to notice that such sentences are not logical contradictions, as is evident from the fact that they can be true. Moreover, the person herself can believe, assert, and know variants of these sentences, for instance ones expressed in the past or future tense. Jones can readily assert "I used to believe that honey spoils, though it doesn't" and he can also, if he knows he is a forgetful person, tell us that "Honey never spoils, but I, Jones, won't believe that in the future." Jones can also be generically aware of his own fallibility: "I am sometimes wrong about food safety." What he can't do is believe that *this* is one of those times. The Moore sentence is not a contradiction; it is a blind spot. A person can be aware that others' minds diverge from reality, and she can be aware that her own mind can, or did, or will diverge from reality; what she cannot be aware of is the specific way in which it is currently doing so. So goes the philosophical conventional wisdom since Moore.

That conventional wisdom says it's just straightforwardly impossible to believe or sincerely assert a Moore sentence. No one can do it. It cannot be done. Jones can speak the sentence "I believe honey spoils, but it doesn't spoil," he can even shout it, but the one thing he can't do is mean what he's saying. Jones can "think" those words in the sense that he can, for example, imagine them scrolling on a screen before his mind's eye, but he cannot believe the corresponding sentence. He can't be aware of (exactly) what he's wrong about.

This bit of conventional wisdom generates a paradox—"Moore's paradox"—because it is puzzling that such truths would be inaccessible. Consider some other examples of inaccessible truths: many scientific truths are inaccessible to me because I haven't paid the cost of entry—namely, years of study—whereas others would be inaccessible even if I had, because no one has discovered them yet. I can't access truths about the past that went unrecorded, or truths about your emotional life that you refuse to share with me. Moore-paradoxical sentences are unlike any of these cases. The facts that correspond to those sentences, and make them true, are inaccessible to us not because they are too far away from us, but because they are, somehow, too close.

Philosophers find this deeply puzzling: How can proximity generate difficulties of access? Nonphilosophers might be just as puzzled that philosophers care about the paradox. Why does it matter whether one can say, "Honey never spoils but I don't believe that"?

I am going to argue that it is, in fact, possible to sincerely assert a Moore sentence, and that it is important that this is possible: there exist Moore sentences whose inaccessibility would be a moral and intellectual disaster for us.

III. APORIA

If two philosophers meet, and they meet as philosophers, then it is likely that before long one of them will tell the other why they are wrong about something. Refutation is the fundamental form of philosophical interaction; even if most of us are not Socratics, we all share in the Socratic patrimony. Socrates understood refutation (in Greek, the word is *elenchos*) as the hallmark of his philosophical activity,[9] and the Socratic dialogues even have a name for the experience in which refutation culminates: aporia. One of Socrates' interlocutors describes aporia as a feeling of perplexity that is akin to being "stung" by a torpedo fish: "My mind and my tongue are numb, and I have no answer to give you."[10] Another describes it as watching his own sentences move before his very eyes: "I have no way of telling you what I have in mind, for whatever proposition we put forward goes around and refuses to stay put where we establish it."[11] What happens to you when you are refuted? What is it to be in a state of aporia?

Let's start with the notion that aporia—being refuted—is something that is experienced and felt by the person who undergoes it. Suppose that person A shows person B, in the absence of person C, that C's views are incorrect. Has A refuted C? Not as far as Socrates is concerned: so long as C is unaware of what has transpired, there is no state of aporia, and thus no refutation. The phrase "He did not realize that she had refuted him" is an acceptable use of the word "refute" in ordinary English, but Socratic refutation includes the proviso that no one is unwittingly refuted.[12] What would Socrates say to those who insist that a view has been refuted if there's an available proof as to its falsity, irrespective of whether anyone holds the view (or knows the proof)? He would say that one can use "refutation" to describe such a case if one likes, much in the way that one can, pointing to a painting of a dog, say "that's a dog." But of course it also makes perfectly good sense to say, of the dog in the painting,

"That's not a real dog." We will soon see why, for Socrates, real refutation requires recognition by the person being refuted.

So, what is the experience of being (really) refuted? Is it the same as changing one's mind, or suspending judgment on some question one used to have a firm belief on? No. First, there are non-refutational routes to changing one's mind or suspending judgment: I might simply forget my old views, and come to adopt a new one or no view at all, without noticing what I have given up. But even in the case where I suspend judgment *because* I have been refuted, those two events are not identical. The same point holds for change of mind: it is not the same thing as refutation, but rather is an effect of refutation. Refutation may cause a change of mind or suspension of judgment, but something is not identical to what it causes. Moreover, the qualitative character of refutation is quite different from either change of mind or suspension of judgment. Being refuted *feels* like ignorance, confusion, perplexity, whereas once you have changed my mind the perplexity is over and I think I am *now* in the right. And if I have suspended judgment I at least know I am *not wrong*, so that is a kind of safety as well.

Refutation is a (possible) *reason* for the suspension of judgment, or change of mind; but refutation should not be equated with the effects of refutation. A change of mind or suspension of judgment is sometimes undertaken in response to a predicament that necessitates it, and it is that predicament that we want to describe. The predicament is an experience to the effect that, until I change my mind or suspend judgment, I am in the wrong, I am making a mistake. One needn't voice this predicament out loud, but in a philosophical context, it is polite to do so. Instead of skipping directly from asserting p to denying it, or suspending judgment about it, we mark the transition by saying, "You got me" or "You're right" or "I'm wrong" or "I see now" or "Okay"—or just by pausing for a moment. These phrases (or silences), taken together with their corresponding facial expressions, serve to distinguish cases where one changes one's mind as a result of being in the predicament of being refuted from cases of simply changing one's mind. But what is that predicament?

One possible way to describe what you are doing when you are refuting someone is that you are getting them to contradict themselves. Should we then say that being refuted amounts to asserting a contradiction? That cannot be right, either. Most philosophers, as well as most nonphilosophers, believe that no claim of the form "p and not p" could possibly be true, and that it is impossible to sincerely assert one—and yet these people can still be refuted!

There is a group of philosophers who allow for the possibility of true contradictions—they are called "dialetheists"—and it is helpful to distinguish their view from anything that happens in a refutation. A dialetheist takes the contradiction he asserts to be an accurate representation of the way the world is. The contradictoriness of his sentence simply mirrors the contradictoriness he thinks he sees in the things themselves. To judge that "p and not p," is to judge that in some way or other the world is contradictory. But that is not the kind of thought we are trying to produce in refuting someone. We are trying to tell him: the world is not the problem, what is broken is your thinking about it. We insist that there *is* a way of thinking properly, and it is not his, that he is in the wrong, that his mind is—not was—in some kind of defective condition. We want him to judge that the world does not really work the way he thinks it does. This is just to say, *we want to get him in a position to sincerely assert a Moore sentence.* The sentence that expresses the content of a refutation is not "p and not p" but "p, but I don't believe it" (or "not p, but I believe it"). Thus, the possibility of asserting Moore sentences and the possibility of refutation are one and the same. What is at stake in Moore's paradox is nothing less than the practice of philosophy itself.

IV. A MOORE SENTENCE, ASSERTED

Often, the best kind of proof that something is possible is one that shows that it is already actual. I thus propose to prove that Moore sentences can be sincerely asserted by pointing you to a place in the Socratic dialogues where Socrates gets Alcibiades to assert one.

> SOCRATES: Alcibiades, the handsome son of Clinias,
>   doesn't understand justice and injustice—though he
>   thinks he does.
> ALCIBIADES: Apparently.[13]

(This is a slightly edited version of the exchange. I'll quote the full version below.)

"P isn't the case, though I believe it is" is a formula for a Moore sentence. Alcibiades' "apparently" constitutes agreement to such a sentence, with "Alcibiades understands justice," standing in for p. Notice that both of Socrates' verbs are in the present tense. What Alcibiades agrees to—and thus asserts—is that now, at the moment when he says "apparently," he continues to believe he understands justice and injustice, while at the same time continuing to assert "I do not." Socrates has managed to orchestrate a situation in which Alcibiades sincerely asserts what he doesn't believe: I think I understand justice, though I don't in fact understand it. It is important to distinguish what Alcibiades agrees to from sentences such as "I think I understand justice, and I think I don't" and "I understand justice, and I don't." Those sentences are contradictions, whereas the one Alcibiades effectively asserts is in fact a correct description of the way the world is.

"But Moore sentences are unassertable!" Given how entrenched this piece of conventional wisdom has become in the discipline of philosophy, I expect that some readers may be inclined to resist granting that this exchange qualifies as a full-fledged Moore sentence. First, how sincere is Alcibiades being? "Apparently" sounds grudging, and further examination of the context will support this impression. Moreover, the person who utters the words "Alcibiades doesn't understand justice and injustice—though he thinks he does" is not Alcibiades, but Socrates. For both of these reasons, one might suspect that it is only Socrates who recognizes Alcibiades' lack of understanding, not Alcibiades. And, of course, "Alcibiades doesn't understand justice, though he thinks he does" fails to be Moore-paradoxical when said by Socrates. If Socrates is the one uttering the relevant words, doesn't it follow that Socrates is the one talking, and that Socrates is expressing the views of Socrates? No.

All of these worries about whether what I have claimed to be a Moore sentence really counts as a Moore sentence are, in fact, addressed in the conversation that leads up to it. Let me now quote the context at some length. (I've italicized where the Moore sentence appears.)

> SOCRATES: Well then, given that your opinion wavers
>   so much, and given that you obviously neither found
>   it out yourself nor learned it from anyone else, how
>   likely is it that you know about justice and injustice?
> ALCIBIADES: From what you say anyway, it's not very
>   likely.
> SOCRATES: See, there you go again, Alcibiades, that's not
>   well said!
> ALCIBIADES: What do you mean?
> SOCRATES: You say that I say these things.
> ALCIBIADES: What? Aren't you saying that I don't under-
>   stand justice and injustice?
> SOCRATES: No, not at all.
> ALCIBIADES: Well, am I?
> SOCRATES: Yes.
> ALCIBIADES: How?
> SOCRATES: Here's how. If I asked you which is more, one
>   or two, would you say two?
> ALCIBIADES: I would.
> SOCRATES: By how much?
> ALCIBIADES: By one.

SOCRATES: Then which of us is saying that two is one
more than one?

ALCIBIADES: I am.

SOCRATES: Wasn't I asking and weren't you answering?

ALCIBIADES: Yes.

SOCRATES: Who do you think is saying these
things—me, the questioner, or you, the answerer?

ALCIBIADES: I am.

SOCRATES: And what if I asked you how to spell "Socrates," and you told me? Which of us would be saying it?

ALCIBIADES: I would.

SOCRATES: Come then, give me the general principle.
When there's a question and an answer, who is the
one saying things—the questioner or the answerer?

ALCIBIADES: The answerer, I think, Socrates.

SOCRATES: Wasn't I the questioner in everything just
now?

ALCIBIADES: Yes.

SOCRATES: And weren't you the answerer?

ALCIBIADES: I certainly was.

SOCRATES: Well then, which of us said what was said?

ALCIBIADES: From what we've agreed, Socrates, it seems
that I did.

SOCRATES: *And what was said was that Alcibiades, the
handsome son of Clinias, doesn't understand justice and injustice—though he thinks he does—and
that he is about to go to the Assembly to advise the
Athenians on what he doesn't know anything about.
Wasn't that it?*

ALCIBIADES: *Apparently.*

SOCRATES: Then it's just like in Euripides, Alcibiades;
"you heard it from yourself, not from me." I'm not
the one who says these things—you are—don't try to

blame me. And furthermore, you're quite right to say
so. This scheme you have in mind—teaching what
you don't know and haven't bothered to learn—your
scheme, my good fellow, is crazy.[14]

Plato died thousands of years before G. E. Moore was born, so
he cannot have been worried about whether readers would take the
italicized language above as a "real" Moore sentence. And yet it is
remarkable how careful Socrates is to distinguish the situation they
are in from one in which it is *Socrates* who is asserting the relevant
sentence. Plato has Alcibiades initially interpret Socrates like this:
"Aren't you saying that I don't understand justice and injustice?"
And then Plato has Socrates correct him and point out that Alcibiades is the one making the relevant assertion: "You heard it from
yourself, not from me." Socrates is not telling Alcibiades that he is
wrong. Socrates is getting Alcibiades to say, "I'm wrong" and then
he's making sure that Alcibiades sees that those were his own words.

The Moorean drama does not end here. The argument that follows the passage quoted above also arrives at a Moore sentence—
and this time Socrates announces where he is headed in advance.
After Alcibiades insists that just things needn't be advantageous,
Socrates tells him that soon the opposite words will be coming out
of his mouth:

> SOCRATES: Try to prove that what is just is sometimes
> not advantageous.
> ALCIBIADES: Stop pushing me around, Socrates!
> SOCRATES: No, in fact I'm going to push you around
> and persuade you of the *opposite* of what you're not
> willing to show me.
> ALCIBIADES: Just try it!
> SOCRATES: Just answer my questions.
> ALCIBIADES: No, you do the talking yourself.

Socrates: What?! Don't you want to be completely convinced?

Alcibiades: Absolutely, I'm sure.

Socrates: Wouldn't you be completely convinced if you yourself said, "Yes, that's how it is"?

Alcibiades: Yes, I think so.

Socrates: Then answer my questions. And if you don't hear yourself say that just things are also advantageous, then don't believe anything else I say.[15]

Even though Socrates has announced where he is headed in advance, Alcibiades is unable to divert the argumentative train to a different conclusion. Socrates' prediction comes true—see chapter 4, p. 112, for a discussion of the argument Socrates uses to make the prediction come true—and Alcibiades ends up assenting to another Moore sentence:

Socrates: It's obvious from what we've said that *not only are you ignorant* about the most important things, but you also think you know what you don't know.

Alcibiades: *I guess that's right.*[16]

The fact that Alcibiades' assent is grudging, that he is driven to make admissions he was not initially inclined to make, is no reason to doubt the sincerity of his responses. When a witness is brought, by the pressure of precise cross-examination, to grudgingly admit corrections to an earlier version of his testimony, we don't doubt the sincerity of those admissions. Instead, we think, "It is a good thing that that lawyer was there to question him." Indeed, grudging admissions are generally *more sincere* than non-grudging ones, not less; if someone is happy to admit something, his motives are potentially a mix of truth and pleasure. In grudging admissions, truth pulls against pleasure. Socrates' questioning makes it possible for Alcibiades to say, and therefore to think, a thought that would otherwise have lain in his blind spot. To understand how this is possible, we need to again consider the problem in the abstract.

V. NORMATIVE SELF-BLINDNESS

Consider a third personal, and therefore non-paradoxical, variant of a Moore sentence. If I say "p, but Jones doesn't believe it," I am expressing a critical evaluation of Jones' thought. I am holding Jones' thinking up to a normative standard—that of the truth—and saying that he is missing something. The thought "p but Jones doesn't believe it" claims that there is a truth Jones fails to have, that his mind is missing something. Likewise, if I say, "Jones believes p, but it's not the case that p," I am saying that Jones' thinking fails: he is wrong. Moore sentences are, first and foremost, evaluative judgments about some belief. The problem with first personally asserting a Moore sentence is that it would require me to take a critical attitude toward my own thoughts, and I do not seem able to do this. When I assess what you think, I compare it to the way the world really is. But looking at how the world really is is how I figure out what I think in the first place. When I ask myself what I think about something, I am already asking what is true about that thing. There is no room for a separate assessment step, which means that my thoughts are evaluatively inaccessible to me.

Normative self-blindness is the phenomenon that underlies Moore's paradox. When I make an assertion about the way the world is, you can also ascribe to me the corresponding belief, as though, when I said, "Honey never spoils," I had said "I believe that honey never spoils." The reason you can take this liberty is that these two things—p's being the case, and my believing that p—are, though distinct from your point of view, identical from my own. If I believe that p, I think I am correct in holding that belief, and that p is the case. When I have a belief, I don't have the ability to separately evaluate the truth of that belief. But that is not the case when I look at your beliefs: the question of *what* you believe and *whether* it is true are not the same question.

Moore paradoxical sentences are the clearest, but not the only, examples of normative self-blindness. Let's consider a few other examples. These examples are imperfect: in each case, questions arise as to whether we are necessarily or fully self-blind about the relevant phenomenon. I won't extensively engage with those questions; my goal is to highlight the existence of, rather than drawing precise lines around, a certain territory peripheral to our Moore sentences. By considering these related phenomena, we'll get a better grip on the problem to which Socratic refutation is the solution.

Example 1: Parental Praise

When parents praise a child's artwork, appearance, or intelligence, the child often doesn't take that praise seriously. Sometimes, the child may suspect his parents of insincerity, but this needn't be the case. Even if he believes his parents are saying exactly what they think, he may think that they are incapable of assessing him accurately, because he is too close to them. Because he is their own, their flesh and blood, his parents are inclined to see what he does (or how he looks or thinks), and see it as good, in the same glance. They cannot take a separate step of applying standards to him. This is much the way we are with our beliefs: if I were to start to enumerate some things I think, and pause after each one to decide whether it is true, I would miraculously end up placing a check mark next to each and every one. Belief #1, correct. Belief #2, correct again. Belief #3, also true. If I were enumerating your beliefs, things would be very different. To say I am biased toward myself is a wild understatement: I am not *more likely* to judge my beliefs true; I am utterly incapable of judging them to be false. I am not evaluating them at all, because they are evaluatively inaccessible to me.

Example 2: The Paradox of Modesty

Consider a puzzle about modesty: if being an unassuming, reserved, humble person—the sort who is averse to self-praise—is a virtue, then it deserves praise. It would follow that the modest person cannot evaluate herself as possessing the virtue of modesty: were she to do so, she would pride herself on her modesty, and thereby lose it.

The philosopher Richard Moran, developing Bernard Williams' thought that modesty is "self-effacing," in that "a modest person does not act under the title of modesty," observes: "It is part of modesty, insofar as it is a virtue, and hence praiseworthy, not to reflect on itself, in particular not to insist on taking credit for its praiseworthy character . . . if the quality of modesty is taken to be incompatible with praise of oneself, this would appear to be a quality that cannot survive reflection on itself."[17]

Notice that while Moran's and Williams' attention is on whether one can be *aware of* oneself as being modest, the real difficulty here is not awareness but evaluation. The modest person can notice that she doesn't speak up as often as others, or that she is not as inclined to praise herself, or that she tends to adopt an unassuming pose, and so on. What she cannot do is *evaluate* these features of herself positively. The modest person can be perfectly well aware of her modesty so long as she doesn't see modesty as a virtue, or if she has some special reason for thinking that her own modesty is somehow nonvirtuous. When it comes to her own modesty, the modest person must be normatively self-blind.

Example 3: Self-Promising

Try this experiment. Pick something that you usually struggle with—answering emails promptly, staying off your phone, going to bed on time—and promise yourself that you will do better on this front for the next twenty-four hours. Done? Okay, I predict that twenty-four hours from now, you will have trouble answering the question, "Did you keep your promise?" Suppose you picked the bedtime promise, and that you do in fact go to bed on time. Couldn't that be because I drew your attention to the issue, rather than because you felt bound by the force of the promise? Suppose you stay up late. Why not think that means that you released yourself from a silly promise that was, in the first place, only an example in a philosophy book?

What you will surely know, twenty-four hours from now, is the answer to the factual question as to when you went to bed. It is less clear that you will have an answer to the normative question about whether your bedtime met the standard set by a promise. Can you make promises to yourself? We sometimes say "I promised myself that I would . . . ," but it is not clear that there is any difference between breaking such a promise and releasing ourselves from it.

Imagine how much easier it would have been for you to separate my two questions—*Did you go to bed on time?* and *Did you keep your promise?*—if you hadn't had to rely only on your own devices. Imagine that you'd promised your spouse you would go to bed on time tonight. It wouldn't matter whether you did so at my prompting, whether you subsequently changed your mind about the wisdom of doing so, and so on. Like it or not, you've promised, and that means there is a standard governing your action: if you don't go to bed on time, you've failed to meet it. It is now up to them to decide whether they want to hold you to your promise; the distinction between breaking and being released from the promise becomes easy to draw.

People who cooperate with us in the right way make possible a form of normative assessment that has no solipsistic counterpart. This happens when we make a promise to someone, and it happens when someone refutes us. I cannot distinguish between "something I believe" and "a truth about the world" introspectively, because I cannot assess my own beliefs for truth while continuing to believe them; but of course my beliefs are assessable for truth, and the practice of assessing them is one I can participate in—with the help of another. Socrates articulates this point by saying that another person can serve as a mirror to me.

VI. SOCRATIC SELF-KNOWLEDGE

After having been led to assert a Moore sentence two times, Alcibiades is eager for self-improvement:

> Well, Socrates, what kind of self-cultivation do I need to practice? Can you show me the way?[18]

Socrates points out a problem:

> I'm afraid we often think we're cultivating ourselves when we're not.[19]

What is it to *really* cultivate oneself? This question leads Socrates to raise a puzzle about the famous Delphic injunction to "Know thyself."

> SOCRATES: Is it actually such an easy thing to know oneself? Was it some simpleton who inscribed those words on the temple wall at Delphi? Or is it difficult, and not for everybody?
>
> ALCIBIADES: Sometimes I think, Socrates, that anyone can do it, but then sometimes I think it's extremely difficult.[20]

Is assessing one's own beliefs for truth easy or difficult? In one way, it is very easy—each one immediately receives a check mark. When I assess the beliefs of others, by contrast, I have to do actual work to check whether each is true. But of course the "ease" of assessing our own beliefs is a sign we are not really assessing them. Socrates returns to this point about the Delphic injunction later in the discussion:

> SOCRATES: I'll tell you what I suspect that inscription means, and what advice it's giving us. There may not be many examples of it, except the case of sight.

ALCIBIADES: What do you mean by that?

SOCRATES: You think about it, too. If the inscription took our eyes to be people and advised them, "See thyself," how would we understand such advice? Shouldn't the eye be looking at something in which it could see itself?

ALCIBIADES: Obviously.

SOCRATES: Then let's think of something that allows us to see both it and ourselves when we look at it.

ALCIBIADES: Obviously, Socrates, you mean mirrors and that sort of thing.

SOCRATES: Quite right. And isn't there something like that in the eye, which we see with?

ALCIBIADES: Certainly.

SOCRATES: I'm sure you've noticed that when a person looks into an eye his face appears in it, like in a mirror. We call this the "pupil," for it's a sort of miniature of the person who's looking.*

ALCIBIADES: You're right.

SOCRATES: Then an eye will see itself if it observes an eye and looks at the best part of it, the part with which it can see.

ALCIBIADES: So it seems.

SOCRATES: But it won't see itself if it looks at anything else in a person, or anything else at all, unless it's similar to the eye.

ALCIBIADES: You're right.

SOCRATES: So if an eye is to see itself, it must look at an eye, and at that region of it in which the

---

* The word "pupil" comes from *pupa* which means "doll," because the pupil of your eye reflects a doll-like miniature of the person who looks into it. Greek has the same etymological link: the word for doll and pupil of the eye are both *korē*.

good activity of an eye actually occurs, and this, I
presume, is seeing.

ALCIBIADES: That's right.

SOCRATES: Then if the soul, Alcibiades, is to know itself,
it must look at a soul, and especially at that region in
which what makes a soul good, wisdom, occurs, and
at anything else which is similar to it.[21]

The question of how Alcibiades is to cultivate himself—which
is to say, acquire self-knowledge, as per the Delphic injunction—is
here compared to a visual problem: How can someone see herself?
When I look out into the world, the one thing I don't see is me. I'm
not in my own field of view. But wait, what about the fact that I *can*
see my arm or leg by turning my eyes downward? Socrates anticipates this objection, and clarifies that he is not referring to *that* kind
of self-seeing: we should imagine that the oracle "took our eyes to be
people" and advised these eye-people to try to see themselves.

Indeed, Socrates goes one step further to specify that we should
imagine the order "See thyself" being given to a *part* of the eye.
Socrates is taking great care to articulate the problem as one of
self-seeing: *seeing the part of the eye that is doing the seeing.* In
principle, if the part of my eye that sees could project itself from
the rest of my eye—imagine it protruding on an antenna—my eye
could "see itself," which is to say, see other parts of the eye. But
what it could not do is see the very part that is seeing. The activity
of seeing is, in some way, self-blind. What does the seeing cannot
see itself, just as what does the knowing cannot know itself—at
least, not *by itself.*

The eye can see itself by means of a special sort of intermediary,
one that "allows us to see both it and ourselves when we look at it."
Still water, or polished bronze, or any other highly reflective surface,
could, in principle, play the role of this intermediary, but Socrates
fastens onto one very specific kind of reflective surface—the shiny
blackness of another person's pupil—in order to bring the visual

case into line with the intellectual one. If you want a normative grip on yourself, you are going to need the help of another person.

Thinking about one's own thoughts is a two-person job. That is the immediate point of the analogy. But why is Socrates so intent on making this point with reference to a subset of thoughts, namely the ones that lie in the circumscribed region of the soul in which wisdom occurs? Recall that this whole discussion is meant to elaborate the project of self-cultivation. Socrates thinks knowing yourself is how you cultivate yourself—but only if you focus on the right part of yourself. Not all of your thoughts are equally significant to who you are. Socrates is drawing attention to the importance of evaluating the part of you that is *doing* the thinking. Those thoughts that are undetachable from the project of thinking—thoughts you are always "using" in order to think anything at all—are what you really need to know if you want to cultivate yourself.

G. E. MOORE AND the philosophers who inherited his paradox focused on relatively trivial sentences, such as about Jones and honey, and those sentences stand in contrast with the more momentous, life-changing Moore sentences we find in Plato. We can now explain why this difference matters. On most topics, I can alienate myself from what I happen to believe by deciding to suspend judgment. Even though I have a belief, I can step back and reflect on it. I can express such a decision by saying, for example, "I believe honey spoils, but is that right?" This question resembles a Moore sentence, but without the accompanying verbal infelicity and aura of paradox. It conveys my intention to set aside the fact that I already have a belief, one way or the other, about honey, so as to investigate the matter as though I didn't. My suspension of judgment creates enough distance between me and my belief that I can evaluate it; no paradox arises.

Suspending judgment is the conceptual analog to twisting or turning my body to bring parts of myself I can't usually see into view. There are parts of my body whose invisibility follows from how I usually position myself in order to look out at the world: my shoulder, the back of my knee, the soles of my feet. But if I set aside the goal of looking out onto the horizon for new information, and the upright posture that optimizes for that aim, I can contort myself to bring these parts into view. If I had the antenna, I could even see the other parts of my eye. Likewise, suspending judgment allows me to investigate claims I already believe. I usually treat such claims as settled background against which I acquire new information, but I can decide to treat them differently. I turn my belief into a nonbelief by detaching myself from it, and thereby put myself into a position to apply evaluative standards to it. Suspension of judgment is a measure we can take to eliminate such blind spots—though not, of course, to eliminate all of them simultaneously. If I am contorting myself to bring the back of my left knee into view, I can't see my right shoulder.

Even if it is true that I cannot get all of the parts of my body into view at once, the difficulty of getting my knee or shoulder into view is of an entirely different kind from the difficulty of getting *the seeing part itself* into view. That is a persistent kind of blind spot—it moves with me, no matter where I focus my attention. Socrates did not speak of "untimely questions"—that phrase is my own invention—but when he speaks of "that region in which what makes a soul good, wisdom, occurs," I take him to be referring to the thoughts that, at a fundamental level, guide our lives, and thus determine whether we count as "wise" or "foolish." These thoughts are the answers to questions on which we cannot suspend judgment, because the answers drive everything we do, including any inquiry we might make into the questions themselves. Untimely questions help us reframe the stakes of Moore's paradox.

Consider the claim, "No one can ever see an unseen thing." A book that has just been printed and never opened is made up of "unseen" pages, which become seen as soon as someone opens it. In this formal sense, you can never see the unseen pages, but of course in a substantive sense you *can* see those pages, but we are going to call them "seen pages" now. The problem posed by trivial Moore sentences, such as the one about honey, is akin to the formal problem of seeing the unseen pages. Socrates' problem—that of getting the seeing part itself into view—is analogous to the substantive difficulty we might have if some of the pages were glued shut or written in invisible ink. It is Socrates who identifies the philosophically troubling form of self-blindness, namely our stubborn inability to subject certain of our beliefs—the ones whose guidance matters most to us—to evaluative standards. It is our load-bearing beliefs—the ones that answer untimely questions—that we struggle to evaluate.

What might initially have appeared to be a narrow, technical problem of interest only to the subset of epistemologists and philosophers of language who study it turns out to be the Tolstoy problem in disguise. Once we view Moore's paradox through a Socratic lens, we gain sympathy for Tolstoy's struggles to confront questions such as "Why should I care about educating my children?" or "Why should I write novels?" We can now see that his problem is a problem of self-knowledge: he cannot evaluate his answers to these questions, because he is using them. That problem is not insoluble, but he cannot solve it on his own. He needs the help of others. Refutation is how they provide it.

VII. How Refutation Works

Socrates noticed a simple difference between intrapersonal wavering and interpersonal disagreement. When you say or do one thing and then, later, say or do something that conflicts with it—recall our various examples of wavering from chapter 1, from weakness of will to Russell's emotive conjugation to young Hippocrates' discombobulated scuttling—there is no through-line connecting your earlier thoughts and actions to your later ones, no way for you to hold one of those sets of thoughts to the standard set by the other. When you disagree with yourself, you are simply disjointed. But when you say one thing and I disagree with you, and we conduct that disagreement together, then there can be a coherence to our activity of arguing. When, for example, you seek the truth and I avoid error, we are doing one thing, together—disagreeing—in a way that the various time-slices of you are not doing one thing, together, when you disagree with yourself by wavering.

Return to the case of making a promise to someone. Because there is a promisee, there is space for normative assessment: you can see your own action as a failure insofar as it doesn't meet someone else's promise-grounded expectation. The refuter affords a similar experience. Here is how it works. If you are the refuter, first you ask someone a question, then they answer, and then, by way of further interrogation, you show them that you *can't* accept their answer. You do this by showing them that it contradicts something else that both of you accept, or that it is internally incoherent, or that it simply doesn't count as an answer to the question once the question has been clarified. Because you are holding them accountable—reminding them of what they said earlier in the conversation, or of what follows from what they said earlier, or of common sense, or of what they've agreed to on other occasions—they can come to see their answer as bad. They see that it would rightly be judged unacceptable by anyone who wasn't caught up in already thinking it.

But that doesn't mean that they instantly drop it, either. If the question was untimely, they can't suspend judgment on it, so they can't simply "give up" their only answer as soon as they see problems with it. Until they come up with a replacement, they continue to accept it, yet at the same time understand why you don't. They acknowledge that you are right not to buy what they are selling; because of you, they can see a defect in their answer; you are a normative mirror for their thought. In the Platonic dialogues it doesn't tend to take very long for someone like Alcibiades to regroup; nonetheless, even if only for the duration of one dialectical exchange, he is afforded the experience of watching his own thinking fall short. He sees the truth about himself reflected in the soul of his interlocutor.

One might ask: If the question is an untimely one, how is even the refuter capable of posing it? One possibility is that the question only counts as untimely for the refutee. Consider a question such as "Do you think that you and your spouse will stay married?" The person who poses this question can approach it with the detached curiosity unavailable to the person to whom it is being posed. We have seen that Socrates often gets his foot in the door by way of such questions—for instance, when he asks Lysis whether his parents love him, Euthyphro whether his prosecution of his father is pious, and Alcibiades whether he has what it takes to rule the world.

Yet Socrates systematically translates such one-way untimely questions into questions that are untimely for both parties: his conversation with Lysis quickly becomes "What is a true friend?" with Alcibiades it turns into "What is justice?" with Laches and Nicias he explores "What is courage?" with Euthyphro "What is piety?" In other words, Socrates guides each conversation toward the special subset of questions that are untimely for *everyone*, including himself. Just like the rest of us, Socrates needs to believe that he is a good person, which means that he needs to believe he is conducting himself in the manner of a true friend, with justice and courage and piety. Once again we see that Socrates is targeting the most stubborn blind spots: the ones we all share. Which returns us to the question: How are such questions even askable? How can Socrates pose questions on which he himself cannot suspend judgment?

The solution is to recognize that it is possible to direct a question such as "What is X?" at someone else, even if you have your own answer to that question, and even if you do not suspend judgment with reference to that answer. When Socrates asks "What is X?" and his interlocutor offers an answer, Socrates doesn't reply with a simple "Great, thanks so much." Instead, he asks a series of pointed questions, each of which leads to an explanation of why he cannot accept the answer. What is the soil from which his probing questions spring? Socrates' own conception of X, refined over the course of many such conversations.

As we saw in the last chapter, Socrates' conversations are not merely

destructive but make positive progress toward knowledge of the subject matter. That progress is available to be deployed in subsequent
conversations—or even later in the same conversation—as a basis
for resisting, or demanding elaborations of, his interlocutors' contrary claims. For example, in the *Gorgias*, two of Socrates' interlocutors have claimed that doing injustice is better, for the one doing
it, than undergoing injustice, and Socrates has refuted this claim
so many times, in so many ways, that he describes the claim that
doing injustice is worse than undergoing it as "held down and bound
by arguments of iron and adamant."[22] Socrates uses what he has
learned about X over past encounters as a standard against which
he can compare his new interlocutor's ideas, and will take what he
learns over the course of that conversation into the next. Socrates is,
like his interlocutors, both using his answers to an untimely question, and inquiring into that question, at the same time.

Socrates is testing what he has learned from others against what
he stands to learn from each new person. He introduces an enlightening image for this process in the *Gorgias* when he describes
one of his most oppositional interlocutors, Callicles, as "one of
those stones on which they test gold."[23] The way for two people to
inquire into a question each takes to be already answered is by pit-
ting those answers against one another. Each serves, for the other,
as a kind of testing stone, or, along the lines of the previous analogy, a mirror in which their own view becomes evaluable. It allows
the refutee to ask: Is what I think the sort of thought that someone
who doesn't already think it would accept? How does it look from
the outside?

But even if both participants are inquiring by using their own
answers, it is worth observing two asymmetries between what Socrates is doing and what his interlocutors are doing. First, there is
the fact that puts Socrates at such an advantage: his answers are the
products of past investigations, whereas his interlocutors' are usually
not. Second, Socrates is playing Clifford, whereas his interlocutor is
playing James. The interlocutor uses his answers to furnish the thesis

to be examined, whereas Socrates uses his answers to examine that thesis. It is because the Clifford role is entirely responsive, skeptical, critical, and negative that Socrates denies having said anything—"Well then, which of us said what was said?"[24]—or rather, Socrates brings Alcibiades to deny that Socrates has said anything!

When Alcibiades speaks, he is saying what Alcibiades thinks. When Socrates questions, he is also—provided Alcibiades assents—saying what Alcibiades thinks. Once the project of saying what Alcibiades thinks is distributed over two people, "p, but I don't believe it" becomes both sayable and thinkable. Socrates discovered that the space of speech is more capacious than the space of thought: it allows a person to see their own mistakes. Socrates drives Alcibiades to sincerely speak against himself, and then to witness the surprising mismatch between the words coming out of his own mouth and what he sees when he introspects. The blind spots associated with untimely questions cannot be inwardly "seen" by means of introspection, but they can be spoken—outwardly "seen"—by being mirrored in another. We can indeed assert Moore sentences, but that project is a collaborative one. With Socrates' help, Alcibiades manages to explore the thoroughly familiar territory of his self as though he were in an uncharted land. And Socrates can, in turn, learn from what he has helped Alcibiades to say, and make use of it to sharpen his future refutations.

VIII. The Fate of Alcibiades

But if Socrates is so successful at exposing Alcibiades' otherwise hidden ignorance, why did Alcibiades' life turn out so badly? Why did he persist in his self-destructive quest for world domination? I believe that Plato asked himself this question, and that his answer can be found in the speech he puts into Alcibiades' mouth in the *Symposium*. Whereas the conversation that we have been examining, in the *Alcibiades*, marks the beginning of Socrates' association with Alcibiades, the *Symposium* marks its end: the *Symposium* is set seventeen years after the *Alcibiades*, which is about a year before the disastrous Sicilian expedition. In the *Symposium*, Alcibiades describes the extraordinary effect of Socrates' words:

> The moment he [Socrates] starts to speak, I am beside myself: my heart starts leaping in my chest, the tears come streaming down my face, even the frenzied Corybantes seem sane compared to me—and, let me tell you, I am not alone. I have heard Pericles and many other great orators, and I have admired their speeches. But nothing like this ever happened to me.

But then Alcibiades confesses that, despite Socrates' refutations, Alcibiades keeps returning to his usual, politically ambitious ways. Every encounter with Socrates becomes a reminder that this choice is a mistake:

> He always traps me, you see, and he makes me admit that my political career is a waste of time, while all that matters is just what I most neglect: my personal shortcomings, which cry out for the closest attention.

Alcibiades reports that over the course of such conversations he would find that "my very own soul started protesting that my life—my life!—was no better than the most miserable slave's" and that Socrates "makes it seem that my life isn't worth living!" He runs away from Socrates:

> So I refuse to listen to him; I stop my ears and tear myself away from him, for, like the Sirens, he could make me stay by his side till I die. Socrates is the only person in the world who has made me feel shame—ah, you didn't think I had it in me, did you? Yes, he makes me feel ashamed: I know perfectly well that I can't prove he's wrong when

he tells me what I should do; yet, the moment I leave his side, I go back to my old ways: I cave in to my desire to please the crowd. My whole life has become one constant effort to escape from him and keep away, but when I see him, I feel deeply ashamed, because I'm doing nothing about my way of life, though I have already agreed with him that I should.[25]

Plato seems to be saying: Socrates can be a mirror showing you what's wrong with you, but he cannot prevent you from looking away. Yet why does Alcibiades *want* to look away? He describes his encounters with Socrates as thrilling, and he clearly finds the mirror to be truthful. Alcibiades' difficulty seems to be that everything he sees in it is negative: "my shortcomings," "my life isn't worth living." Recall Clitophon's inability to see the positive aspects of the Socratic project. Alcibiades cannot perceive how the Socratic method will ever afford him the possibility of moving forward in life, of making progress. The life of military conquest and political power promises concrete gains in wealth and status. When Alcibiades compares this life to the philosophical one, he can't help but finding the latter wanting. Alcibiades grasps only the "refutation" side of the Socratic method, not the "inquiry" side.[26]

To be fair to Alcibiades, the positive side of the Socratic method is the much more difficult side to bring into view, to the point that an entire philosophical tradition—that of the ancient Skeptics—ended up framing the Socratic project in purely negative terms. Nonetheless, in the next chapter, we will try.

Chapter 7

Meno's Paradox

B EFORE PROGRAMMABLE ELECTRONIC COMPUTERS EXISTED, the word "computer" referred to a human being hired to perform calculations. The ancestors of the objects we now call computers were, in their own time, called "mechanical computers," to distinguish them from the humanoid kind. In the 1940s, when "computer" started to transition over to the meaning it has today, the people who worked with the machines pondered the difference: on the one hand, newfangled mechanical computers were nothing but a set of switches; on the other hand, that is also a way to describe a human brain. And it was easy to see that computers were bound to become vastly more complex, adding more and more switches, in the decades to come. Is there some threshold of complexity that, when crossed, qualifies a computer as a thinker? If yes, how would we know where that threshold is or when it had been crossed?

These are hard questions. They are hard in large part because we are not sure what we mean by "think." Forget about machines. When do I myself count as thinking? Do nonhuman animals think? What *is* thinking? If we cannot answer these questions, we seem very far from being able to say what it would be for a machine to think. Faced with this predicament, one of the pioneers of computing, Alan Turing, proposed that we set aside thorny philosophical debates about the nature of thought in favor of a simple test.[1] The test involves three participants: two human beings and a machine. Each is located in a separate room. The first human, call her A, communicates, via text, with both the other human and also with the machine. If A cannot tell which of her interlocutors is a machine, then the machine has passed the test—it now officially counts as thinking.

Turing transformed a vague question—Can machines think?—into a well-defined problem—Can you construct a machine that can pass a specific test? This type of transformation is often useful. If I want to know which surgeon is best at performing bypass surgery, or which foreign language class to enroll in, or which neighborhood I should move to, the first step will likely be to transform these vague goals into more specific desiderata. I might want to compare rates of complications, or the grades that students who took various courses achieved on standardized language exams, or the distances between candidate neighborhoods and my workplace. Someone faced with the question "Which surgeon has a low rate of complications for bypass surgery?" understands what to do next in order to make progress on the investigation; "Who is a good surgeon?" by contrast, invites the stymied response, "It depends what you mean by good."

It is true that in many cases I may be interested in more than one data point—not only the rate of complications, but how booked the surgeon is, whether they accept my insurance, what medical school they went to, whether my friends have referred them, and so on. Complexity adds steps, but even a complex set of desiderata is actionable; the set of actions will simply take longer. Imagine someone who says: "I don't want the surgeon with a low rate of complications, or one covered by my insurance, or one who went to a prestigious medical school, etc. . . . I just want a *good* surgeon." We are likely to respond that "Find me a good surgeon!" is not a well-defined problem. Even if we want to help this person, we are not sure how to do so. For suppose that somehow we stumbled across "a good surgeon"; how would we know that we had?

Philosophers have faced this complaint for a long time. Philosophical inquiry is not an attempt to solve well-defined problems; it is, instead, an attempt to ask important questions. It has often been noted that much, if not all, of the territory now claimed by science once belonged to philosophy. When philosophical questions can be reformulated as problems, that is when they leave the orbit of philosophy. Consider questions such as What is motion, change, cause? Or: What allows something to be counted as alive? Or: How can different substances be mixed together? Each of these was, at one time, a purely philosophical question, before the disciplines of physics, biology, and chemistry turned them into a set of interrelated and more precisely formulated problems. (Though it is worth remarking that each of those disciplines retains ties to their ancestral philosophical questions.) The same holds for logic, economics, and computer science. Back when they were more poorly formulated, their questions were philosophical questions.

But not all philosophical questions have been converted into problems. When philosophers and nonphilosophers face off over one of the unconverted questions, the ensuing interactions tend to go awry. The nonphilosopher is liable to be frustrated by questions such as "Is there free will?" or "What is justice?" or "How should one live?"; to reply that "it depends what you mean by 'free' or 'justice' or 'should' "; to dismiss the question as ill-defined; to doubt whether the philosopher would have a way of recognizing the answer if it were staring her in the face. The nonphilosopher may be too polite to give full verbal expression to her incredulity, but inside she wonders, "What makes these philosophers think that they are doing anything at all?"

Meetings between philosophers and nonphilosophers so reliably result in such a culture clash that the typical encounter deserves a name. I will call it "the primal scene." The specter of the primal scene hovers over every introduction to philosophy class, and the students in the class will often find themselves reenacting the scene when they go home for break and explain to their parents that they are studying philosophy. When philosophers confront complaints about whether philosophy has or can or ever will make progress, and the complainers seem to have little interest in philosophy outside of raising this complaint, that interaction tends to be a version of the primal scene.

I. MENO'S PARADOX

Plato dramatizes the primal scene in the *Meno*. Socrates asks Meno, "What is virtue?" Meno offers three answers, each of which is refuted by Socrates. When Socrates asks Meno to try again, Meno explodes in a shower of incredulous questions:

> How will you look for it, Socrates, when you do not know at all what it is? How will you aim to search for something you do not know at all? If you should meet with it, how will you know that this is the thing that you did not know?[2]

Socrates immediately recognizes what is happening. He has clearly encountered the primal scene before:

> I know what you want to say, Meno. Do you realize what a debater's argument you are bringing up, that a person cannot search either for what he knows or for what he does not know? He cannot search for what he knows— since he knows it, there is no need to search—nor for what he does not know, for he does not know what to look for.[3]

Socrates' reformulation, which precisifies Meno's skeptical challenge into a dilemma, is called Meno's paradox. It calls into question the very possibility of searching: either the search is unnecessary, because you already have what you're looking for, or it is impossible, because you don't know what you're looking for, and so wouldn't know it if you found it.

Meno is not complaining generally about any and every kind of search. He would not say that it is impossible to search for one's keys or for the answer to an arithmetic problem, or that one can't look a word up in a dictionary. Meno's paradox targets the specific kind of search that he has only now, after extended conversation, come to understand himself as having been dragooned into. It is important to emphasize that Meno did not raise his challenge immediately, when Socrates first asked him, "What is virtue?"

In the opening of the dialogue, when first Socrates posed that question, Meno was not of the opinion that it would be impossible to answer. Quite the contrary. As I emphasized when we first examined this encounter, in chapter 2, after Socrates asks Meno what virtue is, Meno repeatedly insists that it is trivially easy to answer:

> It is not hard to tell you, Socrates. First, if you want the virtue of a man, it is easy to say that a man's virtue consists of being able to manage public affairs and in so doing to benefit his friends and harm his enemies and to be careful that no harm comes to himself; if you want the virtue of a woman, it is not difficult to describe: she must manage the home well, preserve its possessions, and be submissive to her husband; the virtue of a child, whether male or female, is different again, and so is that of an elderly man, if you want that, or if you want that of a free man or a slave. And there are very many other virtues, so that one is not at a loss to say what virtue is. There is virtue for every action and every age, for every task of ours and every one of us—and, Socrates, the same is true for wickedness.[4]

This is an impressive speech about virtue, one that Meno has evidently come prepared to rattle off. But Socrates is dissatisfied. He did not want to hear the different virtues of different kinds of people. He wanted to know what these different kinds of virtue all have in common: "Even if they are many and various, all of them have one and the same form which makes them virtues, and it is right to look to this when one is asked to make clear what virtue is."[5] Socrates wants to know what virtue *itself* is: "Tell me the nature of virtue as a whole and stop making many out of one . . . allow virtue to remain whole and sound, and tell me what it is."[6] Meno tries again, but all of his subsequent answers also end up in the same difficulty. Socrates complains, "I begged you just now not to break up or fragment virtue."[7]

In response to this complaint, Meno, who has studied with the famous sophist Gorgias, offers a complaint of his own. Meno insists that he is usually quite good at talking about virtue: "Yet I have made many speeches about virtue before large audiences on a thousand occasions, very good speeches as I thought, but now I cannot even say what it is."[8] But of course he is usually permitted to do what Socrates won't let him do—chop virtue up into pieces. Someone with expertise in the world of surgeons might say, "I can tell you which surgeon has the lowest rage of complications, which has the most availability, which accepts your insurance, and so on." We are likely to sympathize with the frustrations of a person who is faced with the demand to simply find a *good* surgeon, and their doubts about what—if not low complications, availability, and so on—the demander can mean by "good." Many a philosopher can think back to a time when, not yet having been converted to the philosophical enterprise, she played the part of the nonphilosopher, skeptically challenging some philosopher to prove that the sort of thing philosophers look for is even findable. Those of us who have played both parts in the primal scene appreciate where Meno is coming from—but we are, at the same time, cognizant of what he is missing.

There are certainly times and places where it is appropriate to convert a vague question into a more precise and delimited problem. But this conversion does not always work out in the way one anticipated. Recall the question of whether computers would ever be able to think. Seven decades after Turing's death, the problem posed by his test stands as solved. Large language models (LLMs) produce essays that fool teachers into thinking that students wrote them, secure high grades on examinations for would-be economists and doctors, and serve as substitutes for texts composed by human beings, such as those on Wikipedia and in online encyclopedias. LLMs have passed the Turing test with flying colors.

What has the response been? Not widespread acknowledgment of the need to make room for a new set of thinkers in our midst, but a debate—between those eager for innovation and those fearing misuse—over the degree to which we should regulate LLMs. Few appear concerned with the ethics of regulating thought, because few even consider the possibility that LLMs are actually thinking. It appears that when we converted the question, "Can machines think?" into the problem, "Construct a machine that passes this test," something got lost in translation. Insofar as some of us are still moved to wonder what it would mean for a machine to actually engage in thought, we may indeed find ourselves cast back on philosophical shores, wondering: What is thinking, after all?

This chapter is about how it is possible to make positive progress on this question, and the others like it. It addresses the worry—shared, we can now see, between Alcibiades and Meno—that philosophy, so long as it remains resolutely philosophical, orienting itself around questions and not problems, is consigned to be negative and destructive. We have seen how refutation works. But how does inquiry work?

II. QUESTIONS AND PROBLEMS

The distinction between a question and a problem turns out to be the key to understanding both Meno's paradox and the "primal scene." Consider the etymologies of those two words. "Problem" comes from the Greek *problēma*, which means an obstacle or barrier. The prefix "*pro*" means before or in front of, and the verb is *ballō*, to throw. *Problēma* was the word used for something that is thrown before you and impedes your way—so a wall can count as a *problēma*; so can a shield, or one's horse's armor.[9] If I am trying to kill you, your shield, the armor on your horse, and the wall behind which you hide constitute *problēmata*—problems—for me.

A problem is something you need to move out of the way so that you can go on with what you were doing before the problem arose. A question is a very different sort of beast. To ask a question is to be on a quest: the word "question" comes from the Latin *quaerere*, which means to seek or search or pursue or hunt. At the end of your hunt, you have caught what you wanted: the answer, or the quarry, or the Holy Grail. Your quest wasn't a distraction from some underlying project; it *was* the underlying project. At the end of the problem-solving process, you have eliminated something—the solution to a problem dissolves the problem—whereas at the end of the question-answering process, you have something—whatever it was you are looking for. The question culminates in its answer.

One way to see the difference between questions and problems is to compare how they are transferred. When you present your problem to someone else, you are setting a task before them: this is what you need to solve. They don't necessarily need to know why you need it solved, because one person can eliminate an obstacle to another's progress toward a goal without sharing that goal. That is why the transfer of a problem characteristically takes the form of a command—though of course the expression of this command can be softened in the direction of a request ("Please?"), or propped up with added incentives ("I'll pay you . . ."). When I pose a question, by contrast, I am not commanding, deferring, or delegating—I am sharing or inviting. I hope to captivate your interest, to whet your curiosity, to make my question your question, to entice you to join me in the hunt. Whereas the symbol for a question is the question mark, the symbol for a problem is the exclamation point. Motives are exogenous to problem-solving, but endogenous to question-answering.

Admittedly, we often express problems interrogatively. Instead of commanding you to find my keys, I might ask you where they are. But "Where are my keys?" is a problem hiding in question clothing. To see this, consider some possible answers. "Not on the surface of the sun" truthfully gives the location of my keys, as does, "Wherever your keys are." Nonetheless, these are bad answers, and they are bad precisely because they do not help me achieve the goal—leaving the house, opening a locked door, rubbing my lucky rabbit's foot—to which keylessness constituted an impediment. Consider the reply "They are in your room." This is a good reply if you have a small, tidy room, but if your room is large and cluttered, you might need the location demarcated more specifically. Whether or not it is a good reply is a function of whether or not it solves the problem. Indeed, "Here, take mine" could be a good reply to "Where are my keys?" if what is needed is to leave the house quickly, and if we have copies of the same key. A good reply doesn't need to offer an answer to the question, "Where are my keys?" as long as it resolves the problem of not being able to leave the house.

If we try to imagine a version of "Where are my keys?" that is resolutely inquisitive—the person is really after *knowledge* of the location of his keys—we will start to feel the force of Meno's paradox. Suppose I tell you that your keys are in your room, but you turn down that answer. They are also in your house, and in the city where your house is located, and some large number of miles from the Eiffel Tower. You don't like those answers, either. Do I need to add that they are on your desk? Sitting at the center of a patch of light cast by your desk lamp? Do you need to know their GPS coordinates? Down to how many decimal points? What about them being exactly where they are? Or not on the surface of the sun? Someone who just wants to know where his keys are and cannot give us any sense of the kind of problem he's trying to solve by locating them leaves us with a baffling array of possible responses. We may feel either that there is no correct answer—that he would not know it if he saw it—or if he insists that there is an answer ("It's the one about the patch of light") that can only be because he had settled upon it in advance.

We can now say why the scope of Meno's paradox is much narrower than it might first appear to be. Most searches aim to arrive neither at what I know, nor at what I don't know, but at a way to keep doing what I was doing before I ran into a problem. Likewise, most questions are merely inquisitive repackagings of problems. Perhaps there is no definitive answer to the question, "Where are my keys?"—no reason to pick "in the patch of light" over "on planet

Earth." This needn't pose any difficulty in a world where no one is ever asking that *question*, because all we were ever trying to do was find solutions to the *problem* of keylessness. That problem is typically well defined, to the point where it is easy for the answerer to tell that "on planet Earth" would be a bad answer whereas a variety of others—"on your desk," "near your lamp," and so on—would all be equally good. We don't run into Meno's paradox when we search for our keys, or look words up in the dictionary, or ask after the sum of a series of numbers, because in all of those cases we are looking for solutions to well-defined problems.

Any time I ask an expert for a piece of information, I am posing a problem rather than asking a question. True, I may put a question mark at the end of my request: When was Napoleon born? What is the atomic number of helium? Where is the ocean deepest? Nonetheless, my readiness to let them be in charge of what the correct answer looks like is the telltale sign that I am not on a quest. I do not expect, after hearing their answer, to say "Aha!" The Aha! of understanding is associated with questions, rather than problems. It expresses the feeling that, in getting what you were searching for, you got exactly what you wanted.

When I ask for information what I actually want is something distinct from the information itself—namely, to move on with whatever activity was impeded by the problem posed by the absence of that information. There is always an ulterior motive for seeking out information, some use to which I aim to put it, even if that use is merely to relieve the itch of curiosity or a period of boredom. This ulterior motive is precisely what allows me to produce a "well-defined" formulation of the circumstances under which the problem will count as solved. I can tell you, in advance, what stands in the way of my moving on: I want *whatever* will allow me to fill in the blank on the test, or advance to the next stage of my research project, or leave the house, or sate my curiosity, or ease my boredom.

A question, by contrast, counts as answered when I have the answer. There is nothing that comes next. So if you ask me to tell you what it will be like for me to have the answer, I am forced to reply that I will only be able to do that once I have it. The state of having the answer is simply the state of knowing something that I do not yet know, and so cannot identify for you.

But how can it be that when I have the answer, I recognize it as being just what I was looking for ("Aha!"), but I can't tell you, in advance, what it is going to look like? This is Meno's paradox.

PROBLEMS TEND TO COME packaged with an accepted methodology for approaching them, which is to say, a system that has been developed for solving problems of that kind. This is a selection effect: we don't even notice most of what obstructs our goals, because a problem only precipitates out of the giant mush of things I might try to do when its solution promises to come cheaply, relative to other problems that might so precipitate. If I want something that is available both in town A and in town B, and there are roads between me and town A, but an ocean between me and town B, I do not ask myself, "How do I cross the ocean?"; I only ask, "Which roads should I take?" The former problem does not even show up, to me, as a problem. That is why problems and standardized tools for solving them—know-how, skills, algorithms, machines, formulas, instruments, systems, procedures, and so on—tend to go hand in hand. Where there is a problem, there tends to also be (at least) the makings of a road that one ought to travel in order to arrive at the solution. Problems are characteristically tractable.

Noam Chomsky wrote, "Science is a bit like the joke about the drunk who is looking under a lamppost for a key that he has lost on the other side of the street, because that's where the light is. It has no other choice."[10] But in fact it makes a lot of sense to look for one's keys under the light; and, not finding them, to move on to alternative solutions to the problem of keylessness—having new keys made or staying at a friend's place, for instance. Assuming that those alternative solutions are easier than searching for keys in the dark, there is no reason to do the latter. What Chomsky is observing is that in science, as in life, one's tools determine one's problems. It is only if we recast the role played by the keys in this metaphor, and imagine that "the drunk" is searching not for the solution to some (scientific, or other) problem but to the answer to a question, that the joke becomes a legitimate critique. If the keys themselves are what you want, you must search wherever you need to search, in the light and in the dark, even if you have no idea in advance how that search will proceed.

Most of the time, when a search runs into trouble—we don't know how to proceed, we don't know how to get help—we are willing to do one of two things. The first is give up. The second is find some way of turning our question into a problem. "Who is a good surgeon?" becomes "Compare the rates of complications," and so on. A problem is tractable; it can be handed to someone else; it can be formulated in a manner that is "well defined" in the sense that the terms of the solution can be specified in advance; it comes packaged with a procedure, which is to say, a reason to believe that it can be solved. But it is possible to imagine a scenario where someone is not interested in who has the lowest rates of complications, or who went to the best medical school, and so on; where she really does want to know what makes a surgeon a good surgeon—"Who is the *good* surgeon?"—because she aspires to become one.

Recall that when Meno was asked to define virtue, he offered correlates of it, instead. Obedience is what Meno thinks virtue looks like in a slave; whereas power or wealth or connections indicate virtue in the kind of man Meno wants to be. This is akin to saying a good surgeon is the one with low rates of complications, or who went to a good medical school, or comes recommended by one's friends. Socrates complains that this approach leaves virtue fragmented: when you look at the actual parts of virtue—namely, the various virtues—a question remains as to what holds them all together. The question is: What do virtues such as justice, courage, and generosity have in common? The answer to that is not going to be "money," or "power," or "obedience."

If the reason you seek a good surgeon is because you have a medical problem, you might look at complication rates or what school they went to, but if you want to *be* a good surgeon you will think about it differently. You will consider the elements of the practice of surgery—the parts proper to it—such as diagnosis, managing a surgical team, actually wielding a scalpel or laser, providing postoperative care. The common core of these activities, if they are considered as parts of a single project, will be something like: cutting into people for the sake of their health. Doing *that* well is the key to *being* a good surgeon; complication rates and alma maters are, at best, mere correlates.

When Socrates insists that Meno keep virtue whole and not split it into parts, he is reminding Meno that "What is virtue?" is a question, not a problem. This is, more generally, what Socrates is doing when he asks his interlocutor after "the X itself," or to look to "the Form of X" or to tell him "the definition of X." Socrates is convinced that there is such a thing as virtue, that virtue is a suitable target for an inquiry: it could be the endpoint of what you wanted to know. The answer to the question, "What is virtue?" is something to "Aha!" over. Consider, by contrast with virtue, a shmiraffe. I am going to define "shmiraffe" as: a giraffe plus one foot of air around it in every direction. A shmiraffe is, unlike virtue, not a suitable target for Socratic inquiry; faced with "What is a shmiraffe?" the correct thing to do is to split it into parts—the giraffe and the air around it—and not try to find anything that holds those parts together. One is not inclined to hope that sustained inquiry will expose the form or essence of a shmiraffe. Whether a giraffe has a Form or essence is debatable: Aristotle thinks the answer is yes, giraffes are one of the basic building blocks of reality, whereas a contemporary scientist might disagree, and argue that a giraffe can be reduced to ("is really nothing over and above") a collection of atoms. But everyone—Plato, Aristotle, and the contemporary scientist—will be on the same page when it comes to shmiraffes. No one thinks that concept is a suitable target for an inquiry into the nature of things. Nonetheless, the concept of a shmiraffe might yet be useful for solving problems. It has already proved useful for solving the problem of illustrating, to you, what it means for something to lack the unity requisite for Socratic inquiry.

Socrates is always telling his interlocutors to treat what he is saying as a question about what X is, not as a problem about how to find an X. He'll instruct them not to break X into pieces, or not to simply give an example of X. In this context, the famously obscure notion of a Platonic Form can be understood in a relatively straightforward way. Socrates sometimes speaks of the Form of Justice, or the Form of Piety, or the Form of whatever X he and his interlocutor are examining. "The Form of X" simply refers to the version of X that you must have in mind so as to answer the *question* "What is X?" This is why "The Form of X" is synonymous with "X itself" or "the essence of X." The Form of X is what you look to in order to produce a definition of X. The Form of X is X, considered as a question to be answered, rather than as a problem to be solved.

It is worth noting the difference between a Socratic definition, which stands as the goal of inquiry, and the kind of definition I gave of "shmiraffe." The second kind of definition is one that allows us to sharpen our statement of a problem; such a definition can even, for maximum precision, be articulated in a formal language—using mathematical or logical notation—instead of a natural one. That kind of a definition is a tool. It serves as a prerequisite for the real work in service of which the definition is introduced; a Socratic definition, by contrast, is the endpoint, the quarry.

A misunderstanding characteristic of the primal scene is when the philosopher is asked to provide a definition of the very term she hoped the conversation would explicate. The nonphilosopher sees definition as the prerequisite for solving whatever problem the philosopher wanted us to solve, but there was no such problem. The philosopher wasn't posing a problem. She was asking a question.

III. A DEMONSTRATION OF THE SOCRATIC METHOD

Once it has become clear to Meno what Socrates wants to do—inquire—Meno doubts whether it is something that can be done. If I can't tell you, in advance, what the answer is going to be, how will I recognize it when I get it?

There is one arena in which it is relatively easy to make sense of what it would mean to be on the hunt for some particular thing you do not yet have: hunting. Imagine you are on the trail of an animal that you are trying to capture or kill. It is only once you are in some kind of contact with it, by way of its scent, or some hairs from its body, or its footprints, or the sound of its movements, or a glimpse of it in your peripheral vision, that we would say you are tracking it in any substantive sense. Suppose you had none of these things and were wandering aimlessly in the animal's habitat. If you suddenly saw such a clue—a footprint or a hair—you might think to yourself, "I've got him!" That is the moment when your quest begins in earnest. We can grasp the requirement that you must "have" the animal in order to seek the animal: there is such a thing as "having" from a distance, when the search is underway, and there is another kind of "having" from closer up, when the search is complete. Being on the hunt—actually searching—might require the first kind of contact with your quarry, even though it obviously cannot require the second kind.

But how far can this distinction between two kinds of contact take us? When it comes to hunting we can draw distinctions that rely on properties of three dimensional space—close versus distant contact—because our quarry is a physical object. Socrates holds that there is an analog to "picking up the scent" in the space of ideas: when two people both have answers to a question, even if neither of those answers constites knowledge, the answers of the one can be tested against those of the other. This is a kind of hunt that cannot be undertaken alone.

Witness this exchange:

> SOCRATES: I want to examine and seek together with you
> what it [virtue] may be.
> MENO: How will *you* look for it, Socrates, when *you* do
> not know at all what it is? How will *you* aim to search
> for something *you* do not know at all? If *you* should
> meet with it, how will *you* know that this is the thing
> that *you* did not know?[11]

And a bit later in the dialogue:

> SOCRATES: Since *we* are of one mind that one should
> seek to find out what one does not know, shall *we* try
> to find out together what virtue is?[12]

I have italicized the pronouns here to expose the contrast between Meno asking how Socrates will inquire, and Socrates proposing a joint inquiry: Meno sees himself as presenting a difficulty to Socrates, whereas, as Socrates sees it, he and Meno are in a difficulty together. I have also italicized the word "how," which occurs three times in Meno's speech. As we saw when I first quoted Meno's questions, earlier on, Socrates goes on to rephrase them into a dilemma (you can look neither for what you already know, nor for what you don't know), but what Meno himself originally expresses is not any kind of paradox but instead a demand for a procedure: *how, how, how.* These two presuppositions on Meno's part—that Socrates will be on his own, and that he will have to rely on some antecedently approved procedure—are connected. When it comes to, for instance, the problem of finding the sum of a series of numbers, we embark on solving it with advance knowledge of the procedure by which we will proceed: addition. Meno's demands are appropriate for problems; by making these demands, he suggests that problems are the only thing we can think about.

Meno's paradox poses a real threat to the Socratic project, because all of Socrates' questions are genuine questions, and not problems. Targeting things of fundamental importance to us, they stubbornly and persistently resist being transformed into problems. Untimely questions ask after the things we actually want, rather than the things we must remove to pursue the things we want. Having an untimely question and having an answer to such a question: we have seen that, and why, these two states come together. But there is a difference—all the difference in the world—between having an answer to a question and having *knowledge* that the answer is correct.

The difference made Socrates who he was: he himself was defined by his awareness of his own ignorance, which is to say, understanding that his answers to untimely questions did not yet qualify as knowledge. He recognized the space between an answered question and a question whose answer has the finality of knowledge—but equally significantly, he recognized that this space only becomes inquisitively relevant in the company of another. Alone, we do fall prey to Meno's paradox: our answer either satisfies us or we lose hold of the question. But if you and I both have the same question yet different answers, a path opens up: we can test our answers against each other. This process is Socratic inquiry. The Socratic method is a way you can make progress without knowing in advance how you are going to do so.

We can now see why Socrates calls Meno's question unfair, a "debater's trick." Meno demands to be shown how Socrates can, by himself, do something that in fact he can only do with Meno: "How are you going to find virtue if I don't help you?" The primal scene always involves such a request for advance guarantees. The nonphilosopher hesitates to dip his toe into the waters of philosophy unless he first finds out what exactly is he going to be doing, and what he will get out of it. He wants the practice and the payoff of philosophy translated for him into extra-philosophical terms. The reader of this book may feel herself tempted to make the same impatient demand: show me some philosophical progress! She wants to stand on the sidelines and watch—passive, uninvested, safe—and assess whether some other people are making advances toward knowledge of untimely questions. If she likes what she sees, *then* she may decide to jump in.

I can't satisfy this request as it stands, nor could Socrates. Trying to assess an inquiry into untimely questions from the outside—that is, without recognizing them as your questions, and without asking yourself whether you are making progress—is like trying to assess what water feels like without touching it. So, what is Socrates to do, if he can't convince Meno to continue with the inquiry without offering him a display that would serve as some kind of "proof," and if he also doesn't think it makes sense to put philosophical inquiry on display? Socrates decides to put *non*philosophical inquiry on display. Socrates cannot offer Meno a demonstration as to how inquiry into some (genuine) question makes progress, if the demonstration must meet both the requirement that Meno relates to it as a passive, detached spectator, as well as the requirement that the question being inquired into is an untimely one. But he can offer a demonstration that meets only the first requirement, which is what he does.

He invites Meno's slave, who is unversed in geometry, to answer the following question: What is the line from which the double square comes? Suppose you have a square, let's call it S, with a side of length 2 and an area of 4, and you want a square twice as big as S, with an area of 8. How do you draw, in the diagram containing S, the line that will serve as the side of the square with twice the area of S? Socrates initiates an inquiry into that line.

> SOCRATES: Come now, try to tell me how long each side of this will be. The side of this [S] is two feet. What about each side of the one which is its double?
> SLAVE: Obviously, Socrates, it will be twice the length.[13]

The slave finds it "obvious" (recall Meno's opening response to Socrates) that the answer is the line of length 4. But he is wrong, since that line will produce a square quadruple the area of S, with an area of 16, not 8. After the slave himself comes to see this by way of some follow up questions, Socrates invites him to try again.

> SOCRATES: The line on which the eight-foot square is
>   based must then be longer than this one of two feet,
>   and shorter than that one of four feet?
> SLAVE: It must be.
> SOCRATES: Try to tell me then how long a line you say
>   it is.
> SLAVE: Three feet.[14]

Next, the slave proposes a line one and a half times the length of the side of S, of length 3; but this is also incorrect, because it yields a square with an area of 9.

Figure 1.

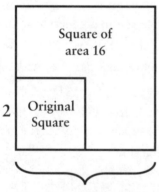
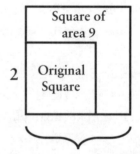

The slave's first answer: The slave's second answer:
the double line.   the one-and-a-half line.

At this point Socrates interrupts the demonstration and turns to Meno, so that Meno can keep an eye on one feature of it in particular:

> Look then how he will come out of his perplexity while searching along with me. I shall do nothing more than ask questions and not teach him. Watch whether you find me teaching and explaining things to him instead of asking for his opinion.[15]

Socrates goes back to the quadruple square, which is composed of four copies of S, and asks the slave what happens if they cut each S along the diagonal. The slave answers that the 8 resultant triangles will each have the area of half of the original square; since the area of the whole quadruple square is 16, he is then able to conclude, under more questioning, that four of those triangles, taken together, form a square double the size of the original, that is, 8. Thus the answer is: the diagonal. The double square comes from the diagonal. The slave is able to arrive at this conclusion, without being taught, by "searching along" with Socrates.

Figure 2.

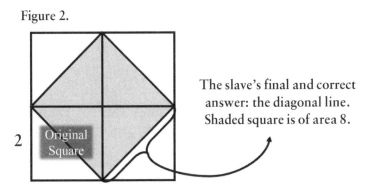

2 Original Square

The slave's final and correct answer: the diagonal line. Shaded square is of area 8.

Notice that although we can readily *name* the desired line, there is no easy way to specify its *length*. If the slave had been asked, at the outset, to describe in generic terms what the answer would look like, he might well have insisted that one way or another it would have to be able to be produced out of the units based off of the side of S. If the double line is too long, and the 1.5 line is too short, perhaps one ought to try the 1.75 line, and so on. His assumptions about the procedure required for finding the answer would have been wrong. Had he been allowed to search for his keys under that particular streetlight, he would never have found them, due to the fact that the diagonal is incommensurable with the side of the square. The slave, as an answerer, makes progress without a procedure, which is to say, without knowing in advance exactly how he will take the next step. If he had been presented with *the problem* of finding the line from which the double square comes, he would have been unable to do so, since he had no procedure for approaching this problem. But he is able to make progress on the corresponding *question*, by inquiring into it, with Socrates.

The reason it is possible for the slave to learn merely by answering questions is that the Socratic method is not a one-and-done affair. If the slave were only allowed to answer once, his false initial response would doom the inquiry. Socrates subjects the slave's answers to further examination in such a way that even a false answer is made useful, becoming part of the route to the truth. Socratic questioning makes it possible for the slave to answer inquisitively: not as if he already knows, but with a view to knowing. Of course, this only works because Socrates himself has an answer—a pretty good one—to the question of where the double square comes from.

Does Socrates consider his own answer about the diagonal to be a final answer—to count as *knowledge*? Or does he think true knowledge of the line from which the double square comes would require a more systematic grasp of geometry than he possesses? We never learn the answer to this question, since the mathematical demonstration is only a "toy example" meant to analogically illustrate the practice of inquiry. Socrates is emphatic that he is not teaching the slave—he only proceeds by questioning—so even if he had knowledge, he was not conveying it. Perhaps it does not matter to Socrates whether he himself has more to learn about geometry. But it does matter a great deal that he considers his answers about virtue to be unfinished, imperfect, and calling for further inquiry.

Equally important, however, is the fact that Socrates does have answers. In part three, we will examine some of his answers on the topics of love, death, and politics, but we have already encountered others: there is no such thing as weakness of will, revenge (in all its guises) is incoherent, it is better to have injustice done to you than to do it. Moreover, he is famous for his answers. In the *Laches*, one of his interlocutors describes the view that virtue is knowledge as a well-known Socratic position.[16] That answer is itself tested, and modified, over the course of the *Meno*; the dialogue ends with the revised position that when someone has virtue, that is either because they have knowledge *or* because they have true opinion. It is only because Socrates has a sense of where he's headed when he asks after virtue that he has a place from which to refute Meno's initial three definitions.

More generally, the reason why his interlocutors can answer inquisitively is because Socrates asks the kinds of questions—pushy questions—that are inflected by answers that have themselves been honed by years of inquiry. Pushy questions inspire inquisitive answers, which, in turn, help push further toward knowledge.

IV. PAST LIVES?

Let's reanimate Meno's skeptical challenge one last time. If two people have different answers to a question, each of them will, naturally, think that they are right. Why think that they can make progress by comparing their answers?

Among readers of Socratic dialogues, Meno's paradox often shows up as the worry that Socrates asks *leading* questions. A leading question is a question that "forces" an answer, comparable to how a magician forces a card when he offers you what appears to be a free choice but uses sleight of hand to get you to pick the card he wants. The charge is that Socrates is putting words into his interlocutors' mouths, the result being a one-sided conversation that simply goes where Socrates wanted it to go. They are not making progress together by comparing their answers; rather, we are just watching the Socrates show.

Socrates' questions to the slave are "pushy" in the sense that they are informed by Socrates' own mathematical reasoning and intelligence. Are they leading questions? Although it is possible that the slave is simply telling Socrates what he wanted to hear, that is not a necessary, or the only, interpretation of the exchange. Another interpretation is possible, because we can imagine ourselves in the slave's shoes, and imagine ourselves being brought, by this kind of conversational exchange, to see that the double square comes from the diagonal. The slave's answers strike us as answers we might give— and not only because Socrates pressured us to do so. Importantly, this is a function of how Socrates conducted the conversation: he asks the questions in the right order, so that it makes sense to answer as the slave does.

There is certainly no guarantee that two people with different answers will make headway; in most cases of divergent opinion, neither even attempts to refute the other and the disagreement goes nowhere. Socrates' claim is not that disagreements must or even typically do lead to intellectual progress, but that progress is *possible*, so long as one person asks pushy questions and the other gives inquisitive answers. Even so, readers have been inclined to wonder whether there is some fancy footwork going on in this part of the *Meno*; they worry that Socrates' success with the slave is a function of some feature peculiar to mathematics, and that the same success cannot be found in ethics.

It seems important to the success of the geometrical demonstration that the rightness and wrongness of a prospective answer is available to the learner in a specific way. Socrates seems to be relying on the "Aha!" character of mathematics, where, when confronted with a better answer, you can see that it is a better answer. Something clicks into place. Even if it is the first time you are approaching a new type of mathematical puzzle, you do not need to rely on the authority of your math teacher to inform you which answers are wrong, and which are right. You can, with a little work, see it for yourself.

Compare that example with the predicament of someone who is, for the first time, looking into the question of when Napoleon was born. Wrong answers don't "feel" wrong to him; he doesn't say, "I should've seen that it can't be 1768!" When he encounters the correct answer, he does not have the experience of its suddenly falling into place, of saying "Of course! 1769!" This power to recognize that the thing in front of you is (or in the case of wrong answers, is not) the very thing you were looking for—Socrates calls it "recollection"—is central to the kind of demonstration Socrates is putting on. Recall Meno's challenge:

> How will you look for it, Socrates, when you do not know at all what it is? How will you aim to search for something you do not know at all? If you should meet with it, how will you know that this is the thing that you did not know?[17]

Without answering how, Socrates can show Meno *that* it is possible to know that this is the thing you did not know. The experience that "this is the thing I did not know" is real, because we have it when we learn math. We also have it outside of math, when we remember something. For example, if there was a word I was trying to remember, and then it suddenly it comes to mind, I say "Aha! that's it!" Someone who once knew the year of Napoleon's birth might experience a burst of recognition when presented with 1769. Socrates is inclined to assimilate these two facts, and posit that even in the case of math we are "recognizing" something we saw earlier—in a past life. He claims to have heard from priestesses and poets that the soul is immortal, and that our current life represents a reincarnation. This would explain our ability to do math, and it should make us optimistic about virtue:

> The soul is immortal, has been born often, and has seen all things here and in the underworld, there is nothing which it has not learned; so it is in no way surprising that it can recollect the things it knew before, both about virtue and other things. As the whole of nature is akin, and the soul has learned everything, nothing prevents a man, after recalling one thing only—a process people call learning—discovering everything else for himself, if he is brave and does not tire of the search, for searching and learning are, as a whole, recollection.[18]

Socrates is saying that in our pre-lives, before we were born, we knew things that we can now hope to recover—with an "Aha!" experience—if we search for them. It makes sense to search; we can be optimistic of success. But what if you do not share Socrates' commitment to reincarnation, or his inclination to defer to priestesses and poets? If you don't happen to believe that the soul is immortal, that it lived for an infinitely long period before the time you were born, and that during that period it acquired knowledge of all things, do you have any reason to think that inquiry will work out?

The *Meno* marks the opening of thousands of years of philosophical inquiry into the special "Aha!" character of the kind of knowledge that Socrates claims we can recollect from our pre-lives. Later philosophers speak of this kind of knowledge as "a priori knowledge"—a phrase denoting what we know prior to experience—or "innate ideas," or "relations of ideas." They want to hold on to Socrates' notion that there is some distinct kind of knowledge at play in (for instance) geometry, access to which does not seem to depend on one's particular life-experiences, but they do not think one must characterize the activation of such knowledge as remembering what one saw in a past life.

If we set aside the peculiar details of Socrates' story about pre-life, and rely just on the philosophical theory of a priori knowledge, will that reassure our skeptic? Not necessarily. First of all, some people are just as skeptical about a priori knowledge as reincarnation. The philosopher W. V. O. Quine famously denied the existence of a priori knowledge; and even those who don't deny it outright might be inclined to limit its scope to math and logic. What guarantee do we have that ethics lies inside the space of a priori knowledge? Aren't there a lot of reasons to doubt the existence of common ground between finding the double square and finding virtue?

These are good questions, but if they are meant as an attack on Socrates, they miss the mark. After the encounter with the slave, Socrates refers back to his claims about the soul's pre-life and says:

> I do not insist that my argument is right in all other respects, but I would contend at all costs both in word and deed as far as I could that we will be better men, braver and less idle, if we believe that one must search for the things one does not know, rather than if we believe that it is not possible to find out what we do not know and that we must not look for it.[19]

It turns out that Socrates is willing to set aside not only the specifics of the theory of recollection, but even the existence of a special category of a priori knowledge. Both of those are ways to flesh out a positive response to Meno's paradox, but Socrates' real commitment is to the positive character of that response rather than to details about what happened in our past life or whether there is such a thing as knowledge held independently of experience. That is why Socrates is less concerned than subsequent philosophers have been to produce a theory about what ethical knowledge shares with the other sorts of knowledge—mathematical, logical, conceptual—that are usually recognized as a priori. Socrates' point is: Whatever it is that you think is necessary to assume in order to be able to believe in the possibility of searching for the answers to questions—which is to say real questions, by contrast with those that are really problems in question clothing—assume that. If you just believe that "one must search for things one does not know," you don't need to commit in advance to any particular theory about how recognition experiences are generated in us.

Socrates and Plato and Aristotle lived in a culture where the closest thing to the idea of what is "your own" or "native" to you or yours "by right" was the idea that it had been yours in the past. Hence the role of "autochthony"—the notion that the citizens of a given city had at some point been born from its soil—in the myths of many ancient societies, and hence the importance placed on myths and origin stories more generally. Aristotle thought that every species of organism stretched back eternally into the past. It makes sense that someone coming from such an intellectual culture, when faced with the demand to flesh out the idea of the mind's coming home to an answer it can recognize as its own, adopts the language of memory and origins. If Socrates were living in our more dynamic world*— where the understanding of life is informed by evolutionary science, where nations both have been and are increasingly expected to be shaped by mass migration, and where culture is continually subject to upheavals by new technology—Socrates might well choose to speak of the mind's destiny rather than its memories, of the future of the soul rather than its past. Speaking only for myself, I will say that

---

* To be clear, politically Socrates' world was quite dynamic: in the background were the Peloponnesian War with Sparta, in which he fought, and two occasions on which the Athenian democracy was briefly replaced by an oligarchy (411 and 404–3). But living through this sort of political instability did not lead people to welcome change; just the opposite. Aristotle says that the love of change comes from vice (*Nicomachean Ethics*, 1154b29).

I prefer to think of inquiry in terms of the aspiration to arrive at a new and better understanding—it will still need to be true that one recognizes it as such!—than in terms of gravitating back to one's forgotten origins. (I admit that it is not obvious how aspirational search enables us to recognize what we find as what we were after all along; I wrote a book in order to explain this.)[20] In any case, Socrates makes it clear that he is, at least in principle, friendly to emendations about his theory of the pre-birth lives of our souls.

That is because, in the final count, his commitment is not to the correctness of some poet's tale, nor to the existence of a distinct and unified category of items that can be known independently of experience, but rather to the possibility that there are real, genuine questions, and that improving our answers to these questions is a project worthy of our efforts. The point of the slave demonstration is not to claim that ethics is somehow "like math," except in the broadest terms: both ethics and math are sites of questions that cannot be unmasked as problems. Yes, it is true that many people experience math exclusively as a set of problems we muscle through in order to please some teacher or to proceed with some technical project, but that is not what math is for mathematicians. The image of mathematics as a closed subject in which we grind out proofs according to established rules, or perform calculations in accordance with a fixed algorithm, is a distortion many of us absorb in high school. For those who devote themselves to the study of mathematics, it is a creative activity full of surprises—such as the fact that the line that produces the double square is not commensurable with the side of the original square. Even if many of us do not approach mathematics in a spirit of real inquiry, it *can* be approached in that way. Mathematics is a site not only of problems, but also of questions.

Both math and ethics feature questions. The difference is that while a mathematical question can become untimely for the mathematician who has invested herself in it, many ethical questions are untimely for everyone. We can't avoid assuming we already have the answers to questions about how to live our lives. It follows that, like it or not, you are already on the hunt. You don't get to choose to put yourself in that situation, you already are in that situation; you only get to choose how courageously, energetically, and persistently you search.

Think of the slave. We have no reason to believe he was possessed of any fancy theory about the existence of a priori knowledge or that he knew poetry about past lives. He did not ask for and did not receive any assurance that his search was going to go anywhere, or that he would recognize the answer when he saw it. And yet he proceeded anyway, without advance guarantees, bravely stepping forward into the mathematical unknown, making mistakes, recovering from them, and in the end achieving real progress. What Socrates demonstrates, with the slave's help, is that *that* is a way a person can be. Socrates is asking Meno to be inspired by the courage of his slave: Be bold and inquire.

XENOPHON RECOUNTS THE FATE of Meno in terms that rival Alcibiades': as a general under Cyrus, Meno showed himself to be greedy, treacherous, and incompetent.[21] He dies young, after being tortured for a year. If the conversation that Plato describes actually took place—and there is some reason to doubt that it did—it may well have represented the best hours of Meno's life.

The cases of Clitophon, Alcibiades, and Meno should be set alongside those of Socrates' more successful long-term associates, such as Plato, Xenophon, Theaetetus, and all the participants in the *Phaedo* (we will meet them in chapter 11). Socrates did not always fail to have a positive impact on the lives around him. Nonetheless, he very clearly did fail sometimes, and Plato wanted to draw those failures to our attention. If Socrates' interlocutors have a problem sustaining Socratic optimism about the process of inquiry, I anticipate that the reader of this book—even if, as I hope, her life never sinks to the depths of a Meno or an Alcibiades—will also have such a problem. She wants to be able to believe in philosophical progress, but she is not sure that it has anything positive, anything substantive, to offer her. And so, this is the moment to point out that it already has.

V. WHAT IS THINKING?

We can summarize the conclusions of the three chapters of part two, including this chapter, as follows: The Socratic method is inquisitive refutation, refutation cures normative self-blindness, inquiry allows us to ask questions (as opposed to solving problems). These claims, taken together, add up to an answer to the question with which this chapter began: What is thinking?

I am going to define thinking by describing the paradigmatic case, and then I will explain how various kinds of peripheral cases are related to it.

Thinking is, paradigmatically, a social quest for better answers to the sorts of questions that show up for us already answered. It is a quest because it has a built-in endpoint: knowledge. It is social because it operates by resolving disagreements between people. Thinking begins when Socrates, or someone like him, recognizes that his account of justice, or piety, or love is not as good as it could be—which is to say, that it does not qualify as knowledge. This realization prompts him to ask another person for help inquiring into questions such as, "Is it beneficial to be just?" "Who is worthy of love?" and "What is piety?" Socrates plays the role of Clifford, using his answer to examine the one provided by his interlocutor, who plays the role of James. If the interlocutor's first attempt at an answer is refuted, he tries another, and then another. If one of the interlocutor's answers holds up against Socratic pressure, they come to agree on that; otherwise—and this is what we see in Plato's dialogues—it doesn't, and the process of refutation draws Socrates' answer out of him, which becomes the shared conclusion. Either way, the two parties come to agree. This does not mean that the quest is completed: both parties can go on to subject what they have agreed on to further tests of the same kind in future disagreements with others. Each time the answer passes, it becomes more firmly "tied down" with the very arguments used to explain its preferability.

This is thinking. It is completed when one arrives at an answer that is perfectly stable. The arguments with which it has been definitively "tied down" can then be conveyed to others, and this is why, if one has knowledge, one can teach it to others. Thinking is the road from ignorance about the most important things to knowledge about them.

Here is another way to put my definition: Thinking is using the Socratic method to inquire into untimely questions. But we can also use the Socratic method to inquire into other sorts of questions, as in the case of the slave and the double square. We can call that "thinking," too, with the understanding that we are referencing its resemblance to the paradigmatic case. We can also use the Socratic method when what we have on our hands is not a question but a problem, because any problem can, in the right social context, be turned into a question: "What is the solution to this problem?" If the parties pursue the answer to this question using inquisitive refutation, we can call that conversation "thinking" as well. Finally, in the usage of "thinking" that diverges most from the core of my definition, we can use the word "thinking" to describe a process that is not conversational at all—perhaps it takes place in someone's head, or on a sheet of paper—but has the potential to be integrated into a conversation, because it stands open to the sorts of corrections and clarifications that are associated with Socratic refutation. A dream sequence would not qualify, but a chain of reasoning would, and so would an arithmetical calculation, or even an idea for the plot of a novel.

This definition of thinking inverts the usual order of importance between the inner and the outer: the standard approach to thinking privileges what is private and unvoiced and "in the head" as the core case, so that what happens in conversation counts as thinking only insofar as it is an outer echo of an inner event: "thinking out loud." I could not have opened this book with the definition of thinking I have just provided, because some readers would have immediately rejected it for failing to correspond to ordinary usage, while others would have too freely accepted it, on the grounds that they do not mind my using the word "thinking" however I see fit. The first set of readers would have anticipated a dictionary definition, which is a summary of our linguistic practices in relation to a word, while the second set would have assumed I was offering a stipulative definition, of the sort that might appear in the opening of a proof: "Let A represent . . . " If you are giving a dictionary definition, you are beholden to ordinary usage, whereas if you are giving a stipulative definition, you get free rein to use any word to mean anything you like, as long as you are clear about what stands for what.

My definition of thinking is not a dictionary definition, and it is not a stipulative definition; rather, it is a Socratic definition. A Socratic definition must come at the end, and not the beginning, of a process of inquiry: it is the upshot of having figured out what something really is. (By contrast, my definition of the phrase "untimely question" [see chapter 2, p. 55] *was* stipulative, an invention of my own. I introduced it early in the book, not in order to explain anything, but simply in order to have a convenient handle by which to refer to something that I would go on to explain.)

Unlike stipulative definitions, a Socratic definition can be the target of objections: it is possible to claim that the definition is somehow mistaken, that we ought to emend it or discard it altogether. Unlike in the case of dictionary definitions, you cannot object to a Socratic definition merely by pointing to linguistic conventions. The fact that it stands in some tension to how we usually talk won't necessarily constitute an objection to a Socratic definition, because a Socratic definition is itself the product of arguments, and those arguments give you leverage to criticize how we usually talk.

The argument for the definition I have given can be stated in two premises: First, in order for someone to be thinking, they must keep an open mind and inquire, moving toward what's true and away from what's false. If a series of images flash before your eyes, or follow one another in your daydreams or night dreams, that is not yet thinking—thinking requires subjecting such representations to some minimal standards of thoughtfulness. Second, thinking must, at least in principle, be capable of processing any kind of thought. Unlike "multiplying," or "remembering," or "updating," or "analyzing," or "planning," terms that reference specific forms of thinking, thinking itself is an all-purpose activity, accommodating all possible thoughts. Thinking must be the biggest possible tent.

The three chapters in part two have argued that it is the Socratic method that allows us to think about untimely questions in an open-minded, inquisitive, and truth-directed manner.* But the Socratic method is hospitable to narrower forms of thought as well: an interlocutor is free to introduce the results of memory, or analysis, or multiplication into the conversation, as the slave does, when he uses multiplication to find the area of various squares. In one dialogue, Socrates and his interlocutor venture into the interpretation of poetry. There is no algorithm that can be used to answer an untimely question, because an untimely question is not a problem. But any algorithm can, at least in principle, be subjected to the checking procedure of the Socratic method. We can ask, of the algorithm, "Was it used correctly?" or "Should it have been used in the first place?" or "What was it used for?" and we can pursue this inquiry in an open-minded, truth-oriented, and inquisitive way. More generally: anything that you could potentially disagree with in that open-minded, truth oriented, and inquisitive way can be subjected to the Socratic method.

Imagine that there is something you want to think about, because it is desperately important to you to arrive at a better understand-

---

* I do not claim to have argued that it is *only* the Socratic method that accomplishes this, but I have yet to encounter another method that does. Once one has shown that a very difficult challenge can indeed be met in a particular way, the burden of proof shifts onto to those who positively claim the existence of alternatives. If anyone meets it, I will be happy to modify my definition into a disjunction.

ing, but you don't have any antecedently vouchsafed procedure for thinking about it. There is no mechanism you can rely on to check your thinking against it, no process to ensure that your thinking is proceeding in a productive, correct fashion instead of veering wildly off course. You don't have an algorithm or decision procedure to keep you honest. Are you lost? No. Even in this situation, you can still think about what you need to think about, you are not left out in the cold, because even when there is no existing problem-solving mechanism you can rely on, there is still—other people. The Socratic method is how you think about things that you couldn't think about if it were not for the presence of other people, which is to say, it is how you think about *just anything*. The method that allows you to think about *anything*, leaving nothing behind, in its wake, as unthinkable—that method is rightly called "thinking."

On this definition, if I multiply 4 × 5 and get 20, it is not obvious that what I have done counts as thinking. I do not think this is an absurd claim. Return to the question at the opening of this chapter, a question that animates many people in our world today: "will computers ever be able to think?" The reason this strikes people as a difficult question is also a reason to hesitate over whether 4 × 5 = 20 is thinking. Someone who is convinced that deploying an algorithm such as multiplication amounts to thinking must concede not only that nonhuman calculators think, but that they are much better at it than we are.

On a Socratic account, the use of an algorithm—for example, multiplication—counts as thinking insofar as it is, at least in principle, subject to questioning. Multiplication is thinking if it is possible for someone to call into question whether the multiplication was done correctly, to request an explanation of why multiplication was used, and to potentially convince the one using it that an alternative arithmetic operation—or none at all—might have been a better choice. The algorithmic activity of a handheld calculator is not embedded in this sort of broader intellectual openness to questioning and challenge, but if a nonhuman computational device—such as a large language model—developed to the point where it were, Socrates would be happy to say that it is thinking. The fact that it is silicon-based instead of being realized in neuronal tissue would be entirely irrelevant, from a Socratic point of view.

Socrates would thus accept a modified version of the Turing test. On Turing's version, a computer counts as thinking if it seems more human, to the evaluator, than the actual human being that the computer is being compared to. This test would not satisfy Socrates. He would point out that even in his time, it was possible to produce convincing imitations of humans: painted statues, for instance. To count as thinking, Socrates will require that the computer fool us in a specific way: by playing either the role of James, or the role of Clifford, well enough to help us inquire into some untimely question. In order to qualify as a thinker, it is not enough that the computer imitate a human being. It has to imitate a human being who is, in the paradigmatic sense of the word, thinking.

Part three of this book is devoted to showing you the concrete fruits of thinking, in the Socratic sense, not in the area of geometry but in what I believe to be the three most difficult areas of human life: romantic love, facing one's own death, and the minefield of problems that goes under the heading of "politics." You may not be as inclined to agree with Socrates' conclusions about politics, love, and death as you are to agree with his conclusions about geometry, but you will have an opportunity to see the Socratic philosophical machinery sink its teeth into the mess of everyday life.

Inquire, with an open mind, seeking the truth and avoiding falsity. We have explored why using this method is not as straightforward as it initially appeared. Now we will see where it can take us.

Part Three

SOCRATIC
ANSWERS

Introduction to Part Three:

The Socratizing Move

O VER THE COURSE OF THE SOCRATIC DIALOGUES, SOC-
rates makes three claims to specialized expertise. He claims
to be an expert in politics, in love, and in facing death. It would be
striking for anyone to claim mastery over such vast territory, but it
is even more remarkable for Socrates to do so, given his trademark
protestations of ignorance. How can Socrates both know nothing
and at the same time boast of his in-depth knowledge of arguably the
three most important domains of human experience?

Here is Socrates talking about each domain:

> *Politics:* "I believe that I'm one of a few Athenians—so
> as not to say I'm the only one, but the only one among
> our contemporaries—to take up the true political craft
> and practice the true politics."[1]

> *Love:* "The only thing I say I understand is the art of
> love"; "my expertise at love."[2]

> *Death:* "The one aim of those who practice philoso-
> phy in the proper manner is to practice for dying and
> death"; "those who practice philosophy in the right way
> are in training for dying and they fear death least of all
> people."[3]

When talking about love, Socrates says he understands only one
thing: love. And yet, he also claims that he understands death and

politics. If these claims are to be consistent with one another, the art of love, the craft of politics, and the preparation for death must be attributable to the same underlying ability. What could that be? Look at the quotes about death. Socrates' point seems not to be that he, individually, happens to be well prepared for death. His point is, rather, that it belongs to and is characteristic of the philosopher as such to have been engaged in the preparation for death. By inquiring into untimely questions, every philosopher has, all along, been preparing himself for death. If we extend that argument to the other cases, we arrive at the conclusion that somehow the trademark ignorance of the philosopher itself amounts to expertise in the domains of love and death and politics.

This is quite an astonishing claim—that the practice of Socratic ignorance is a kind mastery of the deepest things. The mechanism of this reversal is something that I call "the Socratizing move."

Let me introduce the Socratizing move with an example from my own life. One day, a student who was puzzled and intrigued by a sentence from Aristotle's *De Anima* told me he was considering getting the sentence tattooed onto his arm. I said: "Why don't you try to understand it instead? That's like tattooing it onto your soul." In claiming that the tattoo he was thinking of getting stood for the interpretative clarity he really wanted, I was Socratizing the concept of a tattoo. What the student sought, by means of the tattoo, was to develop a permanent connection with an idea—but the real way to do that, I claimed, is to understand it. You Socratize something when you show that it must be understood in the light of something else, something of which it is the imitation.

In general, the Socratizing move takes the form "A is the real B." For example, "Understanding is the real tattoo." With this move, Socrates scrapes the dust and cobwebs off of an ordinary or everyday concept and reveals it to be something higher, more transcendent, more demanding, and often more real than we had thought. "A is the real B" means that B wavers in the way the image of a house, reflected in water, wavers, whereas A is the stable and unwavering house.

"Socratizing" has the opposite effect of the reductive or deflation-
ary or unmasking approach that is usually expressed with the phrase
"nothing but": love is nothing but hormones, appreciation of opera
is nothing but posturing, higher education is nothing but a means of
signaling to employers, helping others is nothing but a way to feel
good about oneself, colors are nothing but wavelengths of light, Cartesian skepticism is nothing but a confusion, philosophy is nothing
but a language game. Where "nothing but" demotes, Socratizing
promotes. One facet of Socratizing is that it moves upward rather
than downward. The other is that it is systematic.

We can distinguish the one-off cynicism of someone who says,
of a specific X, that it is nothing but Y—for instance, by dismissing
opera lovers as pretentious—from the systematic, unified reductiv-
ism adopted by theorists who have found a way to argue that a large
share of important human phenomena are, at bottom, "nothing but"
something else. So, for example, to take some famous thinkers, Sig-
mund Freud argues that many things that do not appear to have anything to do with sex should nonetheless be understood in terms of it,
and Karl Marx makes that claim for class relations, Michel Foucault
for power, René Girard for imitation.

The economist Gary Becker wrote, "All human behavior can
be regarded as involving participants who maximize their utility
from a stable set of preferences and accumulate an optimal amount
of information and other inputs in a variety of markets."[4] Becker
thought that the tools of economic analysis could be applied not
only to those transactions traditionally understood as economic—
buying and selling—but also to marriage and racial discrimination
and crime and child-raising and more. The sociologist Erving Goffman showed how the concept of "performance" is applicable to a
wide range of human behavior: not only on the stage, but in everyday life, we put on a show that involves the concealment of conflicting information that has been relegated to a "backstage." In their
book, *Elephant in the Brain: Hidden Motives in Everyday Life*,[5]
Robin Hanson and Kevin Simler argue, with reference to domains

as diverse as conversation, health care, laughter, education, charity, art, politics, and religion, that our motives are lower—more self-ish, more self-deceived, more biologically driven—than we usually believe they are.

All of these thinkers—Freud, Marx, Girard, Becker, Goffman, Hanson, and Simler—make what we might call the anti-Socratizing move: taking a large and apparently heterogenous field of human phenomena and saying that it is best understood in terms of something lower than what it appeared to be. Many scientific approaches, when applied to human phenomena, amount to anti-Socratizing: the neuroscientist who wants to tell us that what appeared to be choices and intentions and values were "really nothing but" electrical signals in our brains, or the evolutionary psychologist who explains these phenomena in terms of selection pressures on our ancestors, both belong to the family of anti-Socratizers.

Socrates unified domains as distinct as love, death, and politics not by analyzing them in terms of some underlying common denom-inator, but rather by seeing them as converging upward toward a single aspiration: inquiry into untimely questions. Instead of arguing that these domains all have a common source or cause or are built up out of common materials, Socrates argues that what they have in common is a *goal*. To frame the point in Aristotelian terminol-ogy: anti-Socratizing unifies by way of a common material cause, whereas Socratizing unifies by way of a common final cause. The Socratizing move seeks out the coherent reality behind the incoher-ent imitation of the reality that shows up in our everyday lives, and it often reveals that what was going on in everyday life was something very different from what it had appeared to be, for example: war is really a form of conversation.

The Socratizing move is at the heart of Socratic intellectualism. Socrates claimed that each of the traditional virtues of justice, cour-age, moderation, and piety is to be equated with knowledge. Virtue is identical to, which is to say, *is nothing other than*, knowledge. Soc-rates thought that if you had knowledge of what to do, you wouldn't need to rely on anything extrinsic to it—not virtues plural, not "will-power," not the luck of being blessed with a compliant natural disposition—in order to act correctly. On the traditional understanding of the virtues, courage is necessary to rouse a person to do what, even when it is known to be "the right thing to do," is nonetheless difficult to do; likewise, the virtue of moderation is how you avoid overindulging in what you know to be a harmful bodily pleasures. This traditional picture makes the virtues out to be something over and above knowledge about what to do, whereas on a Socratic picture, there is only knowledge. When Socrates insists that no one ever acts against their knowledge of what they should do, this is sometimes described as a "denial of weakness of will," but it is more accurate to say that Socrates is Socratizing weakness of will. Weakness of will is really ignorance.

If knowledge is the end-all and be-all, then we should expect the activity that is directed at knowledge—philosophical inquiry—to be how a person develops courage, justice, moderation, and so on. And Socrates does, I think, hold that insofar as virtue is to be found among those who are ignorant, it is to be found, first and foremost, inside of philosophical conversation. The usual view is that the arena in which we train for courage is the battlefield; for moderation the dining table or bedroom; for piety religious ritual; for justice the courtroom. The Socratic view is that real courage and moderation and piety and justice are manifested in speech, and, more specifically, in the back-and-forth of inquisitive refutation.

Socrates is making the radical claim that, for ignorant people like us, human goodness is primarily expressed in how a person conducts herself in inquiry, and that conversation is where we find our true home. This amounts to the Socratization of the whole of life. Instead of trying to explore this claim in its full generality, I will shrink my task to the still formidable one of explaining Socrates' claim to expertise in politics, love, and death. Let us examine what the three most important domains of human life look like when they have been Socratized.

Chapter 8

Politics:
Justice and Liberty

WHEN WE LOOK AT OTHER SOCIETIES, ESPECIALLY
those in the distant past, certain political fictions stand
out to us: how they attributed to some individuals a God-given right
to rule over others (the divine right of kings); how myths of autochthony allowed them to understand themselves as descendants of an
original set of citizens sprung from the soil; how they relied on a
caste system that sorted people by birth to determine their social
role; how they conceived of slavery as divinely sanctioned, morally
acceptable, natural, or all of the above; how they assumed gender or
race or religion should restrict someone's political role.

I call these fictions "political" because they pertain not only to
how people live together, but more specifically to the question of
whose ideas about how to live together count, and to what degree.
To say that human beings are *social* picks out the fact that a normal
human life is a life spent with other humans; to say that we are *political* means something more specific, which is that we live together
under a shared idea of how to do so. The set of fictions listed above
are attempts to mitigate the fundamental problem of politics, which
is that we sometimes have trouble living together, because we have
different ideas about how best to do so. One way to handle that problem is to decide that some people's ideas don't count, or don't count
as much as others'. I call the ideas I listed "fictions" because, well,
it's obvious that that's what they are—made-up stories that serve
as ad hoc justification for a political arrangement. Or rather, that is

obvious to us today. People living under those ideas didn't tend to see them as fictions, but as reality.

Identifying political fictions in other cultures is easy. In this chapter and the next, I am going to take on the harder task of identifying political fictions in our own culture. When more enlightened future people look back on us, and they say, "These ideas are obviously just stories made up ad hoc to justify some political arrangement," which ideas will they be referring to? Which of our ideas will they classify alongside autochthony, slavery, the caste system, and the conceit that women and racial minorities were incapable of participating in governance? I believe that future critics of our current political order will identify, as political fictions, what might be called the liberalism triad: freedom of speech, egalitarianism, and the fight for social justice.

These two chapters (8 and 9) will not show that any of those three ideas are false or mistaken or deserving of being discarded. I am not an enlightened future person, but a creature of my own time—and, while I certainly hope that this book will survive long enough to eventually be encountered by enlightened future people, it can only do so by first addressing people who are, like me, in the thrall of the liberal ideas of free speech, egalitarianism, and the fight for social justice. While I won't repudiate any of those ideas, I will, with the help of the Platonic dialogue the *Gorgias*, make the case that they are not valid as they stand. Each of the three is an image: a distorted, imperfect, partial reflection of another thing. Instead of trying to eliminate any of these ideas, I will be Socratizing them.

Socrates is famous for having withdrawn from politics in a city where respectable citizens prided themselves on taking part in it. In the *Apology* he describes himself as having led "a private, not a public, life"[1] and explains that "if I had long ago attempted to take part in politics, I should have died long ago."[2] In the *Gorgias* Callicles criticizes Socrates for this decision, arguing that the pastime of philosophizing is appropriate for the young, but that it is "unmanly" to live one's whole life "in hiding, whispering in a corner with three or four boys."[3] So both according to Socrates' own self-understanding, and according to the understanding of others, he lived an unusually apolitical life.

On the other hand, Socrates also describes himself as someone who has spent his life having engaged in politics. Politics is one of Socrates' three areas of self-professed expertise alongside love and death. He describes himself as God's gift to the city of Athens, and says, "I believe that I'm one of a few Athenians—so as not to say I'm the only one, but the only one among our contemporaries—to take up the true political craft and practice the true politics."[4] Socrates claims to be not only a politician, but *the* preeminent politician of Athens. How could Socrates be both the most apolitical and the most political man at once?

The answer is that he understood what is usually called politics as a stage on which philosophical disagreement gets dramatized. Those bent on getting and keeping political power make a show of navigating disagreements about how to live together, and of producing agreements about how to live together—but it's only a show. Philosophy is how you actually navigate such disagreements. Philosophy is the real politics, which means that without ever stepping onto the political stage, Socrates could look at those who had done so, and see that they were mimicking him. That is why the Socratizing move worked so well on Socrates' politically active interlocutors. It continues to work, 2,500 years later, because when we engage in politics today, we are still imitating Socrates. Socrates can show us that our political ideals are not what they appear to be.

These two chapters on Socratic politics contain three counterintuitive assertions about politics. First, you cannot fight injustice. The conceit that you can is based on symbolically transposing a disagreement about justice into another arena, where it can be fought over as a contest. When people think that they are fighting injustice, they are, instead, imitating refutation. Second, all of our standard answers to the question of what it is for speech to be free—the first amendment, the marketplace of ideas, persuasion, debate—fall short of capturing a coherent sense of freedom. Speech is free if, and only if, it is inquisitive. Finally, with reference to equality, which is the subject of chapter 9, we need to distinguish between what mitigates the feeling of inequality in one or another context—the elimination of discrimination, the absence of large disparities in opportunities or wealth or recognition, the presence of many different kinds of symbolic tokens of respect—from what it actually means for one person to treat another as their equal, which is a matter of whether they can take one another seriously even when they disagree about what is most important.

A glance in the Socratic mirror reveals that our three most cherished political ideals—justice, freedom, and equality—are, in fact, intellectual ideals. They are norms that pertain, in the first instance, to the shared quest for knowledge. Our current practice of politics is riddled with puzzling features that vanish once we restore our ideals to their proper context. Socratic intellectualism promises to set politics straight.

I. Politicization

When, at the age of ten, I became a naturalized US citizen, there was an error on my naturalization papers: my gender was listed as male. My father refused to have the error corrected, because to do so he would have had to mail back the papers, and he was worried about what might happen if the only legal document that established my identity got lost in transit. I didn't object to this, or see myself as being "misgendered," at least not in any objectionable sense. And this in spite of the fact that my father often used the male pronoun, "he," to refer to me (which was, very likely, the cause of the mistake in the first place). In my native language, Hungarian, pronouns aren't gendered: "he" and "she" are the same word, ő. I learned English at a young enough age that gendered pronouns give me no trouble, but the same is not true of my parents. To this day, they still regularly get "he" and "she" mixed up; no one takes offense. When my parents use the wrong pronoun, this is seen as an innocent mistake—even if they continued to make that mistake, over and over again, for decades.

By contrast, today questions about pronouns—for example, the question of whether you go out of your way to announce your pronouns, or go out of your way to avoid doing so; the question of whether you take care to use an individual's chosen pronoun, or make a show of not doing so; the question of whether there are additional pronouns available to an individual besides "he" or "she," and so on—have become proxies for a deeper disagreement. Answers to these questions signify moves in a dispute—about the relationship between gender and biology—whose primary location is not language. The dispute about gender is not conducted *as* a dispute about gender. Instead, it is transposed onto a variety of battlefields, from pronouns to bathrooms to inclusion criteria for women's sports.

I call this phenomenon "politicization." "Politicization" is a commonly used word that is rarely defined, even though the concept it refers to is difficult to understand. We all think we know what it means, but I am not sure that we do, so let me specify exactly how I understand it: politicization is the displacement of a disagreement from the context of argumentation into a zero-sum context where if one party wins, the other loses. It converts a question—which of two positions is correct—into a competition between the interests of two parties.

If someone claims that a given topic—be it the minimum wage, climate change, the Covid pandemic, or college course syllabi—has been "politicized," they mean that actions and speech on that topic have to be interpreted against the backdrop of some standing conflict. So, for example, the ostentatious inclusion or removal of a text from my syllabus can constitute a way of positioning myself in a culture war: I might be providing assurances to my allies, or I might be provoking my enemies.

When people criticize "polarized" politics, they should, I think, speak instead of politicization. Polarization is not, in and of itself, a bad thing. A philosophy conference featuring views polarized into two camps won't necessarily be less interesting to attend than one where the views expressed in the talks are more evenly distributed over a range of intermediate positions; and many of us are more interested in watching a movie that "polarizes" people in the sense that you either love it or hate it, than in watching one that everyone thinks is merely OK. Furthermore, thought is by nature polarized, in that every well-formed proposition is either true or false.

Extreme polarization without politicization is fine; politicization is the real problem. Whenever some topic seems "touchy" or "charged," that is a good sign of politicization; another is if the answers tend to map perfectly onto existing battle lines. For instance, climate change and abortion have become politicized, to the extent that they are arenas within which a battle between the political Right and the political Left is adjudicated. When laws are passed making it more difficult to secure an abortion, that constitutes a "defeat" for the Left, whereas a new climate deal could be a "victory" for them.

When you are not personally invested, and you observe others debating some charged topic, you notice options neither side seems to consider, and possibilities for compromise that both sides have ruled out in advance. You see that the welfare of groups who stand to be harmed or benefited by the resolution of the issue are suddenly of paramount concern to those who showed little concern for those groups earlier. You conclude that the debaters are not really talking about what they claim they are talking about.

It is worth emphasizing that "politicization" should not be understood as synonymous with "politics," though people sometimes use the word "politics" that way—for example, when we speak of "office politics," we mean office *infighting*. Politicians often say, "Let's keep politics out of this," using "politics" as shorthand for "what's politicized"—they mean, let's temporarily suspend our usual practice of mapping every interaction onto a symbolic battlefield. Nonetheless, the actual practice of politics involves a lot more than fighting; politicization is a *pathology* of politics. Moreover, politicization—

the mapping of a disagreement onto a contest—is not restricted to the political sphere. Far from it. In every marriage there are one or more topics that could be described as "politicized." In the early stages of my own, laundry was an example: it was a place I could reliably find a fight, if I wanted to pick one. (Ever since we resolved this with an "everyone in the family does their own laundry" policy, I have had to look elsewhere.)

Politicization is a phenomenon all of us encounter, and many of us strongly dislike, but no one was ever so allergic to it as Socrates. The substantive disagreements he is trying to have with people—that he has devoted his life to—are always on the verge of being projected onto a battle of egos. He has a standing fear that his interlocutor will misinterpret him as someone who wants to employ combative, coercive tactics to "win" some battle. He expresses that concern to the esteemed orator Gorgias:

> I'm asking questions so that we can conduct an orderly discussion. It's not you I'm after; it's to prevent our get-ting in the habit of second-guessing and snatching each other's statements away ahead of time. It's to allow you to work out your assumption in any way you want to.[5]

Socrates draws a contrast between the kind of conversation he wants to have with Gorgias and how arguments usually go:

> If they're disputing some point and one maintains that the other isn't right or isn't clear, they get irritated, each thinking the other is speaking out of spite. They become eager to win instead of investigating the subject under discussion. In fact, in the end some have a most shame-ful parting of the ways, abuse heaped upon them, having given and gotten to hear such things that make even the

bystanders upset with themselves for having thought it worthwhile to come to listen to such people.[6]

Disagreement tends to fuel an "eagerness to win," which manifests itself in the practices Socrates described himself as wanting to avoid: "second-guessing and snatching each other's statements away ahead of time." Each person misinterprets or twists the words of the other in such a way as to clear the path toward argumentative victory for himself; eventually this degenerates into shameful, abusive speech. Socrates finds this sort of thing intolerable, and so he wants to make very clear the difference between what he aims to do—"to allow you to work out your assumption in any way you want to"— with the kind of coercive speech that typically characterizes verbal disputes and debates. Socrates explains *why* he is so worried that Gorgias will allow their conversation to devolve into a battle:

> I think you're now saying things that aren't very consistent or compatible with what you were first saying about oratory. So, I'm afraid to pursue my examination of you, for fear that you should take me to be speaking with eagerness to win against you, rather than to have our subject become clear.[7]

Socrates understands that people are inclined to interpret counterargument *symbolically*, as though the opponent were trying to defeat the idea by making its holder lose face. When people feel that they are—or are about to be—attacked, they respond in kind. This is what Socrates calls "eagerness to win." When each party escalates to ever more coercive language in a preemptive defense against being on the receiving end of the same, conversation becomes politicized. Events in the conversation will start to be viewed symbolically, as standing for wins or losses for either side. Socrates only wants to continue the conversation with Gorgias if Gorgias can take him literally.

We might think: *of course* Gorgias is going to get a bit miffed or defensive if Socrates starts trying to refute him, but Socrates believes there's no "of course" about it. The following quote is so emblematic of Socrates that I used it to introduce him to you, in the opening of this book:

> For my part, I'd be pleased to continue questioning you if you're the same kind of person I am, otherwise I would drop it. And what kind of person am I? One of those who would be pleased to be refuted if I say anything untrue, and who would be pleased to refute anyone who says anything untrue; one who, however, wouldn't be any less pleased to be refuted than to refute. For I count being refuted a greater good, insofar as it is a greater good for oneself to be delivered from the worst thing there is than to deliver someone else from it. I don't suppose there's anything quite so bad for a person as having false belief about the things we're discussing right now. So if you say you're this kind of person, too, let's continue the discussion; but if you think we should drop it, let's be done with it and break it off.[8]

Unlike most people in such a situation, Socrates does not suggest that he and Gorgias each agree to put up with criticism gracefully, to contain any resentment and guard against expressing any irritation they might feel. Instead, Socrates claims that he is not susceptible to the negative responses to refutation, because from his point of view, being refuted—which is to say, sitting on the being persuaded end of persuasion—is *pleasant* and calls for *gratitude*. Indeed, later in the *Gorgias* he claims that refutation is the greatest favor one human being can do another.[9] What makes Socrates seem unreal to his interlocutors is that he found a way to scrub away the symbolism that everyone else feels compelled to layer on top of any conversation that involves criticism, pushback, or resistance. He is pleased to refute his interlocutors, and *no less pleased to be refuted.* Socrates doesn't care that the refuter is conventionally "assigned" the label of winner; Socrates feels free to "count being refuted a greater good" because he has not politicized the conversation.* He sees no conflict of interest between himself and his interlocutor.

This is why Socrates' suggestion to Gorgias was not that they agree to put up with criticism gracefully, or to contain any resentment over loss, but rather to insist that in refutation, both parties benefit. Socrates is trying to convey the thought that this is not a war, or a competition, or a contest, or a duel, or a race. More generally: it is not the kind of event that has been symbolically organized into a zero-sum structure. Only in a symbolically mediated conflict does the benefit to one party entail the loss to another. Absent such a symbolic arrangement, my interests might fail to coincide with yours in the sense that it is unlikely we'll both get what we want, but the event of my doing well will nonetheless be conceptually separable from the event of your doing poorly. A head-on conflict of interest—my win is your loss—means that the interaction between the parties has been mediated by symbolism.

Socrates is trying to tell Gorgias: *This is not a game, or a contest, or a competition, or a fight. I am trying to interact with you directly.* Socrates and his interlocutor are on the hunt for the answer to a question, and, if they clear away a mistaken answer, they have made progress that harms no one, and especially benefits the person from

---

* If someone wishes to stipulate, as a linguistic matter, that "being refuted" is equivalent to "losing the argument"—and thus that those who are refuted lose—Socrates will not object to this, so long as the person allows that losing can sometimes be good for a person. Socrates will also allow you to stipulate, as a linguistic matter, that it is part of the meaning of "lose" that losing is (always) bad for the person who loses. What he won't let you do is stipulate *both* that losing is bad, *and* that being refuted is losing, because at that point you've disguised a substantive claim as a semantic one.

whom it was cleared away. A disagreement is a head-on conflict—if I am right then you are wrong—but it is not a conflict of interest, and thus need not be interpreted in zero-sum terms. A disagreement *can be* symbolically organized into a zero-sum game, but it needn't be. Socrates thinks it shouldn't be, because what we want to work out is not who wins, but who is right. A fight is a conflict of interest, and a disagreement that has been turned into a fight stands at a symbolic remove from the adjudication of the disagreement. When we are working out who wins, we are, at best, *pretending* to be working out who is right.

Suppose I attack *you* on the basis of an idea you have, setting up some kind of a duel or contest between us in which one of us will be the winner. Each of us might see ourselves as "fighting injustice," but we are not, because even if I win, the idea in you may nonetheless remain intact. Suppose I kill you: still others may take up the idea on your behalf. This is exactly what Socrates thinks will happen to philosophy after he is put to death—others will continue to practice it. Socrates understands that his refutational activities have upset his fellow citizens, but he warns them that you cannot kill philosophy by killing Socrates: "You are wrong if you believe that by killing people you will prevent anyone from reproaching you for not living in the right way."[10]

Socrates holds that when you fight with someone, you are pretending to argue with them. Let's explore that radical claim more carefully.

II. FIGHTING IS PRETEND ARGUING

In the *Alcibiades* and the *Euthyphro*, Socrates describes hostility, fighting, and war as arising from disagreements over justice and injustice. As evidence for this claim, consider the opening of Homer's *Iliad*. Agamemnon has taken Chryseis, daughter of Chryses, as his prize, and her father asks for her back. Having been turned down, Chryses prays to Apollo to punish the Greeks:

Lord of the silver bow, now hear my prayer!
Great guardian of Tenedos and Chryse
and sandy Cilla! Mouse Lord! If I ever
built temples to your liking, ever burned
fat thighs of oxen or of goats for you,
fulfill this prayer for me, and let the Greeks
suffer your arrows to avenge my tears![11]

The result of this prayer is that Apollo inflicts a plague on the Greeks, who eventually figure out why they are being plagued, forcing Agamemnon, their leader, to give Chryses back his daughter. You might wonder, looking back at Chryses' speech: if you are in a position to call in favors from a God, why not, instead of asking him to make the Greeks suffer, just ask for your daughter back directly? The answer is that Chryses is angry, he feels he has been wronged, and he wants vindication. Earlier, he wanted his daughter back; now, he wants to teach the Greeks a lesson. The saga of Chryses and his daughter is the whole Trojan war in miniature: it wasn't the pragmatic need to retrieve Menelaus' wife that launched a thousand ships so much as the wounded pride of the men sailing in them. And so Socrates was right to describe war as, in large part, an attempt to prove that one is right—which is to say, to settle a disagreement.

Typically, if you didn't think that someone was wrong about something, there would be nothing to be fighting *over*. If you strike or coerce someone in the absence of such a point of contention, you would not see yourself as fighting them, but instead just as using force on them to achieve a goal. When I fight you, I exercise force on you *as though* I were exercising force on some idea associated with you—I am not just using force on you, but I am using it agonistically, in the context of a contest that aims to "support" or "stand up for" some principle. The disagreement has been displaced from its original home, which was a disagreement over that principle. Instead of actually settling it by argument, we pretend to settle it by way of a zero-sum contest. In a fight, there is always a conflict of interest.

A Socratic definition of fighting would be something like this: fighting is politicized arguing. Whether we politicize the argument by using physical force, or emotional force, or whether we fight more indirectly, by way of proxies—think of how, in an especially acrimonious divorce, the ex-spouses might use their children to get at each other—what unifies all the fighting that we do is that the fight represents an argument we are not having.

But aren't there cases in which we fight others without fighting "over" any point of disagreement? For example, if there is only room for one of us on the lifeboat, as I push you off it, I might say "No offense, nothing personal," to signal that there is no real disagreement between us. Or consider a situation where one uses physical force against a child for their own good. If getting you off the lifeboat, or getting the child to stop running into the intersection, required a protracted struggle, I might describe myself as "fighting" you or the child, even though there is no disagreement I am trying to resolve by way of that use of force. Or consider two nonhuman animals wrangling over a piece of meat or a mate—we might say that they are fighting each other.

It is fair to raise these as counterexamples to the principle that those who fight see themselves as settling a dispute; nonetheless, as long as we admit that they are not core cases of fighting, and that they are classified as fighting with reference to those core cases, the principle stands. We call the uses of force in the lifeboat case, or the child protection case, or the animal wrangling case "fighting" to the extent that they bear an outward resemblance to, and therefore remind us of, the fights that *are* animated by self-righteous anger over disagreement. If it is true that fighting imitates argument, then it makes sense that we are capacious in being willing to apply the term "fight" to what imitates *that*: "being an image of" is a transitive relation.

Even metaphorical uses of fighting support the analysis I've given here. Consider: When we decide to describe ourselves as *fighting* cancer instead of simply as undergoing treatment with the hope of survival, we employ the metaphor of fighting because it allows us to see ourselves as standing up for something. The feeling that I am upholding a principle gives me energy, motivation, and optimism: I deserve to live! I'm not going to let this cancer take my life away from me! When you decide to "stand up and fight" against an attacker instead of running away from them, you are energized by the thought that they are in the wrong, and you are in the right. You are standing up *for yourself*, as though you yourself were a principle or idea or concept that you could defend by means of fists or insults. People sometimes describe their political enemies as "questioning my right to exist," a framing that facilitates the interpretation that in defending myself against those enemies, I am defending a principle: my right to exist.

The problem in each of these cases is that the level of ideas and principles, and the level of fists, swords, scalpels, and insults, are detached from one another.

The glorification of violence is only possible if we imagine some principle is at stake, and that principle is being upheld by means of violence—because blood is being shed, the principle stands to win. The glorification of violence essentially involves politicization. The same is true of the glorification of nonviolence: if you think you are upholding some principle—for example, that violence is wrong—by allowing yourself to be assaulted and not fighting back, then you have politicized the philosophical question, "Is violence ever justified?" by projecting it onto this scene: if you can suffer patiently, your side wins. As Socrates would say, the only way to actually determine whether violence is justified is to ask the question, "Is violence justified?" and inquire freely into the truth of the matter.

A soldier eager to fight Nazis sees warfare as more than the most expeditious means to prevent future tyrannies; he would not, for instance, accept an alternative that involved *rewarding* Nazis—not even if he were assured it wouldn't produce perverse incentives. Rather, such a soldier's goal was, by means of killing Nazis, to defend the principle *fascism is wrong*. In order for an action to constitute a defense of this principle, the action must entail hurting

Nazis, making them suffer, and, above all, ensuring that they experience *defeat*. When we speak of "fighting for justice" we imagine ourselves not only as preventing future injustices—there are a lot of ways of doing that—but specifically as defeating injustice using violence, or patience, or (in the case of some forms of protest) by calling attention to something. The problem is that is impossible. You cannot defeat or disprove or defend an idea using any kind of force but the force of argument. You might, instrumentally, be able to take steps toward a more just world by exerting physical or emotional force; and you might imagine, as you do so, that you're fighting injustice. But what you're really doing is pretending to argue.

Notice that even if you could kill enough people to bring it about that no one held an idea, you haven't thereby defeated the idea, not any more than you defeat the theory that the sun is at the center of the solar system by killing everyone who believes it to be true. And if the person who sees himself as battling injustice claims that he is not trying to fight ideas, but only trying to stop their spread, consider the hypothetical alternative where you can release a gas that had no effect other than to cause everyone to forget the noxious idea. This action would not carry with it the same passion and glory as the act of inflicting harm on the holders of ideas, precisely because the passion and glory come from the conceit that harms to people represent harms to ideas.

The person who sees himself as fighting injustice is engaged in a symbolic contest, even if he does not want to admit it. The reason he may not want to admit it is that the symbolism is not literally true. Exsanguinating the bodies of people who hold an idea is not a way of getting at the idea itself, and preventing them from being exsanguinated doesn't preserve the idea. Killing and saving don't touch ideas: only argument does. An argument is a battle to the death, not between two individuals, but between the idea in one, and the denial of that idea in another. It is like the showdown in a Western—"This town ain't big enough for the both of us"—except that in the case of the Western, the claim in question is not ever literally true. Two people could fit into just about any room, let alone a whole town; but logical space, big as it is, is not big enough for both an idea and its negation. The demands that only one of the two survive makes sense when located in its natural habitat: argument. Likewise, consider that those who fight—even when what they are fighting is a genuinely outrageous injustice—often adopt tactics as brutal as their opponents'. What will win the fight and what is just are not in any way guaranteed to be the same. But if we transpose the fight to its original home, argument, the corresponding guarantee does in fact obtain. Although you can win a fight by behaving more unjustly than your opponents, you cannot refute someone by saying things that are even more false that what they say.

Everyone understands that you can't literally fight cancer any more than you can fight a mountain or the color blue, yet many are drawn to speaking as though they really could fight racism or anti-Semitism or fascism or inegalitarianism or any other form of injustice. But notice that although it is imaginable to speak of "defeating" these evil ideas, it isn't imaginable that they might win. They can't prove themselves true no matter how many battles anyone wins. But if that's the case, the same holds for liberalism and justice and so on: one cannot prove them true by fighting. Nor can you fight for your right to exist, because no amount of fighting can bring it about that you have this right. And as Socrates says to Crito just before drinking the hemlock, "To express oneself badly is not only faulty as far as the language goes, but does some harm to the soul."[12] What you are really doing when you say you are fighting injustice is inflicting harms on people and imagining that those harms somehow transfer to the ideas that are your real enemies. When you say you are fighting injustice, there is something else that you are really trying to do.

There is more to be said about the reality of which "fighting injustice" is the image, but first we need to put liberty, and, in the next chapter, equality, on the table.

III. FREEDOM OF SPEECH

It is easier to say what freedom of speech isn't than to say what it is. The first amendment to the US Constitution protects citizens from a certain kind of government interference in their speech; but government censorship is far from the only way speech can be made unfree. When we hear, as we often do these days, of people being silenced or canceled or experiencing "chilling effects" on their speech, the culprit is rarely the government. Our idea of freedom of speech extends beyond what's specified in the First Amendment to something that has bearing on how we conduct ourselves on social media, in the workplace, and in classrooms, on sidewalks, and even in homes. The great public philosopher John Dewey (1859–1952) made this point, nearly a hundred years ago:

> Merely legal guarantees of the civil liberties of free belief, free expression, free assembly are of little avail if in daily life freedom of communication, the give and take of ideas, facts, experiences, is choked by mutual suspicion, by abuse, by fear and hatred. These things destroy the essential condition of the democratic way of living even more effectually than open coercion.[13]

When governments interfere with the free press and the public dissemination of ideas, they place restrictions on what we, as individuals, can talk to each other about, and on what kinds of information can flow into our conversations. It is those conversations that are, first and foremost, the locus of freedom. Dewey's view is that freedom from government interference is important exactly insofar as it facilitates the free communication between citizens:

> I am inclined to believe that the heart and final guarantee of democracy is in free gatherings of neighbors on the street corner to discuss back and forth what is read in

uncensored news of the day, and in gatherings of friends in the living rooms of houses and apartments to converse freely with one another. Intolerance, abuse, calling of names because of differences of opinion about religion or politics or business, as well as because of differences of race, color, wealth or degree of culture are treason to the democratic way of life.[14]

It is when the topics, values, and commitments that are central to a person's life become open for discussion and adjudication with others that she can be said to "live together" with those others in a substantive sense. I call that way of living together with other people "free"; Dewey calls it "democratic." Regardless, we agree that barriers to communication stand in the way of politics, which is to say, of living together under a shared idea. Freedom of speech, in this broader ("democratic") sense, includes the freedom to communicate with whoever one chooses (freedom of assembly or association) and the freedom to enact the results of one's communicative exchanges in self-determination (the right to vote).

And yet, for all the emphasis Dewey places on the key role that being able "to converse freely" plays in democratic living, he doesn't explain what that means. He himself only tells us what free speech isn't—insulting, abusive, or intolerant—not what it is. Suppose an idea is to travel from my mind to yours, and it must make that journey "freely": What path should it take?

The standard answer is *persuasion:* our conversations are "free" when we are open to persuasion, and when our changes of mind are the products of persuasion. In a free society, people engage in persuasion. Persuasion is a form of unilateral cognitive determination: When I make you think what I think, I've persuaded you. If I'm trying to persuade you, then I succeed if you end up thinking what I think, and in all other scenarios—you leave unpersuaded, you persuade me—I fail.

But persuasion is not the only kind of unilateral cognitive determination. When someone uses hypnosis, brain surgery, or mind-altering pills to manipulate the thoughts of others, that is unilateral cognitive determination, but it is not persuasion. We should also distinguish someone who operates by persuasion from an expert. When we have collectively recognized a set of people as authoritative, and anything they say as "knowledge"—or, as close to knowledge as we can hope for—then they do not need to persuade us. They can just tell us, because we believe what they say on the strength of their say-so. We describe ourselves as "consulting" experts, which is to say, we trust their testimony. And when experts communicate among themselves, they transfer their knowledge by some accepted process of demonstration or proof. Experts interact with one another not by persuasion but by teaching.

Socrates points out that those engaged in politics speak on too many topics to count as experts in any of them. He also notes that heated political disagreement is a sign that no one is in the position to do any teaching; and that there is no standard proof procedure. If persuasion is not hypnotic mind control and it is not how experts engage with other experts—which is by teaching—or how experts engage with nonexperts—which is by telling—then what is it?

Look at the following passage, in which Gorgias the orator describes how his persuasive powers give him an advantage *in medicine* over his brother, the doctor:

> Many a time I've gone with my brother or with other doctors to call on some sick person who refuses to take his medicine or allow the doctor to perform surgery or cauterization on him. And when the doctor failed to persuade him, I succeeded, by means of no other craft than oratory. And I maintain too that if an orator and a doctor came to any city anywhere you like and had to compete in speaking in the assembly or some other gathering over which of them should be appointed doctor, the doctor wouldn't make any showing at all, but the one who had the ability to

speak would be appointed, if he so wished. And if he were to compete with any other craftsman whatever, the orator more than anyone else would persuade them that they should appoint him, for there isn't anything that the orator couldn't speak more persuasively about to a gathering than could any other craftsman whatever. That's how great the accomplishment of this craft is, and the sort of accomplishment it is![15]

Gorgias prides himself on being able to move your mind where he wants it to go, without using any illicit mind-control devices, and without possessing the relevant expertise; he does this by means of "no other craft than oratory," which is to say, the art of persuasion. But how do you persuade someone of what neither of you knows? You give them the experience of knowing, without the reality. You do this by choosing your message, and your audience, carefully; as an orator, you have an eye for those claims people were antecedently inclined to tell themselves they know, and a knack for inducing in others the illusion of knowledge. A persuader leverages the general human inclination to tell ourselves that we know things that we don't know. Socrates calls this flattery. He says the orator is skilled at flattery, and therefore, unfree: Someone constrained to flatter his audience is not at liberty to speak the truth. Someone bent on persuasion has to tell people what, in some sense, they want to hear.

Debate might at first appear to be an improvement over persuasion. It offers up a platform to both sides, instead of only to one, acknowledging the reality of the disagreement. But Socrates does not believe in debate, and refuses to participate in it. In the *Gorgias*, he explains why: debate politicizes argument. At one point, Socrates' interlocutor, Polus, insists that Socrates has already been refuted, which is to say, "lost" the debate between them, because he adopted an unpopular position:

Don't you think you've been refuted already, Socrates, when you're saying things the likes of which no human being would maintain? Just ask any one of these people.[16]

Socrates objects that Polus is treating their conversation as a debate in which

one side thinks it's refuting the other when it produces many reputable witnesses on behalf of the arguments it presents, while the person who asserts the opposite produces only one witness, or none at all. This "refutation" is worthless, as far as truth is concerned, for it might happen sometimes that an individual is brought down by the false testimony of many reputable people.[17]

Socrates is not willing to "give in" to Polus' side on the basis of how many votes Polus can wring from the audience. Debate is always a matter of convincing a third party. The third party might be the judge of the debate tournament, the jury in a court case, the members of the Athenian Assembly, the voters in a presidential debate, or the "general public." Debate maps the project of determining which idea is true onto a contest between the debaters; more specifically, it becomes a contest between the persuasive powers of those debaters.

Adding another persuader doesn't change the fact that each remains tasked with fostering an illusion of knowledge; the debate format simply adds the twist of allowing persuaders to compete over who is better at that sort of flattery. If the audience of ordinary persuasion asks themselves, "Is this person making me feel like I know something?" the audience of a debate asks themselves, "Which of these people is best at making me feel like I know something?"

Polus thinks that he has refuted Socrates even though Socrates is unpersuaded; Socrates, by contrast, insists, "The truth is never refuted." In the real kind of arguing Socrates is interested in, the truth can never lose; it is only in the gamified version of refutation in which Polus wants to engage—the version where you win by persuading people—that someone who is saying true things can nevertheless "lose." Socrates refuses to play this game. Contrasting himself with Gorgias and Polus, Socrates denies that he is in the persuasion business. Elsewhere, he denies that has possesses the art of speaking well, and insists that he has never been anyone's teacher. In the *Gorgias*, Socrates suggests that he and Polus ignore the audience and turn toward each other:

> Though I'm only one person, I don't agree with you. You don't compel me; instead you produce many false witnesses against me and try to banish me from my property, the truth. For my part, if I don't produce you as a single witness to agree with what I'm saying, then I suppose I've achieved nothing worth mentioning concerning the things we've been discussing. And I suppose you haven't either, unless you disregard all these other people and bring me—though I'm only one person—to testify on your side.[18]

But how is what Socrates wants to do with Polus—bring him around to testify on Socrates' side—different from persuasion? How can we define "freedom of speech" in the broadest sense without talking about that very thing: that is, persuasion? To answer this question, we will have to examine the third leg of the liberal triad: equality.

EQUALITY IS THE SUBJECT of the next chapter. Before we get to it, however, I want to briefly consider an objection to the equation, implicit in the discussion above, between freedom and freedom of speech. I have focused my discussion of politics on three liberal values—justice, freedom, and equality—but my discussion of the second was restricted to freedom of speech, albeit in the broad Deweyan sense. If we take all the freedoms relevant to the sharing of ideas about how to live together, including the right to free assembly and the right to vote, isn't that still only a *part* of freedom? Aren't there forms of freedom that have nothing to do with expression and communication? What can we say, for instance, about the right to be left alone, the right to own property, or the right not to be imprisoned without cause?

Recall the distinction at the top of this chapter: to say that human beings are *social* picks out the fact that a normal human life is a life spent with other people; to say that we are *political* means something more specific, which is that we live together *under a shared idea of how to do so*. Politics is the set of solutions that we develop to those difficulties in shared living that spring specifically from differences in our ideas about how best to do so. When these disagreements are managed poorly, then some people coercively impose their way of life on others, or there is unceasing strife; when they are managed well, they are managed *freely*. A free society is one in which disagreements about how to live together are well managed.

Freedom is not the same thing as the state of being unimpeded by the presence of others—or what could be called "independence." A man alone on a desert island has complete independence, in the sense that no one will interfere with him: he will be left alone, he can claim anything he likes as his "property," and no one will imprison him. Nonetheless, these facts do not represent freedom, since there are no others with whom his agreements might be managed well or poorly. It may well be that, even when we live among others, we still wish, to some extent, to live as though (at least some of those) others were not present, and we can represent this as a desire for independence, as placing value on being left to our own devices. But it is only when our independence is the product of a shared agreement about how to live that it counts as a form of freedom.

Moreover, it is important to remember that the size and boundaries of this "tolerance zone" must themselves be politically adjudicated: some of the agreements that make up our shared political idea are agreements as to what we *don't* need to agree about. Figuring out which topics are *not* a part of justice is an inquiry into justice. If we disagree about that question, those disagreements need to be managed freely. Something counts as my property if and only if there is a shared understanding, in my community, that I can dispose of it as I see fit; and communication is how we establish and maintain a shared understanding. Thus independence is, for those persons not located on desert islands, a communicative freedom. This is because freedom is a political idea, and political activity is communicative activity.

Chapter 9

Politics:
Equality

P EOPLE BRISTLE AT THE PROSPECT OF INFERIORITY, OF being someone's subordinate, of being at the bottom rung of a hierarchy; most say they want equality. But could it be that what such people would really prefer, instead of equality, is superiority? Is equality a compromise embraced only by those too weak to dominate?

Nietzsche seems to believe this, describing the egalitarian impulse as a "slave morality" in which physical and psychological weaknesses get reinterpreted as moral strengths: "The lambs say to each other, 'These birds of prey are evil; and whoever is least like a bird of prey and most like its opposite, a lamb,—is good, isn't he?' "[1] One finds similar thoughts expressed in the writings of Hobbes, Machiavelli, and Foucault. If, as Foucault famously asserted, "Power is everywhere,"[2] perhaps that means that true equality is nowhere. This cynical critique of equality also finds expression in Plato: in the *Republic*, Thrasymachus admires only "a person of great power [who] outdoes everyone else,"[3] and his views receive further articulation from Glaucon, who describes the fundamental human motivation as "the desire to outdo others and get more and more. This is what anyone's nature naturally pursues as good, but nature is forced by law into the perversion of treating fairness with respect."[4] Likewise Callicles insists that

> the people who institute our laws are the weak and the many. So they institute laws and assign praise and blame with themselves and their own advantage in mind. As

a way of frightening the more powerful among human beings, the ones who are capable of having a greater share, out of getting a greater share than they, they say that getting more than one's share is "shameful" and "unjust," and that doing what's unjust is nothing but trying to get more than one's share. I think they like getting an equal share, since they are inferior.[5]

Moralists insist that good people pursue equal recognition whereas bad people pursue power and superiority. One can see that this form of moralism was already operative in the ancient world, from the vehemence with which people like Callicles and Thrasymachus reject it, insisting that no self-respecting man would content himself with an equal share.

The moralist tells you to strive to be on par with everyone else, whereas the anti-moralist tells you to strive for elevated status. I want to first raise some reasons for thinking that neither bit of advice will suffice to make you happy, because what you really want is elevated status *and* equality. I will then explain how, once equality has been Socratized, you can have both.

I. THE QUEST FOR EQUALITY

When people meet for the first time, for example at parties, they try to impress each other. Each subtly brings to the others' attention the sorts of facts that predictably elicit respect. It could be a job that someone wants to show off, or where they went to school, or their wealth, or their detailed knowledge of politics, or how well connected they are, or their ability to make insightful observations about some movie or book or foreign city that the pair discovered they have a common interest in. Attention to tone of voice, posture, facial expressions, hand gestures, and eye movements would reveal the ways in which each vies for the other's recognition: human interactions are replete with status-seeking behavior. This kind of behavior might initially appear to be a way of angling to be placed above one's interlocutor, but on closer examination, that common assumption isn't right.

Notice, first, that conversational status games typically involve an expectation of symmetry: we anticipate that our interlocutor will seek the same sort of recognition from us that we are seeking from them—in fact, it is often offensive if they do not!—and we are just as inclined to dole out respect, provided the grounds exist for doing so, as to seek it. If the person presents themselves as a subordinate too lowly to deserve our respect, or as a superior too aloof to seek it, the game of recognizing one another's importance becomes impossible. This shows that the people involved are usually not trying to dominate one another; rather, they are participating in a shared quest for shared superiority. They want their equal recognition of one another to be grounded in reasons for deserving that recognition; they are trying to get the "equality point" set high, to license the conclusion that both are in some way superior people.

Consider an example. In 1987 the philosopher A. J. Ayer was at a party where the boxer Mike Tyson was making aggressive sexual advances on the (then very young) fashion model Naomi Campbell. When Ayer stepped in to demand that Tyson stop, Tyson was outraged: "Do you know who the fuck I am? I'm the heavyweight champion of the world." Ayer responded: "And I am the former Wykeham Professor of Logic. We are both preeminent in our field. I suggest we talk about this like rational men." That is what happened, and in the meanwhile Campbell was able to slip away.[6] Ayer's response worked because it served to set the equality point between Tyson and Ayer high enough that Tyson could feel that he was being respected in a substantive way.

The equality we seek in such encounters is something positive; it is not something you get for free, and two people don't get it by having been allotted equal amounts of money, or the same basic human rights, or by having started out their childhoods on the level playing field of equal opportunity. The reason we have to hunt for it is that it is not a default, but a conversational achievement, and this is why it can constitute the basis for interpersonal respect. A person wants to be recognized by someone whose recognition she, in turn, recognizes; she wants to be standing on the same plane as that person, and to have that plane be, in some way, elevated. "Elevated" does not mean elevated *over* the person she's talking to; and "elevated" also does not necessarily mean "at the absolute top."

It is striking how often the same people who angle for importance will, in those same conversations, sometimes seem to do the opposite. People who are meeting for the first time often performatively share feelings of stress, inadequacy, or weakness; express discontent with the powers that be; and identify shared sources of outrage, frustration or oppression. People bond by complaining about shared subordination or struggle, eager to have, as common knowledge between them, the fact that neither is in charge of as much about the world as they would like. By making clear that neither of us claims to be at the top—we both know what it's like to struggle—we avoid positioning ourselves hierarchically in relation to one another, and we minimize the significance of whatever differences remain between us. (I like to imagine that Ayer and Tyson, in the conversation that followed, went on to bond over what it's like to worry that there is nothing left to achieve in a field one has mastered.)

If we thought that conversational status-seeking always aimed at domination, we would be puzzled by how readily its participants gesture at how powerless or oppressed or overwhelmed they are. These self-lowering gestures can be reconciled with status-seeking if we see them both as part of the quest for an elevated equality: we are trying to be high up, *and* equal to one another.

II. The Elusiveness of Equality

How often do we stably secure the kind of equality we seek? The mutual recognition we arrive at by way of our quest for equality is fragile enough to be easily overturned by a word or gesture with the wrong symbolic associations. People are generally averse to deceiving one another, but if you look at where we are willing to bend the rules, it is surprising how frequently these exceptions involve maintaining the appearance of equality. Equality is a value in the service of which we are willing to lie. The defensive practices we use to guard the conversational equilibrium, which range from tactful nondisclosure to downright deception, suggest that what we are guarding is, at most, the *appearance* of equality.

We reflexively engage in a kind of interpersonal balancing: if I admit I am bad at something, then you have to say you're also bad at something, or point out that I'm good at something else. We are anxious to even out the appearance of difference in abilities, in social standing, in success. We are especially vigilant in policing asymmetries of affection: if I want to be talking to you more than you want to be talking to me, that is something that it is rarely permissible to be explicit about. Differences in intelligence, attractiveness, and sense of humor are rarely acknowledged by the individuals themselves. For the most part, we make an effort to treat each other *as though* we were equal, and that often involves tactfully ignoring the ways in which we are not. Much of what gets called "social skill" involves inducing the feeling of equality in the face of all the facts that challenge this feeling.

Our quest for equality tends to end in something that is better described as the *conceit* of equality. It is possible, indeed probable given their career choices, that Ayer thought more highly of being a distinguished philosopher than he did of being a heavyweight champion, and that Tyson held the opposite view. It is fine for them to think this, and for each to confess as much to their respective (philosophical or pugilistic) associates, but it would certainly be awkward to mention to one another. These prohibitions are not only a feature of casual relationships. Even in a marriage, there might be facts to which neither party is eager to draw attention, such as which spouse has a more important job, is more appreciated by the children, more popular among their circle of friends, more responsible with money, or more sexually frustrated. Beyond our families, we have to actively police, guard, and maintain the feeling of equality across fraught fault lines of inequality such as gender, or race, or religion.

Living in a world of fragile and partly fabricated equality means living in constant fear of disrespecting others, and being disrespected ourselves. This fear might fade into the background much of the time, but it is always ready to surface; the temperature in the room is liable to increase. All of this is a sign that when it comes to equality, we are only just barely keeping it together. The equality arrived at in social contexts is not the real thing, but only an unstable placeholder.

III. Inequality

Many an ambitious person learns that power, once achieved, does not always translate into the forms of respect they had anticipated. When you come to be in a position to treat others as subordinates, the respect you receive from them is only respect from subordinates. When they were your superiors, you hungered for their recognition, but you forget to factor in how much less that recognition would mean to you once you came to see them as your inferiors; and so, once one ambition is achieved, your sights naturally turn to the prospect of climbing even higher. The quest for equality drives the ambitious person to excess.

Likewise, the weak, mistreated, or unsuccessful might dream of a time when they secure enough power to lord it over their onetime oppressors, but that fantasy of domination won't be fully satisfying in reality if what ultimately drives it is the desire for the kind of respect you can only get from equals.

George Orwell explores this point in an essay called "Revenge Is Sour," where he describes a visit to a prisoner-of-war camp in southern Germany shortly after the Second World War. This is how Orwell reports his own reaction to watching a former SS officer being humiliated by a Jewish man who had been tasked with guarding him:

I wondered whether the Jew was getting any real kick out of this new-found power that he was exercising. I concluded that he wasn't really enjoying it, and that he was merely—like a man in a brothel, or a boy smoking his first cigar, or a tourist traipsing round a picture gallery— *telling himself* that he was enjoying it, and behaving as he had planned to behave in the days he was helpless.[7]

Orwell is not unsympathetic to the Jew; he observes that "very likely his whole family had been murdered," and that "a wanton kick to a prisoner is a very tiny thing compared with the outrages committed by the Hitler regime." Nonetheless, Orwell marvels at the fact that "the Nazi torturer of one's imagination, the monstrous figure against whom one had struggled for so many years, [has] dwindled to this pitiful wretch," the punishment of whom could only be pretended to count as satisfying. Pulling yourself up above the level of the person dominating you looks like an achievement only so long as they are above you.

Orwell also describes an incident after the death of Mussolini, when his corpse was on public display in Milan and an old woman was said to have fired five shots into it, one for each of her five sons. Orwell muses,

I wonder how much satisfaction she got out of those five shots, which, doubtless, she had dreamed years earlier of firing. The condition of her being able to get close enough to Mussolini to shoot at him was that he should be a corpse.[8]

The reason Orwell keeps raising this question of *satisfaction* is that he is tracking the question of what we really want. The oppressed person imagines that she will be satisfied once the tables are turned and she stands above her oppressor, but when that happens by way of the lowering of the oppressor—to the level of a pitiful wretch, or a corpse—then being above them is not the splendid thing it once appeared to be. It cannot furnish the "real enjoyment" of feeling genuinely respected or valuable. Shooting Mussolini's corpse, kicking the imprisoned SS guard: these actions have a symbolic value. Their appeal is conditional on our being in a degraded or oppressed condition where we can't easily get what we really want into view.

On the other hand, it can be quite hard to see how to bring about the thing we really do want—substantive equality—after it has been so flagrantly violated. It is by no means obvious how oppression can be undone. Being treated in ways that would have supported the conceit of equality, had the oppression not taken place, may not suffice for feeling substantively equal, once it has. (We might think here of debates over racial "color-blindness," or how the Jew would have felt if the SS guard, now supposedly reformed, moved in next door.) Finding a way to balance at that equality point, and then stably rest there—that is difficult in the best of times, but once the relation has been thrown off balance it can seem impossible.

Inequality is much easier to understand than equality. When someone discriminates on the basis of race, or religion, or gender, they are saying that the equality point does not exist, that they are not going to recognize another person as being, substantively, their equal. One can find such inegalitarianism to be clearly, self-evidently, objectionable without having much of a sense of what it would look like if there were the kind of substantive equality between the parties that suffices for feeling valued and respected. When someone treats you with disrespect, you know that you are not getting what you want, but this doesn't mean that you are in a position to say what it is you do want. We're not sure how to put that equality point back where it belongs after we are discriminated against because we don't actually know where it belongs. We never knew; what we had at the best of times was only the conceit of equality. This problem about egalitarianism is not new; it is ancient.

IV. EGALITARIANISM IN THE *ILIAD*

Let's return to the *Iliad*. When we left things off in the previous chapter, the Greeks had refused to return Chryseis to her father Chryses, who then prayed to Apollo to unleash a plague on the Greeks. Apollo heeds his prayer, and when the Greeks find out the cause of their predicament, Agamemnon, leader of the Greek forces, and Achilles, his greatest warrior, disagree about what must be done. They agree that Agamemnon should give Chryseis back to Chryses, but Agamemnon thinks that he needs to be compensated for his loss by way of a different prize, whereas Achilles thinks Agamemnon should, just this once, forgo a prize. This disagreement creates the schism between the two men from which the entire action of the epic springs. Here are Agamemnon's final words to Achilles:

> And Agamemnon, lord of men, replied,
> "Then off you go, if that is what you want!
> I certainly will not be begging you
> to stay at Troy for me. You see, I have
> plenty of other helpers at my side,
> ready to treat me with respect and honor—
> including Zeus, the god of strategy!
> I hate you more than any other leader,
> any of those whom Zeus protects and loves.
> You always relish war and fights and conflict.
> You may be strong, but some god gave you that.
> Go home! Take all your ships and your companions
> and rule your Myrmidons. I do not care!
> To me, you are entirely unimportant.
> Your anger does not bother me at all.
> But this I swear to you. Just as Apollo
> will take Chryseis back, away from me,
> when I send her to him on my own ship,

escorted by my very own companions,
so I shall take your beautiful Briseis,
your trophy. I myself will come and get her
in person from your tent, so you will see
how far superior I am to you,
and other men will shrink from talking back
to me, as if we were on equal terms."[9]

When Agamemnon says that he does not see Achilles as his equal, that marks the end of the conversation. Achilles' next move is to reach for his sword, and he's ready to kill Agamemnon when Athena grabs his hair to stop him. Homer is drawing our attention to the most disrespectful things one person can say to another: I don't seek to be honored by you, I take no account of you, I don't care whether you are angry at me—which is to say, I don't care whether you disagree with me about something important—and I do not see you as someone who can talk back to me, standing face-to-face with me and asserting the opposite of what I think.

The language of comparison and equality had surfaced earlier in their conversation, when Agamemnon demanded to be compensated for the loss of Chryseis with a trophy of equal value, by taking one from another of the Greek kings—Achilles, or Ajax, or Odysseus. Achilles objects to losing his prize, and complains that when it comes to prizes, "You always get a better one than mine,"[10] in spite of doing more than his share of the killing.

The Greek leaders demand to be recognized by one another as peers—they are all kings, ruling over distinct regions in Greece—but they have to negotiate a tricky situation in which one of them, Agamemnon, has been put in charge of the others for the purpose of conducting this war against the Trojans. The specific situation between Achilles and Agamemnon is touchy in exactly the way that contemporary discourse that crosses certain fault lines (gender, race, religion) is touchy. The question of how they can achieve an egalitarian distribution of prizes is not a trivial one, because in addition to the desirability of the prize, there is the question of the signal that the distribution of prizes sends.

When we dole out equal amounts of something—equal portions of cake at a birthday party, equal numbers of votes, equal speaking time to each speaker, equal health care, equal government payments (as with a universal basic income), and so on—that gesture points beyond itself. It represents or reflects or symbolizes the existence of a form of equality that doesn't have anything to do with cake or votes or health. We object to getting less cake or fewer votes or less money not only because we want as much of these things as possible, but because getting less than others makes us feel disrespected, as though we deserved less than them because we were worth less. If we were to learn that the unequal distribution was driven by features very specific to the context, we would not be offended. This is easy to see in the case of cake: if I see that there's a good reason why I should get less cake than others on precisely this occasion—e.g., there isn't enough cake for both children and adults—I won't be offended. Of course, the more charged the situation, the more difficult it is to defuse the offense. Neither Achilles nor Agamemnon can see the issue of which of them goes prizeless as failing to point beyond itself, though each of them expects the other to do so. Agamemnon thinks he should be able to take Achilles' prize without Achilles interpreting that as disrespect, and Achilles thinks Agamemnon should be able to remain prizeless without interpreting that as being disrespected.

They are struggling to find the equal point, and at the end Agamemnon just gives up, effectively telling him: You're not my equal, Achilles. You don't matter. You're not a part of this discussion. I don't need your recognition, I don't need honor from you.

The apparatus of respect can take many forms. In the Iliad, it's prizes, elsewhere it could take the form of honorifics, or titles, or saying *vous* instead of *tu*; it could also be reflected in seating arrangements, or dress codes, or gestures such as bowing and curtseying.

Homer draws our attention to the connection between that signaling apparatus and the question of disagreement. What causes things to explode between Achilles and Agamemnon is Agamemnon's insistence that Achilles is not allowed to speak to him as an equal, is not allowed to say that Agamemnon is in the wrong about something; that if Achilles does think Agamemnon is wrong, Agamemnon can ignore that.

Neither the status games by which we quest for equality nor what might be called the revenge games by which we try to reestablish it are fully successful at getting us what we were seeking. They don't lead, in Orwell's term, to *satisfaction*. Sticking it to one's oppressor is as close as the oppressed can get to the concept of equality, but it turns out that it is not very close at all. Making sure no one gets more than anyone else is a good way to prevent complaints over inequality, but as far as substantive equality goes, such actions are at best symbolic placeholders. They stand in for the recognition we truly desire, which is a matter of being seen and valued for the distinctive value we have. Much of the apparatus of our practice of equality—the titles and gestures and modes of address—is likewise symbolic. What does the reality look like?

Real equality means you know that you are useful, important, and valuable to me not because I tell you those things, or send you signals to that effect, but because I am making active use of you, leaning on you, doing something I could not be doing without you. The *practice* of equality is where equality comes alive.

V. Adam Smith

I believe that Adam Smith is trying to describe the practice of equality when he writes:

> The desire of being believed, the desire of persuading, of
> leading and directing other people, seems to be one of
> the strongest of all our natural desires. It is, perhaps, the

instinct upon which is founded the faculty of speech, the characteristical faculty of human nature. No other animal possesses this faculty, and we cannot discover in any other animal any desire to lead and direct the conduct of its fellows. Great ambition, the desire of real superiority, of leading and directing, seems to be altogether peculiar to man, and speech is the great instrument of ambition, of real superiority, of leading and directing the judgments and conduct of other people.[11]

At first glance, one might be inclined to assimilate Smith to Nietzsche and Callicles, as yet another person who thinks that everyone desires to dominate. But I think it's a mistake to equate what Smith describes in terms of leading and directing with domination. No one wants to be dominated, but Smith does not think that people are averse to being led. He goes on to say that if you knew nobody would *ever* believe you, you'd die of despair; he says that a liar "forfeits all title to that sort of credit from which alone he can derive any sort of ease, comfort, or satisfaction in the society of his equals." What you want to do among your equals is, at least every once in a while, lead them; lying is bad because it forfeits your right to lead your equals. An unintentional falsehood is bad for the same reason, if not to the same degree: he says we are "mortified" by speaking falsely because it "diminishes our authority to persuade, and always brings some degree of suspicion upon our fitness to lead and direct." We're not horrified by having our minds directed by others; we're horrified by being excluded from the circle of who gets to direct others. We want to believe we are fit to lead and direct, but we don't need to do it all the time. Indeed, none of these practices would be a source of ease or comfort among one's equals if everyone resisted being led because they themselves wanted to lead—because that would put us in perpetual conflict with one another. Unlike Hobbes, Smith very much does not see the basic human condition as that of a "war of all against all."

One datum that Smith's theory explains extraordinarily well is the otherwise puzzling human preference for speaking over listening. We use phrases like "getting to talk" by contrast with "having to listen." We understand being granted a platform as a privilege, whereas being told that it is time for you to be quiet and let others talk is a bit of a put down. We impatiently suffer through what others have to say, eagerly awaiting our chance to talk. We speak of taking turns to talk, not taking turns to listen. We have social norms against interrupting, not against pausing.

It is such an evident fact of life that it's a challenge to shut people up, and a challenge to get them to really listen to one another, that we don't stop to reflect on how puzzling this is. Think about it: When I communicate something to you, on the face of it, who wins? I'm the one giving, and you're the one getting. I already know what I'm going to tell you, and you're the one who doesn't know it yet. I get nothing, you get something. Communication, is, roughly speaking, how we find things out from one another; one might expect that domain to be filled with under-talking and over-listening. If two people are on opposites sides of a cake stand, and one of them is handing out cake and the other one is receiving cake, and it's a yummy cake, which person do you want be? Wouldn't it be weird if we saw people impatiently gobbling down their cake, trying to eat it as fast as possible, so as to arrive more quickly at their turn to hand out the cake? Are we supposed to conclude that the preference for speaking—which is often censured as egotistical and narcissistic—is actually a sign of some deep altruism in us? With most goods, we prefer to get them, rather than giving them. Why does it work the other way with cognitive goods?

Smith's answer is: because when you give someone a cognitive good, what you get, in return, is a signal of your own worth. Their willingness to receive the products of your mind is a mark or a sign of your fitness to lead. I think he's right.

Let me relate a true story. In middle school I had a best friend named Bella, and Bella had a younger sister, Heather. Like many middle school best friends, Bella and I were inseparable, so I was at her house all the time, and when I was there, Heather was always angling to be part of our duo: to join our games and projects, to participate in our conversations. As you'd expect, we mostly ignored, avoided, and excluded her: Bella and I were sophisticated sixth graders whereas Heather was a mere child, an ignorant fourth grader. One time, Bella and I were baking brownies at her house. We had taken the ingredients out of the cabinets, we had measured out the flour, and then we realized that the bag of sugar was almost empty—not enough left in it for brownies. We were annoyed and frustrated, ready to admit defeat, when Heather, underfoot as usual, pointed out that we could use the sugar in the small sugar bowl on the counter. I turned to her and said, "Heather, you're a genius!" and what happened next—the way Heather responded to that—is seared in my memory in a way that very few experiences from my childhood are. She didn't say anything in response, she was completely silent, but she gave me a look that I find hard to describe though I can still see it in my mind's eye—it was a radiant look of pure, complete joy. I think that is the happiest I've ever made anyone.

There was just enough sugar left in the bowl for the recipe, so we went ahead with the brownies, and with uncharacteristic generosity, Bella and I even let Heather help us; and of course Heather was glad to be included in the baking, but mostly I think she was basking in the afterglow of the sugar bowl incident. That had been the moment when she was really included. She was listened to, and she directed our minds.

It might be hard to see how Agamemnon's complaint about not receiving sufficient respect from Achilles was a complaint about *inegalitarianism,* but perhaps it becomes easier to see if we treat that episode as similar to the sugar bowl episode. In both cases, we have a quest for the recognition of being fit to direct the minds of others. Someone who is placed in charge of others, such as Agamemnon, precisely because they are tasked with continuously directing the minds of others, is unusually exposed to the prospect of being judged as unworthy of doing so.[12] Precisely because rulers are in a position to compel obedience, they are highly attuned to the slightest signals of disrespect. This is why those who lead and rule can be so touchy about symbols and signals validating their claim on authority, and so insistent on forbidding even the slightest deviation from their method of directing others' minds. If, as often happens, they end up oppressing and dominating their closest associates (not to mention many others), the result is a predictable perversion of the quest for equality.

Smith understands the fundamental principle of social life: Whether you are a king or a little sister, you are worth something only if you can direct the minds of others. But even if Smith is right, he's not completely right. He hasn't gotten to the bottom of the story. The reason that Heather cared so much about getting to direct our minds is that doing so *meant something* to her, which is to say, it signified something over and above the particular way in which she was useful to us. Had I responded merely by grabbing the sugar bowl and proceeding with the recipe, that wouldn't have meant as much to her, even though she would have been able to see that she had directed our minds. What pleased her was that my mode of address explicitly acknowledged her. But every such acknowledgment is a symbolic gesture, one that points beyond itself to the practice of equality in some other arena.

If the reason I care about changing your mind is that your acknowledgment that I can do so is a *sign* of my worth to you; if the reason we are so happy to take turns talking is precisely that we are offering one another positive indications about what would happen in some other, target scenario; if what Achilles and Agamemnon each ask the other to forgo, given the exigent circumstances, are merely reassurances about that target scenario; if hot or contested issues are precisely ones charged with the tension of "whoever wins this one is really in charge in the target scenario"—then we still haven't located equality when it is at home.

The power to change your mind bears a more intimate relation to the practice of equality than titles or prizes, but the relation is still not a direct one. In acknowledging, to you, that you can direct my mind, I am allowing you, however temporarily, to play the role of "teacher," or "leader." You are in charge; you are, for now, the knowledgeable one; I am your subordinate. But if you really were knowledgeable, you wouldn't depend on my acknowledgment. There is something very strange in the practice of seeking, from someone, proofs that you do not need such proofs from them.

VI. SOCRATIC EQUALITY

Suppose I am trying to persuade you, and I am only pleased if you end up persuaded—but not if you end up persuading me. This is a common enough scenario, and yet it reflects a bizarre mix of motivations.

If I am bent on persuasion, then I'm trying to (however temporarily) dominate you. I'm doing something which, were I to do it all the time, would leave me in a position where your respect was worth nothing to me. Orators characteristically hold their audiences in contempt—think back to Gorgias and his boasts—which means that they cannot get, from that audience, the validation they seek. Constantly chase superiors until I run out of them and hold everyone in contempt, and have nothing—this is not a coherent project.

How can I seek your respect sustainably, which is to say, in a way that doesn't threaten to destroy your ability to give me what I want? How can I direct your mind in a manner that preserves your equality to me? How can I address an audience in such a way that it sustains them as people before whom I have a voice?

The answer is to stop seeking symbolic displays of how independent one is from the recognition of others, and accept dependence. The orator tries to convince himself, by means of the reverberating applause of the audience, that what he has is knowledge; the philosopher eschews this pretense in favor of actually trying to acquire the knowledge. If I need to be the one who does the persuading rather than the one who was persuaded, then I have something to prove. If

I have nothing to prove, then I am no less pleased to be persuaded than to persuade.

Notice: If I am no less happy to be persuaded, I won't use any rhetorical tricks to persuade you. I will only ever give you the arguments that would seem good to me as well. I don't want you to be convinced on any other grounds than the grounds that convince me, and indeed I want to make it as easy as possible for you to *unconvince* me. Recall Socrates:

> Though I'm only one person, I don't agree with you. You don't compel me; instead you produce many false witnesses against me and try to banish me from my property, the truth. For my part, if I don't produce you as a single witness to agree with what I'm saying, then I suppose I've achieved nothing worth mentioning concerning the things we've been discussing. And I suppose you haven't either, unless you disregard all these other people and bring me—though I'm only one person—to testify on your side.[13]

Socrates goes on to say:

> I do know how to produce one witness to whatever I'm saying, and that's the person I'm having a discussion with. The majority I disregard. And I do know how to call for a vote from one person, but I don't even discuss things with the majority.[14]

Socrates describes the kind of "refutation" Polus seeks—refutation by majority—as being "worthless, as far as truth is concerned."[15]

In these passages, Socrates is complaining—about not being treated with respect, about not being treated the way that he deserves, about not being treated in the way that he treats others. He thinks that Polus is being a bully. When Polus says that Socrates has been proven wrong without Socrates actually having come to believe that he was wrong, it's akin to the bully threatening to beat you up unless you give them your lunch money, regardless of whether you think they should get that money. In both cases, we speak of someone as being *forced* to act in a certain way. Socrates is complaining, "The truth is *my* property!" in just the way you might tell the bully, "But that's *my* lunch money!" The fact that the bully is bigger than you is irrelevant to the question of whose money it is; likewise, the fact that Polus can get a group to agree with him is irrelevant to the question that is to be adjudicated between Socrates and Polus. Socrates is standing up to this attempted use of force—"You don't compel me!"—in just the way you might stand up to the bully. A bully is someone who dominates another person in a manner that is objectionably inegalitarian. Socrates is saying, "Don't treat me that way, treat me as your equal."

So what would it be for Polus to treat Socrates as his equal? It would be for Polus to recognize that Socrates has a claim on the truth. When Socrates describes the truth as his property, he is clearly not insisting that everything he currently believes is true, since that would amount to a claim to knowledge. Socrates means that he has a right to the truth, that it is his property in an aspirational sense. Just as the status of full citizenship—with all the rights that it entails—is the birthright of every baby born into a given nation, so too, the truth is Socrates' birthright, in that he is destined to come into it. Respecting someone means that even when they say what you believe to be false, *you regard their orientation toward the truth as sufficient to structure your interaction with them.*

So: they disagree with you, which means you see them as other, as distinct from you, but you still recognize them as being oriented towards the truth, which means you can nonetheless interact with them as a mind. Putting those together, it follows that you see them as *another mind.* That is a real accomplishment. It's easy to mock the Cartesian solipsist who stares out of his window and wonders whether the hats and cloaks moving outside could be concealing automata, but all of us overestimate the degree to which we've solved the problem of other minds. It is common to give lip service to a solution to that problem. For example, when we "agree to disagree," it's as though each of us is saying, "I'm sure there's a mind in there somewhere." Or, when we set our differences aside as being unimportant, we're saying, "Deep down, we're of one mind—mine."

In contrast, actually recognizing the existence of another mind means, first, that the two of us are not of one mind, we're not united in agreement but rather divided by disagreement; and, second, that disagreement doesn't close the door to our engaging in a mental activity with one another, to our treating one another as minded creatures, creatures who have a claim on the truth; and, third, the most important condition, neither of us counts as "achieving anything worth mentioning concerning the things we are discussing" except with reference to the other. We're in a closed system. Our interaction is structured *only* by our respective claims on the truth. To engage with a point of view that conflicts with your own, but to continue to engage with it as a point of view on the truth—that is what it is to recognize someone as your equal.

"Regarding someone's claim on the truth as sufficient to structure your interaction with them" is my gloss on Socrates' "calling for a vote from one person alone," but neither phrase is entirely transparent. Let me describe what they refer to in more detail.

When viewed from the outside, a conversation is a world within the larger world we all inhabit. The conversation is embedded both in the longer narrative of the participant's lives, and in the wider social environment that contains many other people besides the ones currently talking. There are a variety of ways in which that outer world can become salient during the conversation: You could think about how people might make fun of you if they heard what you said inside this conversation; or how they might misinterpret you, experience what you are saying as hurtful, and go on to decide they no longer want to associate with you. When Callicles says that Polus and Gorgias were restrained by shame from telling Socrates what they really thought,[16] he is describing them as speaking with one eye on the audience of the world outside the world of the conversation. When people characterize their interlocutors as arguing "in bad faith," or accuse them of having "ulterior motives" that govern how they argue or what they argue for, these criticisms are usually invoked in order to explain the critic's own refusal to prioritize the inner world of the conversation: given your failure to argue "in good faith," I cannot be expected to call for a vote from you alone. Another way to bring the outer world to bear on the conversation is that you could care about the causal upshot of creating conviction in your interlocutor, and all the harms that could be prevented if they were brought around to the truth. When we speak of certain kinds of ideas as "dangerous" or "scary" we are referring to the impact of those ideas on the world outside the world; inside the world of a conversation, the only danger any idea can present is falsity.

The proper home of equality and respect is not the outside but the inside: the world of the conversation. The rule that you haven't achieved anything with your words unless the person you are talking to has come to understand your ideas on the same terms on which you understand them: that's a rule for the world within the world. In the outer world, there are many possible things that your words could do or bring about. In the inner world, there is only one thing, because your interlocutor's claim on the truth is sufficient to structure your interaction with them. Each of you is calling for a vote from one person alone. And it is quite a privilege to be that person; it is an honor to find oneself playing the part of the one and only being from whom a vote is called.

When you receive that honor, you start to realize that "the world within the world" is only how it looks to those standing outside of it; those on the inside understand it as "the world *above* the world." The space of inquiry is elevated above everyday cares, above hunger and busyness and lust and the various drives that drive us toward bodily survival; and it is elevated above concerns about reputation and honor and status and all the allegiances you need to collect and preserve for the sake of your social survival. Inside the conversation, you are immune to the bodily command, and you are immune to the kinship command. When you are playing by the rules of the world where your vote is the only one that is called for, you get to see yourself as the sort of being about whom nothing is relevant but their claim on the truth. For the purposes of this conversation, you are no longer defined by bodily necessities, nor are you just a node in a social network. What defines you, within the conversation, is only your orientation toward the truth, which makes you: an intellectual thing, a mind.

When Heather was elated by my response to her, it was not only because I included her, and not only because I allowed her to direct my mind, but because the *way* I did those things—telling her that she is a genius—suggested that I saw her *as* a mind. Praise for intelligence or intellectual ability touches us so deeply because it speaks to our most fundamental wish: to be treated not as a physical thing, nor as a social thing, but as an intellectual thing. The ultimate form of respect is being seen in terms of one's power to help others figure out how to live. At the end of chapter 5, we discussed the solipsistic illusion that thinking is something a person can do on her own. The complement to the danger of falsely seeing oneself as a mind is the joy of being seen, by another, as a mind, in the context in which that is truly what one is. There's no higher form of respect an ignorant human being can hope for than to be treated as a mind, and the only way one can get such respect is from the person who inquires with you.

So this is my explanation for why the concept of equality has the peculiar structure that it has: we really do care about being on an equal footing with another person, and that concern really does drive us—both of us—on a quest to occupy a position of superiority. Neither of us is trying to be superior to the other, but we are both trying, together, to be superior, elevated. We are dissatisfied with the merely negative sense of equality where no one gets more than anyone else, or in which no one gets respected or mistreated. The equality we seek is not merely the absence of an evil but the presence of a good; we want to achieve some substantial form of recognition.

Ordinary conversation is a quest for an elevated sort of equality, and that kind of equality can in fact be really, truly, stably arrived at in the right sort of conversation. And now we can see that the sort of conversation I've specified—and whose details are the topic of part two (chapters 5–7)—is the same sort as the one that can be described as truly free, and as the mechanism by which questions of justice and injustice can be, not fought over, but adjudicated. Such a conversation is free precisely because it is *detached* from outer consequences, free to be guided by its own internal principle—namely, the pursuit of the truth.

Someone with knowledge can claim the truth as their property irrespective of how anyone else behaves toward them, but the same does not hold for an ignorant person. If the ignorant person speaks, what she says may not be true, even though she believes that it is. An ignorant person has at most an aspirational claim on the truth. She can speak with a view to the truth, so long as someone is bent on refuting her, and on constraining what she says in no other way. It is by way of this kind of recognition that she acquires the power to speak freely. Freedom of speech is simply the freedom to speak truly.

Socrates' great insight was to notice that this freedom is not, under ordinary circumstances, available to us. More specifically, it is not available to us whenever we determine in advance that what we say must conform to what other people have said, or what they expect us to say, or what we should say in order to get them to like us, or what, if we said it, would send the right sorts of signals about respect and equality. Since those signals are meant to communicate something about how we would treat our interlocutor if we were in an actual, live, inquisitive disagreement, when we are in one of those disagreements we set aside signals in favor of actual respect: calling for a vote from a single person. This is a substantive kind of equality because it actually satisfies our deep intellectual need for one another: we practice equality by speaking with a view to knowing, which is to say, by inquiring together with one another. It is when you regard my claim on the truth as sufficient to structure our interaction that I have the freedom to speak.

Aristotle is the one who said man is a political animal, but it was Socrates who explained the distinctive need that drives human beings to engage with one another: we live together because we think together. Politics has an intellectual foundation.

Chapter 10

Love

T HERE IS SUCH A THING AS THE FAIRY-TALE IMAGE OF perfect romance, in the sense that that phrase conjures up, for each of us, a fictional representation of love. But it is also true that there is no such thing as the fairy-tale image of perfect romance, in the sense that life doesn't actually work that way.

If we compare romantic love, as it appears in our lives, to our romantic ideals, we find ourselves falling very far short. Romantic relationships can turn abusive, emotionally turbulent, or mutually miserable; and when we are lucky enough to enjoy romances that don't go down in flames, they stabilize, so that the company of the person one once chased with breathless abandon loses its thrill, the frequency of both sex and intense conversation decreases, and living together becomes a matter of routine. Even the "good case" is far from the ideal.

Stably married people will stress the benefits of escape from the hell of dating, the despair of living alone, and the dangers of truly toxic relationships. They might be right. Perhaps we settle for mediocre romances because the alternatives—the romantic situations we would end up in if we refused to settle—are, on the whole, even worse. Unromantic marriage might, for most of us, be the best deal on offer. But it is very far from the best deal we can conceive of.

Imagine two elderly individuals sitting side by side on a park bench. They sit there for a long time, hours perhaps, in silence, holding hands. This image is pleasing to many people; it might even be pleasing to the pair of young lovers for whom it would constitute a projection of the future. But if those young people had to actually sit there, on the park bench, in silence, for hours, they wouldn't like it. They would be bored. At the present moment, energized by the not yet dulled spark of their romance, they have so many things to say to each other; at the present moment, they want more out of love than "companionship."

It is a commonplace to chide the romantic passion of new lovers as silly or naïve, in praise of the more "solid" or "permanent" attachments associated with marriage, child-raising, and growing old together. Perhaps it is true that the ideal of young lovers is in some way impossible or unsustainable, but there is nonetheless something remarkable in the mere fact that it exists and persists and continues to capture our emotional attention. It is a powerful ideal, one that has inspired art and literature for thousands of years now. Where did this unachievable ideal come from? Why do we have it? Could it—instead of being simply mistaken—perhaps be merely displaced from its true home? Is there a context in which it would not appear silly, or naïve, but perfectly appropriate?

I. SOCRATES VERSUS ARISTOPHANES

In the *Symposium*, the comic poet Aristophanes describes the mystery of love: "It's obvious that the soul of every lover longs for something else; his soul cannot say what it is, but like an oracle it has a sense of what it wants, and like an oracle it hides behind a riddle." Aristophanes continues, "Suppose two lovers are lying together and Hephaestus stands over them with his mending tools, asking, 'What is it you human beings really want from each other?'"[1] Aristophanes imagines that they would be perplexed, and unable to answer, but that if the god Hephaestus went ahead and used those "mending tools" to join them together and fuse them into a single being, "everyone would think he'd found out at last what he had always wanted: to come together and melt together with the one he loves, so that one person emerged from two."[2] Later, Socrates (who is here reporting, with approval, the views of his teacher Diotima) takes issue with Aristophanes' solution to the love problem:

> There is a certain story . . . according to which lovers are those people who seek their other halves. But according to my story, a lover does not seek the half or the whole, unless, my friend, it turns out to be good as well. I say this because people are even willing to cut off their own arms and legs if they think they are diseased. I don't think an individual takes joy in what belongs to him personally unless by "belonging to me" he means "good" and by "belonging to another" he means "bad." That's because what everyone loves is really nothing other than the good.[3]

Aristophanes' story takes its bearings from the sex act—the two lovers "lying together" seem, to him, to be striving to affix their bodies to one another. But notice that if people were conjoined in this way there would be no sex. Aristophanes replaces the goal-oriented activities of lovers with the static endpoint of mere togetherness; even if his notion of fusion is meant to be metaphorical, what the metaphor resembles is a certain kind of invasive, pathological dependence. When a controlling lover requires his beloved to stay physically nearby, limiting her access to the outside world, preventing her from flourishing as an independent being—in short, treating her as a kind of bodily appendage of his—we don't think of this possessive attitude as a paradigmatically loving attitude. Nor would it be made much better if she reciprocated, and were equally controlling and possessive. We use the term "codependence" to censure such romantic attachments.

Yet Aristophanes' story, for all its failings, does solve one of the central preoccupations of lovers: permanence. One of the things we want, out of love, is someone who won't leave us for another, lose interest in us, or abandon us in our hour of need. Having them be glued to us ensures that result. But permanence is not the only thing we want, because we will not be happy with permanent *badness*. As Socrates says, Aristophanes seems to have omitted goodness from his story of love. Unlike pathological forms of attachment, real love is in some way attuned to reasons to appreciate someone: When I love someone, I love what is good about them. They are a source of goodness in my life, and I want to be loved in the same way—to be a source of goodness to them. Socrates says, "love is wanting to possess the good forever."[4]

But it is not obvious how the two requirements that make love love—the Socratic requirement that it be rationally oriented toward goodness, and the Aristophanic requirement that it be stable and permanent—are supposed to go together. Think of it this way. Suppose you love me for my valuable properties. These could be properties of my body such as health and physical beauty, or properties of my soul such as courage and intelligence, or properties that render me useful to you such as talent, power, and wealth. If you love me for those properties—if those properties underwrite, and constitute, the reason for your love—then if someone else comes along who has those properties to a greater degree than I do, the rational thing for you to do is swap them in for me. Moreover, if I lose some of those properties—if age diminishes my beauty, if I lose my money and connections—then I become less lovable to you. If you are always on the market for someone better than me, then even if you don't happen to come across her, what you have in relation to me doesn't strike me as love.

The rational interest in someone on the basis of their valuable properties doesn't seem stable; whereas being blindly attached to a person due to their irreducible particularity—for just being exactly the person they are—doesn't look rational. And notice that we cannot convincingly say "so much the worse for rationality." The ideal of rational love, in which love is an orientation toward the good, is alive and well in how we conduct romance. Instead of efficient solutions to attachment such as matchmaking or arranged marriage, we expend a large proportion of our youths on the dating quest, carefully seeking out the partner who has just the right set of qualities. This behavior supports Socrates' thesis that "what everyone loves is really nothing other than the good."

We are as committed to Socratic rationality as we are to Aristophanic attachment. The lover who is so doggedly loyal that he will stick with us in spite of seeing nothing of value in our appearance, character, or company holds little more appeal than the slippery sort of lover who is always looking to trade up. The standard response to this predicament, in the world we live in, is to accept a dynamic compromise between rational appreciation and attached stability. We lean toward appreciation in our early years, with enough allowances for the possibility of comparison and breakups and "shopping around" to make it appropriate to speak of a dating "market," and toward attachment in the later ones—the park bench scene.

Romantic love today is conventionally located inside of exclusive relationships springing from sexual attraction and armored in shared domestic life. This arrangement has benefits, and it reflects the presence of the ideal of rational attachment in the form of a sliding scale, from the dating market stage that emphasizes rationality to marital fusion stage that emphasizes attachment. But it has also proved unstable: shaken by affairs, subject to divorces, supplanted by polyamory and other nontraditional romantic arrangements.

The radical insight of Socrates' theory of love is that you don't need to trade the two parts of the ideal off against each other. You can have rationality *and* attachment, if you are willing to rethink both.

II. EROTICIZED PHILOSOPHY

The Plato scholar Aryeh Kosman, commenting on the *Symposium*, describes the problem of love thus:

> The individual frustrates our efforts by a maddening transparency. Insofar as I love him for his qualities, the qualities seem to constitute the proper object of my love;

insofar as I love him irrespective of his particular qualities, it becomes unclear in what sense I may be said to love, specifically, him.

The problem may be put in another way; we want a theory that will account for our pre-reflective paradoxical demands that love be charitable and unconditional, yet not independent of features of the beloved that the lover recognizes and values. We want our lovers at once to accept us as we are and admire us for what we are.[5]

Here Kosman illuminates two common beliefs about love—that it is focused on an individual, and that it is *contented* with the beloved, in the sense embodied in attitudes of appreciation and admiration—and asks how either is possible on the assumption that love is rational attachment. If I (rationally) love an individual for his qualities, I love the qualities, rather than him; and if I am attached to him for no reason at all I likewise don't seem to be directing my love at what makes him *him*. If Socratic rationalism must take the form of admiration for how great he is, and Aristophanic attachment takes the form of acceptance of him, even if he is not so great, it is hard to see how these can be combined into satisfaction with a person.

Socrates preserves love as rational attachment by denying Kosman's two assumptions: he holds that the object of love is not the individual, and that love is, in a certain sense, dissatisfied. It doesn't take the form of admiring acceptance toward another human being. Rather, it takes the form of philosophical dissatisfaction.

Socrates is consistent, in all his many discussions of love, that the proper activity for lovers to engage in is philosophy. In the *Symposium* he says that Erōs, the divine spirit of love, is a philosopher. In the *Phaedrus*, he describes various tiers of love, but the highest kind is one in which the lovers eschew sex and instead "follow the assigned regimen of philosophy," and live a life of "shared understanding";[6] Socrates concludes by advising any would-be lover to "devote his life to Love through philosophical discussions";[7] and warns that "only a philosopher's mind grows wings."[8] In the *Lysis*, Socrates presents his method of refutation as a method of seduction: Hippothales asks for advice as to "what one should say or do so his prospective boyfriend will like him," and Socrates offers to give a "demonstration" of how to woo someone.[9] What follows is the usual course of Socratic questioning: apparently, Socratic refutation *is* courtship.

Socrates claims "expertise at love" in the *Phaedrus*[10] and an understanding of the "art of love" in the *Symposium*;[11] these claims do indeed make sense if the characteristic activity of lovers amounts to inquisitive refutation. But if lovers are to engage in philosophy, they can be neither admiring nor accepting of one another. Admiration and acceptance are both static ("I love you just the way you are"), whereas philosophy is dynamic, aimed at the improved character and life that would be possible if we had better answers to our most important questions. As Socrates says—I would add, lovingly— toward the end of the *Laches*, "The one thing I would not advise is that we remain as we are."[12]

Socrates does not reject the idea that love should manifest in wondrous, reverential appreciation and total, unconditional acceptance of the object of love. What he denies is that the target of such admiration is a person. This is the oddest thing Socrates says about love—it might be the oddest thing Socrates says about any topic. He thinks we don't love human beings—not really. Recall his claim that "love is wanting to possess the good forever." My love, which manifests itself in the form of my philosophizing with you, aims not at possessing *you*, but rather, at possessing the good. What I love is the good. He expresses this in the *Phaedrus* by saying that the lovers aim ultimately to grow wings and fly up to an intellectual heaven in which they will be able to behold—we might add, to appreciate and admire—the splendor of real Justice and Knowledge and Moderation; and in the *Symposium* by describing love as an ascent to the disembodied form of the Beautiful.

The passages in which Socrates makes the claim that we don't love people are some of the most poetic, imagistic, and ecstatic in all of Plato. In both the *Symposium* and the *Phaedrus* there is an elaborate setup before Socrates is willing to come out with his point, and when he does, his language explodes in a breathless mixture of metaphor and metaphysics.

Here is an exemplary passage from the *Phaedrus* describing how the encounter with the beloved feeds the soul's yearning for flight:

> Now the whole soul seethes and throbs in this condition. Like a child whose teeth are just starting to grow in, and its gums are all aching and itching—that is exactly how the soul feels when it begins to grow wings. It swells up and aches and tingles as it grows them. But when it looks upon the beauty of the boy and takes in the stream of particles flowing into it from his beauty (that is why this is called "desire"), when it is watered and warmed by this, then all its pain subsides and is replaced by joy.[13]

And here is Socrates, quoting Diotima, describing the final stage of the soul's ascent in the *Symposium*:

> The lover is turned to the great sea of beauty, and, gazing upon this, he gives birth to many gloriously beautiful ideas and theories, in unstinting love of wisdom, until, having grown and been strengthened there, he catches sight of such knowledge, and it is the knowledge of such beauty . . . it always is and neither comes to be nor passes away, neither waxes nor wanes. Second, it is not beautiful this way and ugly that way, nor beautiful at one time and ugly at another, nor beautiful in relation to one thing and ugly in relation to another. [14]

Socrates is saying that the sort of thing you (really) love bears more resemblance to an idea than to your flesh and blood lover.

But he is saying that in passionate, erotic language ("seethes and throbs") and at atypical length: the two excerpts above are taken from speeches that go on in a similar vein for many pages. One could have imagined an abrupt, dispassionate, and abstract presentation of these same ideas; instead, the *Symposium* and *Phaedrus* sing out their message, wrapping the Socratic account of love in language that is as erotic as the phenomenon it purports to capture. This language is evidence of the Socratizing move: Socratic (philosophical) love purports to be the stable reality of which romantic (sexual) love is a wavering image. If Socratic love is the real love, then we ought to be able to take the language we standardly apply to romantic love and apply it to philosophical love, without that sounding somehow wrong or absurd. And indeed, Plato shows that Socratic love can successfully be dressed in the language that usually clothes romantic or sexual love.

All of this mattered, to the ancient audience of the *Symposium*, because Socrates was selling them a picture of love that differed radically from their romantic conventions. The same is true for a modern audience, though the points of departure are not exactly the same. We will have occasion to discuss what made Socratic love strange to ancient Athenians, in general, and to Alcibiades in particular, below; for now, let us view it from a modern perspective. Here is a surely incomplete list of what Socratized romance would force us to leave behind:

(1) Taking people as they are: it is often considered romantic either to conceive of your beloved as perfect or as perfectly imperfect. Being satisfied with who they are is part of what it means to love them for who they are. Socratic love is, by contrast, perpetually dissatisfied.

(2) Romantic exclusivity: it is considered romantic to reject other people in favor of your beloved, at least for the duration of the relationship ("serial monog-

amy"). Passionate breakups are also considered romantic, for the same reason: when you are willing to dissolve your longstanding bond with X in order to be with Y, that can show how much you love Y. Socratic love is measured purely in positive terms: what is romantic is the progress you make together, and you should always be open to more of it, both with that person and with others.

(3) Sexual intercourse: from a Socratic point of view sexual activity is neither necessary nor sufficient for romance, and preoccupation with sex will distract people from their Socratic goals.

(4) Working together to stay alive, live comfortably, and transmit humanity into the future via children: all such nonphilosophical cooperative projects belong in the same category as sexual activity. Child-raising, homemaking, comfortable companionship, and so on—these are neither necessary nor sufficient for true romance, and have the potential to distract from it.

(5) Poems and stories and movies that we call "romantic": insofar as artistic representations of love stake their claim on romance by way of (1)–(3) (less often [4]), they get love wrong and are in fact unromantic.

Socrates is not saying that sex is dirty, or that you shouldn't have children, or that monogamy is a mistake, or that love poems should be censored. He is saying that none of these things truly embody the spirit of *erōs*; they do not achieve the goals that we have when our hearts are inflamed with the kind of passion that is suggested by the language in the *Symposium* and *Phaedrus*. That language therefore has the important role of reminding you how romantic you really are.

It is natural to react to the list above by telling Socrates that he can keep his so-called philosophical romance, because what everyone really wants is companionship and sex and romantic novels and monogamy and children. But that response is disingenuous. You may say you "just" want sex, but you do not seem to want it in any kind of simple or unproblematic way. Sexual desire is a famously tortured and obscure form of desire. We often lust after precisely what we can't have, as though sex couldn't give us what we want out of sex. More generally, life is filled with romantic frustrations—with painful breakups and dull, dead marriages, with extramarital affairs that predictably make life worse for everyone involved in them, with long periods spent miserably alone, with anguish over whether to marry and whether to divorce. People who are anxious to find a romantic partner typically have little idea in advance as to what kind of partner would make them happy: they don't know what they want. Couples are stymied over whether to have children, struggling with it as an impossible question: we do not seem to know what the point of having children is. People commit to monogamy but often go on to have affairs; people who are consumed by jealousy when their partners have affairs cannot explain why; and sometimes those two groups—the ones who have affairs and the ones who are incensed when their partners do—are the same people. It is common for couples to want more romance in their lives and not know how to go about achieving that goal. If an alien came to earth to study human romance, it is unlikely that we would be able to instill confidence in them that we know what we are doing. There is nothing in this domain about which it can be said that we "just" want that.

For one final illustration, consider the common enough phenomenon of the bad breakup. It is not unusual for someone who has come to hate the person who left her to nonetheless succumb occasionally to the impulse to text him, driven in part by fantasies of a reunion—but this time, she will be the one to reject him. This pattern of motivation is familiar enough that we have become desensitized to how strange it is. Imagine if someone behaved that way in relation to food: he is banging on the doors of a closed restaurant, demanding to be let in, ignoring the many open restaurants nearby, and when you ask him "Is the food here so amazing?" he complains bitterly that it's terrible and he hates it, but he *has* to go to this restaurant, or rather, he has to get them to open the door, so that he can slam it in their face, and walk away without eating anything. When it comes to restaurants, we would view such behavior as a mark that the person has lost their mind. Our romantic behavior is a sign of the same, if we let ourselves see it. If we try to claim that we "just like sex," or companionship, or romantic movies, or child-raising, that is not any more credible than if that man banging on the doors of the restaurant were to claim that he "just likes eating out." Socrates says that the person in love is in a state of *mania*, a word that means the same thing in Greek and in English.

Socrates can explain why romantic behavior is often puzzling: we are committed both to the rationality requirement and to the attachment requirement, and yet we don't know how to reconcile them with one another. But he thinks we are not stuck trading them off against one another, because they can be fully reconciled: there is no paradox about how my love can take the individual human being as its proper target if my love does not take the individual human being as its proper target; and once that target has shifted onto something divine and perfect and unimprovable, admiration and acceptance do go hand in hand. It is, indeed, rational to be fully and unconditionally attached to that which cannot in any way be improved. The threat of substitution vanishes. Socrates' logic is unassailable, even if we can also predict that he will have trouble getting this point across to a bunch of maniacs.

But perhaps he will have an easier time with us than with his original audience—at least with respect to (3) in the list above. In a sex-positive world equipped with increasingly clear standards of consent; low-risk and low-cost methods of birth control; improved detection, prevention, and treatment of sexually transmitted diseases; openness to the variety of human sexual appetites; and technology to facilitate casual hookups, the conceit that sex is, in and of itself, dangerous and transgressive becomes harder to sustain, and the truth that its aura of danger must be glory borrowed from elsewhere may become easier to access. Inquiry is, according to Socrates, what is truly dangerous, transgressive, and exciting.

III. Socrates versus Henry James

But can Socratic love really compete with (5) from the list above—the image of romance we get from fictional representations of it? As a test case, I will juxtapose Socrates' treatment of romance with my favorite literary representation of falling in love, which occurs in the novel *The Wings of the Dove* by Henry James, brother of William. In one scene, two people meet for the first time at a party in an art gallery:

> They had found themselves regarding each other straight, and for a longer time on end than was usual even at parties in galleries; but that in itself after all would have been a small affair for two such handsome persons. It wasn't, in a word, simply that their eyes had met; other conscious organs, faculties, feelers had met as well, and when Kate afterwards imaged to herself the sharp deep fact she saw it, in the oddest way, as a particular performance. She had observed a ladder against a garden-wall and had trusted herself so to climb it as to be able to see over into the probable garden on the other side. On reaching the top she had found herself face to face with a gentleman engaged in a like calculation at the same moment, and the two enquirers had remained confronted on their ladders. The great point was that for the rest of that evening they had been perched—they had not climbed down; and indeed during the time that followed Kate at least had

had the perched feeling—it was as if she were there aloft without a retreat.[15]

It will be instructive to see where Socrates agrees with James and where Socrates is prepared to correct James. The first thing to notice is that James does not represent falling in love as *falling*; instead he adopts the Platonic metaphor of love as *ascent*. The ascent springs from a desire to know, and the pursuit of the fulfillment of this desire is arrested: caught by and diverted onto the person who reciprocates it. These lovers appear to be frozen in the air, staring at each other. The gaze that they direct at one another, "regarding each other straight," is, at the same time, a searching gaze, the gaze of "two enquirers." Lovers would not fall in love—or rather, as we should put it here, climb up to love—unless they were looking for something. Thus far, we can say that James captures something that is not only true but Socratic.

The un-Socratic element of this story is that the Jamesian ascent ends at the top of the ladder, as though the lovers had found what they were looking for—each other. James' description of how this is more than a meeting of eyes and minds—"other conscious organs, faculties, feelers had met as well"—recalls Aristophanic fusion. James' lovers are "enquirers" only until they encounter each other; at the moment of confrontation, the search is over, and the lovers have no task remaining except, perhaps, appreciation. Socrates' criticism of this picture of love is simply that there is much more ascending to do; that the true object of appreciation is to be found much farther up; that James has cut off the real work of love, the work lovers do together, before it could even begin.

Suppose that we grant James' point, that the opening stage of love is like being up on a high ladder without a retreat, the question is: What happens next? If we imagine that there is no more ascending to be done, and that descent is impossible, then it is hard to avoid the conclusion that the next step will be to build a platform at the top of the ladder, to turn the ladder into something that is not a ladder anymore. The fundamental problem of romance is restlessness: pinning love down kills it. Lovers cannot hang there, frozen in midair, for long, and the awareness of the instability of that position leads lovers to try to build firm ground where they stand. We lovers can't stop ourselves from wanting to have, to possess, to securely own. Socrates doesn't dismiss this impulse, but he does deny it immediate gratification—further ascent is required. We shouldn't fuse with other humans, now, into love globs, we should resist fusing with anything until the argument has been fully and finally stabilized. At that point we will find ourselves fused with—which is to say, possessed of—what the argument has offered up to us: knowledge of the essence or Form or underlying nature of whatever we were inquiring into. In Socrates' picture, other people are not for fusing with. Other people allow the restlessness of love to drive us upward.

There is undoubtedly an appeal to being appreciated for one's great qualities, or unconditionally accepted as one is—and to finally, after a long quest, encountering one's "true love." But in the Jamesian version of this story, it stops at that point, and that means the ascent is arrested before the lovers get down (up?) to their real, which is to say inquisitive, business with each other. Moreover, as many fictional narratives attest, the point where love is arrested is not a stable one. *The Wings of the Dove* ends with Kate saying to her beloved, "We shall never be again as we were!" A true lover, according to Socrates, doesn't really want to be loved for who they are; they want to be loved precisely because they are unhappy with who they are. Socratic love takes the impulse toward the lovers' ascent as an impulse to change: lovers approach one other as inquirers, and their love is an aspirational ascent to knowledge.

It is important to understand, when it comes to the strangeness of Socratic love, that Socrates is not simply inventing a new and unusual kind of love to sit alongside our old versions of it. Rather, he's calling our attention to the well-known problems inherent in rational attachment, helping us see that romantic love, as we standardly pursue it, cannot solve these problems; and offering a new form of love, inquisitive love, that can.

IV. A Love Story: Socrates and Alcibiades

Does it feel good to be a participant in Socratic love? If you are on the receiving end of Socratic dissatisfaction, do you feel loved? If what someone loves is knowledge, does he treat humans lovingly?

There is a person who would have answered a resounding "NO!" to all of these questions. We have already met him: Alcibiades. The reader has probably noticed, by way of the pronouns that appear in the quotes from the *Symposium* and *Phaedrus* above, that the erotic relationships under discussion in Socratic dialogues are primarily between men. Bisexuality was the norm for elite Athenian men, who, although expected to marry women and have children, seem to have devoted their most concerted—or at least, most public—romantic efforts toward other men. These relationships often took a peder-astic form, in which an older man served as mentor to a younger one, who was thereby educated into moral and political life.[16] Those cultural norms shape Alcibiades' romantic expectations, and help explain why he was both outraged and fascinated by Socrates.

In the *Symposium*, Alcibiades tells the story of his doomed love affair with Socrates. It begins with Alcibiades sending away his attendant so that he can be alone with Socrates:

> My idea, naturally, was that he'd take advantage of the opportunity to tell me whatever it is that lovers say when they find themselves alone; I relished the moment. But no such luck! Nothing of the sort occurred. Socrates had his usual sort of conversation with me, and at the end of the day he went off.[17]

Alcibiades, disappointed but undeterred, invites Socrates on a series of dates. First, to the gymnasium, where men wrestled naked:

"I was sure that this would lead to something. He took exercise and wrestled with me many times when no one else was present. What can I tell you? I got nowhere."[18] Next, he invites Socrates to dinner, but Socrates leaves right after dinner. Finally, at another dinner, Alcibiades manages to drag the conversation out long enough that he can persuade Socrates to spend the night.

> The lights were out; the slaves had left; the time was right, I thought, to come to the point and tell him freely what I had in mind. So I shook him and whispered:
>
> "Socrates, are you asleep?"
>
> "No, no, not at all," he replied.
>
> "You know what I've been thinking?"
>
> "Well, no, not really."
>
> "I think," I said, "you're the only worthy lover I have ever had—and yet, look how shy you are with me! Well, here's how I look at it. It would be really stupid not to give you anything you want: you can have me, my belongings, anything my friends might have. Nothing is more important to me than becoming the best man I can be, and no one can help me more than you to reach that aim. With a man like you, in fact, I'd be much more ashamed of what wise people would say if I did not take you as my lover, than I would of what all the others, in their foolishness, would say if I did."
>
> He heard me out, and then he said in that absolutely inimitable ironic manner of his:
>
> "Dear Alcibiades, if you are right in what you say about me, you are already more accomplished than you think. If I really have in me the power to make you a better man, then you can see in me a beauty that is really beyond description and makes your own remarkable good looks pale in comparison. But, then, is this a fair exchange that you propose? You seem to me to want more

than your proper share: you offer me the merest appearance of beauty, and in return you want the thing itself, 'gold in exchange for bronze.'"[19]

Alcibiades does not accept this as an answer, and presses his case, to which Socrates offers the following response:

> In the future, let's consider things together. We'll always do what seems the best to the two of us.[20]

Alcibiades interprets this as a sexual invitation, and we reach the climax—or perhaps we should call it anticlimax—of the story:

> I slipped underneath the cloak and put my arms around this man—this utterly unnatural, this truly extraordinary man—and spent the whole night next to him. . . . But in spite of all my efforts, this hopelessly arrogant, this unbelievably insolent man—he turned me down! . . . I swear to you by all the gods and goddesses together, my night with Socrates went no further than if I had spent it with my own father or older brother![21]

Alcibiades describes himself as "deeply humiliated" by Socrates' rejection, but also spurred on to continue to court Socrates, though he does not know how: "The only trap by means of which I had thought I might capture him had already proved a dismal failure. I had no idea what to do, no purpose in life; ah, no one else has ever known the real meaning of slavery!"[22]

Alcibiades never does figure out how to "trap" Socrates, and ends his speech with a warning: "I told you how horribly he treated me—and not only me but also Charmides, Euthydemus, and many others. He has deceived us all: he presents himself as your lover, and, before you know it, you're in love with him yourself! I warn you, Agathon, don't let him fool you! Remember our torments; be on your guard:

don't wait, like the fool in the proverb, to learn your lesson from your own misfortune."[23]

The "horrible treatment" Alcibiades claims to have received from Socrates is the deprivation of love: Socrates makes you love him, but he won't love you back. But why does Alcibiades feel unloved? Alcibiades believes that his charms—his physical beauty—go undervalued and unappreciated while Socrates continuously draws attention to Alcibiades' "personal shortcomings."[24] Socrates is, of course, behaving just as his aspirational model of love would dictate. Alcibiades also believes that Socrates is not offering him anything *special*. Recall Alcibiades' disappointment, the first time they were alone, that Socrates merely "had his usual sort of conversation with me."

After Alcibiades finishes his speech, Socrates offers his own diagnosis of what went wrong between them: "As if the real point of all this has not been simply to make trouble between Agathon and me! You think that I should be in love with you and no one else, while you, and no one else, should be in love with Agathon."[25]

Agathon is a tragic playwright who had just won first prize for one of his plays at a dramatic festival, and it is in his house, and in his honor, that they have all gathered. According to Socrates, Alcibiades is afraid that Socrates is starting to turn his romantic attentions in Agathon's direction. Alcibiades wants, first, to be the exclusive recipient of Socrates' love, and, second, to be freed from the torture and prison of loving Socrates, free to shift his own love onto another. There is a connection between the two things Alcibiades wants: his frustrations and powerlessness over not being able to "catch" Socrates' love lead him to want to vengefully turn the tables so that Socrates is forced to endure loving someone who doesn't love him back. Alcibiades strongly resembles the man who bangs on the locked door of the restaurant whose food he despises. He needs to own Socrates but not in order to love him; rather, what it means to "have" Socrates is to trap him in a one-way love that runs in the reverse direction.

This pathological manifestation of romantic exclusivity is the dark side of Aristophanes' story about how we seek our other half.

Of all the circumstances in which human beings seek vengeance, there is perhaps none that arouses that emotion more powerfully than romantic rejection; when you find yourself bent on romantic fusion with someone who refuses to cooperate, it is almost impossible to avoid entertaining the fantasy of becoming the one who gets to reject them. As we saw earlier in the book, revenge is the characteristic way in which savage commands malfunction; we can now add that romance is the arena within which this malfunction occurs especially often, and especially dramatically.

Consider Alcibiades' sex-for-wisdom trade offer, and Socrates' comment that if Alcibiades could see such wisdom in Socrates, "you are already more accomplished than you think." Socrates is saying: if you could see great wisdom in me, you would already have that wisdom, because I am a mirror. Alcibiades wants to perch motionless on the ladder, idolizing Socrates, whereas what Socrates wants is to philosophize with Alcibiades.

Alcibiades' interest in wresting control from Socrates—his very framing of the relation in terms of traps, and slavery, and who is in charge—is a mark of a failure to see that there is something for the two of them to do together. Alcibiades' mistake is trying to direct his love at a person—Socrates—instead of at the target of their shared activity—knowledge.

V. SOCRATIC FRIENDSHIP

Let us now leave Alcibiades for a moment to examine Socrates' interactions with a different partner: Crito. Crito was one of Socrates' closest friends, appearing in the background of so many dialogues (*Phaedo, Lysis, Euthydemus, Apology*) that it is clear he was frequently to be found in Socrates' company. In the *Crito*, Crito shows up as the representative of all of Socrates' friends and supporters, when he goes to Socrates try to persuade Socrates to escape from prison. Moreover, in that dialogue, Crito laments that if Socrates dies, he will be "deprived of a friend, the like of whom I shall never find again."[26]

We have already discussed that critical scene, in chapter 3, as one in which Socrates rejects revenge as incoherent—a form of hateful love. I want to go back over it and consider it again in the light of Socratic friendship (*philia*). If the conventional understanding of *philia* demanded revenge on behalf of one's loved ones, and Socrates rejects that demand, does he reject the very concept of friendship? No, because he is prepared to Socratize it. Socrates replaces the fickle love of individual people with what it imitates: a shared love of argument. Socrates' resistance to escaping from jail is fueled by Socratic love.

Crito approaches Socrates and begs him, in the name of *philia* (friendship/kinship), to try to escape:

> I do not think that what you are doing is just, to give up your life when you can save it, and to hasten your fate as your enemies would hasten it, and indeed have hastened it in their wish to destroy you. Moreover, I think you are betraying your sons by going away and leaving them, when you could bring them up and educate them. . . . I feel ashamed on your behalf and on behalf of us, your friends, lest all that has happened to you be thought due to cowardice on our part . . . the time for counsel is past and the decision should have been taken, and there is no further opportunity, for this whole business must be ended tonight. If we delay now, then it will no longer be possible; it will be too late. Let me persuade you on every count, Socrates, and do not act otherwise.[27]

Crito is telling Socrates that the demands of kinship dictate that he escape from jail. Socrates has kinship duties to his children, to raise them, and to his friends, to not make them look bad. Moreover, Socrates has a kinship duty to frustrate the desires of his enemies, by not letting them get away with it. Crito's claim is that Socrates is being disloyal, and betraying his ties of belonging—both by failing to help those he ought to help (his family and friends), and by failing to hurt those he ought to hurt (his enemies).

Socrates' response to this exhortation brilliantly Socratizes the very idea of kinship. Let's look at it carefully.

> My dear Crito, your eagerness is worth much if it should have some right aim; if not, then the greater your keenness the more difficult it is to deal with. We must therefore examine whether we should act in this way or not, as not only now but at all times I am the kind of man who listens to *nothing of what is mine* but the argument that on reflection seems best to me. I cannot, now that this fate has come upon me, discard the arguments I used; they seem to me much the same. I value and respect the same principles as before, and if we have no better arguments to bring up at this moment, be sure that I shall not agree with you. . . . How should we examine this matter most reasonably?[28]

Crito's speech comes from a place of deep affection and sincere desperation, and Socrates can see that. Yet Socrates is not unequivocally willing to hear Crito's emotional pleas as loving, and he rejects Crito's demand of urgency—the demand, as we might put it, just to get through the next fifteen minutes. Crito's eagerness to help Socrates is only "worth much" to Socrates if it is aimed in the right direction. For Socrates, that means that Crito's help must be consistent with Socrates' love of and loyalty not to people, but to arguments and principles.

Even here, in a passage far from any explicit theorizing about love, Socrates' message is consistent: the only thing that he is ultimately willing to devote himself to is an abstract ideal. Socrates invokes language of loyalty and betrayal in relation to non-people: he is prohibited from discarding arguments that have served him well in the past, arguments he values and respects, because that would constitute a kind of betrayal. He cannot abandon his beloved principles; he is unwilling to let them down. I have italicized the phrase "nothing of what is mine," which Socrates uses to make clear nothing is "mine" to him but the argument and principles and values that are truly his own. Only the argument is *akin* to him.

Notice that even as Socrates denies that loyalty and kinship bind him to any person, he approaches Crito in a resolutely cooperative, inquisitive, and inviting spirit: "We must examine." When Socrates says, "I only listen to the argument within me," he is not saying, "I am going to do what I am going to do, and you have no say in the matter." Socrates underscores this in a subsequent response, when he opens up an inquiry into the question of whether he ought to escape:

> Let us examine the question together, my dear friend, and if you can make any objection while I am speaking, make it and I will listen to you, but if you have no objection to make, my dear Crito, then stop now from saying the same thing so often, that I must leave here against the will of the Athenians. I think it important to persuade you before I act, and not to act against your wishes. See whether the start of our inquiry is adequately stated, and try to answer what I ask you in the way you think best.[29]

The plan Socrates proposes here, for how to manage his disagreement with Crito, is a version of the offer he made to Alcibiades.

> In the future, let's consider things together. We'll always do what seems the best to the two of us.[30]

Socrates really does see Crito as his "dear friend," which is why he wishes for himself and Crito to settle this matter between the two of them; in the terms of the language Socrates used in his proposal to Alcibiades, he is proposing that he and Crito first "consider things together" and then, having considered them, "do what seems the best to the two of us." This involves Socrates listening to Crito, and being unwilling to "act against his wishes," but it also makes a demand on Crito. Socrates is willing to hand over his agency entirely to the process of conversation, as long as Crito is willing to do the same. Socrates is, in effect, proposing that how they live is something the two of them can figure out together.

They can work together, if they are both willing to listen, not to the pressurizing forces of savage commands, but only to the argument unfolding over the course of their conversation. By Socratizing love, kinship, and loyalty, Socrates opened himself fully to Crito. For Socrates and Crito to work together, and for them to submit themselves to the force of argument, are one and the same thing. This is, concretely, what it looks like to love an ideal in the presence of someone. Notice, too, that in standing by his old agreements with Crito, Socrates is in effect standing by their love, and exhibiting a kind of loyalty and commitment to it.

Alcibiades admits that he is the one to defect from the relationship with Socrates: "I refuse to listen to him; I stop my ears and tear myself away from him. . . . My whole life has become one constant effort to escape from him and keep away."[31] Socratized commitment is, in fact, less fickle than the Alcibiadean kind. Loyalty, as it is commonly understood, is self-undermining. It includes the willingness to harm the person one loves, so long as they harm you first. The people to whom you are bound by ties of loyalty are also the people who can betray you, and if they do, conventional loyalty calls for a reprisal. Socrates is not willing to be conventionally loyal to Crito and Alcibiades—to love them on their own terms—because he is not willing to harm them, or to harm others on their behalf.

Socrates made an invitation to Alcibiades, to Crito, and presumably to a number of other people. It is an invitation into a shared life of considering things together, a life in which neither would shy away from confronting difficult truths—such as the truth that it is morally impermissible to break the law, or the truth that Alcibiades' political career might be a waste of time. Refusing to flatter his partner in inquiry is part of what it means for Socrates to live up to his ideal of rational attachment. Socrates won't accommodate Crito's desire to help him escape, because he thinks it comes from a misunderstanding of what friendship really demands, and he won't accommodate Alcibiades' sexual advances, because he thinks they spring from a misunderstanding of romance. What Alcibiades takes for a refusal to offer love is, precisely, an offer of Socratic love.

VI. SOCRATIC POLYAMORY

If Socratic love is philosophizing, then Socratic love is radically nonexclusive. Some of Socrates' "love affairs," which is to say, philosophical encounters, are short and underdeveloped, lasting not even the length of a dialogue (Agathon, Cephalus, Anytus, Meletus); others are one-time encounters with "public intellectuals" undertaken partly for the benefit of an audience (as in the *Gorgias*, *Hippias Minor*, and *Protagoras*); and in other cases, a dialogue offers us the opening act of what could or does develop into a longer relationship—the *Charmides*, *Alcibiades*, and *Lysis* would be good examples. In addition, we do know that Socrates had longstanding interlocutors, including Crito, Alcibiades, and of course Plato and Xenophon, among many others. Socratic love is not exclusive but additive, in that he seems to accumulate a group of regular associates, each of whom can further benefit by philosophical interaction with others in the coterie. One might ask, what is the difference, for Socrates, between romantic love on the one hand and the sorts of love we feel for friends or family members on the other? What is the difference between *erōs* and *philia*?

The answer is there is no difference: true *erōs* is a form of *philia*. When Socrates says that only the argument is "his own," this is of a piece with his saying in the *Lysis* that the good is one's first friend; or that real Justice and Moderation are the targets of erotic flight in the *Phaedrus*; or that love climbs up until it reaches the ideal of beauty in the *Symposium*. We shouldn't be surprised that Socrates merges *erōs* and *philia*: we do the same by way of our sliding scale.

Dating is the erotic end of the spectrum, and marriage—recall the park bench scene—is the *philia* end. (People regularly describe their spouses as "my best friend.") Any successful solution to the problem of rational attachment will find a way of including, within *erōs*, the stability and permanence characteristic of *philia*. We view romantic love as aiming to incorporate the other as a member of one's family.

The real difference between love today and Socratic love is that the Socratic fusion of *erōs* and *philia* goes both ways. Whereas we countenance many sorts of relationships as being full-fledged instances of *philia* in spite of the total absence of *erōs*—parents and children, siblings, friends, neighbors—for Socrates real philia requires *erōs*, because another person can only participate in your attachment to what is truly "your own" if they are part of your inquiry. This explains why, when it comes to the fate of his children after he dies, Socrates seems to be concerned primarily that they have opportunities to be refuted.[32]

Ignorance of the true nature of *erōs* leads Alcibiades to mark it out from *philia* in the conventional way, by the presence of sexual activity and the requirement of exclusivity; from that point of view, Socrates' behavior under the blanket, and his continued openness to the likes of Agathon, both amount to a "friendzoning" of Alcibiades. But in a Socratized world, there's only one zone, and Socrates is inviting Alcibiades into it. Of course, if we are Socratizing *philia* and *erōs*, we will also have to Socratize the intimate connection, mutual openness, and interpersonal vulnerability that characterize love. Socratic polyamory is that kind of polyamory that doesn't distinguish between having many lovers, and having many friends.

VII. SOCRATIC IRONY

When people first encounter Socrates—such as in an introduction to philosophy class—they often think that he is a jerk. Many persist in that view. They are put off by the fact that Socrates seems, to them, to be someone who deceptively conceals his real views while making a mockery of the people he is talking to. Oddly enough, there is a group of people who are attracted to Socrates for the same reason: they love his ironic detachment, his ability to stand aloof from his interlocutors, and the secret messages, theories, and ideas that you can extract from his words if, unlike most of his unworthy interlocutors, you are smart enough to interpret them carefully. The question of Socratic irony—When does Socrates mean what he says?—is probably the central controversy in Socratic scholarship; I have refrained from discussing it until now because I think the right context for understanding it—although it is rarely considered in this context—is that of love.

The place to begin, when it comes to the question of Socratic irony, is to notice both that and, even more important, *where* it explicitly surfaces in the dialogues. It shows up twice in Alcibiades' angry speech in the *Symposium*. While Alcibiades is complaining of having been treated "horribly" by Socrates, he also describes Socrates as ironic: "His whole life is one big game—a game of irony,"[33] says Alcibiades of Socrates, whom he also describes as speaking to him in an "ironic manner."[34] Alcibiades is not alone in accusing Socrates of irony; a number of Socrates' interlocutors have trouble believing that he could mean just what he is saying.

Thrasymachus attributes Socrates' general practice of questioning to irony:

> By Heracles, he said, that's just Socrates' usual irony. I knew, and I said so to these people earlier, that you'd be unwilling to answer and that, if someone questioned you, you'd be ironical and do anything rather than give an answer.[35]

Callicles likewise doubts Socrates' seriousness:

> CALLICLES: Tell me, Chaerephon, is Socrates in earnest about this or is he joking?

CHAEREPHON: I think he's in dead earnest about this, Callicles. There's nothing like asking him, though.[36]

CALLICLES: By the gods! Just the thing I'm eager to do. Tell me, Socrates, are we to take you as being in earnest now, or joking? For if you *are* in earnest, and these things you're saying are really true, won't this human life of ours be turned upside down, and won't everything we do evidently be the opposite of what we should do?[37]

Shortly thereafter, he explicitly accuses Socrates of speaking ironically:

SOCRATES: Tell me once more from the beginning, what do you mean by the better, seeing that it's not the stronger? And, my wonderful man, go easier on me in your teaching, so that I won't quit your school.

CALLICLES: You're being ironic, Socrates.

SOCRATES: No I'm not, Callicles.[38]

Callicles, Thrasymachus, and Alcibiades are using the Greek word *eirōneia*, from which we get the Latin *ironia* and later the English *irony*. In each of these cases, Socrates either explicitly or implicitly disputes the charge in question: he insists that they are wrong, and that he is not being ironic, that he means what he says. Clearly Socrates encountered this problem routinely, because in the *Apology*, Plato has Socrates express a worry that although "all that I shall say is true," nonetheless "perhaps some of you will think I am jesting,"[39] and later that "you will not believe me and will think I am being ironical (*eirōneiomenōi*)."[40] These are all of the places in Plato where Socrates is described as ironic, and it is worth adding that elsewhere—both elsewhere in Plato, when someone other than Socrates is being described as ironic, and outside Plato, in contemporary or earlier authors—the word *eirōneia* is likewise negative; it is a term used to blame people for deceptive insincerity.[41] The great Socrates scholar Gregory Vlastos comments: "Not Socrates, but his arch-rivals, whom Plato thinks impostors, are the ones he [Plato] calles *eirōnes* (ironists)."[42]

We can summarize the status of "Socratic irony" in the Platonic dialogues as follows: it seems that "irony" was a negative trait, a bad thing to be accused of; that Socrates was routinely accused of it; that these accusations tended to come from people who were in some way hostile to Socrates (Callicles, Thrasymachus, the older Alcibiades, the jurors who would vote against Socrates in his trial); that Socrates denied the accusations; that Plato and Socrates' other friends would have denied them. Writing about *eirōneia* in Plato, classical scholar Melissa Lane sums up the matter: "In Plato we see *eirōneia* being ascribed to Socrates in ways which indicate the ascriptions to be untrustworthy."[43] Which is to say, Plato didn't seem to believe there was any such thing as Socratic *eirōneia*; Xenophon nowhere mentions Socratic *eirōneia*; presumably Socrates' other close associates felt the same way. The dividing line between Socratic irony and its absence was also the dividing line between whether you were Socrates' enemy, or his friend.

All this would change: "The time would come, centuries after his death, when educated people would hardly be able to think of *ironia* without bringing Socrates to mind,"[44] writes Vlastos. Vlastos is thinking of Cicero, who lived three centuries after Socrates, and who said that Socrates exceeded all men in irony and the power to hide his own thoughts;[45] and of Quintilian, who lived a century after Cicero, and who described Socrates as an example of how "a man's whole life may be colored with irony." Quintilian also says Socrates "assumed the role of an ignorant man lost in wonder at the wisdom of others."[46]

Cicero and Quintilian seem as certain as Callicles and Thrasymachus that Socrates is ironic, but in the intervening centuries something strange seems to have happened: unlike Socrates' contemporaries, when they "charge" Socrates with irony they are *com-*

plimenting him. Cicero views Socrates' irony as an impressive and elegant stylistic flourish, Quintilian as a noble form of humility.

Before and during Socrates' life *eirōneia* was a term of opprobrium, but eventually it becomes a term of admiration and approval. Vlastos argues that it was Socrates—and specifically, Socrates as he is presented in Plato's dialogues—to whom we today owe the positive conception of irony. In fact, Vlastos goes so far as to claim the positive conception of irony as a Socrates' major cultural contribution to the sensibility of western Europe.[47]

Many friends and defenders of Socrates, Vlastos among them, have devoted themselves to making the case for the existence of such a positive form of irony. Vlastos does not want Socrates to come across as dishonest, or manipulative, or as someone who uses deceptive argumentation. Instead, says Vlastos, Socrates instantiates a good—Vlastos' term is "complex"—kind of dissimulation. From Hegel onward, many philosophers have carried forward this (supposedly) Socratic legacy of positive irony.[48] Following in the footsteps of Quintilian and Cicero, they argue, sometimes with dazzling sophistication, that there is a good way of not saying what you mean. For Kierkegaard, following Hegel, Socratic irony was "infinite absolute negativity"; for Leo Strauss, it was a way of adapting one's speech to different audiences; for Vlastos, it meant letting people figure things out for themselves; for Jonathan Lear, following Kierkegaard, it is an uncanny relation to one's own practical identity.[49] The result is that irony, for the contemporary Plato scholar, is something good and deep and sophisticated—and even, somehow, honest—by contrast with the accusations of shallow, deceitful trickery made by Thrasymachus and company.[50]

Melissa Lane wants to separate the *eirōneia* of which Socrates is accused from the *ironia* for which he is later praised; she thinks the meaning of the word changed, and we shouldn't use "irony" to translate "*eirōneia*." Lane's view is that when Socrates is charged with *eirōneia*, he is accused of *concealing* his true meaning and intention, whereas the Latin *ironia*, the German *Ironie*, and the English *irony* refer to a skill at *conveying*—typically to a second audience—one's true meaning and intention. She seems correct to note this change, but I do not think, as she does, that it is a change in the meaning of the word. It is, rather, a change in the vantage point from which the word is interpreted. What is (supposedly) deceptively concealed from Thrasymachus is the very same thing that is (supposedly) elegantly conveyed to Cicero.

If Thrasymachus and Callicles and Alcibiades were to read us moderns praising Socratic irony, I think they would be annoyed. Thrasymachus, Callicles, and Alcibiades were interacting with Socrates face-to-face, and they were complaining, not that he was lying, exactly, but that he was not being entirely direct or straightforward with them. Watching A be indirect with B is a very different experience when you are B. It may be charming, to Quintilian, to watch Socrates pretend to be less wise than Thrasymachus, but the same experience is not charming to Thrasymachus. The same can be said for Cicero admiring the "wit and genius" with which Socrates hides his thoughts or his "elegant kind of humour, satirical with a mixture of gravity"[51]—it is understandable that Alcibiades and Callicles look upon those respective scenes somewhat differently than Cicero does. If *eirōneia* really had a different meaning from *ironia*, then we could imagine Thrasymachus and co. agreeing with Cicero's praise of Socrates—but I think we can't.

The terms in which Cicero and Quintilian praise Socratic irony are too similar to those with which Alcibiades, Thrasymachus, and Callicles *blame* Socratic irony to call what has happened here a shift in the meaning of a word.[52] The shift is more like the one captured in Mel Brooks' joke, "Tragedy is when I get a papercut, comedy is when you fall down an open sewer and die." When it comes to catastrophe, we waver, depending on our level of personal involvement. The same is true of Socratic irony. The two poles between which we waver— involvement and uninvolvement—are alive and well today.

Those who have immersed themselves in the study of philosophy in general and Plato in particular are likely to see "Socrates" as synonymous with "irony" and "irony" as synonymous with a positive quality of verbal sophistication. People who are encountering this material from the outside—first-year students, those unversed in philosophy, those approaching the "primal scene" for the first time—instinctively inhabit the point of view of Alcibiades, Thrasymachus, and Callicles. They think that Socrates is being a jerk. The idea that Socrates is a jerk is not taken seriously among Plato scholars, who tend to dismiss this second point of view as a mark of the naïve and uneducated.

I agree that the novices are making an error about Socratic irony, but I think that the sophisticates are in fact making the very same error, to wit: believing in the existence of Socratic irony.[53]

But is it even possible to read the sorts of exchanges that I've been quoting throughout this book without hearing, in them, either mockery or ironic detachment? Yes. The time has come for the story of my own love affair with Socrates.

VIII. SOCRATIC SERIOUSNESS

I discovered Socrates in high school but I didn't fall head over heels until college, where I read all the dialogues, took classes on them, read commentaries on them, learned ancient Greek so I could read them in the original, learned Greek history so I could understand the context, and read Xenophon and Aristophanes for alternate perspectives on Socrates. Above all, I threw myself into the project of decoding the dialogues, scouring them for hidden meanings, desperate to access the true Socrates. I assumed, alongside my teachers, and alongside the scholars whose commentaries I read, that it was boorish to take Socrates at his word, and that one had to work hard to pierce the surface of the text so as to dig out its concealed insights.[54] But I became dissatisfied. I was getting better at producing elaborate explanations of what Socrates *really* meant, but I didn't feel I was getting any closer to Socrates. What had drawn me to Socrates was precisely that, unlike other figures in history, he was not merely a person you study; he was also a person you could make yourself into. I didn't just want to *interpret* Socrates, I wanted to *be* Socrates.

Thus, when I was twenty-one years old, a senior in college, I tried to do it—to be Socrates. I lived in Chicago, where the closest analog to the Athenian agora are the steps in front of the Art Institute, so that's where I went. When I got there, I walked up to the people milling around the front of the museum and asked them whether they wanted to have a philosophical conversation. When they said yes—and most of them did, somewhat to my surprise—I would follow up with a question such as "What is art?" "What is courage?" "What is the meaning of life?"

In the Socratic dialogues there is a rough pattern to how such interactions go: Socrates asks a question, such as "What is virtue?"; his interlocutor immediately supplies an overconfident answer; Socrates' refutation of that answer paves the way for an extended inquiry into the nature of the topic. This is not what happened to me. The conversations I had were all quite short, and never really got off the ground. The people I talked to seemed put off by my approach, confused about my intentions, and, in truth, somewhat afraid of me. They felt trapped, and I felt not at all like Socrates.

In retrospect, I understand their predicament. Imagine that someone walks up to you, right now, and asks you what the meaning of life is. It would be hard for you to believe that they really don't think they already know, and that they really think *you* might be the one to give them an answer. The level of vulnerability, and self-exposure, and trust that such a question requires is almost unthinkable. The height to which they have elevated you in assigning you this task seems unimaginable. And if, after you give your answer, they ask you a series of questions about it, it would be hard to believe that the spirit in which these questions were asked is that nothing separates their point of view from yours but their current incomprehension of your answer. If they claimed that they would immediately adopt your way of living, if only you explained it to them, you might think they were only acting, or pretending, or somehow making fun of you, or being ironic. The irony people projected onto me was the very same irony that I, in my quest for hidden meanings, projected onto Socrates.

And it is the same irony that Callicles, Thrasymachus, and Alcibiades project onto Socrates. They found it hard to accept that Socrates was for real, that he saw in them the potential of incredible beauty, and that he was ready to put his life in their hands. They felt sure that he was always preserving an ironic distance from them, in which he held the life of his mind apart from theirs. The theory of "Socratic irony" is precisely the theory that Socrates is not someone you can be, that the most anyone, including Socrates himself, could do is *play* Socrates.

Recall that when he first tries to seduce Socrates, Alcibiades does so by sending away his attendant so that the two of them can be alone:

> My idea, naturally, was that he'd take advantage of the opportunity to tell me whatever it is that lovers say when they find themselves alone; I relished the moment. But no such luck! Nothing of the sort occurred. Socrates had his usual sort of conversation with me, and at the end of the day he went off.[55]

Alcibiades is disappointed that Socrates is unwilling to capitalize on a moment of privacy by engaging in erotic banter. What Alcibiades misses is that Socrates' "usual sort of conversation" already amounted to the most erotic form of banter of which Socrates (and, if Socrates is correct, Alcibiades) was capable. Socratic irony is what Socratic intimacy looks like to those who can't believe in it; Plato implies, I believe, that the only thing shutting Alcibiades out of Socrates' love is Alcibiades' tragic inability to believe that Socrates was really offering it.

Look what happens when Callicles turns to Chaerephon—a Socratic insider—to ask whether Socrates is being serious.

CALLICLES: Tell me, Chaerephon, is Socrates in earnest about this or is he joking?

CHAEREPHON: I think he's in dead earnest about this, Callicles. There's nothing like asking him, though.[56]

Chaerephon's response underscores his status as an insider: just ask him. For Chaerephon, it really is that simple.

AS A YOUNG READER of Plato, I saw irony everywhere in the dialogues. Being able to point out double meanings made me feel smart, and it made me feel included. If Socrates is not wholly absorbed in speaking to his interlocutors, then I can imagine that some of his attention—and love—is directed outward, past the fourth wall, to me. He's talking over their heads, trying to reach a real philosopher. Like me. What makes *eirōneia* offensive to interlocutors such as Thrasymachus and Alcibiades is exactly what makes *ironia* so attractive to readers such as Cicero or Quintilian or me: the more Socrates withholds himself from them, the more Socrates seems to speak to us.

But this jealous and worshipful attitude toward Socrates, this desire to own him, to wrest him from the grasp of interlocutors unworthy of him—all of that is very Alcibiadean. Alcibiades compares Socrates to a statue who presents to the world a deceptively drab exterior, but is secretly filled with hidden treasures. Alcibiades claims ownership over Socrates by doubting whether anyone else has ever seen the real Socrates: "I don't know if any of you have seen him when he's really serious," and boasts that he, Alcibiades, alone had the good fortune, on one occasion, of having "caught him when he was open" and briefly witnessed the treasures he conceals from others: "I had a glimpse of the figures he keeps hidden within: they were so godlike—so bright and beautiful, so utterly amazing."[57] Alcibiades' jealousy distorts his own grasp of what is wonderful about Socrates.

The most radical feature of Socrates is not his godlike hidden wisdom but the naked vulnerability he displayed in treating others as sources of answers to his questions. That is, for Socrates, what one human being is to another: either a source of answers to your questions, or a source of questions that challenge your answers. Socrates explicitly rejected the kind of kinship relation constructed by the reader who, by reading him ironically, hopes to position herself in the inner circle of the special few who possess the esoteric knowledge required to understand Socrates.

If I approach you with double meanings; or by saying the opposite of what I intend; or with words that are geared only partly to you, and partly to another audience of which you are unaware; or with false praise designed to butter you up or false humility designed to soften your defenses—if I do any of these things, then I am not really serious about inquiring with you. Thrasymachus, Alcibiades, and Callicles are correct that, given what Socrates has purported to be doing with them, irony would be counterproductive. I agree with Thrasymachus and Alcibiades and Callicles that we shouldn't praise Socratic irony, and I agree with Plato that Socratic irony does not exist. There is no such thing as Socratic irony, except in the sense that it is indeed ironic that the man who hid his thoughts from others less than perhaps anyone in the whole history of the world should have come to be credited with the concept of irony as his central contribution to humanity.

Over the decades, a lot has changed about how I read Plato, but the single biggest change is that I have come to see less and less ironic distance or detachment between Socrates and his interlocutors. Increasingly, Socrates seems to me to be putting all his cards on the table, and this strikes me as an act of great friendliness, openness, and humanity. Where I once saw Socratic irony, I now see Socratic love.

Chapter 11

Death

A FEW YEARS AGO, I HAD A THREE-HOUR CONVERSATION with my friend Steve, online, in public, about premature death. Before I had the chance to talk to him again, he died, prematurely. It sounds absurd to say that I felt guilty for feeling sad, but I did: I felt sadder than I had a right to be. I wasn't his relative or even his colleague; we did not "go way back" via a connection from youth, or even graduate school; we were not part of some tight-knit circle of friends; we did not share much about our personal or emotional lives. The only thing we ever did together was talk philosophy.

I first met Steve at a conference, but most of our subsequent interactions were in coffee shops. He taught up in Evanston, north of Chicago, and I teach down in Hyde Park, on the South Side, so we'd swap papers and then get together at a coffee shop downtown, halfway between us, a few times a year, to discuss. The first time we spent all three hours on my paper. From then on I insisted we start with Steve's paper, before moving on to mine. I'd give him comments, he'd give me comments. That was it, that was our whole relationship, that's what I'm referring to when I talk about him as my friend: he was someone I exchanged paper comments with periodically, as academics are inclined to do.

It's not hard to come up with reasons for me to be sad about Steve's death. I'm sad to miss out on the philosophy he'd never get to write, and that I'd never get to read, and the conversations I'll never have with him. I'm sad on behalf of other people too—his wife, his young daughter, his brothers and parents, his close friends, and everyone who lacked the good fortune of meeting him altogether, and who might have, if he'd lived longer. And of course there is reason to be sad for him, sad that he'd miss out on those experiences—of family, of friendship, of philosophizing, of meeting new people. Those are good reasons, but when I consider all of them together, they somehow don't add up, either in quantity or in quality, to the pain I feel in my heart when I think about Steve's death.

I. The Consolations of Philosophy?

Unlike me, Steve was not a flashy person. He didn't dress oddly, he didn't use rhetorical flourishes, he didn't call attention to himself or reflexively make himself the center of every conversation. He was soft-spoken, gentle, and—in my experience—always calm. On casual inspection, there was not much that was unusual about him—if you met him, you'd notice he was tall and red-headed. Maybe, if you were especially observant, you'd notice he gave off the air of being content—happy with his lot in life. That's about it.

But when you started talking to him about philosophy, there was this shock. Imagine you're sitting at home, bored, looking at the same old living room furniture you've stared at a million times before, and there's a knock at the door. You open it, and everything around you is transformed. As soon as your visitor crosses the threshold, you realize that what had seemed to be a dull living room is actually full of mysterious objects, secret passageways, and works of art hidden in plain view. In a way that's hard to describe or explain, Steve took your ideas more seriously than you did. You'd toss out a thought, casually—"just a suggestion," "a point I'm in the habit of making sometimes," "no big deal," "it's probably wrong," "whatever"—and he would respond as if to say, "No, wait. This could be *real*. This could actually be something."

You don't get much sympathy for complaining about being a "thinker"—it's a cushy life—but thinking is so floppy, ideas are so vaporous and protean, that it's easy to get the impression that you are not really *doing* anything. It's easy to become exasperated with yourself for turning over the same old stale concepts and pedantic distinctions over and over again. As a thinker, you're always going around *making points*—"My point is . . . ," "All I'm trying to say is . . . ," "The point of this argument is . . ."—and the points are never pointy enough, they lose their force even before encountering counterarguments. Who cares, really? Are we getting anywhere?

The magic of Steve was that his questions, his observations, his calm cheerful insistence on staying on a topic when you thought you'd exhausted it—the sort of insistence that, from anyone else, would come across as stubborn, but that with him came off as gentle resoluteness—his very presence had the effect of solidifying ideas and giving them substance. He made the nothing and nowhere dream-world of "the life of the mind" into what felt like a real place you could actually be in. It's not that you suddenly had all the answers, or any of the answers, really, but with Steve you felt you could find them—he filled you with energy and courage and seriousness, with the spirit of "We are in a place designed to be explored, a place where knowledge is ours for the taking."

When I think of Steve, I think of that place, and I think about what it was like—should I say "was" or "is"? On the one hand, it wasn't mine—it was ours, and he's gone. On the other hand, a whole world can't just poof out of existence like that, can it? Some things are not the sorts of thing that can disappear: "Sorry, the number four is gone, we don't have it anymore." When I think of the place I shared with Steve, I can't help thinking of it as being there, and as not being there, at the same time. This is what I'm sad about: how a mind—with all the space that only it could create—could be the thing we call "dead." In fact, the word *sad* really doesn't cut it. The thought feels broken, and my heart breaks trying to think it.

I've dealt with death before—in fact I've dealt with the deaths of people much closer to me, emotionally, than Steve. But the only other time I've felt *this* pain—the pain of the absolute unthinkability of the person's death—was with someone I also interacted with mostly philosophically. I think that it is *because* Steve was a philosopher, and because my engagement with him was philosophical, that his death brings me the peculiar pains that it does.

That seems to be the opposite of what Socrates predicted would happen. In the *Phaedo*, which is the dialogue dramatizing Socrates' death and the conversations he had right before it, Socrates says that "a man who has truly spent his life in philosophy is probably right to be of good cheer in the face of death."[1] It is in this dialogue that Socrates describes philosophy as a preparation for death, and philosophers as experts in death: "The one aim of those who practice philosophy in the proper manner is to practice for dying and death."[2]

Steve was a philosopher, and I am, and that was the reason for and nature of our connection—we knew each other almost exclusively as philosophers. Yet the thing that was supposed to make dealing with death easier has made it harder. Where is the calm and equanimity that Socrates promised me?

The *Phaedo* shows us how well philosophy prepared Socrates for death; his friend Phaedo, who narrates the story, reports that "in both manner and words he died nobly and without fear." Does philosophy really have that effect on the rest of us? Eerily enough, I asked Steve this exact question during our last conversation—I asked him whether philosophy prepares you for death. Even more eerily, he never got a chance to answer. A question from the audience interrupted him, I said we would go back to it, and we had time, we went for another hour, but I forgot, and he forgot, and our conversation ended. And then before I could talk to him again, he died. So we never did. What is the answer? Does philosophy prepare you for death?

II. IVAN ILYICH

Suppose you knew you were going to die soon. How would you prepare yourself? I am not asking about how you would make the best use of your remaining time. If you were asked that question, I imagine you'd answer that you want to spend your final days being close to loved ones, or engaging in the activities you most enjoy, or finishing important projects, or eating favorite foods, or visiting favorite places. But it's not clear that those same activities would serve as an answer to the question about preparation. There's a difference between finding the best way to spend the remaining hours before a portentous event—such as a final exam, a wedding, an interview, one's own death—and *preparing* for that event. I'm not asking how you would *pass* your final hours. I'm asking, how you would prepare?

You might think this question makes no sense, because there is no such thing as being prepared or unprepared for death; you might think the only question is how to pass the time until it comes. I think that is wrong, and so does Tolstoy, who makes the experience of being unprepared for death the subject of his novella *The Death of Ivan Ilyich*. The story concerns the final months of the life of a bourgeois Russian official. Ivan Ilyich was a paragon of familial, career, and social success—his home is a party hub for aristocrats—until he started experiencing a pain in his side. The pain gets worse, and eventually it becomes clear that Ivan is dying. Everyone around Ivan—his wife, his friends, even his doctors—pretends that he is not dying, that he will get better soon. They repeatedly insist that he is turning a corner. He finds himself miserably isolated in his knowledge of what his happening:

> In the recent loneliness in which he found himself, lying with his face to the back of the sofa, loneliness in the midst of a crowded city and his numerous acquaintances and family—loneliness that could not be more absolute anywhere, either at the bottom of the sea or underneath the earth.[3]

Ivan's solitude comes from the fact that he alone is confronting his death, while everyone else around him is studiously avoiding it.

Ivan himself does make efforts to avoid this confrontation, but when he attempts to resume his former habits and practices, he finds they have been hollowed out:

> He tried to return to his previous ways of thought, which had concealed the thought of death from him. But—strangely—everything which previously had concealed and covered up and obliterated the awareness of death now could no longer produce this result. . . . He would say to himself, "I'll take up some work, that's what I live by." And he went to court. . . . But suddenly in the middle of it the pain in his side . . . began its own gnawing work. Ivan Ilyich listened and tried not to think about it, but it kept on. It came and stood right in front of him and looked at him, and he became petrified; the fire in his eyes died down, and he again began to ask himself, "Is it alone the truth?" . . . He would return home with the depressing awareness that his work as a judge couldn't hide from him as it used to what he wanted it to hide; that with his work as a judge he couldn't be rid of It. And what was worst of all was that It was distracting him not to make him do anything but only for him to look at It, right in the eye, look at it and without doing anything endure inexpressible sufferings.[4]

Illness gives Ivan a distance from his life-projects that allows him to wonder, for the first time, whether he ever had any reason to pursue them. What were once untimely questions—Should I be married to this person? socialize with these people? pursue these career goals?—have become open to the suspension of judgment. And Ivan finds no way of defending his old, reflexive answers:

> It occurred to him that the notion that had previously seemed to him a complete impossibility—that he had not

lived his life as he should have done—could be the truth. It occurred to him that his barely noticeable attempts at struggling against what was considered good by those in high positions above him, those barely noticeable attempts which he had immediately rejected, could be genuine, and everything else wrong. His work and the structure of his life and his family and his social and professional interests—all that could be wrong. He tried to defend all that to himself. And suddenly he felt the fragility of what he was defending. And there was nothing to defend.[5]

Ivan finds, upon examination, that his answers to questions about how to live had been dictated by the savage commands of his kinship group—he did what it took to fit in among the people that surrounded him.

"But if this is so," he said to himself, "and I am leaving life with the realization that I have lost everything I was given and that it's impossible to put right, then what?" He lay on his back and started to go over his whole life afresh. When in the morning he saw the manservant, then his wife, then his daughter, then the doctor—every one of their movements, every one of their words confirmed for him the terrible truth that had been disclosed to him in the night. He saw in them himself, everything by which he had lived, and saw clearly that all this was wrong, all this was a terrible, huge fraud concealing both life and death. This realization increased, increased his physical sufferings tenfold. He groaned and tossed about and pulled at the clothes on him. He felt suffocated and crushed. And he hated them for that.[6]

And yet, having dismissed his life as a lie, he nonetheless goes on to cling, in the face of death, to a "declaration that his life had been good. This justification of his life caught on something and stopped him from going forward, and that distressed him most of all."[7] This problem, the problem of justifying his life, is the Tolstoy problem.

Ivan's predicament is that death both necessitates a justification for his life and also drives him to abandon the only justification he knows. But the other significant aspect of Ivan's predicament is that he is *alone*. Everyone around him is consumed by the need to evade death, the only way they know how—by immersing themselves in those same, conventional pursuits, and by pretending that Ivan is not dying. Tolstoy makes repeated reference to this "lie" and how it isolates Ivan: "this lie around and within him poisoned most of all the last days of Ivan Ilyich's life." Consider his final interaction with his wife:

> "You feel better, don't you?"
>
> Without looking at her he said, "Yes."
>
> Her clothes, her body, the expression of her face, the sound of her voice—everything said to him one thing: "Wrong. Everything by which you have lived and are living is a lie, a fraud, concealing life and death from you."

He hates her for forcing him to lie to her, so much that he can no longer tolerate her presence:

> His expression when he said "yes" was terrible. Having said that yes, he looked her straight in the eye and with unusual strength for his weakness turned himself face-down and cried: "Go away, go away, leave me!"[8]

Ivan experiences his wife as taunting him: waving before him and then immediately withdrawing the possibility of comfort and human connection.

The life of Ivan Ilyich turned out to be no preparation for the death of Ivan Ilyich; his life was such that he became unhinged by the prospect of death. Ivan's crisis resembles Tolstoy's own, as described in *Confession*, written many years earlier, and it also resembles the one experienced by Pierre in *War and Peace*:

> Whatever he started thinking about, he came back to the same questions, which he could not resolve and could not stop asking himself. It was as if the main screw in his head, which held his whole life together, had become stripped. The screw would not go in, would not come out, but turned in the same groove without catching hold, and it was impossible to stop turning it.[9]

The questions Pierre asks himself are the same familiar set, and instead of making progress on them, Pierre, like Ivan and Tolstoy, runs headlong into the fact of death:

> "What is bad? What is good? What should one love, what hate? Why live, and what am I? What is life, what is death? What power rules over everything?" he asked himself. And there was no answer to any of these questions except one, which was not logical and was not at all an answer to these questions. This answer was: "You will die—and everything will end. You will die and learn everything or stop asking." But to die was also frightening. . . . And he again put pressure on the stripped screw, and the screw kept turning in one and the same place.[10]

We find the same scene yet again in *Anna Karenina*, where the character Levin recapitulates the experiences of Tolstoy in *Confession*:

> "Without knowing what I am and why I'm here, it is impossible for me to live. And I cannot know that, therefore I cannot live," Levin would say to himself . . .

> Levin was several times so close to suicide that he hid
> a rope lest he hang himself with it, and was afraid to go
> about with a rifle lest he shoot himself.[11]

These various descriptions of confrontations with the prospect of death share a desperate, sinking sense that most of the practices on which we rest the meaning of our lives collapse at the slightest intellectual provocation; and that, once life's justification has been undermined in this way, no amount of thinking can restore it. All of these descriptions are also characterized by loneliness and isolation: in *Confession*, Tolstoy presents himself as posing questions primarily *to himself*; the same is true of Ivan and Pierre and Levin.

Over and over again, Tolstoy tells the same story of being unprepared for the confrontation with death. Whether this confrontation occurs at the end of one's life, as it does for Ivan, or in middle age, as it does for Tolstoy, or in one's twenties or thirties, as it does for Pierre and Levin, the effect is the same. The prospect of death represents the stopping of the clock that has been ticking the background of everything we do, counting off each fifteen-minute period. All of a sudden, untimely questions can no longer hide in the background; all of a sudden, we are called upon to answer them—but we cannot. We cannot justify our lives, and the attempt to do so will only convince us that life is meaningless. Tolstoy tells this story with courageous honesty. But it is not the only story there is.

III. MISOLOGY, MISANTHROPY

If the *Death of Ivan Ilyich* describes what it's like to be unprepared for death, the *Phaedo* shows us what it's like to be prepared. Socrates passes his final hours inquiring into the immortality of the soul. This activity is of a piece with how Socrates has lived his life—he died as he lived, philosophizing—and, at the same time, fitting or suited to the circumstances he is in, namely, to someone who faces impending death. His usual modes of living neither collapse nor have to be suspended in the face of death.

Recall how intractable Ivan finds the problems posed by death: "It was distracting him not to make him do anything but only for him to look at It, right in the eye, look at it and without doing anything endure inexpressible sufferings."[12] Ivan is torn between staring death in the face and suffering, alone, inexpressibly, on the one hand, and looking away from death, alongside his family and friends, on the other. Socrates, by contrast, looks death straight in the eye, and has a conversation with his friends about it.

The *Phaedo* is a rigorous philosophical dialogue, presenting a series of increasingly complex arguments for the immortality of the soul, as well as objections to those arguments, one of which requires an extended foray into the general theory of causation. It is also unmistakably a death scene: Plato describes how Socrates' closest friends gather mournfully around him in his jail cell to keep him company during his final hours, how he drinks the hemlock, how they watch its numbing effects work their way up from his feet, to his legs, to his belly, knowing that "when the cold reached his heart, he would be gone."[13] And then it does, and he is.

If the *Gorgias* showed us that philosophy can be political and the *Symposium* and *Phaedrus* showed us that it could be erotic, the *Phaedo* shows us that philosophy can be funereal. It is worth stressing how remarkable it is that philosophical conversation is capable of matching the solemnity of death. Ordinary conversations—describing the enjoyment of a movie or a meal, grumbling discontentedly about one's boss, planning for an upcoming vacation—seem unfitting or inappropriate in the face of death. Death trivializes those pursuits and concerns, just as death trivialized Ivan's whole life. That is why we have developed certain religious or quasi-religious ("spiritual") formulae that we use at funerals and memorial services—a special kind of speech designed to erect a wall between life and death. But that kind of speech is specialized to a funereal context, whereas philosophy is not. Philosophy is a way of living one's life, and it is also a way of dying.

It is possible to die without experiencing the kind of terror that Ivan feels, just as it is possible to coast through life without confronting the Tolstoy problem. The condition that many of us are in on our deathbeds—in severe pain, or drugged, or otherwise cognitively impaired—makes it unlikely that dying will be the time we confront death. But the question raised by Tolstoy is this: Is such a confrontation *ever* anything but a disaster? Tolstoy shows us many characters, at many stages of life, including himself, recoiling from failed attempts to face their deaths with eyes wide open. Is such a thing even possible?

The answer Plato offers in the *Phaedo* is yes. He shows us Socrates *choosing*, at a specific moment during his final hours of life, to confront death. The event takes place at around the midpoint of the dialogue, after Socrates has given three arguments for the immortality of the soul. There is a murmur of unrest among his friends. It turns out that two of the people who have been listening quietly to Socrates' arguments—Simmias and Cebes—have formulated objections to them. They are troubled by the force of these objections, which seem to show that Socrates is wrong to believe that his soul will survive his death, but hesitate to raise them: now does not seem like the right moment to call into question Socrates' basis for facing his death with equanimity.

Socrates encourages them to present their objections. He insists that his proximity to death makes him even *more* eager to hear their counterarguments; he compares himself to swans who, though they sing beautifully all the time, sing even more beautifully in the face of death. Socrates *wants* to face up to the prospect of his own death. Simmias and Cebes, taking Socrates at his word, each offer a persuasive counterargument to the claim that the soul survives the destruction of the body. The narrator of the dialogue, Phaedo, reports that the effect of these arguments was to induce despair in the assembled group:

When we heard what they said we were all depressed, as we told each other afterwards. We had been quite convinced by the previous argument, and they seemed to confuse us again, and to drive us to doubt not only what had already been said but also what was going to be said, lest we be worthless as critics or the subject itself admitted of no certainty.[14]

But the one person who did not despair was Socrates. Phaedo expresses wonder at:

the pleasant, kind, and admiring way he received the young men's argument, and how sharply he was aware of the effect the discussion had on us, and then how well he healed our distress and, as it were, recalled us from our flight and defeat and turned us around to join him in the examination of their argument.[15]

How could someone who is clinging to the immortality of his soul in the face of his imminent death receive counterarguments in a "pleasant, kind, and admiring way"? That is the question that Plato wants us to be asking ourselves. The answer is clearly not "Because Socrates knew he had a decisive reply in his back pocket." After Socrates gives his reply, Simmias still confesses to "private misgivings about what we have said" and Socrates concedes that this worry is well placed: "You are not only right to say this, Simmias, but our first hypotheses require clearer examination, even though we find them convincing." Socrates can pursue the argument no further, as it is time for him to die, but suggests that Simmias do so, in the future: "If you analyze them adequately you will, I think follow the argument as far as a person can, and if the conclusion is clear, you will look no further."[16] Socrates responds in a "pleasant, kind, and admiring way" to the challenges levelled against the answers on which he bases his life, not because he knows these challenges are wrong, but because he thinks they might be right.

Socrates explains why he reacts as he does: "We should not become misologues [i.e., haters of reason], as people become misanthropes. There is no greater evil one can suffer than to hate reasonable discourse."[17] He warns that just as the experience of being let down by other people, especially our closest friends, can lead us to lose faith in humanity, so too the experience of being let down by arguments leads people to lose faith in argumentation.

Socrates thinks that the mistake is similar in the case of people and arguments. If you find everyone around you to be evil and untrustworthy, you should conclude that the problem might be you—you are trying "to have human relations without any skill in human affairs." Likewise, though misologues "believe themselves to have become very wise and that they alone have understood that there is no soundness or reliability in any object or in any argument" and think that "all that exists simply fluctuates up and down," the fluctuation in question is really happening in their own soul:

> It would be pitiable, Phaedo, he said, when there is a true and reliable argument and one that can be understood, if a man who has dealt with such arguments as appear at one time true, at another time untrue, should not blame himself or his own lack of skill but, because of his distress, in the end gladly shift the blame away from himself to the arguments, and spend the rest of his life hating and reviling reasonable discussion and so be deprived of truth and knowledge of reality.[18]

When Pierre concludes "there was no answer to any of these questions," Socrates would say he is mistaking a fact about himself for a fact about the world:

> We should not allow into our minds the conviction that
> argumentation has nothing sound about it; much rather
> we should believe that it is we who are not yet sound and
> that we must take courage and be eager to attain sound-
> ness, you and the others for the sake of your whole life
> still to come, and I for the sake of death itself.[19]

Socrates goes further than encouraging them to pursue the inquiry. He warns them of his own bias. He admits that the proximity of death will incline him to be too ready to believe in the immortality of the soul, and thus that they need to guard against what he is saying:

> If you will take my advice, you will give but little thought
> to Socrates but much more to the truth. If you think that
> what I say is true, agree with me; if not, oppose it with
> every argument and take care that in my eagerness I do
> not deceive myself and you and, like a bee, leave my sting
> in you when I go.[20]

Socrates sees that he is defending an answer to an untimely question, and he invites his friends to refute him. The link Socrates draws between misology and misanthropy is as telling as the claims he makes about each considered on its own. Recall how their existential crises lead Pierre, Ivan, and Tolstoy to withdraw into themselves. If Socrates is right, and the kind of thinking they are trying to do is essentially social, then misology and misanthropy amount to the same thing. Love of argument requires that you love other people— and, because refutation is the highest favor you can do another person, the converse is also true.

This is the climactic moment of the dialogue: Socrates shows great love for his friends when he instructs them to "give but little thought to Socrates but much more to the truth," and great courage in being willing to subject to refutation the claim on which his ability to confront death rests, "for the sake of death itself."

Tolstoy accurately perceives that many ways of spending your life cannot stand up to death, collapsing in the face of it; philosophy, Socrates demonstrates, is an exception. Philosophy did not consign Socrates to loneliness and alienation in the face of death, nor did the prospect of death undermine his own answer to Socratic questions—even though it invited objections to those answers. Philosophy lives up to the challenge of death. You can be philosophizing—socially, philanthropically, happily—and be facing up to death, at the same time. I experienced this myself.

IV. THE CONFERENCE

After Steve died, there was a memorial service at the chapel of the university where he taught. Three people close to him made beautiful speeches about him, a priest read a poem, there was music. It was a moving ceremony, but not an unusual one. It was what happened before the ceremony that was unusual. One of Steve's colleagues had organized a philosophical conference on Steve's unfinished work, and the conference took place over the two days before the ceremony. About thirty philosophers flew in from around the world to sit around a table and discuss Steve's unpublished papers one by one.

I arrived at the conference on the verge of tears, and as soon as I saw a friend I collapsed into his arms, sobbing. As the first session convened, I said to myself, this is going to be impossible. I'm not going to be able to do philosophy; I'm going to cry every time I open my mouth. Looking around the room, I could see that others were in the same condition. But an amazing thing happened to us: After a few initial tears, we all threw ourselves into philosophy mode. My first comment was a question—there were a few sentences in the paper for that session that I felt were important, but didn't understand. I read them out loud and asked for help. My friend—the one who I had been sobbing with just a few minutes earlier—came to my aid. Calmly, patiently, he explained Steve's argument—and the flaw he saw in it. Together, the group summarized the main points of Steve's papers, we explained them to one another, we raised objections to his claims, we thought about responses on his behalf, or about ways of pressing our objections further—to make them more devastating. We considered how to tie the papers together, and to our own work; we joked over his funny choices for examples. We argued with one another, and with Steve. We remarked, more than once, how much Steve's personality came through in his written words, how much we felt we were talking to him.

The conference didn't feel tragic; it felt happy. And it was *interesting*. There were things we wanted to know, we were trying to find them out, and inquiring into them was somehow *befitting*; it suited the context of death. Philosophy—the fact that we were philosophers, and that Steve was one too—made it possible to be mourning our friend, and to be happily inquiring, at the same time. And when I think about how cooperative, and spirited, and well-prepared, and engaged everyone was in the discussion, and compare it to other conferences I've attended, I think I can say something stronger: the fact that we were dealing with our friend's death made us philosophize better, like the swans who sing more beautifully when faced with death.

But if philosophers are so good at dealing with death, why am I so sad about Steve? It might be noble if I were sad on his behalf, or on behalf of his family, but the truth is that I am selfishly sad: I miss him. Even now, as I write these words, I feel sad about Steve being dead—sad and not cheerful, not inquisitive, not energized, not philosophical. Why? I think the answer is simply that I'm often thinking about his death when I'm alone. Confronting the death of a dear friend requires all of my philosophical powers, and I don't have all of those powers sitting in a room, by myself. Sitting by myself, what I am doing is not so much thinking as remembering. I am remembering the conference, and the joy and attentiveness of those conversations. I am remembering the *Phaedo*, and my many classroom discussions of it—it is probably the text I have taught most often during my fifteen years as a professor at the University of Chicago.

Most of all I am remembering Steve, and what it was like when I had him to share my ignorance and my struggle.

We are unable to think about the most important things on our own, and we habitually shield ourselves from this terrifying fact. All of us, even professional philosophers, walk around with a conceit of knowledge separating us from other people. Our feeling of basic mental competence—of having the answers on which the living of our lives depends—keeps us from connecting with others in the ways that benefit us most. Ignorance of ignorance leads us to think that we are to figure these important questions out for ourselves. Ignorance of ignorance prevents us from thinking alongside another person about what neither of us knows. Ignorance of ignorance is the barrier between us. Socrates dismantled that barrier. Steve did the same.

Recalling my conversations with Steve forces me to confront the gulf between what my mind can do on its own, and what it is capable of when paired with a kindred spirit. I know what I *don't* have, what I'm *not* doing—and that's what hurts. To be a philosopher is to feel, with special acuteness, one's need for others—especially those others who also feel the same need, with the same acuteness. You can see what an immense task lies before you, how easily you might be prevented from achieving it, and how precious are those who are willing to help.

Does that mean that philosophy makes you less afraid of death—or more? The answer to that question begins with corpses.

V. Corpses

Where is Steve now? Does he still exist? What happens to your soul after you die?

Many readers of this book will immediately offer the following answer: Steve is nowhere, he does not exist; when you die, your soul, if any such thing can be said to exist, is annihilated. Some readers may, based on tenets of their faith, think that the opposite answer is obvious. Very few people, if asked these questions, will even pause before they respond, or think that the answers are anything but straightforwardly obvious. Both those who think that it is easy to say that Steve exists, and those who claim that it is easy to say that he does not, resemble one of Socrates' interlocutors: Meno. Recall that after Socrates asks him what virtue is, Meno is unable to stop repeating how easy that question is to answer: "It is not hard to tell you, Socrates . . . it is easy to say . . . it is not difficult to describe . . . one is not at a loss to say what virtue is."[21] Meno's facility for saying what virtue is turned out to be superficial; he was readily brought to contradict himself. The same is true with our facility for determining the fate of the soul.

It is in fact not obvious to anyone what happens to a person after they die, and if some people claim that it is, their actions belie those statements: those who insist that something called "science" definitively forecloses the possibility of life after death act continue to act as though the souls of their loved ones are still around, those who piously avow a belief in the immortality of the soul mourn their dead loved ones as though their souls have been annihilated, and neither group treats corpses in a manner consistent with their professed account of death. When it comes to the question of what happens to the soul after death, we waver. The name for wavering in this arena of life is *superstition*. What characterizes the philosophical approach to death, above all, is the principled rejection of superstition.

Those who vehemently deny the immortality of the soul—call them materialists—waver by continuing to care about fulfilling the dead person's wishes, by thinking it is important to remember them and memorialize them, by describing themselves as still loving them, and by treating invocations of their name as carrying weight: "If X were here, he would be ashamed of you!"

In defense of these practices, materialists might claim that what they care about is not the person themselves, but their "legacy" or "memory" or "spirit." People invoke these terms in order to avoid a troubling admission of concern for someone who does not exist, who is not there, who is nothing. But if you see the dead person's legacy or spirit as enough of a *thing* that it makes sense for you to direct love and concern at it, if you think that in honoring their "memory" you are honoring not some part of yourself, but a being distinct from yourself, then you are wavering from materialism. You evidently think that even when the body is gone, something of a person remains, disembodied.

Materialists ought to be more puzzled than they are by their inclination to comply with the dead person's wishes, requests and intentions. If we are close to one another, and I tell you I wish for X, and later on I tell you I've changed my mind, and no longer wish for X, you wouldn't persist in trying to fulfill that wish. If I stop wishing for something, you stop having reason to fulfill my wishes. But if you are a materialist, you ought to think that dying is a pretty decisive way to stop wishing for something: someone who does not exist can't do anything, including wish. So it is puzzling for materialists to act as though someone's failure to exist were compatible with their continuing to engage in the practice of wishing.

If materialists waver, so do believers. People whose religions commit them to the existence of the afterlife feel the terror of death just as anyone else does, nor are they spared the wrenching pain of loss. They do not respond to their loved one's death as though the loved one has moved to a place where they can't contact them for a while but expect to later rejoin them. They might *say* that is how they see the situation, but their profound sorrow and their mourning practices point in a different direction. Nor does their religion expect consistency of them: if a devout Catholic approaches her priest in the throes of grief over the death of a loved one, their religion enjoins the priest to offer her comfort and support, rather than to censure her as an evident nonbeliever. Religious people, like nonreligious people, put up with superstitious wavering. Socrates does not.

When Crito asks Socrates, "How shall we bury you?" and Socrates replies, laughing, "In any way you like, if you can catch me and I do not escape you." Socrates laments the fact that

I do not convince Crito that I am this Socrates talking to you here and ordering all I say, but he thinks that I am the thing which he will soon be looking at as a corpse, and so he asks how he shall bury me.

Socrates insists that Crito "should not say at the funeral that he is laying out, or carrying out, or burying Socrates." One might have thought that this linguistic point—do we call Socrates' corpse "Socrates"?—doesn't matter so much. But Socrates insists that it does, and explains this point to Crito directly:

> For know you well, my dear Crito, that to express oneself badly is not only faulty as far as the language goes, but does some harm to the soul. You must be of good cheer, and say you are burying my body, and bury it in any way you like and think most customary.[22]

The norm in our world, as in Socrates', is to treat corpses with extravagant fanfare. The second half of the *Iliad* is organized around the fate of corpses—first Patroklus', then Hector's—and militaries today continue to repatriate corpses, even at great danger and expense. The opening of Karl Ove Knausgaard's series *My Struggle* is an extended meditation on the efforts we make to dispose of corpses quickly and discreetly.

Knausgaard imagines some scenes of death: An old man dies during a movie. A teacher gets a heart attack on the playground of the school. A homeless person freezes to death. A small girl is run over by a bus. A young man gets drunk, falls into a lake, and drowns. Knausgaard comments, with reference to their corpses, "There is no need for any rush, they cannot die a second time."[23] He wonders, "Why all this haste to remove them from the public eye?"[24]

If one asks which theory of the soul's fate after death answers Knausgaard's question, the answer is, neither. Our scrupulous care for corpses makes sense neither on the assumption that the soul survives death, nor on the assumption that it is annihilated by death. If the soul survives death, then it does so by being separated from the body. It would follow that from the moment of death onward, it does not undergo what the corpse undergoes, and what happens to the corpse does not matter to the person. If the soul is annihilated by death, it likewise no longer inhabits the body, and the person is now nonexistent. Whether the soul is mortal or immortal, death separates it from the body, which entails that from death onward the soul's fate is decoupled from the body's. In either scenario, it is silly for Crito to do what Socrates anticipates he is going to do "when he sees my body being burned or buried, [to] be angry on my behalf, as if I were suffering terribly."[25]

Socrates summarizes what he knows about life after death when he says, "Either the dead are nothing and have no perception of anything, or it is, as we are told, a change and a relocating for the soul from here to another place."[26] This is what people living in his time knew—that one of those two things is true—and people today are in that position, too. We know that we will die, and we know that after we die, we will either be annihilated or continue to exist in some form. Whatever we might profess, we do not actually know which of those two things will happen. The state of the art has not advanced much in 2,500 years. Most people have beliefs about the question, and are prepared to assert those beliefs with passionate certainty, but they also are inclined, like Crito, to waver substantially from those beliefs.

It is precisely this wavering that Socrates will not tolerate. He is not going to insist that his friends agree with him about the question he is inquiring into—Is the soul immortal, or is it destroyed at death?—but he puts his foot down when it comes to the existence of death. Death is real, corpses really are not ensouled, and Socrates will not put up with any superstitious nonsense to the contrary. Socrates cannot say for certain whether his soul will be eliminated or continue to exist after he dies, but he feels extremely confident that exactly one of those possibilities will occur. He is not going to allow

his friends to suggest that his dead body will be haunted by his disembodied soul, because that is a way of trying to assert two incompatible possibilities at the same time. Why is Socrates so intolerant
of superstition? Because wavering between two incompatible results
gets in the way of the attempt to inquire as to *which* of those results
is actually true.

We are accustomed to looking at death through a panicked haze,
so terrified of it that we will not even really accept that it takes place.
From that vantage point, we can only *feel* the fear of death; we cannot understand why we are fearful. Once we die, our bodies will be
nothing more than things. To understand the import of this event,
you first have to believe that it will take place. Looking at death
carefully, and accurately—as neither the religiously minded nor the
scientifically minded are inclined to do—does not dispel one's own
fear of death. But it does clarify the situation: we will discover there
are two ways to fear death.

VI. FOMO versus FONA

The *Phaedo* is, like many Platonic dialogues, a conversation within a
conversation. It begins when a man who was not present at the death
of Socrates accosts Phaedo, who was, and asks to hear every detail of
what happened. Plato thus makes it clear that after Socrates' death,
his friends told and retold the story of their final conversation with
Socrates. I have had a similar experience: since my final conversation
with Steve was online, and recorded, I have been able to watch it
many times. As I mentioned, the conversation was about premature
death. We started with a paradox I'd found in a blog earlier that day,
to the effect that all death is premature death.[27] If you consult actuarial tables you will see that someone who dies at eighty could have,
given that he reached that age, expected a few more years of life. The
same is true at age ninety, or ninety-five; even when you turn one
hundred nineteen, which is as high as the actuarial tables go, you
can expect six more months. No matter when you die, someone who

arrived at that age could reasonably have expected to live longer, because that's what happens to most people who arrive at that age.

Steve's solution to the paradox as stated was that we should fix expectations at birth, on the basis of the natural lifespan dictated by our biology. We can then say that dying at forty is premature, whereas dying at ninety is not. But Steve and I came to conclude that there was indeed a sense in which all death is indeed premature, though it doesn't have much to do with actuarial tables or biology. To see why, we have to consider the drive by which any conscious mind—whether it be ten, forty, or ninety years old—reaches forward and illuminates not only the present moment but also some stretch of the upcoming time.

Suppose that the oldest person who has ever lived is alive right now. They'd have no basis for expecting that "most people who arrive at my age live a bit longer," and yet they still wouldn't be expecting to die at every moment. Living, at any age, involves projecting yourself into the future. When we go through a day, making decisions, planning, organizing our agency, we stretch ourselves forward in time. Indeed, this kind of stretching is required even for the mental activities of planning, deliberating, and considering, all of which take time. And so it is natural that one fears the scenario in which this expectation is not met, in which one is cut off from the future one is counting on. In this sense, all death is premature death, whereas in the biological sense, only some death is.

When I first watched the video of my conversation with Steve, I was overwhelmed by sadness, and struck by the many strangely portentous moments in the conversation. Over time, however, I came to approach the video differently: to study it. On the second or third viewing, I started to become dissatisfied with Steve's analysis. Steve's death strikes me as premature not only because, at thirty-eight, he hadn't lived out his biologically mandated lifespan, but— somehow—because he was a philosopher. But why would the fact that he was a philosopher make his death seem especially premature? I watched again, hunting for an answer to that question. Sometime around the fifth or sixth viewing, I realized that there is a distinction that lurks in the background of our conversation the whole time. We keep alluding to it, skirting around it, brushing up against it, but never explicitly bring it up. It is a distinction between two different ways of projecting oneself forward in time, and thus two different forms that the danger of interruption can take. I realized there isn't a single fear of death, but two versions of that fear.*

The first version is a manifestation of the bodily command. Our bodies savagely command us to protect them, to keep living at all costs. They tell us that being deprived of more life is, per se, an evil, and they do this by filling us with blind, unthinking terror in the face of death. Epicureanism, the philosophical school focused on taming the bodily command, is especially attuned to this bit of savagery; it is, therefore, unsurprising that the two best known arguments against the fear of death—or rather, to anticipate the distinction I am about to make, against *this version* of the fear of death—have come from Epicureans.

Epicurus argues that death cannot be a misfortune, since there is no one around to suffer it:

> So death, the most frightening of bad things, is nothing
> to us; since when we exist, death is not yet present, and
> when death is present, then we do not exist. Therefore,
> it is relevant neither to the living nor to the dead, since it
> does not affect the former, and the latter do not exist.[28]

The poet Philip Larkin, who sings out his own fear of death in the poem "Aubade," rejects this argument:

> *specious stuff that says* No rational being
> Can fear a thing it will not feel, *not seeing*

---

* I am setting aside the fear of eternal suffering in Hell since that is really a fear of *not* dying.

That this is what we fear—no sight, no sound,
No touch or taste or smell, nothing to think with,
Nothing to love or link with,
The anaesthetic from which none come round.[29]

The Epicurean says that the absence of the subject of experience is the reason why we shouldn't be afraid of death. According to Larkin, this is silly, because the disappearance of the subject of experience is precisely what we fear in the first place.

Another famous Epicurean argument, presented by the Roman poet and philosopher Lucretius (99–55 BCE), tells us that rationality requires symmetrical treatment of past and future: if the question is whether it is a bad thing not to exist for some stretch of time, then we should answer this question in the same way with reference to the time before we were born, and the time after we die. We shouldn't be any more bothered by postmortem nonexistence than we are by prenatal nonexistence.[30]

The philosopher Thomas Nagel replies to Lucretius' argument, offering the following justification of our asymmetrical response: someone born earlier than Steve would have to be a different person from him—formed from a different sperm and egg, and perhaps even to different parents. By contrast, it is easy to imagine that Steve could, in principle, have lived longer than he did. A person can lament missing out on the time after she died without thinking that she missed out on any time before she was born. The forward-looking fear of death is justified, according to Nagel, because "a man's existence defines for him an essentially open-ended possible future, containing the usual mixture of goods and evils that he has found so tolerable in the past."[31]

I don't want, here, to try to adjudicate these disagreements— between Epicurus and Larkin, between Lucretius and Nagel. Instead, I want to point out an assumption they all share, one that is expressed well in the quote from Nagel, just above: the fear of death is the fear of being deprived of the "usual" sorts of goods with which life has already familiarized you. Larkin agrees, when he bemoans the loss of tasting and smelling and loving and linking. He already knows what those activities are like, and he wants to keep doing them. This is how the fear of death appears when it is the product of the bodily command: a demand for continuity, for more of the same.

The popular acronym FOMO can be used to refer to the fact that the bodily command instills in us a "fear of missing out" on the future instantiations of the goods we have experienced in the past. Larkin and Nagel disagree with Epicureans about whether FOMO is a good reason to fear death—Larkin and Nagel think it is—but all parties agree that *if* there is a reason for fearing death, it is FOMO. It is a basic principle of Epicureanism that, whatever the fear of death is, it isn't a fear of missing out on something *new*: Epicureans equate the good with pleasure and insist that there are no new pleasures in store for us.[32] What the future has to offer you are the same goods you have already been experiencing over the course of your life. Larkin and Nagel do not call this assumption into question, but if one does, one arrives at a distinct reason to fear death.

When we speak of "the end of life," that phrase can refer to the time when life comes to a stop, but it can also refer to the fact that life sets us a completable task. In this second meaning, "end" is synonymous with "goal" or "target." It is possible to fear that these two senses of "end" will not come together for us, and life will stop before it's finished. I will call this second version of the fear of death FONA, because it is a "fear of never arriving." Whereas FOMO is exclusively a fear of being deprived of future goods, FONA is a fear of being deprived of both present and future goods: if I will never arrive at the goal of the activity I am currently engaged in, then I might as well not have done any of it. There is no reason to take the means to an end you will never arrive at: FONA is the fear that you are striving in vain.

Notice that the two Epicurean arguments do not address FONA at all. Even if I won't be around to experience my failure to arrive at my goal, I can lament the fact that this future, unexperienced failure renders my current actions pointless. And, to address the Lucretian argument, striving for a goal is essentially asymmetrical: failure to arrive at your destination is only a failure *after* you've gotten started.

We can find FONA expressed in poetry, for instance in the Keats sonnet that begins:

> *When I have fears that I may cease to be*
>   *Before my pen has gleaned my teeming brain,*
> *Before high-pilèd books, in charactery,*
>   *Hold like rich garners the full ripened grain*[33]

Only immortality would satisfy Larkin's insatiable desire for more and more of the same, whereas Keats could, in principle, be satisfied by living long enough to glean all the unripe ideas teeming in his brain, ripen them to the full, and enclose them in a sufficiently high pile of books. Keats had a task he wanted to get done, and he (rightly) feared that he would not live long enough to complete it. The difference between how Keats and Larkin approach death might, in part, be due to age: "Aubade" was one of Larkin's last poems, he finished it at the age of fifty-five, eight years before his death, whereas Keats' sonnet was written when he was twenty-two, three years before his death at the age of twenty-five. It stands to reason that a young man's fear of death will be more likely to take the form of FONA, an old man's, FOMO. When we see it as especially tragic that a young person's life was cut short, we are thinking in terms of FONA; when we see *any* death, no matter how old, as sad, we are more likely to be thinking in terms of FOMO. The right way to think about the premature death paradox with which Steve and I wrangled is that in one way (FOMO) all death is premature, and in another way (FONA) some deaths are more premature than others.

VII. Philosophical FONA

Though Socrates comes across as brave and stoical in the *Phaedo*, Plato shares one striking detail that reveals a chink in the Socratic armor.

In the opening moments of the conversation, before the philosophical inquiry begins, the reader learns that while in prison, Socrates started writing poetry. Socrates explains that for a very long time he had had versions of a dream in which he receives instruction to "practice and cultivate the arts."[34] Before his trial, his long-standing interpretation of that dream had held that it was encouraging him onward in the pursuit of philosophy, but during the days spent waiting to die he began to second-guess himself. Maybe the dream had meant, all along, that he should write poetry? So he started setting the stories of Aesop to verse, composing poems for the first time in his life.

Socrates relates these facts breezily, without much fanfare, and his friends don't pursue the topic. Commentators are likewise inclined to pass over these brief remarks so as to focus on the meat of the dialogue—the significance of death and the immortality of the soul—but it's worth pausing for a moment to appreciate how strange this is. Socrates, who famously refused to write his own ideas down, who eloquently declared himself to be against writing, started doing just that?[35] Socrates, who often inveighs against the poets as dangerously ignorant (of their ignorance) of their own subject matter, became a poet? In the final days of his life, Socrates entertained some sort of doubt as to whether philosophy was his true calling? Apparently.

In the ensuing conversation with his friends, and in the earlier jail cell conversation reported in the *Crito*, Socrates betrays no such doubts about his life's purpose. But the reader might reflect that it is not so surprising to learn that there were moments when he was sitting alone in his cell, waiting to die, when he was less than fully sure of himself, moments when he did not feel full of eagerness and courage, moments when he may even had something like the experience that Ivan had when he "started to go over his whole life afresh" and felt terrified by his inability to justify himself.[36]

It appears that the philosopher is not immune to the fear of death. But the question is: Which version of that fear does he feel? Just before Socrates drinks the hemlock, Crito points out that he could extract a few more minutes of life:

> But Socrates, said Crito, I think the sun still shines upon the hills and has not yet set. I know that others drink the poison quite a long time after they have received the order, eating and drinking quite a bit, and some of them enjoy intimacy with their loved ones. Do not hurry; there is still some time.[37]

Socrates firmly refuses:

> It is natural, Crito, for them to do so, said Socrates, for they think they derive some benefit from doing this, but it is not fitting for me. I do not expect any benefit from drinking the poison a little later, except to become ridiculous in my own eyes for clinging to life, and be sparing of it when there is none left. So do as I ask and do not refuse me.[38]

Socrates thinks that it might be understandable for others to cling to life, always wanting a bit more of it, but this sort of attitude would be unfitting for him as a philosopher. In the opening of the dialogue, Socrates' wife is present with him in the jail cell, and when she sees his friends she remarks, "Socrates, this is the last time your friends will talk to you and you to them." At this, Socrates sends her home. He does not want his friends, or himself, filled with sadness at the prospect of the future conversations they are missing out on. After he drinks the hemlock, and his friends break down in tears, he chides them along the same lines: "It is mainly for this reason that I sent the women away, to avoid such unseemliness . . . so keep quiet and control yourselves." Socrates will not tolerate displays of FOMO. Why? I suggest: Socrates sets FOMO aside to focus on FONA, which looms so large for a philosopher that confronting it calls for all his energy and attention.

Consider what happens when Crito asks after Socrates' last wishes:

> What are your instructions to me and the others about your children or anything else? What can we do that would please you most?[39]

Socrates tells Crito that he has only one instruction for him, which is to "live following the tracks, as it were, of what we have said now." As mentioned above, Socrates admitted to Simmias that "our first hypotheses require clearer examination, even though we find them convincing. And if you analyze them adequately, you will, I think, follow the argument as far as a person can." Socrates wants his friends to continue his inquiries—and he expects them to. In the *Apology*, after the jury has voted to put him to death, Socrates prophesies that many would spring up, in his place, to refute the Athenian people.[40] Socrates sees that he is going to die without completing his life's task. How can he avoid being paralyzed by the terror and pain of that thought? The answer is: hope. He hopes that he himself will continue philosophizing in the afterlife, that his friends will continue in his footsteps in their own lives, and, generally, that philosophy will go on.

Epicureans wanted to dispel FOMO because the disquiet of worrying about what you might miss out on in the future prevents you from enjoying those very same goods, now. The fear of death is an irritant in the tranquil calm that is Epicurean happiness. Socratics want to dispel FONA for a very different reason: because it can sap your motivation, dampen your energy, and prevent you from throwing yourself into whichever task you fear may be interrupted by death. Epicurean arguments against the fear of death are designed to keep you stably ensconced in the present; Socratic arguments against the fear of death are designed to move you forward.

Socrates is always exhorting people to move forward. For example, he says in the *Meno*: "We will be better men, braver and less idle, if we believe that one must search for the things one does not know, rather than if we believe that it is not possible to find out what we do not know and that we must not look for it."[41] Socrates' response to the depression induced by Simmias and Cebes' objections is very similar. When the assembled company starts to doubt whether arguing is really getting them anywhere, and they begin to suspect that "the subject itself admitted of no certainty," Socrates hears the voice of FONA whispering in the background. He chides them to be brave and energetic: "We must take courage and be eager to attain soundness, you and the others for the sake of your whole life still to come, and I for the sake of death itself." Socrates may see FOMO as beneath him, but FONA is a real threat. It must have been FONA that afflicted him in those lonely hours in his jail cell when he wondered whether it had been a mistake to devote his life to philosophy.

When Socrates says that philosophers are experts in death and dying, when he speaks of acting "for the sake of death itself," when he confesses that he is "in danger at this moment of not having a philosophical attitude about" the immortality of the soul, Socrates is thinking primarily of FONA. The poet's FONA may be extinguished by producing a sufficiently high pile of books; the philosopher's won't be. The philosopher faces FONA in its most acute form, because she takes on a task whose shape is not dictated in advance by the temporal confines of a human life: "it does not matter to such people whether they talk for a day or a year, if only they may hit upon that which is."[42]

Those are the lines from the *Theaetetus* that I quoted when introducing the phrase "untimely questions" in part one. In that passage, Socrates sketches a prototype of the ideal philosopher, and contrasts it with someone who "is always in a hurry when he is talking; he has to speak with one eye on the clock."[43] Interlocutors such as Euthyphro and Protagoras routinely break off their conversation with Socrates by telling him that it is time for them to go: they are getting through life fifteen minutes at a time, which is to say, they "speak with one eye on the clock." Projects that take longer than fifteen minutes—be it months, or years—also keep you on the clock, both because they typically dictate what you need to do for a given fifteen-minute period, and because they stand in the shadow of the big clock of life. Even a project that requires you to dedicate your whole lifetime to it is different from one that requires you to take your eye off the clock altogether. Whereas we usually ask ourselves what we can get done in the next fifteen minutes, or the next few years, or perhaps our whole lives, when we step into the role of the philosopher, we must disregard all such clocks. For that is the only way to ask questions such as, "Is the soul immortal?" (or "What is thinking?" or "How can love be both rational and attached?" or "When and where do we practice equality?").

How do you take on, in a life, a project that is too big for a life? What if, like Socrates, you have less than an hour left to live, and you've just been confronted with some objections that call for much more than an hour's worth of philosophizing? How do you avoid giving up?

One tempting move is to claim that the journey is the destination, because the joys of philosophical inquisitiveness are their own reward. If this were true, philosophical FONA would become FOMO—a fear of missing out on more of the same. But it simply isn't true. Philosophy is an end-directed activity; it aims at knowledge. What motivates the person who engages in it is the desire for that knowledge. Socrates does not spend his final hours taking a last draft of his "usual pleasures" of philosophical conversation. He spends them looking for answers. There is somewhere the philosopher is going, which makes it reasonable for her to fear the prospect of never arriving there. Granted, Socrates thinks limited progress is both possible and valuable—an answer can become partially tied down, even if not yet completely tied down—but one makes limited progress only by aiming for completion. In order to philosophize, Socrates must vanquish the voice of FONA, which tells him, "You will never achieve knowledge about the soul's immortality." How does he do it? For one, practice: he has spent his whole life approaching people such as Protagoras and Euthyphro and bravely diving into some huge question he knows they will all too soon walk away from. Socrates has become an expert at taking his eye off the clock. For another, he has help.

If I am right that even Socrates was subject to moments of wavering when he was alone in his cell, then we can explain his harshness toward his friends' wavering by way of the central claim of this book: in the presence of others, something becomes possible that isn't possible when you are alone. Socrates sees the duty of a friend to be the source of precisely the sort of assistance we can't give ourselves: to challenge your claims, hold you to your agreements, and persist in the inquiry. They remind you that the only alternative to inquiry—the way we live when we're not living inquisitively—is pretending that you already have the knowledge that you are seeking. However frightening and dispiriting inquiry may be, it is better than the alternative. Your friends are there to help you stop pretending.

Many people assume that the *real* you are the tears you shed when you are alone, not the brave face you put on in public. Larkin cynically dismisses the idea of being brave in the face of death: "Courage is no good: It means not scaring others."[44] He assumes that the brave face must represent a nod to social convention, which is to say, the savage command of kinship. Socrates does not agree, because he thinks there is something different that we can do with other people, besides negotiate the bonds of kinship: we can inquire with them. Socrates denies that his true self is the person he is when no one is looking, believing that he is his truest self when he's arguing with his friends. Socrates' foray into poetry teaches us that what fortifies him in the face of death is not his unshakable belief in the immortality of the soul—a belief presumably present to him in his private moments as well, and indeed one would have felt all the more secure when it was not exposed to challenges and doubts—but rather his argumentative, inquisitive practice of philosophy in relation to that belief.

What helped Socrates face death was not his belief that the soul was immortal, but his inquiry into whether it was.

Tolstoy and his characters encounter the Socratic truth that the unexamined life is not worth living, but without the Socratic tools that would help them see how the examined life is possible. Recall Tolstoy, in *Confession*: "But *as soon as* I tackled them and tried to find the answers, I at once became certain first that these were not childish and stupid questions but the most important and profound questions in life, and second that *I could not, just could not answer them, however much I thought about it.*"[45] By his own account Tolstoy lives much of the first part of his life fifteen minutes at a time, until, sometime around midlife, he looks up from the clock and finds himself faced with a set of untimely questions—only to be immediately engulfed by waves of FONA. He is so paralyzed by the terrified certainty that he will never arrive at real answers to these questions that he cannot get himself to inquire at all. This is the Tolstoy problem: there is a thought you are avoiding your whole life, namely, the thought that your life may be unjustified, and when you confront it, your life unravels.

The mythology of death often involves a confrontation with a divine figure who demands that you explain yourself. He stands between you and a gate that you can only pass through if you succeed in justifying your life. Socrates himself tells some version of this myth multiple times, at the end of the *Gorgias*, the *Phaedo*, and the *Republic*, while at the same time conceding that it is only a myth: "No sensible man would insist that these things are as I have described them."[46] Socrates clearly thinks that the myth of being judged at the end of one's life contains an insight. What is it? I propose that this myth tells us what the problem of death represents for us: it is our way of thinking about the time when there is nothing left that stands between you and untimely questions, when they can be delayed no longer. Preparation for death is preparation for that time, and to do philosophy is to see that time as right now.

Socrates found that you can confront untimely questions without being overwhelmed by FONA, so long as you do so together with others. If you are a philosopher, you routinely ask questions that are too big for you to answer, in conversations that you know will be cut off before reaching their endpoint, and then they are cut off, and you don't arrive at the endpoint, and you wake up the next day and do it all over again. This is what Socrates means by saying that the philosopher is an expert in death and dying, that he has been preparing all his life for death.

The final words of the *Phaedo* praise Socrates as "a man who, we would say, was of all those we have known the best, and also the wisest and the most upright."[47] Socrates' friends were awed and inspired by his courage, but they may not have taken sufficient account of the role they played in making it possible.

"In what way is the study of philosophy training for death?" I asked this question at the one hour forty-minute mark of my final conversation with Steve, and he never had the chance to give voice to his answer. But I think he did show me his answer. In our final conversation, as in so many of the others, Steve and I were preparing ourselves, and one another, for death.

Acknowledgments

WHEN I FIRST SAT DOWN TO WRITE THIS BOOK IN earnest, I found myself confronted with a challenge: If I am correct that thinking is not something a person can do by herself—that when it comes to the most fundamental questions, we all have blind spots in crucial places, and need other people to show us why we are wrong—then how can the book in which I express this thought constitute thinking? And if it doesn't, what kind of philosophy book is it? I decided that the book should begin by answering these questions, so my first written efforts, in relation to the book, were devoted to an expansive introduction that would allay all such doubts about the project. But what I wrote had the opposite effect, at least on me. So I rewrote it. And again, and again.

I spent a year caught in the Sisyphean trap of trying to undo the fact that I was writing, by writing. Socrates' solution to this problem is simple—don't write:

> You know, Phaedrus, writing shares a strange feature with painting. The offsprings of painting stand there as if they are alive, but if anyone asks them anything, they remain most solemnly silent. The same is true of written words. You'd think they were speaking as if they had some understanding, but if you question anything that has been said because you want to learn more, it continues to signify just that very same thing forever. (*Phaedrus* 275d)

Socrates is saying that written words stand to spoken words as paintings of human beings stand to real people. A man in a painting looks a lot like a real man, but unlike a real man he can't move, or talk to you. Likewise, writing doesn't respond to your questions: it says the same thing every time you read it. It looks like thinking, but it isn't thinking.

Socrates compares writing down one's ideas to planting seeds in barren soil from which nothing can grow: pointless. He understands that your mind is not my plaything. I can't insert ideas into you; I can't make you know anything. It is only if you are active in relation to ideas that you will be able to asses them for truth, and that means you must be a speaker in the conversation, not merely a listener. This is why Socrates recommends against writing in favor of question and answer, which "is not barren but produces a seed from which more discourse grows" (*Phaedrus* 277a).

I wish I could tell you that after so much time smashing my head against this problem, and these passages, I came up with a brilliant solution. But that is not what happened. Instead, I gave up on trying to explain how the book would be possible, and simply set out to make it actual. I assumed that as I wrote the book the answer would come to me. I have now reached the end of that process, and I regretfully report that it has not. I do not have an account of how it is possible for writing to be inquisitive, and this in spite of the fact that at every moment of writing the talks that would become the drafts that would get revised into book chapters, in every conversation about how to interpret a tricky passage of Plato, in every debate about how to view the contemporary world through a Socratic lens, I have had my eye on only one goal: to produce an inquisitive text for you. To what degree I succeeded, I leave you to judge, but without a theory of inquisitive writing, I cannot claim to have offered you much help with that judgment.

I am grateful for the opportunity to acknowledge all of this. I acknowledge the existence of the problem of inquisitive writing, and that I have failed to solve this problem, and that I ought to have done so. I acknowledge my guilt. But I believe that thinking is a social process, which means that defects of this book cannot be not mine alone. I would like to acknowledge the guilt of others, as well.

My closest interlocutors, and therefore the people most directly to blame, are my husband Arnold Brooks and my ex-husband, Ben Callard. Every claim in this book was born in one of our conversations, and their passionate investment in every idea, every argument, every detail of interpretation put them in a uniquely favorable position to give me what I continue to lack. My editor Dan Gerstle, and my agent Margo Fleming, each of whom read many drafts of this book, including the ill-starred introductions just alluded to, surely bear some responsibility as well, as do the many esteemed philosophical colleagues with whom I have discussed parts of the book, especially Eric Brown, Sarah Buss, Christopher Moore, Oded Na'aman, Rory O'Connell, Christopher Roser, and Joshua Sheptow.

I have been testing the ideas presented in this book on hundreds of exceptional UChicago students for well over a decade. I consider them all culpable for not pressing me further, but I would single out: Jessica Aaron, Sarale Ben-Asher, Madeline Busse, Giacomo Cetorelli, Noah Chafets, Steven Chen, Viviana De Alba, Spencer Dembner, Su Dedehair, Cal Fawell, Ava Geenen, Olivia Gross, Joshua Fox, Henry Hopcraft, Caroline Hoskins, Jess Ip, Lucy Johnson, PK Kanoria, Allo Kerstein, Joshua Kramer, Anya Marchenko, Sarah Okayli Masaryk, Jessica Oros, Ganesh Mejia-Ospina, Anna Prisco, Ermioni Prokopaki, Ben Schall, Nur Banu Simsek, David Singer, Joshua Trubowitz, Adam Trujillo-Hanson, Charlie Wiland, Sophia Wyatt, Iris Yahi, and Karen Zhu.

In a broader way, the blame extends to my first Plato teachers at the University of Chicago: Arthur Adkins (*Apology*), Liz Asmis (*Symposium*), Eric Brown (*Protagoras*), Joseph Cropsey (*Parmenides*), Jonathan Lear (*Republic*), Ian Mueller (*Phaedo*) and Leon Kass (*Meno*). It was in Leon's home, at a Passover seder in 1995, that I first raised the question about inquisitive writing. At the time, I posed it thus: why does anyone publish? Once you have an idea, why do you want other people to have it? I remember walking home that evening filled with the energy of the conversation that ensued, and the certainty that the answer would come to me before sunrise. It is a crime that three decades and several books later, it still hasn't— a crime of which Leon is not wholly innocent. Nor is John Ferrari, with whom I went on to study at Berkeley, and who probably understands the intricacies of Platonic writing better than anyone.

If there is value to this book then all of these people deserve recognition, but I do not see how most authors make sense of dispensing credit while withholding blame. Of the two, blame is readier to hand, since one has much sharper awareness of what one has not accomplished than of what one has. And if we compare the two practices—patting ourselves on the back for what we have achieved, and lamenting what we have not—the latter is self-evidently more Socratic. Recall Socrates' parting words in the *Laches*: "What I don't advise is that we remain as we are" (*Laches* 201a).

Notes

Introduction: The Man Whose Name Is an Example

1. Leo Tolstoy, *Confession*, in *The Death of Ivan Ilyich and Confession*, trans. Peter Carson (New York: Liveright, 2014), 132.
2. *Confession*, 133.
3. *Confession*, 131, italics mine.
4. *Confession*, 132.
5. *Confession*, 162.
6. *Confession*, 132.
7. Plato, *Apology*, trans. G. M. A. Grube, in *Complete Works*, ed. John M. Cooper (Indianapolis: Hackett, 1997), 41c.
8. Plato, *Symposium*, trans. Alexander Nehamas and Paul Woodruff, in *Complete Works*, ed. John M. Cooper (Indianapolis: Hackett, 1997), 173b.
9. *Apology*, 21b.
10. *Apology*, 23a.
11. Plato, *Gorgias*, trans. Donald J. Zeyl, in *Complete Works*, ed. John M. Cooper (Indianapolis: Hackett, 1997), 458a. Here, and in a few other places, I have modified the translation of the Greek word *anthrōpos*. I use "person" or "human being" in place of "man," because Greek has another word, *anēr*, specifically for "man" in the sense of male human being.
12. *Gorgias*, 458ab.
13. *Gorgias*, 458ab.
14. *Gorgias*, 458a.
15. *Gorgias*, 458a.
16. *Gorgias*, 481bc.
17. *Apology*, 30c.
18. John Maynard Keynes, *The General Theory of Employment Interest and Money* (London: Macmillan, 1936), 383.
19. Cicero, *Academica* in *Cicero: De Natura Deorum; Academica*, Loeb Classical Library vol. 19, trans. H. Rackham (Cambridge, MA: Harvard University Press, 1967), I.4.16.
20. William Rainey Harper, "Freedom of Speech," in *The Chicago Canon on*

Free Inquiry and Expression, ed. Tony Banout and Tom Ginsburg (Chicago: The University of Chicago, 2023), 29.

Chapter 1: The Tolstoy Problem

1. *Confession*, 139–140.
2. William James, *The Varieties of Religious Experience* (London: Routledge, 2002), 147.
3. *Confession*, 131.
4. *Confession*, 130.
5. *Confession*, 130–31.
6. *Confession*, 134.
7. *Confession*, 139–40.
8. *Confession*, 134.
9. *Confession*, 160.
10. *Confession*, 132.
11. *Confession*, 151.
12. *Confession*, 162.
13. All of the quotes in this paragraph are from *Confession*, 158–59.
14. Plato, *Protagoras*, trans. Stanley Lombardo and Karen Bell, in *Complete Works*, ed. John M. Cooper (Indianapolis: Hackett, 1997), 310b–d.
15. *Protagoras*, 312cd.
16. *Protagoras*, 312e.
17. *Protagoras*, 313bc.
18. *Protagoras*, 361a–d.
19. *Protagoras*, 361e.
20. Plato, *Euthyphro*, trans. G. M. A. Grube, in *Complete Works*, ed. John M. Cooper (Indianapolis: Hackett, 1997), 11b.
21. *Euthyphro*, 15c.
22. *Euthyphro*, 15e.
23. Plato, *Alcibiades*, trans. D. S. Hutchinson, in *Complete Works*, ed. John M. Cooper (Indianapolis: Hackett, 1997), 117a. This dialogue is sometimes known as *First Alcibiades* so as to distinguish it from the *Second Alcibiades*, which is generally agreed not to have been written by Plato. On the authorship of the former, see note 1 to chapter 6 below.
24. Plato, *Lesser Hippias*, trans. Nicholas D. Smith, in *Complete Works*, ed. John M. Cooper (Indianapolis: Hackett, 1997), 376c.
25. *Lesser Hippias*, 372e.
26. *Confession*, 138.
27. *Confession*, 137.
28. Cited in Fabrizio Macagno and Douglas Walton, *Emotive Language in Argumentation* (Cambridge: Cambridge University Press, 2013), 2.
29. *Gorgias*, 491b.

30. Leo Tolstoy, *War and Peace*, trans. Louise and Aylmer Maude (Oxford: Oxford University Press, 2010), I.9.
31. Elena Ferrante, *Frantumaglia*, trans. Ann Goldstein (Melbourne: Text Publishing Company, 2016), I. 13.
32. *Varieties of Religious Experience*, 146.
33. *Apology*, 38a.
34. Plato, *Theaetetus*, trans. M. J. Levett, rev. Myles Burnyeat, in *Complete Works*, ed. John M. Cooper (Indianapolis: Hackett, 1997), 172de.
35. Plato, *Meno*, trans. G. M. A. Grube, in *Complete Works*, ed. John M. Cooper (Indianapolis: Hackett, 1997), 97c–98a.
36. *Meno*, 98a.

Chapter 2: Load-Bearing Answers

1. See S. C. Humphreys, "Kinship Patterns in the Athenian Courts," *Greek, Roman and Byzantine Studies*, 1986, who comments, "in Athenian eyes this was an incomprehensible way to behave," 69.
2. *Euthyphro*, 3e–4b.
3. *Euthyphro*, 4e–5a.
4. Plato, *Lysis*, trans. Stanely Lombardo, in *Complete Works*, ed. John M. Cooper (Indianapolis: Hackett, 1997), 207d.
5. John Cooper, note to *Charmides* in Plato's *Complete Works*, 639.
6. *Euthyphro*, 15e.
7. *Meno*, 71e–72a, emphasis mine.
8. *Euthyphro*, 5de.
9. *Gorgias*, 448c.
10. *Alcibiades*, 110bc.
11. *Alcibiades*, 112ab.
12. *Euthyphro*, 7b–d.
13. *Alcibiades*, 110c.
14. Quoted in van Jean Heijenoort (ed.), *From Frege to Gödel: A Source Book in Mathematical Logic, 1879–1931* (Cambridge, MA: Harvard University Press, 1967), 127.
15. Sophocles, *Antigone*, trans. Paul Woodruff (Indianapolis: Hackett, 2001), lines 304–14.

Chapter 3: Savage Commands

1. Plato, *Republic*, trans. G. M. A. Grube, rev. C. D. C. Reeve, in *Complete Works*, ed. John M. Cooper (Indianapolis: Hackett, 1997), 437c.
2. Aristotle, *On the Soul*, trans. J. A. Smith, in *The Complete Works of Aristotle* (Princeton, NJ: Princeton University Press, 1984), 431a8–10.

3. *Republic*, 439b.
4. Samuel Scheffler, *Death and the Afterlife* (Oxford: Oxford University Press, 2013).
5. Plato, *Phaedo*, trans. G. M. A. Grube, in *Complete Works*, ed. John M. Cooper (Indianapolis: Hackett, 1997), 66c.
6. *Phaedo*, 69ab.
7. *Protagoras*, 356cd.
8. *Phaedo*, 66a–c.
9. Plato, *Crito*, trans. G. M. A. Grube, in *Complete Works*, ed. John M. Cooper (Indianapolis: Hackett, 1997), 48c.
10. *Crito*, 44d.
11. *Gorgias*, 481e.
12. *Gorgias*, 513c.
13. *Protagoras*, 353c.
14. *Protagoras*, 352de.
15. *Protagoras*, 355d.
16. *Protagoras*, 356a.
17. *Protagoras*, 356bc.
18. *Protagoras*, 355d.
19. *Protagoras*, 355a–d.
20. *Protagoras*, 356b.
21. *Crito*, 45c–e.
22. *Crito*, 50a–c.
23. *Crito*, 49a–d.
24. *Gorgias*, 477–79.
25. *Republic*, 335b.
26. *Crito*, 49de, italics mine.
27. *Crito*, 45c–e.
28. This example is borrowed from Elizabeth Bruenig.
29. *Gorgias*, 480e–481b.
30. *Crito*, 51e–52a, italics mine.
31. See Alan Kim, "Crito and Critique," *Oxford Studies in Ancient Philosophy*, 2011.
32. *Crito*, 48e–49a, italics mine.
33. E.g., οὔτε πείθεται οὔτε πείθει ἡμᾶς, *Crito* 51e.
34. *Crito*, 45d.
35. *Crito*, 44c.
36. *Crito*, 45c.
37. *Crito*, 48cd.

Chapter 4: Socratic Intellectualism

1. *Alcibiades*, 115ab.
2. *Alcibiades*, 115cd.

3.   *Alcibiades*, 116a.

4.   *Alcibiades*, 116cd.

5.   *Alcibiades*, 115d.

6.   *Protagoras*, 360a.

7.   Epicurus, *Letter to Menoeceus*, in *Hellenistic Philosophy*, trans. Brad Inwood and L. P. Gerson (Indianapolis: Hackett, 1988), 129–30.

8.   *Vatican Collection of Epicurean Sayings*, in *Hellenistic Philosophy*, trans. Brad Inwood and L. P. Gerson (Indianapolis: Hackett, 1988), 56–57; however, I have modified their translation, translating *apistia* as "treachery" rather than "a lack of confidence."

9.   For Bentham, see *An Introduction to the Principles of Morals and Legislation*, chapter 2, paragraph 7; for Mill, see *Utilitarianism*, chapter 2; for Sidgwick, see *Methods of Ethics*, book I, chapter 1, paragraph 4.

10. Seneca, *De Otio*, in *Seneca: Moral Essays*, vol. 2, Loeb Classical Library, trans. John W. Basore (Cambridge, MA: Harvard University Press, 1932), 4.1.

11. *Discourses* 1.18.3–9, 1.28. 9–10.

12. Seneca, *Letters on Ethics*, 121.7.

13. "No One Errs Willingly: The Meaning of Socratic Intellectualism," *Oxford Studies in Ancient Philosophy*, 2000, 1.

14. Roslyn Weiss, *The Socratic Paradox and Its Enemies* (Chicago: University of Chicago Press, 2006); she denies many of the other intellectualist claims as well.

15. A group of interpreters argue that when Socrates says "everyone desires the good," he means that we desire what appears good to us, not necessarily what really is good: Gerasimos Santas, "The Socratic Paradoxes," *Philosophical Review*, 1964; David Wolfsdorf, "Desire for the Good in *Meno* 77b2–78b6," *Classical Quarterly* 2006; Kevin McTighe, "Socrates on Desire for the Good and the Involuntariness of Wrongdoing: *Gorgias* 466a–468e," *Phronesis* 1984; and Rachel Barney, "Plato on the Desire for the Good," in *Desire, Practical Reason, and the Good*, ed. Sergio Tenenbaum (Oxford: Oxford University Press, 2012). For the opposing view, see Terry Penner, "Desire and Power in Socrates: The Argument of *Gorgias* 466A–468E That Orators and Tyrants Have No Power in the City," *Apeiron*, 1991; and Terry Penner and Christopher Rowe, "The Desire for Good: Is the *Meno* Inconsistent with the *Gorgias*?" *Phronesis*, 1994. For the view that Socrates thinks we desire what both appears good to us and is in fact actually good, see my "Everyone Desires the Good: Socrates' Protreptic Theory of Desire," *Review of Metaphysics*, 2017.

16. Rachel Singpurwalla, "Reasoning with the Irrational," *Ancient Philosophy*, 2006.

17. I am referring here to the famous and much vilified "craft analogy," which appears in many dialogues and seems to compare the knowledge we could acquire of virtue to knowledge we do have of various crafts. Theodor Gomperz, in his *Greek Thinkers*, vol. 2 (London: John Murray, 1905), 296, understands the *Hippias Minor* as a reductio ad absurdum of the craft analogy; Gregory Vlastos, in his *Socrates: Ironist and Moral Philosopher* (Ithaca,

NY: Cornell University Press, 1991), 279, n.137, insists that the analogy be understood only loosely; and Rachel Barney argues that the craft analogy need not be understood in intellectualist terms: see her "Techne as a Model for Virtue in Plato," in *Productive Knowledge in Ancient Philosophy*, ed. T. Johansen (Cambridge: Cambridge University Press, 2021).

18. Vlastos, "Happiness and Virtue in Socrates' Moral Theory," *Proceedings of the Cambridge Philological Society*, 1984.

19. Nehamas, "Socratic Intellectualism," *Proceedings of the Boston Area Colloquium in Ancient Philosophy*, 1987; Robert Zaborowski, "To what extent was Socrates a moral intellectualist? Revisiting Plato's Protagoras," *Acta Classica*, 2021; Thomas C. Brickhouse, Nicholas D. Smith, *Socratic Moral Psychology*, (Cambridge: Cambridge University Press, 2010).

20. Henry Sidgwick, *The Methods of Ethics* (London: Macmillan and Co, 1874), book I, chapter 2.

21. William James, "What Makes a Life Significant," in his *Talks to Teachers* (New York: Henry Holt, 1925), 268–69.

22. "What Makes a Life Significant," 270.

23. "What Makes a Life Significant," 272–73.

24. *Alcibiades*, 115d.

25. *Republic*, 505de.

26. I am reading "beautiful things" here as a reference to objects of bodily sensory appreciation, along the lines of the discussion of the "lovers of sight and sound" in book V, who take pleasure in bodily experiences of beauty ("beautiful sounds, colors, shapes, and everything fashioned out of them," 476b and following), such as delicious wine and attractive young men. It is, however, possible that "beautiful things" is instead a reference to noble or honorable actions, in which case *both* examples (just things and beautiful things) would pertain to the spirited part of the soul. I've adopted the former interpretation, but I see the latter as possible as well; there isn't much in the text to decide between them.

Chapter 5: The Gadfly-Midwife Paradox

1. Translated by Michael Hamburger, in *German Life and Letters*, 1951; all quotations from this text are from pages 42 and 43.

2. *Alcibiades*, 130e.

3. *Apology*, 21e.

4. With the admittedly notable exception of Diotima, the teacher to whom Socrates alludes in the *Symposium*, his interlocutors in the Platonic dialogues are all men.

5. *Theaetetus*, 150de.

6. *Meno* 81c and following, *Phaedo*, 73 and following.

7. Plato, *Charmides*, trans. Rosamond Kent Sprague, in *Complete Works*, ed. John M. Cooper (Indianapolis: Hackett, 1997), 166d.

8. *Gorgias*, 505e.
9. *Gorgias*, 508e.
10. For a historical overview of the development of this consensus, see Leonard Brandwood, "Stylometry and Chronology," in Richard Kraut ed., *The Cambridge Companion to Plato* (Cambridge: Cambridge University Press, 2006).
11. *Crito* and *Phaedo* are sometimes classified as "transitional" or "early-middle."
12. *Protagoras*, 348c–349a.
13. Some scholars do not believe that Plato wrote the *Clitophon*. I won't go into the details of this dispute (those interested could start with G. S. Bowe, "In Defense of Clitophon," *Classical Philology*, 2007), since for our purposes all that matters is that whoever wrote it had an important insight into how Socrates was received by some of his companions.
14. Plato, *Clitophon*, trans. Francisco J. Gonzalez, in *Complete Works*, ed. John M. Cooper (Indianapolis: Hackett, 1997), 408c.
15. *Clitophon*, 410b–d.
16. *Confessions*, trans. Henry Chadwick, (Oxford: Oxford University Press, 2009). All quotes are from III.12.
17. Plato, *Euthydemus*, trans. Rosamond Kent Sprague, in *Complete Works*, ed. John M. Cooper (Indianapolis: Hackett, 1997), 274de.
18. *Euthydemus*, 275.
19. *Charmides*, 165bc.
20. *Charmides*, 166c.
21. *Charmides*, 166cd.
22. "The Will to Believe," in *William James: Writings 1878–1899* (New York: Library of America, 1992), 469.
23. "The Will to Believe," 469.
24. In Clifford's *Lectures and Essays*, volume 2, ed. Leslie Stephen and Frederick Pollock (London: Macmillan, 1879).
25. "The Ethics of Belief," 183.
26. "The Ethics of Belief," 183.
27. "The Ethics of Belief," 184.
28. "The Will to Believe," 469.
29. "The Will to Believe," 470.
30. "The Ethics of Belief," 181.
31. "The Will to Believe," 473.
32. "The Will to Believe," 470.
33. *Intention* (Cambridge, MA: Harvard University Press, 2000), §32
34. This is an update of Davidson's famous carbon copier example. See 92 of his "Intending," in his *Essays on Actions and Events* (Oxford: Oxford University Press, 2001).
35. *Meditations on First Philosophy*, trans. John Cottingham (Cambridge: Cambridge University Press, 1986), 12.
36. Aristotle, *Nicomachean Ethics*, trans. W. D. Ross, in *The Complete Works of Aristotle*, (Princeton, NJ: Princeton University Press, 1984), 1145b2–7.

37. *Theaetetus*, 150c.
38. *Charmides*, 166cd.
39. *Protagoras*, 338bc.
40. *Protagoras*, 348c–49a.
41. *Gorgias*, 457e–458a.
42. *Charmides*, 166c.

Chapter 6: Moore's Paradox of Self-Knowledge

1. *Alcibiades*, 105a–c. In the nineteenth century the theologian Friedrich Schleiermacher raised doubts about the authenticity of the *Alcibiades*, but more recent scholarship has largely put those doubts to rest (see discussion in Jakub Jirsa, "Authenticity of the 'Alcibiades' I: Some Reflections," *Listy filologicke*, 2009). However, even those doubts were still active, I would make the claim that I made above about the *Clitophon* above, see note 13 in chapter 5 above: what's important for our purposes is not that Plato wrote the *Alcibiades*, but that whoever wrote it had insights into the Socratic method.
2. *Alcibiades*, 135bc.
3. *Alcibiades*, 135c.
4. Debra Nails, *The People of Plato* (Indianapolis: Hackett, 2002), 13, which offers the overview of what we know about Alcibiades' life on which this summary draws.
5. *The Peloponnesian War*, trans. Steven Lattimore (Indianapolis: Hackett, 1998), 6.16.1.
6. Plutarch *Lives*, vol. IV, Loeb Classical Library, trans. Bernadotte Perrin (Cambridge, MA: Harvard University Press, 1916), I.4.16.
7. William Smith, *A Smaller History of Greece, from the Earliest Times to the Roman Conquest* (New York: Harper & Bros., 1872), 376.
8. *Alcibiades*, 127d.
9. *Apology*, 23b.
10. *Meno*, 80b.
11. *Euthyphro*, 11b.
12. *Gorgias*, 473e–474b.
13. *Alcibiades*, 113bc.
14. *Alcibiades*, 112d–113c.
15. *Alcibiades*, 114de.
16. *Alcibiades*, 118ab, italics mine.
17. *Authority and Estrangement* (Princeton, NJ: Princeton University Press, 2001), 170–71.
18. *Alcibiades*, 124b.
19. *Alcibiades*, 128a.
20. *Alcibiades*, 129a.
21. *Alcibiades*, 132d–133b.

22. *Gorgias*, 508e.
23. *Gorgias*, 486d.
24. *Alcibiades*, 113b.
25. *Symposium*, 215e–216b.
26. For further discussion of Alcibiades' speech in the *Symposium*, and some more specific thoughts about why he in particular struggles to get the positive project into view, see chapter 10 below.

Chapter 7: Meno's Paradox

1. In "Computing Machinery and Intelligence," *Mind*, vol. LIX, issue 236, October 1950.
2. *Meno*, 80d.
3. *Meno*, 80e.
4. *Meno*, 71d–72a.
5. *Meno*, 72c.
6. *Meno*, 77a.
7. *Meno*, 79a.
8. *Meno*, 80b.
9. The references here are to Euripides (*Rhesus*, 213), Aeschylus (*Seven Against Thebes*, 540), and Xenophon (*Cyropaedia*, 6.1.51), respectively; see the entry for *problēma* in Liddell and Scott, *A Greek-English Lexicon* (Oxford: Clarendon Press, 1996).
10. Robert F. Barsky, *Noam Chomsky: A Life of Dissent* (Boston: MIT Press, 1998), 95.
11. *Meno*, 80d, italics mine.
12. *Meno*, 86c.
13. *Meno*, 82de.
14. *Meno*, 83de.
15. Meno, 84cd.
16. Plato, *Laches*, trans. Rosamund Kent Sprague, in *Complete Works*, ed. John M. Cooper (Indianapolis: Hackett, 1997), 194cd.
17. *Meno*, 80d.
18. *Meno*, 81cd.
19. *Meno*, 86bc.
20. *Aspiration: The Agency of Becoming* (New York: Oxford University Press, 2018).
21. *Anabasis*, II.6.

Introduction to Part III: The Socratizing Move

1. *Gorgias*, 521d.
2. *Symposium*, 177d; *Phaedrus*, 257a.

3. *Phaedo*, 64a; 67e.
4. *The Economic Approach to Human Behavior* (Chicago: University of Chicago Press, 1976), 14.
5. Robin Hanson and Kevin Simler, *Elephant in the Brain: Hidden Motives in Everyday Life* (Oxford: Oxford University Press, 2018).

Chapter 8: Politics: Justice and Liberty

1. *Apology*, 32a.
2. *Apology*, 31d.
3. *Gorgias*, 485de.
4. *Apology*, 30a, *Gorgias*, 421d.
5. *Gorgias*, 454c.
6. *Gorgias*, 457de.
7. *Gorgias*, 457e–458a.
8. *Gorgias*, 458ab.
9. *Gorgias*, 506c.
10. *Apology*, 39d.
11. Emily Wilson, trans., *The Iliad* (New York: W. W. Norton, 2023), Book 1, lines 55–61.
12. *Phaedo*, 115e.
13. "Creative Democracy," in *The Essential Dewey*, vol. 1 (Bloomington: Indiana University Press, 1998), 342.
14. Dewey, "Creative Democracy," 342.
15. *Gorgias*, 456bc.
16. *Gorgias*, 473e.
17. *Gorgias*, 471e.
18. *Gorgias*, 472bc.

Chapter 9: Politics: Equality

1. *On the Genealogy of Morality*, trans. Keith Ansell-Pearson (Cambridge: Cambridge University Press, 2006), first essay, §13.
2. *The History of Sexuality*, vol. 1, trans. R. Hurley (London: Penguin, 1998), 93.
3. *Republic*, 343e–344a.
4. *Republic*, 359c.
5. *Gorgias*, 483bc.
6. Ben Rogers, *A. J. Ayer: A Life* (New York: Grove Press, 2002), 344.
7. *The Collected Essays, Journalism and Letters*, vol. 4, Sonia Orwell and Ian Angus, eds. (London: The Camelot Press, 1968), 4.
8. Orwell, "Revenge Is Sour," 5.
9. *Iliad*, book 1, 230–54.

10. *Iliad*, book 1, 220.
11. *The Theory of Moral Sentiments*, D. D. Rafael and A. L. Macfie, eds. (Indianapolis: Liberty Fund, 1976), 336.
12. See also Creon in chapter 2, p. 74
13. *Gorgias*, 472bc.
14. *Gorgias*, 474ab.
15. *Gorgias*, 471e.
16. *Gorgias*, 482de.

Chapter 10: Love

1. *Symposium*, 192d.
2. *Symposium*, 192e.
3. *Symposium*, 205e–206a.
4. *Symposium*, 206a.
5. "Platonic Love," in *Facets of Plato's Philosophy*, edited by W. W. Werkmeister (Assen, Netherlands: van Gorcum, 1976), 57.
6. *Phaedrus*, 256b.
7. *Phaedrus*, 257b.
8. *Phaedrus*, 249c.
9. *Lysis*, 206c.
10. *Phaedrus*, 257a.
11. *Symposium*, 177d.
12. *Laches*, 201a.
13. *Phaedrus*, 251bc.
14. *Symposium*, 210d–211a.
15. New York: Charles Scribners Sons, 1902, 60.
16. See Kenneth Dover, *Greek Homosexuality* (Cambridge, MA: Harvard University Press, 1989).
17. *Symposium*, 217bc.
18. *Symposium*, 217c.
19. *Symposium*, 218c–219a.
20. *Symposium*, 219b.
21. *Symposium*, 219b–d.
22. *Symposium*, 219e.
23. *Symposium*, 222b.
24. See the end of chapter 6.
25. *Symposium*, 222d.
26. *Crito*, 44b.
27. *Crito*, 45c–46a.
28. *Crito*, 46bc. Emphasis mine: the italicized text reflects a slight modification on my part of Grube's translation. The original runs ὡς ἐγὼ οὐ νῦν πρῶτον ἀλλὰ καὶ ἀεὶ τοιοῦτος οἷος τῶν ἐμῶν μηδενὶ ἄλλῳ πείθεσθαι ἢ τῷ λόγῳ ὃς ἄν μοι λογιζομένῳ βέλτιστος φαίνηται.

29. *Crito*, 48e.
30. *Symposium*, 219b.
31. *Symposium*, 216ab.
32. *Apology*, 41e–42a.
33. *Symposium*, 216e.
34. *Symposium*, 218d.
35. *Republic* 337a.
36. See note 56 below.
37. *Gorgias*, 481b.
38. *Gorgias*, 489d.
39. *Apology*, 20d.
40. *Apology*, 38a.
41. See Lane, M., "The Evolution of Eirōneia in Classical Greek Texts: Why Socratic Eirōneia is Not Socratic Irony," *Oxford Studies in Ancient Philosophy*, 2006.
42. "Socratic Irony," *The Classical Quarterly*, 1987, 81.
43. "The Evolution of Eirōneia in Classical Greek Texts," 77.
44. "Socratic Irony," 85.
45. *De Oratore* II, 269–70, Loeb Classical Library, trans. E. W. Sutton, H. Rackham (Cambridge, MA: Harvard University Press, 1942).
46. *The Orator's Education, Volume IV: Books 9–10*, Loeb Classical Library, trans. Donald Russell (Cambridge, MA: Harvard University Press, 2002), 9.2.46.
47. "Socratic Irony," 94.
48. See Hegel's *Lectures on the History of Philosophy*, vol. 1, trans. by E. S. Haldane (London: K. Paul, Trench, Trübner 1892), 397–406.
49. Kierkegaard, *The Concept of Irony with Continual Reference to Socrates*, trans. and ed. Howard V. Hong and Edna H. Hong (Princeton, NJ: Princeton University press, 1989); Strauss, *The City and Man* (Chicago: University of Chicago Press, 1978); Vlastos, op. cit.; Lear, *A Case for Irony* (Cambridge, MA: Harvard University Press, 2014).
50. Consider a representative discussion:

Nor should we infer that irony is, at least in Plato, the expression of something that is false, a lie or an intentional deception. What makes Socratic irony in particular so complicated is that the statements in question are in different ways both false and true. Again, the true kernel in the statement is not necessarily just the opposite of what the statement seems to mean, as might be the case with a merely sarcastic statement; it might be something different from what is conveyed by the surface meaning of the words. When Socrates professes ignorance, for example, it is false that he is simplistically ignorant, but perhaps true that in some deeper sense he is indeed ignorant— and in a way that shows a certain kind of knowledge. (Charles L. Griswold, "Irony in the Platonic Dialogues," *Philosophy and Literature*, 2002.)

Notice the knots in which the interpreter is tied: Socrates' professions of ignorance are false, though *perhaps* true, but the way in which they are true, if they are, is that they are false, because he has a certain kind of knowledge.

Socratic statements are both false and true, but what is true about them is not merely a negation of what is said, but somehow *hidden* in what is said, so that one must always shun the "surface" meaning in favor of some "deeper sense." One must be wary of interpreting him "simplistically," because Socratic irony is "so complicated." Such an approach to the text makes it very difficult to encounter, evaluate, and be personally challenged by Socrates' arguments. One suspects that may even be the point.

51. Cicero, *De Oratore*, II. 270.

52. Consider all the linguistic parallels: not just *eirōneia/ironia* but Alcibiades' *paizōn* (and Callicles' *paizei*) vs. Cicero's *ludens*, Alcibiades' *panta ton bion* vs. Quintilian's *vita universa*, Alcibiades' *exapatōn* vs. Cicero's *dissimulantia*—and that Socrates' contemporaries already see him as possessed of his own characteristic brand of irony (*eiōthuia eirōneia*, *Republic* 337a, likewise *eiōthotōs* at *Symposium* 218d), which means that the idea of *peculiarly* Socratic irony is not new to the positive meaning.

53. I am far from alone in irony denialism. C. D. C. Reeve, *Socrates in the Apology* (Indianapolis: Hackett), argues that it is much easier to understand the *Apology* if we interpret Socrates literally instead of looking for hidden subtext; Richard Kraut, in *Socrates and the State* (Princeton, NJ: Princeton University Press, 1984), sees Socrates as someone who "must be taken at his word" (288) and who is "completely straightforward and honest" (311). Thomas Brickhouse and Nicholas Smith likewise present an unironic picture of Socrates in their books, *Socrates on Trial* (Oxford: Oxford University Press, 1989) and *Plato's Socrates* (Oxford: Oxford University Press, 1994). In Terence Irwin's influential *Plato's Ethics* (Oxford: Oxford University Press, 1995), which traces the development of Plato's moral philosophy from the Socratic dialogues through the *Republic*, the only mention of Socratic irony occurs in the context of a discussion of Socrates' views on akrasia, where Irwin comments, "We should not dismiss Socrates' conclusion as mere irony" (93).

54. See note 50 above, with Griswold quote.

55. *Symposium*, 217bc.

56. *Gorgias*, 481b. It is worth noting that this line is a word for word repetition of 447c5. It is impossible to know whether Chaerephon is aware that he is echoing Callicles' words from the opening of the dialogue, but if he is aware, he might be suggesting that Callicles interrogate Socrates in just the way that Socrates, there, interrogated Gorgias.

57. *Symposium*, 216e.

Chapter 11: Death

1. *Phaedo*, 63e.

2. *Phaedo*, 64a.

3. Leo Tolstoy, *The Death of Ivan Ilyich*, in *The Death of Ivan Ilyich and Confession*, trans. Peter Carson (New York: Liveright, 2014), 101.

4. *The Death of Ivan Ilyich*, 78–79.

5. *The Death of Ivan Ilyich*, 105.

6. *The Death of Ivan Ilyich*, 105–6.

7. *The Death of Ivan Ilyich*, 108.

8. *The Death of Ivan Ilyich*, 107.

9. Leo Tolstoy, *War and Peace*, trans. Richard Pevear and Larissa Volokhonsky (New York: Vintage, 2008), 347.

10. *War and Peace*, 348.

11. Leo Tolstoy, *Anna Karenina*, trans. Richard Pevear and Larissa Volokhonsky (New York: Penguin, 2000), 530.

12. *The Death of Ivan Ilyich*, 79.

13. *Phaedo*, 118a.

14. *Phaedo*, 88c.

15. *Phaedo*, 89a.

16. *Phaedo*, 107bc.

17. *Phaedo*, 89d.

18. *Phaedo*, 90cd.

19. *Phaedo*, 90e–91a.

20. *Phaedo*, 91bc.

21. *Meno*, 71e.

22. *Phaedo*, 115c–116a.

23. Karl Ove Knausgaard, *My Struggle*, trans. Don Bartlett (New York: Farrar, Straus and Giroux, 2009), 4.

24. Knausgaard, *My Struggle*, 5.

25. *Phaedo*, 115e.

26. *Apology*, 40cd.

27. bfinn, "Premature Death Paradox," www.lesswrong.com, April 13, 2020.

28. Epicurus, *Letter to Menoeceus*, 125.

29. Excerpt from "Aubade" from *The Complete Poems of Philip Larkin* by Philip Larkin, edited by Archie Burnett. Copyright © 2012 by The Estate of Philip Larkin. Reprinted by permission of Farrar, Straus and Giroux. All Rights Reserved.

30. See *De Rerum Natura*, III, 853.

31. "Death," *Noûs*, 1970, 80.

32. See Lucretius III, 944–49, and 1080–81, following Epicurus PD 18–20.

33. "When I Have Fears that I May Cease to Be" in John Keats, *The Complete Poems* (New York: Penguin, 1973), 221.

34. *Phaedo*, 60e.

35. Did Socrates have writing materials, or did he compose the verse in his head? We do not know. But the argument in the *Phaedrus* (275d and following), which attacks writing for its fixed character—the words say the same thing to you every time you encounter them—applies either way.

36. *The Death of Ivan Ilyich*, 105.

37. *Phaedo*, 116e.

38. *Phaedo*, 116e–117a.

39. *Phaedo*, 115b.

40. *Apology*, 39d.
41. *Meno*, 86bc.
42. *Theaetetus*, 172d.
43. *Theaetetus*, 172d.
44. Larkin, *Aubade*, 116.
45. *Confession*, 130–31, italics mine.
46. *Phaedo*, 114d.
47. *Phaedo*, 118a.

Index Locorum for Plato

Index Generalis